Advance Praise for

The Homeowner's Guide to Renewable Energy

Dan Chiras strikes again! With this latest addition to his already impressive list
of titles, Dan makes it as easy as possible for you to effect your own transition
away from fossil fuel dependence. I've never seen a more comprehensive, better
written, or better organized primer on this subject. When you need practical advice
from a warm, smart and informed human being, Dan Chiras is the one to turn to.

— Bruce King, PE Director, Ecological Building Network, and author of
Buildings of Earth and Straw and *Making Better Concrete*

The Homeowner's Guide to Renewable Energy makes abundantly clear the
predicament that humankind has created regarding how we procure and use
energy. Ways that we might extricate ourselves from this predicament are placed
squarely on the shoulders of renewable forms of energy, rather than fossil fuels.
This book shows how we, as individuals, have the power and technology
available now to embrace renewable energy for a bright future.

— Kelly Hart, www.greenhomebuilding.com

Who says home energy improvements have to be complicated, or boring?
Dan Chiras' *The Homeowner's Guide to Renewable Energy* waltzes the reader
gracefully through various efficiency upgrades that put household heat and
coolness in their proper places, then expertly jazz-dances through state-of-the-art
technologies like solar electricity, heat pumps, and biodiesel fuel. This
easy-to-understand, timely book should be distributed by local governments
and utilities to homeowners throughout the country. Imagine how much
less dependent we'd be on uncertain, expensive supplies of oil and natural gas!

— Dave Wann, coauthor of *Affluenza: The All-Consuming Epidemic* and
Superbia! 31 Ways to Create Sustainable Neighborhoods

Dan Chiras is one of the most authoritative writers in the field of renewable energy. His multiple other books create a comprehensive library for homeowners looking to live a lifestyle in harmony with their values. Not only is his style accessible and easy to read but is thorough in what to do, how to do it and why. Dan walks his talk living in a solar, green home and devoting untold hours to sustainable living causes. He is truly one or our national heros!!!

— David Johnston, What's Working: Visionary Solutions for Green Building, and author of *Green Remodeling: Changing the World One Room at a Time*

Dan Chiras has done as much as anyone in America to promote and popularize the use of renewable energy. He works his magic again in *The Homeowner's Guide to Renewable Energy*. As Peak Oil looms, the lucidity and clear thinking of Dan Chiras becomes our first line of defense.

— Stephen Morris, publisher and editor, *Green Living: A Practical Journal for Friends of the Environment*

If you're thinking about investing in a renewable energy system for your home, Dan Chiras' *The Homeowner's Guide to Renewable Energy* helps clarify the decision making process. After beginning with the all important discussion about energy efficiency and conservation, Dan guides you through everything you need to choose which renewable options to integrate into your lifestyle. A great addition to my bookshelf!

— Mick Sagrillo, Sagrillo Power & Light

Books for Wiser Living from *Mother Earth News*

Today, more than ever before, our society is seeking ways to live more conscientiously. To help bring you the very best inspiration and information about greener, more sustainable lifestyles, New Society Publishers has joined forces with *Mother Earth News*. For more than 30 years, *Mother Earth News* has been North America's "Original Guide to Living Wisely," creating books and magazines for people with a passion for self-reliance and a desire to live in harmony with nature. Across the countryside and in our cities, New Society Publishers and *Mother Earth News* are leading the way to a wiser, more sustainable world.

**ACHIEVING ENERGY INDEPENDENCE
through SOLAR, WIND, BIOMASS
and HYDROPOWER**

THE
HOMEOWNER'S GUIDE
TO RENEWABLE
ENERGY

Dan Chiras

NEW SOCIETY PUBLISHERS

Cataloging in Publication Data:
A catalog record for this publication is available from the National Library of Canada.

Cover design by Diane McIntosh. Photos: House image: Russell Illig, Photodisc RF; wind turbine: John Ivanko
Interior illustrations by Jill Haras, unless otherwise credited.
Interior photos by Dan Chiras, unless otherwise credited.

Printed in Canada.
First printing March 2006.

Paperback ISBN 13: 978-0-86571-536-3
Paperback ISBN 10: 0-86571-536-X

Inquiries regarding requests to reprint all or part of *The Homeowner's Guide to Renewable Energy* should be addressed to New Society Publishers at the address below.

To order directly from the publishers, please call toll-free (North America) 1-800-567-6772, or order online at www.newsociety.com

Any other inquiries can be directed by mail to:

New Society Publishers
P.O. Box 189, Gabriola Island, BC V0R 1X0, Canada
1-800-567-6772

New Society Publishers' mission is to publish books that contribute in fundamental ways to building an ecologically sustainable and just society, and to do so with the least possible impact on the environment, in a manner that models this vision. We are committed to doing this not just through education, but through action. We are acting on our commitment to the world's remaining ancient forests by phasing out our paper supply from ancient forests worldwide. This book is one step toward ending global deforestation and climate change. It is printed on acid-free paper that is **100% old growth forest-free** (100% post-consumer recycled), processed chlorine free, and printed with vegetable-based, low-VOC inks. For further information, or to browse our full list of books and purchase securely, visit our website at: www.newsociety.com

NEW SOCIETY PUBLISHERS   www.newsociety.com

This book is dedicated to the founders and hard-working staff and volunteers at *Mother Earth News* and *Home Power* magazine, Solar Energy International, the Midwest Renewable Energy Association, the Colorado Renewable Energy Society, The American Solar Energy Society, the Iowa Renewable Energy Association, the American Wind Energy Association, the Solar Living Institute, and the National Renewable Energy Laboratory. Many thanks for their dedication, hard work, and perseverance.

Contents

Acknowledgments

This book has been made possible by a great many individuals — hard-working, dedicated, and far-seeing people who have spent a lifetime exploring, teaching, and writing about energy efficiency and renewable energy. Their names, and the names of their organizations, too numerous to list here, grace the pages of the resource guide at the end of the book. Without them, this book never could have been possible. Without them, renewable energy would still be a wishful dream. So a world of thanks to all of you! Keep up the amazing work.

I am also deeply grateful to the people who answered my questions, including Johnny Weiss, Randy Udall, Marc Franke, Mick Sagrillo, and Steve Andrews. A special thanks to Johnny Weiss, Marc Franke, Dan New, Mick Sagrillo, and Randy Udall for reading portions of the manuscript, offering their helpful comments and advice, and helping to ferret out inadvertent mistakes. Many thanks to those who provided the photographs that grace the pages of this book.

Finally, I would also like to express my appreciation to my dear friends Chris and Judith Plant at New Society Publishers who signed on to this book and have remained cordial, enthusiastic, and supportive throughout the writing and production of this book and all of the books I've written for their company.

I would also like to thank all of the dedicated staff at New Society Publishers, including my copyeditor Murray Reiss, for his thoughtful and skilled copyediting; Jill Haras for her excellent drawings; Ingrid Witvoet for handling the countless production details; Greg Green for his expert design and layout; and Beth Anne Sobieszczyk and Gail Leondar-Wright for their considerable efforts to publicize this book.

Introduction

For years, Kara Culpepper and her family, all avid Denver Bronco fans, held season tickets, attending every home game like tens of thousands of other enthusiasts. Those were good times, despite the fact that the family often had to brave Colorado's cold winter weather to watch the Broncos play. Several years ago taxpayers built the team a new stadium. Facing much higher ticket prices, Kara and her family decided to give up their season tickets. They hadn't given up on their team, though. They were just going to watch the games on TV in the comfort of their home.

Trouble is, their modest suburban home, which was built in the 1970s, was anything but comfortable. To be truthful, it was an ice box in the winter. Poorly insulated and full of leaks that allowed cold air in on blustery winter days, their home was like millions of residences throughout North America. To watch the games, Kara and her family had to bundle up in jackets and sweaters and don thermal socks or huddle under blankets. Ironically, it wasn't a whole lot different than a December game outside at the stadium.

"The only difference was that in the stadium you could actually get sunrays," remarks Kara.

But those days have changed. Today, Kara and her family watch the game — and other programs — in comfort, no longer bundled up like the Inuit on a cold Arctic night. Today, the family enjoys Bronco games in normal garb. Winters inside their home are no longer just bearable, they've become downright comfortable — thanks to an extensive home energy retrofit. The energy retrofit was made possible by the local utility (Xcel Energy) and a nonprofit organization, the Colorado Energy Science Center, a leader in wise energy use in Colorado.

Kara qualified for the complete energy makeover, worth over $25,000, when her home was selected as one of two winners in a statewide competition. Her family's home was deemed to be one of the two most energy-inefficient homes in an applicant pool of 10,000 homes. The judges believed that her home would, if retrofitted, provide the most significant energy and cost savings.

Being voted one of the most energy-consumptive homes in the state is not a great distinction, but Kara and her family are able to look past that dubious honor, for it earned them a generous retrofit that has slashed their heating bills and increased their comfort levels beyond their wildest imagination. And how has it worked?

Although they've just finished, the family has found dramatic changes. Improved insulation and a host of other upgrades designed to cut their energy use while increasing comfort have already slashed their natural gas bill in half, saving the family $150 per month in the dead of winter. New energy-efficient appliances that replaced older, less frugal models are also bound to cut their electrical bills in the years to come.

The energy upgrades on this home have broader and perhaps even more significant benefits, too. Besides saving energy and money, the work on their home has, as noted above, made their home much more comfortable. It's much warmer in the winter and much cooler in the hot Colorado summers.

In addition, the energy retrofit will also reduce the family's emissions of carbon dioxide, a greenhouse gas that's responsible for the record-breaking heat and wacky and costly violent weather that's been plaguing North America and the rest of the world. All told, their reductions in energy consumption will reduce the family's carbon dioxide emissions by about eight tons a year! "That's roughly equivalent to removing one and a third vehicles

A few hundred dollars can result in amazing energy savings that are good for your pocketbook or wallet and good for your future and the long-term future of your children and theirs. A few thousand dollars will bring even greater benefits!

from the highway every year," writes Amanda Leigh Haag in *Smart Energy Living*.

If you are like most people, you're being hammered by high fuel bills — at home and at the gas pump — and you want to do something about it. Like Kara Culpepper's family, you can reduce your energy consumption dramatically — and you don't have to pay $25,000 to do so! A few hundred dollars, in fact, can result in amazing energy savings that are good for your pocketbook or wallet and good for your future and the long-term future of your children and theirs. A few thousand dollars will bring even greater benefits!

If you are like many other smart, hard-working, and independent-minded people, you may also want to increase your energy independence by joining the growing number of homeowners in urban, suburban, and rural settings the world over who are using energy much more efficiently and even producing some or all of their own from renewable sources like the sun or wind. All across the world people like you are freeing themselves from ever-rising and burdensome utility bills by turning to a variety of cost-effective, reliable, and affordable renewable energy technologies. If this is your dream, this book is for you. It will help you pursue your dreams of greater energy self-sufficiency and a comfortable and affordable life.

This book will, first and foremost, help you understand *all* of the renewable energy options at your disposal. And it will help you develop a sensible, cost-effective strategy to use energy more efficiently and increase your reliance on clean, affordable, and reliable renewable energy.

RENEWABLE ENERGY AND ME

I have to admit to a long-standing love affair with renewable energy. I fell in love with this clean alternative to mainstream energy in the summer of 1977 while visiting Arches National Park in Moab, Utah. It all occurred in the most unlikely spot — in the parking lot in front of the visitors' center. There, park officials, had placed a single solar electric module, shown in Figure 1.

In the baking hot summer sun, this amazing little device cranked out electricity to power a small fan. Park officials had attached small streamers to the fan to dramatize the effect. My immediate interest and affection for this amazing, quiet device was sparked partly because I'd been studying the impacts of generating electricity from coal. I'd heard about solar electricity and seen pictures of various solar technologies, but had never seen a solar electric module in operation. And there it was, this elegantly simple alternative to massive coal plants and the huge surface mines that feed them. It was a perfect example of living in harmony with nature.

I remember thinking that if solar electric modules like these were placed on millions of roofs throughout North America, they could power the entire continent (Figure 2). I remember marveling at the fact that there were no toxic emissions, no mines, and no

Fig. 1: This small display of solar electricity turned my head and started a lifelong commitment to renewable energy. Unfortunately, you can't see the fan and streamers that dramatized the PV's remarkable ability to convert solar energy into electricity.

Fig. 2: These solar electric panels generate electricity from sunlight and are on special tracking devices that allow the array to move as the sun cuts its daily path through the sky. Tracking increases the efficiency of the panels by keeping the solar cells in line with the sun as much as possible.

heaps of slag and ash to get rid of. Just a quiet little device gleaming in the bright desert sun, converting solar energy that takes eight minutes to reach the Earth into electricity. This simple, reliable little device with no moving parts was cranking out electrical energy and sending those streamers and my heart into paroxysms of delight.

Since that day, I have devoted my life to the study of renewable energy, including solar energy, wind power, hydropower, geothermal energy, tidal power, biofuels, and hydrogen. I have written about renewable energy in several books, including my college textbooks. I even published a book titled *The Solar House* that describes how we can heat and cool our homes passively — without costly heating and air conditioning systems and the polluting fossil fuels or dangerous nuclear fuels that power them.

I've done more than write about this potentially liberating energy technology; I have put my knowledge into practice. I retrofitted my very first home with solar hot water panels for domestic hot water, virtually eliminating my hot water bill. I also added insulation in the attic and constructed a small greenhouse on its south side to provide heat to warm the interior. I installed a woodstove and gathered wood for free from a nearby national forest. Together, the insulation, greenhouse, and woodstove virtually eliminated my heating bill.

My second home, purchased many years later, was a passive solar house. Although it worked pretty well, I retrofitted that house to improve its energy performance, reduce my family's energy bills, and achieve greater self-sufficiency. In 1995, I built a super-efficient solar home from scratch. This house, in which I live today, generates 100 percent of its electrical power from photovoltaic panels and a small wind generator, freeing me from those nagging monthly utility bills (Figure 3). (I haven't paid an electrical bill since 1996!) I also have the satisfaction of knowing that I'm dramatically reducing my family's impact on the environment.

My home is passively heated by the sun through south-facing windows, and it is cooled naturally as well. I burn a cord of wood a year as backup heat; all in all, it costs me about $120 per year to supplement the sun's free

Fig. 3: The author's passive solar/solar electric home also obtains energy from a small wind generator.

heat. I have no air conditioner. I don't need one. The house stays cool through the hot summer months thanks to high levels of insulation, energy-efficient windows, earth sheltering, and other features I'll explain later in the book.

You too can dramatically reduce your energy use. You can even achieve nearly total energy independence, eliminating the sting of monthly fuel bills, saving large sums of money, and greatly reducing your environmental impact. This book will show you how. Before we turn our attention to the many ways you can use energy more efficiently, and ways you can tap into renewable energy resources, however, it's important to delve a little deeper into the energy picture. This discussion will demonstrate why energy for use in our homes and automobiles may continue to put a crimp

on your budget and why it is important, indeed essential, to strive for greater efficiency and increased self-reliance now. Let's begin with oil.

WHY SWITCH TO RENEWABLES?

Oil provides 39 percent of the United States' energy. According to numerous oil analysts, global oil production is at an all-time historical high. Production during the new millennium, they say, will very likely never be higher than it is now, which is a polite way of saying that production of oil will very likely soon be on a slippery downward slope (Figure 4).

When the decline will commence, no one knows. Many think that the decline in oil production is already beginning, hence the high cost of home heating oil, gasoline, diesel, and jet fuel. If oil production has not peaked

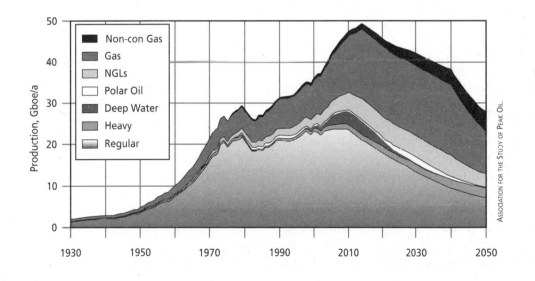

Fig. 4: Oil and natural gas production: past, present, and future.

ASSOCIATION FOR THE STUDY OF PEAK OIL.

and begun its decline already, it will soon. In 2005, Exxon Mobil, the world's largest oil company, quietly issued a statement projecting a peak in oil within five years.

Although most oil analysts think that oil production will follow a bell-shaped curve, reaching a peak and then sliding, I think that the decline, while imminent, will be staved off for a while by energy companies working overtime to compensate for declining production. That is to say, I believe that global oil production could plateau for a while as oil companies seek every avenue humanly and technologically possible to maintain production at current levels.

But even a plateau is not good news. Why?

In simple economic terms: when oil production maxes out, or plateaus, supplies will no longer be able to satisfy ever-increasing demand. Unless demand can be tempered, prices will skyrocket. Some experts predict dire consequences: inflation, economic stagnation, and recession — deep recession.

But even the plateau won't last forever. Sooner or later, the production of oil will begin a steady decline toward oblivion.

A sustained peak or plateau in production and the inevitable decline in production, while potentially devastating, could also spawn some exciting developments — changes that could offset the potential economic catastrophe. In fact, it already has. High prices at the gas pump, for instance, are triggering intense interest in energy conservation by individuals, businesses, and governments the world over.

A neighbor who drives a huge, gas-guzzling SUV called yesterday asking about my Toyota Prius (Gen II), a super-efficient gas/electric hybrid that gets 61 miles per gallon in the city and 51 mpg on the highway. Like many people, he bought one to replace his gas-guzzler SUV.

Energy woes could also result in a shift in North America's energy dependence. As oil supplies peak and then decline, we'll very likely begin to create a more energy-efficient society, powered more and more by renewable energy resources, among them solar energy, wind energy, hydropower, and biomass. To learn more about oil, you may want to read the accompanying textbox, "The Facts Behind Rising Oil Prices."

ANOTHER REASON FOR SWITCHING

As you've just seen (especially, if you've read the textbox), oil supplies here and abroad are in trouble — and so are those of us who depend so heavily on them. But oil's only half of the migraine headache industrial nations are facing. Natural gas supplies are the other half.

In the United States, natural gas supplies about 23 percent of our total energy demand. As most readers can attest, its price is on a meteoric rise, too. In my home state of Colorado, the price of natural gas has risen an average of 100 percent per year over the past three years (2003 – 2005). Nationwide, natural gas prices have tripled in the same period from $2 to $6 per million BTUs. At this writing, they're still rising.

The Facts Behind Rising Oil Prices

Oil prices have begun to increase dramatically over the past few years. This troubling surge in the price of oil, which is reflected in markedly higher prices at the gas pump, comes after a period of relative stability in the late 1980s and early 1990s — a period when some said the world was experiencing an oil glut.

The price of oil and one of its most visible byproducts, gasoline, has soared in large part because demand for oil and oil by-products is at an all time high. The price of any commodity is a function of the interplay of supply and demand. The higher the demand in relation to supply, the higher the price.

The demand for oil and its by-products such as gasoline is so high for a number of reasons. One reason is that Americans, who constitute less than 5 percent of the world's people but consume 25 percent of the world's oil, are using more and more oil and gasoline and diesel than ever before — and demand is continuing to increase. Rising fuel consumption is caused in part by urban sprawl. As cities and towns spread out on the land, Americans are forced to drive more and more miles each year, driving up fuel consumption. Making matters worse, many among us are driving larger, less fuel-efficient vehicles, putting additional demand on the world's limited oil supplies.

But we're not alone. China and other industrializing nations like India are also placing ever-increasing demands on global oil production. In China, for instance, new-found wealth is causing an upsurge in automobile sales. The Chinese who, for years, walked or bicycled to work, are increasingly turning to the automobile — buying a couple of million new vehicles a year now. As more and more Chinese turn from traditional forms of transportation to the automobile, gasoline consumption rises. "China is very important," notes Randy Udall, an expert in US and global energy supplies. "As the Chinese try to live like Americans, it's going to become increasingly expensive for us to continue our profligate ways."

Clearly, demand is up you say, but what about supply? Why can't we crank up production to meet rising demand?

Supply can't meet rising demand, or so say the experts, because global oil production is peaking.

One of the most important and widely respected authorities on global oil production is Colin J. Campbell. Campbell is no miscreant out to disrupt free enterprise. He is a long-time oil man, who has worked for a number of major oil companies in his long and productive career. He has studied and written about global oil reserves for many years, and is author of *The Essence of Oil and Gas Depletion* and founder of the Association for the Study of Peak Oil (ASPO). ☞

Another noted authority on world oil is Kenneth Deffeyes, a petroleum geologist and professor emeritus at Princeton University. He too has written a book on the subject, titled *Hubbert's Peak: The Impending World Oil Shortage.*

Both authors predict an imminent peak in global oil production. Deffeyes thinks the peak may have already occurred. He believes, for instance, that Saudi Arabia's oil production peaked in 2004. If that's the case, says Matt Simmons, head of an international investment banking organization that has financed approximately $50 billion worth of oil and natural gas projects, "World oil production has unequivocally peaked."

Nobody can predict exactly when oil will peak, says Randy Udall, but, "It's enough to say soon, and the foreshocks are already being felt."

A peak in oil production means that oil production cannot keep up with rising demand. Can't we find new oil to ease the crunch?

Unfortunately, we're in a bit of a bind. According to the Association for the Study of Peak Oil, oil companies discover, on average, about four billion barrels of new oil per year. However, the world consumes around 22 billion barrels of oil per year. The only way we can continue our current level of consumption is by tapping into deposits in previously discovered oil fields — oil fields that are, or so it appears, on the decline.

Unfortunately, most oil experts believe that there are no huge oil fields waiting to be discovered. In fact, the world's oil companies haven't found a gargantuan oil field since the 1960s (Figure 5).

Although newspapers and television occasionally report huge oil field discoveries, these "big finds" pale in comparison to the oil fields discovered in the 1960s and earlier. And what is more, they're tiny in relation to global oil consumption. For instance, in 2004 British newspapers and television reported on the discovery of a "huge oil deposit" in the North Sea. What readers and TV viewers didn't realize was that this huge oil deposit contained only enough to fuel the world economy for five and a quarter days.

But what about North American oil supplies? Isn't there enough oil in the United States and Canada to help ease the crunch?

No. In fact, turning to domestic supplies is like grocery shopping in a local outlet the morning before a big hurricane hits. "Three-fourths of all the oil and natural gas wells drilled in the world, have been drilled in the United States. Our continent is like Swiss cheese," remarks Udall.

The shelves are pretty empty. ☞

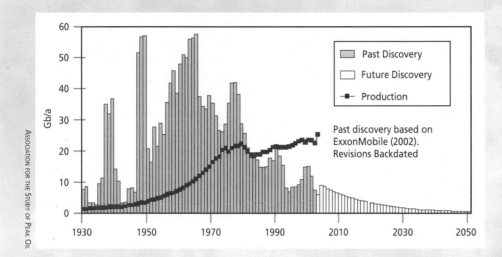

ASSOCIATION FOR THE STUDY OF PEAK OIL

Fig. 5: This graph maps global oil discoveries since 1930. Note that huge oil fields were discovered early on, but since 1970 discoveries of large oil fields have declined while production has continued to climb. In other words, we're living off the previous oil fields. Newer fields are smaller and less productive.

US oil production peaked in the early 1970s and has been on a sharp decline ever since. Our domestic supplies are nearly depleted. Probably about 75 to 80 percent of it is gone, says Steve Andrews, a Colorado-based energy expert. What's left won't even come close to helping ease the crunch.

So that's the oil picture. Sure, there's oil shale and tar sands, but they're costly and highly energy-intensive to develop. The bottom line is that the US is nearly out of oil and global supplies may have peaked or may peak soon. In the not-too-distant future, world oil production is likely to begin to decline, forcing nations to become more efficient and develop clean, reliable, and affordable alternatives.

While much of our attention is focused on oil as a source of gasoline and diesel fuel, it is important to remember that about one-fourth of the oil we use provides home heat. Much of the rest is used to make an assortment of useful products like lubricants, plastics, and synthetic materials for clothing, furniture, and window coverings. Even pesticides and virtually all medicines are made from chemicals extracted from oil. We pay for all of this with plastic credit cards, made from chemicals extracted from crude oil.

If all of this is hard to believe, don't despair; you're not alone in your incredulity. "We have become so accustomed to [the ready availability of oil] that we cannot imagine it to be at risk," says Campbell. If you want to explore this issue in more depth, I encourage you to read about the projections of the experts in Kenneth Deffeyes's book, *Hubbert's Peak,* or Campbell's books or Richard Heinberg's recent work, *The Party's Over.* ∎

To understand what's happening, take a look at the textbox on page 11.

AVERTING GLOBAL WARMING

The imminent peak in oil production and potential shortfalls in natural gas supplies in North America are just two compelling reasons why individuals should be thinking seriously about increasing their energy independence through conservation and renewable energy. Global climate change and its catastrophic impacts — among them drought, devastating and costly weather, and water shortages — are another reason. Already taking a huge toll on human society, global warming is a force to be reckoned with. For example, rising global temperature resulting from the release of greenhouse gases is spawning record-breaking heat waves and drought. Drought and high temperatures, in turn, reduce food production, cause devastating wildfires, and appear to be spawning a dramatic increase in violent weather that is causing tens of billions of dollars worth of damage each year from Texas to Europe to China.

Combine these and other global calamities with oil and natural gas shortages and human civilization could enter into an era of unprecedented economic and social decline. (If you would like to read more about the environmental trends that threaten our future, I strongly suggest you read Lester R. Brown's *Plan B: Rescuing a Planet under Stress and a Civilization in Trouble.*)

IS THERE HOPE?

I believe that individuals can insulate themselves from rising prices and so could the United States and Canada — in fact, any nation — if we act and act soon. One way is to step up energy conservation as I have done in my life. By reducing energy demand, individually and as a nation, we can align energy production and consumption, averting or tempering inflationary pressures while protecting the economy and our jobs.

You can compensate for declining oil and natural gas supplies by increasing your conservation efforts — using less energy and using it more efficiently — and by shifting to renewable energy resources. This strategy, if embraced by large numbers of people, indeed entire nations, could help us avoid the potentially cataclysmic effects of high fuel prices that could lead to runaway inflation and worldwide recession.

A transition to a much more energy-efficient, renewable energy is doable. As many readers already know, North Americans currently acquire only a fraction of the useful energy from the resources we consume, which is a kind way of saying we waste huge amounts of energy in meeting our needs. It wouldn't take much effort on our part to make up for a decline in the production of oil and natural gas through energy conservation, the topic of Chapter 2.

As individuals, businesses, and governments step up efforts to use energy more efficiently, we can also increase our reliance on

The Facts Behind Rising Natural Gas Prices

As shown in Figure 6, US natural gas production peaked in the early 1970s, and has been struggling to stay even for the past 30 years. In Texas, a major source of the nation's declining reserves of natural gas, energy companies drill an estimated 5,500 new wells each year just to keep production from falling, according to energy experts Randy Udall and Steve Andrews in an article published in the July/August 2001 issue of *Solar Today.* As you can see from the graph, natural gas production has plateaued as drillers struggle to keep production from declining.

Some experts believe that US natural gas production will begin to plummet by 2008 after three decades of plateau. This decline, they say, could lead to much higher prices and major economic dislocations that will be felt in every household, every business, and every government in North America, and very likely the world. Like oil, natural gas is vital to our lives and our economies. We use it to heat our homes, cook our food, heat water, and even make fertilizer and some useful chemicals like methanol.

Today, the US currently imports about 15 percent of the natural gas we consume each year from Canada via pipelines. Unfortunately, says Andrews, that 15 percent represents 50 percent of Canada's total annual production. It is doubtful that Canadians are going to ramp up production to supply us ☞

Fig. 6: Natural gas production peaked in the early 1970s and has plateaued since then, despite a massive increase in exploration and drilling. Some analysts believe that US production will begin to decline rapidly after 2008. Global production is expected to peak sometime around 2015.

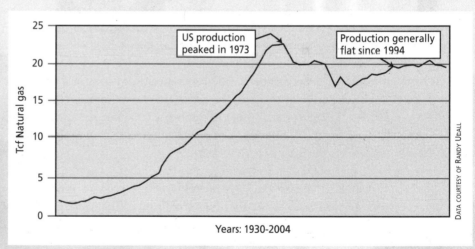

US production peaked in 1973

Production generally flat since 1994

Tcf Natural gas

Years: 1930-2004

DATA COURTESY OF RANDY UDALL

with additional natural gas. Their reserves are on the decline and their climate is colder than ours. It's doubtful that they will expand production to supply their energy-hungry neighbor to the south. Canada has its own future to protect.

Can we stave off the imminent decline in natural gas by tapping into natural gas deposits elsewhere? Unlike oil, the picture on global natural gas supplies is not so clear cut. I've found considerable disagreement on global natural gas supplies. C.J. Campbell, for instance, predicts that global natural gas production will peak somewhere around 2015 (Figure 4). Randy Udall, an internationally renowned natural gas expert, believes that we have a bit longer before we experience a peak in global natural gas production — at least another decade or so beyond Campbell's prediction.

Huge deposits of natural gas lie in the Middle East, but "there are also large deposits in Siberia, Australia, South America, Africa, and Trinidad," says Udall. "We import oil from 30 nations, and could import gas from that many eventually, too." So North America could import natural gas in tankers, ships specially designed to transport compressed natural gas, commonly referred to as CNG.

Natural gas importation to the United States is currently limited, however, by the availability of CNG tankers and by ports that accept this potentially dangerous fuel. At this time, there are only four ports in the United States equipped to accept natural gas from tankers. Importation is, in a nutshell, limited by infrastructure. Making matters worse, a large number of port cities have recently rejected proposals to install facilities that would permit an increase in CNG imports, primarily as a result of safety issues. Some fear that a CNG port might be vulnerable to terrorism; others are concerned that such a facility would pose significant threats to residents of nearby cities. If objections to such facilities are dropped, it could take a decade or longer to obtain approval and to build facilities to increase North America's capacity to import more CNG.

Currently, the United States imports only two percent of its natural gas by ship, say Andrews and Udall. The US Energy Information Agency predicts that the amount of the United States' imports will increase dramatically, up to 20 percent of the country's total natural gas consumption, by 2025. Udall predicts a lesser increase, of 10–15 percent of our total consumption in that time frame. So far, governments have not done much to stave off shortfalls.

For those in North America and elsewhere who depend on natural gas, there's an important lesson in all of this: for at least the next decade homeowners may have to fend for themselves. That is, not only will they need to find ways to use natural gas efficiently, they will need to develop clean, reliable, and affordable renewable energy sources to meet their needs. ■

renewable energy. Abundant supplies of renewable energy could replace declining supplies of nonrenewable oil and natural gas.

As should be clear by now, this plan will require efforts on the part of all stakeholders — individuals like yourself, governments, and businesses. This book, however, focuses on what *you* can do. It will show you what you and your family and your neighbors can do to dramatically improve energy efficiency in your home and to increase your use of renewable energy. If you take these ideas far enough, you could come close to complete energy independence in your home, as I have in mine.

Despite the grim prognostications of some experts, I believe there is hope. Whether you are building a new home or retrofitting an existing residence, you can make significant strides that will help you and your family weather the storm and help create a larger shift toward a renewable energy economy. You can slash your energy bills, help foster the transition to a renewable energy future, and help ensure a strong, vibrant economy and a better future.

KEEPING YOUR EYE ON THE PRIZE

Before we get to the specifics of forging a path of greater energy independence, it is important to underscore a very important guideline to follow as you develop a personal energy plan: remember as you pursue your energy efficiency and renewable energy options to always keep your eye on the prize. That is, always focus on the fuels for which you are seeking replacements and, perhaps more importantly, the services they provide. Seek specific replacements for those services.

Table 1 shows the general uses for oil and natural gas in our society and, more important to you, the specific services these fuels offer us in our homes. As you can see, oil is used in many ways in modern society. It heats many homes in North America, especially in the Northeast and Northwest. It also provides some electricity. Those who depend on fuel oil for home heat will, therefore, want to find alternatives. Oil is the main source of automobile, truck, bus, jet, airplane, and ship fuel, too, and there are alternatives to these uses in Chapter 10 that you can turn to as well.

Natural gas also has many uses in our society, but is much more widely used in our homes. Not only does it provide space heat, it is used to heat water for showers, washing dishes, and cleaning our clothes. It also widely used to cook food. If your home is supplied by natural gas, it is these end-uses on which you will want to focus.

As you can see from the chart, as a homeowner, your main objective in achieving greater efficiency and more independence will be finding alternatives to home heating, domestic hot water, and transportation fuels. However, you may also want to find alternatives to conventional electrical power — generated by coal, natural gas, and oil. This book will discuss your options in this arena as well.

Despite the grim prognostications of some experts, I believe there is hope. Whether you are building a new home or retrofitting an existing residence, you can make significant strides that will help you and your family weather the storm and help create a shift toward a renewable energy economy.

ORGANIZATION OF THE BOOK

This book takes the reader on a journey of discovery. I begin in Chapter 1 with an overview of renewable energy, examining the options available to homeowners. We'll also briefly look at the pros and cons of renewable energy so you enter into this venture with eyes wide open.

In Chapter 2, we'll explore conservation, the cornerstone of any personal energy strategy. You'll learn why I consider energy conservation to be a valuable form of renewable energy.

Table 1 Oil and Natural Gas End Uses			
Fuel	**Products/Services**	**Direct Use in Home**	**Indirect Use**
Oil	Home heating oil in some locales (e.g., Northeastern United States and Pacific Northwest) Gasoline for cars, trucks, lawnmowers, generators, etc. Diesel for trucks and buses Electricity in a few areas Chemicals for pharmaceuticals Chemicals for plastic production Pesticides	Home heating	
Natural Gas	Synthetic fertilizers Industrial processes Domestic hot water Home heating Electrical production	Domestic hot water Home heating	Electrical production

You'll see how much money you can save through home energy conservation, too, and examine a host of other benefits. This chapter concludes with a simple, cost-effective home energy conservation strategy that will save you and your family thousands of dollars, perhaps tens of thousands of dollars, over your lifetime.

In Chapter 3, we'll focus our attention on solar hot water systems for providing domestic hot water. We will examine the types of systems on the market today, and see how they work. I'll provide information, including costs, that will help you decide which system is best for your home. As in other chapters, we'll explore home energy savings as well as the pros and cons of this approach to home energy production.

In Chapter 4, we'll explore space heating options, among them passive solar heating — heating homes without costly nonrenewable fuels and expensive mechanical systems. We'll look at active solar systems as well and study heat pumps, two approaches that could become the mainstay of American home heating in the not-too-distant future. As in many other chapters I'll explain the wisest, most cost-effective strategies in an effort to help you achieve affordable energy independence.

In Chapter 5, we'll explore wood burning as another home heating strategy. We'll examine fireplace inserts and woodstoves as well as pellet stoves. We'll also look at a technology few readers have probably ever heard of: masonry heaters. Like other chapters, this one will include a discussion of the pros and cons of wood heating. I'll also tell you where you can find lots of free wood, even in cities and towns.

In Chapter 6, we will turn our attention to another enormous challenge: cooling a home without costly fossil fuels. We'll explore general strategies as well as specific tools of the trade, and how they can be applied to different climate zones.

In Chapter 7, we will explore solar electric systems. You will learn how this amazing technology works, and the various options that are available to you. We'll even explore ways to help offset the costs of these systems, sometimes substantially.

In Chapter 8, we will turn our attention to yet another means of producing electricity from a renewable energy source, wind power. Although wind generators are not for everyone — certainly not those who live in urban or suburban neighborhoods — you will see that there are ways that you can tap into wind energy *without* installing a wind generator in your back yard.

In Chapter 9, we'll explore microhydroelectric systems, a technology that allows rural residents in some areas to tap into the power of flowing water. Although there are few residential sites available for this approach in North America, those who are lucky enough to live on one will find this to be an excellent choice.

Finally, in Chapter 10 we will take a look at emerging renewable energy technologies and fuels for our homes and our vehicles. Among other topics, we'll study hydrogen, fuel cells, biodiesel, vegetable oil, ethanol, and methane digesters. We'll even explore ways that plants can be used to replace chemicals used to make pharmaceuticals and other products, which are currently derived from oil.

At the end of the book is a list of important resources — websites, books, articles, magazines, videos, organizations, and so on — that provide additional information and support.

What say we get started.

CHAPTER 1

RENEWABLE ENERGY
CLEAN, AFFORDABLE, AND RELIABLE

Contrary to what many think, renewable energy is not a new, unproven invention of modern society. Humans have relied on renewable energy for most of our history — since the very first humanlike creatures roamed the planet over three million years ago. Throughout most of human history, the energy human beings have needed to survive and prosper has come from food molecules, primarily seeds, berries, and roots. The energy in these foods provided the means by which we built early civilizations. Our early ancestors also burned wood to warm their caves and cook their food.

Plants, of course, are renewable resources, capable of regenerating themselves from seeds, roots (as in the case of perennials), or tubers. But plants are here by the grace of three other renewable environmental resources: soil, water, and air.

Although our predecessors, and virtually all other life forms on the planet, received the energy they needed to survive from plant matter, the energy of our botanical companions is not derived from the soil or water or even the air. It comes from the sun.

Plants capture the sun's energy during photosynthesis. In a complex set of chemical reactions, plants synthesize a wide variety of food molecules from three basic "ingredients": carbon dioxide from the air, water from the soil, and solar energy from the heavens. Solar energy that drives photosynthetic reactions is captured and stored in the chemical bonds of organic food molecules. When food molecules are consumed by us, or any other animal for

Contrary to what many think, renewable energy is not a new, unproven invention of modern society. Humans have relied on renewable energy for most of our history.

that matter, the energy is released. Solar energy contained in food molecules and liberated by the cells of our bodies is, in turn, used to transport molecules across cell membranes, to manufacture protein and DNA, to power muscles, and to heat our bodies.

Throughout most of human history, then, humankind's greatest achievements were made by using the sun's energy. The Egyptians, for instance, hauled massive stones from God knows where to build the towering pyramids with nothing but ingenuity and the muscle power of conscripted laborers fueled by organic food molecules courtesy of the sun and plants. The Romans expanded their holdings to build a vast and prosperous empire, too, all with horse and human muscle powered by plant matter and, ultimately, sunlight.

For most of human history, then, renewable energy reigned supreme.

Then came the fossil fuel era.

Lumbering to a start in the 1700s in Europe and the 1800s in North America, the fossil fuel era was first powered by coal, an organic sedimentary rock. It too owes its origin to plants that grew in the Carboniferous era some 250 to 350 million years ago. Coal replaced waning supplies of wood in Europe and fed the industrial machinery that made mass production — and modern society — possible.

For many years, coal reigned supreme. But eventually coal was forced to share its kingdom with two additional fossil fuels: oil and natural gas. Also produced from once-living organisms, notably aquatic algae, these fuels were relatively easy to transport and, like coal, were found in highly concentrated deposits. Over time, oil and natural gas, along with coal, became major components of much of the world's energy diet.

Today, oil supplies 39 percent of the United States' total annual energy demand. Natural gas and coal provide about 23 percent each, bringing the grand total to 85 percent. The remaining 15 percent of the United States' energy diet is satisfied by small amounts of hydropower, solar, wind, geothermal, and nuclear energy — the first four of which are renewable. Canada is also heavily dependent on oil, natural gas, and coal. Oil constitutes about 27 percent of the nation's energy diet, while natural gas provides about 12 percent and coal provides another 12 percent.

Although fossil fuels dominate the energy scene today, their glory days are about to come to an end. As we saw in the introduction, oil and natural gas are soon going to enter their sunset years. The party's over for them, and for us too, unless, of course, we shift to clean, affordable, reliable, and abundant renewable energy alternatives. Fortunately, we have lots of options.

MAKING WISE CHOICES

In order to make the wisest choices as individuals — and as a society — we need to understand precisely what energy resources are endangered, the subject of the introduction to this book. Given the devastating impact and high cost of global warming and a host of other energy-related environmental problems to human society, we also need to determine the energy resources that need to be phased out for social, economic, and environmental reasons.

Oil and natural gas soon will require replacements to satisfy our needs. From an environmental standpoint, coal begs for replacements, too. Although coal is abundant in North America and elsewhere, and its use is bound to increase dramatically as oil and natural gas production peak, coal is the dirtiest of all fossil fuels. Coal combustion not only produces sulfur oxides and nitrogen oxides that contribute to acid rain and snow, it generates millions of tons of particulates that cause asthma and other respiratory diseases. Coal combustion also yields millions of tons of ash containing an assortment of potentially toxic materials. Much of this ash is disposed of in ordinary landfills. Perhaps most important to our future, however, is that coal combustion produces enormous quantities of the greenhouse gas carbon dioxide — far more carbon dioxide per unit of energy produced than any other fossil fuel in use today (Figure 1-1).

Despite industry's frequent mention of an elusive "clean coal technology," a posture by the coal industry to make their inherently dirty fuel appear more acceptable, it's really difficult to make coal clean. Sure, the efficiency of the combustion process can be increased to reduce the amount of pollution per unit of energy produced, and I applaud

any efforts to do so. But pollution is inevitable, and the more coal we consume, the greater the output of potentially harmful gases. Carbon dioxide, for example, is the unavoidable by-product of combustion of any carbon fuel. Much of the sulfur that contaminates coal in varying degrees can be removed before or after combustion by pollution control devices. The sulfur, however, does not magically disappear. It ends up in the environment one way or another. It's a simple mass balance phenomenon: if the chemical ingredients of the pollutants are in the fuel, they've going to be produced as a by-product one way or another. They won't mysteriously vanish because some coal executive tells you so. Much sulfur is removed by smokestack scrubbers, but the sulfur removed by these devices ends up in a

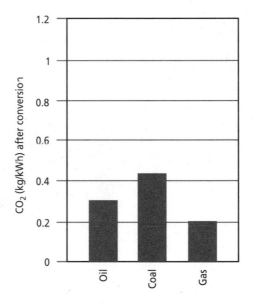

Fig. 1-1: Not all fossil fuels are created equal. Coal has a much higher ratio of carbon to hydrogen than oil, which has a much higher ratio of carbon to hydrogen than natural gas. The more carbon a fuel contains, the more carbon dioxide it produces per BTU of energy released.

toxic slurry that is disposed of in landfills where the toxic components can leach into groundwater.

To make wise choices, we also need to understand the end uses of each fuel because, after all, it is these services that we want to protect, not the fuels themselves. If natural gas supplies are going to decline, we don't necessarily need more gas. Rather, we need to ensure the continuation of the services natural gas provides. For many homeowners, natural

gas is used to provide space heat; to heat water for showers, dishwashing, and laundry; and to cook food. It is these *services* that we need to ensure.

As you read this book, you'll find that there are many options to ensure the services once supplied by now-failing fuel sources. Take space heat — keeping our homes warm. Warm interiors can be ensured by installing additional insulation to the ceilings and walls of our homes and by sealing up those obnoxious and costly heat-robbing cracks around windows, doors, and elsewhere. Space heat can also be provided by retrofitting our homes for passive solar — adding windows on the south sides of our homes to let in the low-angled winter sun. Space heat can also be achieved by installing active solar systems (Figure 1-2). Solar hot water systems generate hot water that can be used for a variety of heating systems that already exist in many of our homes — from baseboard hot water systems to radiant floor systems to forced-air systems. Your options don't end here, however. You can also heat your homes by installing a heat pump, a device that removes heat from the ground or even the air and transfers it to your home.

To make wise choices, you also need to know what options make the most sense. How do we assess the appropriateness of a renewable energy option?

Two of the most important criteria are cost and net energy yield, which often go hand in hand. Consider an example.

Fig. 1-2: Solar hot water panels like these convert solar energy into heat that is used to heat water for domestic uses and to heat homes. These glass tubes contain a small black copper pipe that is heated by the sun.

To replace declining supplies of oil, many fossil fuel advocates suggest that we can turn to oil shale and tar sands. Unfortunately, a huge amount of energy is required to extract the oil from them. The energy required to extract oil from tar sands and oil shale subtracted from the energy of the final product is known as the net energy yield, or simply, energy returned on energy invested. Both oil shale and tar sand oil production have very low net energy yields compared to conventional oil, although new processes have steadily improved the net energy yield of tar sand production. The lower the net energy yield, the more costly the new product. As the price of conventional oil increases, the cost of oil shale and tar sand oil will inevitably rise.

Environmental impact should also be a key criterion when selecting an alternative fuel. To build a sustainable future, we should choose fuels that meet our needs for energy without sacrificing an equally important, though often overlooked, requirement: our need for a healthy environment.

Resource supplies are also vital. From the long-term perspective, it makes sense to pursue those resources that are most abundant. What could be more abundant than a renewable fuel supply?

In sum, when seeking alternatives to waning supplies of fossil fuels, we must proceed with caution and intelligence. We need to develop energy resources that have the highest net energy yield, the most abundant supplies, and the lowest overall cost —

socially, economically, and environmentally. In this book, I present the most up-to-date information I could find on net energy yields to help you sort through the list of options. I'll also look at the pros and cons of various technologies, to help you make the wisest choices.

Before we go much further, though, let us take a brief look at energy itself. To help you understand this elusive entity, I'll cover some basics here, then introduce more concepts later in the book as we explore the various renewable energy systems.

UNDERSTANDING ENERGY

Like love, energy is all around us, but is sometimes difficult to define.

Energy Comes in Many Forms

Let's begin by making a simple observation as a way to help define this term: energy comes in many forms. For example, humans in many countries rely today on fossil fuels such as coal, oil, and natural gas. And some use nuclear energy to generate electricity. In other countries, wood and other forms of biomass are primary forms of energy. (Biomass includes a wide assortment of solid fuels, such as wood, and liquid fuels, such as ethanol derived from corn, and biodiesel, a liquid fuel made from vegetable oils.) And don't forget sunlight, wind, hydropower, and geothermal energy — energy produced in the Earth's interior. Even a cube of sugar contains energy. Touch a match to it and it will burn, giving off heat and light, two additional forms of energy.

When seeking alternatives to waning supplies of fossil fuels, we must proceed with caution and intelligence. We need to develop energy resources that have the highest net energy yield, the most abundant supplies, and the lowest overall cost — socially, economically, and environmentally.

Energy Can Be Renewable or Nonrenewable

Energy in its various forms can be broadly classified as either renewable or nonrenewable. Renewable energy, as noted earlier, is any form of energy that's regenerated by natural forces. Wind, for instance, is a renewable form of energy. It is available to us year after year thanks in large part to the unequal heating of the Earth's surface. When one area is warmed by the sun, hot air is produced. This hot air rises and, as it does, cooler air moves in from neighboring areas. As the cool air moves in, it creates winds of varying intensity. Renewable energy is everywhere and is replenished year after year, providing humankind with a potentially enormous supply ... if only we're smart enough to tap into it.

Nonrenewable energy, on the other hand, is finite. It cannot be regenerated in a timely fashion by natural processes. Coal, oil, natural gas, tar sands, oil shale, and nuclear energy are all nonrenewable forms of energy. Ironically, while most of these sources of energy were produced by natural biological and geological processes early in the Earth's history, and while these processes continue today in some parts of the world, these fuels are not being produced at a rate even remotely close to our rate of consumption. Coal, for instance, may be forming in some swamplands around the world. But its regeneration is taking place at such a painfully slow rate that it is meaningless. Put another way, contemporary production can never replenish the massive supplies that

Renewable energy is everywhere and is replenished year after year, providing humankind with a potentially enormous supply ... if only we're smart enough to tap into it.

were produced over long periods of time many millions of years ago. Because of this, coal, oil, natural gas, and the like are essentially finite.

When they're gone, they're gone.

So now you know two basic facts about energy: energy comes in many forms, and all forms of energy broadly fit into two general categories: renewable and nonrenewable.

Energy Can Be Converted from One Form to Another

Yet there's more to energy than this. For example, even the casual observer can tell you that energy can be converted from one form to another. Natural gas, for example, when burned is converted to heat and light. Coal, oil, wood, biodiesel, and other fuels are also converted to other forms of energy during combustion. Heat, light, and electricity are the most common byproducts of these conversions. But the possibilities don't end here. Visible light contained in the sun's energy can be converted to heat. It can also be converted to electrical energy. Even wind can be converted to electricity or to mechanical energy to drive a pump to draw water from the ground.

Energy Conversions Allow Us to Put Energy to Good Use

Not only can energy be converted to other forms, it has to be for us to derive benefit. Coal, by itself, is of little value to us. It's a sedimentary rock and fun to behold, but it is the heat and electricity produced when coal is burned in power plants that are of value to us. Sunlight is pretty, too, and it feeds the plants we eat, but in our homes and factories, the heat that the sun produces and the electricity we can generate from it are of primary value to us.

In sum, then, it is not raw forms of energy that we need. Not at all. It is the by-products of energy that are unleashed when we process them in various energy-liberating technologies that meet the complex needs of society.

Energy Can Neither Be Created nor Destroyed

Another thing you need to know to deepen your understanding of energy is that energy can neither be created nor can it be destroyed. Physicists call this the First Law of Thermodynamics or, simply, the First Law.

The First Law says that all energy comes from pre-existing forms. Even though you may think you are creating energy when you burn a piece of firewood in a woodstove, all you are doing is unleashing energy contained in the wood — specifically, the energy locked in the chemical bonds in the molecules that make up wood. This energy, in turn, came from sunlight. And the sun's energy came from the fusion of hydrogen atoms in the sun's interior.

Energy is Degraded When it is Converted from One Form to Another

More important to us, however, is the Second Law of Thermodynamics. The Second Law says, quite simply, that anytime one converts one form of energy to another form — for example, when you convert natural gas to heat — it is degraded. Translated, that means energy conversions transform high-quality energy resources to low-quality energy. Natural gas, for instance, contains a huge amount of energy in a small volume; it's locked up in the simple chemical bonds that attach the carbon atom to the four hydrogen atoms of the methane molecules. When these bonds are broken, the stored chemical energy is released. Light and heat are the products. Both light and heat are less concentrated — or lower quality — forms of energy. Hence, we say that natural gas, a concentrated form of energy, is "degraded." In electric power plants, only about 50 percent of the energy contained in natural gas is converted to electrical energy. The rest is "lost" as heat and is dissipated into the environment.

No Energy Conversion is 100 Percent Efficient, Not Even Close to It

This leads us to another important fact about energy: no energy conversion is 100 percent efficient. When coal is burned in an electric power plant, only about one-third of the energy contained in the coal is converted to useful energy — in this case, electricity. The rest is lost as heat and light. The same goes for renewable energy technologies. One hundred units of solar energy beaming down on a solar electric module won't produce the equivalent of 100 units of electricity. You'll

It is not raw forms of energy that we need. Not at all. It is the byproducts of energy that are unleashed when we process them in various energy-liberating technologies that meet the complex needs of society.

only get around 12–15 percent conversion on the most popular modules on the market today.

Energy is lost in all conversions. As another example, most conventional incandescent light bulbs in our homes convert only about five percent of the electrical energy that runs through them into light. The rest comes out as heat.

Each conversion in a chain of energy conversions loses useful energy, as shown in Figure 1-3. Don't forget that. To get the most out of our primary energy sources, we must reduce the number of conversions along the path.

But let's get something straight. Some of you may be wondering if all of this discussion of energy losses is a violation of the First Law, which states that energy cannot be created or destroyed.

The truth be known, the energy losses I've been talking about during energy conversion are not really losses in the true sense of the word. Energy is not really destroyed; it is released in various forms, some useful and others, such as heat, not so useful. Chemical energy in the gasoline that runs a car, for instance, is converted to the mechanical energy of moving parts that propel us forward along

Fig. 1-3: Energy conversions occur commonly in the production-consumption cycle of various fuels. Unfortunately, none of these conversions is 100 percent efficient, so energy is lost at each stage. The key to using energy efficiently is to limit or eliminate conversions.

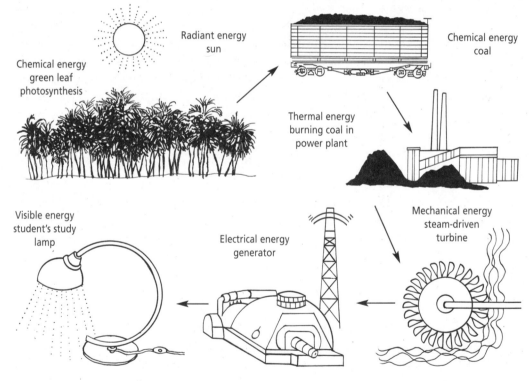

Radiant energy sun

Chemical energy green leaf photosynthesis

Chemical energy coal

Thermal energy burning coal in power plant

Mechanical energy steam-driven turbine

Visible energy student's study lamp

Electrical energy generator

the highway. Some is also lost as heat that radiates off the engine. This waste heat is of little value except on cold winter days when captured, at least in part, to warm the car's interior.

Eventually, however, all heat produced by a motorized vehicle escapes into outer space. It is not destroyed, per se, but it is no longer available to us. Hence, the conversion results in a net loss of *useful* energy.

OK, so now you're cooking with information about energy. You know there are many forms of energy. You know that energy can be renewable or nonrenewable. You understand that raw energy is not as important to us in our homes as are its useful by-products such as electricity, light, or heat. You now also know that energy can be neither created nor destroyed. It can only be converted from one form to another. And you're privy to the fact that no energy conversion is 100 percent efficient, not even close.

You also understand that during conversions useful energy decreases. That fact, in turn, is important for nonrenewable fuels; once they've burned, or reacted in the case of nuclear fuels, their energy is gone forever. The heat radiates endlessly into outer space, heating the universe, as it were.

Renewable energy resources, on the other hand, can be regenerated year after year after year. If we're going to persist as a society in the long term, it is renewable energy resources we'll need to rely on. Unlike fossil fuel energy and nuclear energy, renewable resources can return again and again, making our lives bright and cheery and comfortable so long as the sun continues to illuminate the daytime sky.

With these important points in mind, let's define this thing we call energy.

Energy is the Ability to Do Work

To a physicist, energy is defined as "the ability to do work." More accurately, says engineer John Howe, "Energy is that elusive something that allows us to do work." We and our machines, that is.

Any time you lift an object, for example, or slide an object across the floor, you are performing work. The same holds for our machines. Anytime a machine lifts something or moves it from one place to another, it performs work.

According to physicists, work is also performed when the temperature of a substance, for example, water, is raised. Therefore, your stove or microwave is working when it boils water for hot tea or soup.

Energy, quite simply, is valuable because it allows us to perform work. It powers our bodies. It powers our homes. It powers our society. We cannot exist without energy.

Work and Power

Physicists aren't content simply to define energy; they also like to measure it. Because many of these units of measurement will come in handy when retrofitting your home, let's

Energy, quite simply, is valuable because it allows us to perform work. It powers our bodies. It powers our homes. It powers our society. We cannot exist without energy.

look at a few of the most common ones. Let's focus first on mechanical energy.

If you push a 100-pound box of potatoes 10 feet across a wooden floor, physicists would proclaim that you have performed work. And you'd probably agree. But how much work have you performed?

To calculate the amount of work performed, scientists use a very simple equation:

Work = Force x Distance

In this case work = 100 pounds x 10 feet = 1,000 foot-pounds of work.

Foot-pounds isn't a term that comes in very handy in most home energy applications, but it helps you peer more deeply into energy. Let's go a bit deeper into a realm of more useful energy measurements by examining the rate at which work is performed.

Physicists define the rate at which you or a machine performs work as *power*. An adult, for instance, might be able to push a 100-pound box 10 feet across a floor in 4 seconds. It might take a ten-year-old ten seconds to perform that same amount of work. Clearly, the adult is more powerful. Even though they perform the same amount of work, the adult performs it more quickly.

For the mathematically inclined: power is the force x the distance (or work performed) divided by the time it took to complete the task. Another way of writing this is: Power = Work/Time.

In the case of the adult, power = 1,000 foot-pounds/4 seconds or 250 foot-pounds

per second. In the case of the child, power = 1,000 foot-pounds/10 seconds or 100 foot-pounds per second.

I bring all this up not to torment you with physics, but because you will encounter units of work and power as you study your home energy options. However, in this book most of our attention will focus on thermal and electrical energy.

Thermal or heat energy in homes, for instance, is measured in BTUs or British Thermal Units. Let's get this one out of the way right now: one BTU is the amount of energy it takes to raise one pound of water one degree Fahrenheit. Remember, as just noted, raising temperature is a measure of work.

Furnaces, boilers, and water heaters are all rated by their BTU output. Moreover, energy auditors, whom you may be hiring, typically calculate heat loss in homes in BTUs — usually BTUs per square foot per year. Solar heating specialists calculate heating loads — how much heat your home needs — in BTUs as well.

A single BTU is not much energy when compared to what it takes to provide hot water for a family of four or to heat a home for a year. Most of the time, you will be dealing with tens of thousands of BTUs or, in the case of home heating, millions. A house, for example, can gain tens of millions of BTUs of heat energy from the sun each year.

While BTUs are the measurement of heat energy, electrical energy has its own set of terms. Wouldn't you know it!

You'll need to be familiar with electrical energy terms too if you decide to do something about your home's electrical energy consumption. While I've got you on the torture rack, let's take a look at them now. The pain will ease up shortly.

The electricity in our homes is really the flow of electrons, tiny subatomic particles, through wires. To help students understand electricity, most teachers liken electricity to water flowing in a hose. Water molecules, in this analogy, are akin to the electrons flowing in a wire.

As you know, water can flow slowly through a hose or very quickly, or anywhere in between. How fast water flows through a hose is determined by a force called water pressure. Water flowing out of the hose of a rain barrel, for example, flows pretty slowly. Water flowing through a downspout from the gutter that drains a roof flows more quickly. It is under more pressure than the water flowing out of the rain barrel.

How fast electrons flow through a wire also depends on a force much like the pressure in a hose. We measure this force in volts.

In the world of electricity, electrical power can be calculated using the same equation we used to determine mechanical energy: Power = Force x Distance/Time. In electrical energy the force is the volts. What about the distance and time components of the equation?

Electrons can flow at different rates in wires, too. The number of electrons flowing past a point in the wire at any one time is measured by amps, short for amperes. Multiplying volts (force) times amps (distance/time), therefore, gives you a measure of power. Power is measured in a term familiar to most of us, watts. To simplify matters, physicists calculate watts by the following equation:

Watts = amps x volts

Ok, let's stop here and turn our attention to the shining star of the energy show, renewable energy.

WHAT IS RENEWABLE ENERGY?

Renewable energy, as just noted, is a form of energy capable of being regenerated by natural processes at meaningful rates. Wood, for instance, is a form of renewable energy. It's produced by trees. Sunlight, wind, and flowing water are also renewable energy resources (Figure 1-4). Heat within the Earth's crust is renewable, too, as are the tides.

Fig. 1-4: The energy of falling water can be captured on a small scale or a very large scale. Although this form of energy is relatively clean, damming rivers can create enormous environmental impacts.

Dan Chiras

Our Renewable Energy Portfolio

Solar energy
Wind energy
Biomass
Tidal energy
Geothermal energy
Hydropower

Most of these renewable forms of energy are made possible by the kingpin of all renewables, the sun, the center star of our solar system.

Let's get something out of the way right from the start, however, so we don't live a lie. The sun is really *not* a renewable energy source.

This blisteringly hot ball of gases is a huge fusion reactor, smack dab in the middle of our solar system, 93 million miles from planet Earth. Fusion reactions occur between hydrogen atoms in the sun's interior. When two hydrogen atoms fuse they form a helium atom and enormous amounts of heat, light, and other forms of energy.

That's what makes the sun tick.

And the Earth, too.

Although only two billionths of the sun's energy strikes the Earth, it is enough to power virtually all life on land and sea, and it has been responsible for the build up of vast resources of fossil fuels, now quickly (in geological and human time) sliding toward oblivion.

Technically, though, the sun is a finite resource. Someday its fuel source will run out. But don't fret; there's good news: the sun is going to burn brightly for at least five billion years or more before it dies out on us. And when it does, it will be all over anyway. Life cannot continue on the planet without the sun.

Although the sun is a finite resource, teachers, energy experts, and books on the subject still refer to it as a renewable energy resource. One of the reasons may be that the sun comes up every day and thus appears to provide energy for us day after day, year after year, decade after decade. Perhaps it is just because early advocates didn't understand that the sun was finite.

THE PROS AND CONS OF RENEWABLE ENERGY

Before we immerse ourselves in the details of renewable energy, it is important to step back for a moment to analyze its pros and cons. Entering this venture with eyes wide open will help all of us make the wisest choices. It will also help us find ways to offset some of the problems posed by some of the renewable energy technologies that hold so much promise for our future.

Before we examine the pros and cons of renewable energy, however, it is important — indeed vital — to point out a dangerous trap that many fall into, notably, lumping renewables into a single category. Renewable energy encompasses a half dozen or so fuels: solar, wind, hydropower, biomass, hydrogen, and geothermal.

Understanding the Fine Points

Each of these sources of renewable energy requires various technologies to convert their energy into useful forms. To tap into solar energy to make electricity, for instance, we use solar cells, most of which are now made from silicon (Figure 1-5). Solar cells produce electricity when struck by sunlight. To capture solar energy to produce hot water for heating water in our homes, we rely on solar hot water panels. They capture visible sunlight and convert it to heat. Thermal energy is then used to heat water for domestic uses or to warm swimming pools or melt snow on driveways. Solar panels such as these can also be used to generate heat to maintain comfortable interior temperatures in our homes during the winter.

The upshot of this discussion is that because there are many renewable energy options, it is misleading to lump them into broad categories. It is inaccurate, for example, to speak of solar energy technologies as a single entity; granted, there's one common fuel source —the sun — but a number of different technologies, each with different uses, benefits, challenges, and costs.

Troubles often arise when critics of renewable energy lump these technologies together. For example, opponents of solar energy are fond of saying that "solar energy is too expensive." Such statements do a great disservice to us and to renewable energy. It's a little like saying, "All Americans are idiots," just because there are a few nitwits amongst us.

As you shall soon see, while some solar technologies are indeed expensive, others are quite cost-competitive with conventional fuel technologies. Consider an example. Solar

Fig. 1-5: This tiny solar cell (a) is made of silicon dioxide which comes from sand. It converts solar energy into electricity. Many solar cells are wired together in a module which is mounted on the roof or on a free-standing rack or pole (b).

Fig. 1-6: Emergency phones along a remote northern California highway are made possible by solar electricity. Stringing electrical lines to such locations would be cost-prohibitive.

DAN CHIRAS

electricity is pretty expensive in many places, while passive solar heating is affordable and cost-effective. But even here, a careful review of our options illustrates that qualified declarations can also be misleading. There are, for example, times when solar electricity is actually less expensive than electricity from conventional sources, such as nuclear and coal. In Third World countries, for instance, it's cheaper to install solar electric panels in rural villages than to string power lines hundreds of miles from existing coal-fired power plants to service these remote locations.

Even in industrialized nations, the cost issue is not always straightforward. As a general rule, solar electricity generated by solar electric panels costs around 24 to 27 cents per kilowatt hour. In contrast, electricity from coal-fired power plants in the United States costs about eight cents, give or take a little. Electricity from nuclear power plants costs about 12 to 15 cents per kilowatt hour, give or take a little. Despite these obvious differences, solar electricity can be less expensive than conventional electrical power in some locations. For example, if

you build a home two- or three-tenths of a mile from a power line, you'll find that it is often less expensive to install a full scale solar electric system than it would be to string electric wires from the power line that runs along your property to your home. In fact, it might cost $20,000 to $30,000 just to run an electrical line a couple of tenths of a mile. And that doesn't give you a single kilowatt hour of electricity. All it provides is access to the electrical grid.

As you shall soon see, homeowners can install a pretty impressive solar electric system for $30,000. And if you build more than half a mile from an existing power line, a solar system is hands-down, without question, much less expensive than connecting to the electrical grid — unless your utility picks up the tab for running the wire to your home.

Further clouding the cost picture, some states like California, Illinois, New York, New Jersey, and Colorado offer generous incentives that reduce the cost of solar electric systems. Some offer financial incentives up to half the cost of the system, driving down the cost to around 12 cents per kilowatt hour, making solar electricity much more cost-competitive to homeowners.

Solar electricity also makes sense in cases where grid power is expensive. In California, for instance, electricity from the grid during peak usage periods typically runs from 30 cents to over a dollar a kilowatt hour, far more than the cost of generating electricity from sunlight. Grid power in Germany is currently

75 cents per kilowatt hour, creating a bonanza for US solar cell manufacturers.

When listing the pros and cons of renewable energy technologies, then, we need to be very specific. Keep this in mind when discussing renewable energy technologies with friends, government officials, or opponents. Watch out for others who unfairly lump renewable energy technologies into one group.

With this friendly advice in mind, we can still list some general attributes of renewable energy that constitute its pros and cons.

Let's start with the pros.

The Benefits

First and foremost, renewable energy resources are available year after year in rather steady amounts in all parts of the world. That is to say, they're **fairly reliable resources, and they're renewable.** They're not finite like coal, oil, natural gas, and nuclear.

Another big advantage of renewable energy technologies is that, with few exceptions, the **fuel is free.** It's not under the control of oil cartels or wealthy multinational corporations.

Third, and also vitally important, renewable energy is **clean and nonpolluting**; except for the manufacture and installation of the technologies to capture these forms of energy, there's very little, if any, pollution or environmental damage created by the use of most renewable energy technologies.

Fourth, for the most part the **technologies required to convert energy from renewable sources to useful energy are already available.**

No new breakthroughs are required for their widespread use, although improvements in technology and new developments in some areas could help lower their costs and make some sources more practical.

Fifth, some renewable energy technologies are **cost-competitive with conventional fuels.** Right now, large-scale wind power, passive solar heating, passive cooling, solar hot water, and solar electric production in rural areas or regions with high electric costs are frequently cost-competitive alternatives to fossil fuels and nuclear energy.

Sixth, renewable energy technologies are, for the most part, **decentralized sources of power,** so not as prone to sabotage. They're not controlled by multinational corporations either. Much of the renewable energy business currently consists of smaller companies, with only a few big dogs like BP (formerly British Petroleum), Dutch Royal Shell, and General Electric starting to play key roles.

Seventh, renewable energy **technologies permit individuals to control their own power production.** That is to say, when you install a solar electric system or a wind generator, you become your own plant manager. You're no longer at the mercy of your local power company.

The Disadvantages

As with all things in our lives, there are downsides to renewable energy, many of which we can easily work around or eliminate with a little ingenuity.

For one, renewable energy technologies and renewable energy fuels constitute only a small portion of our current energy production and consumption, so they have **fewer advocates to promote their use**, although that is starting to change with the efforts of progressive governors and other legislators and big companies such as British Petroleum, General Electric, and Dutch Royal Shell.

Closely related to this is the fact that renewable energy is often **actively lobbied against** by powerful segments of the fossil fuel industry, for example, the coal mining industry or the nuclear industry. With such powerful forces working against these vital alternatives, creating a renewable energy future won't be easy without a strong base of support.

Third, renewable energy research and development is **poorly funded in most countries, like the United States and Canada**, compared to conventional fossil fuels. Here again, there are notable exceptions. In Europe, several countries such as Germany, Great Britain, and Holland are making tremendous efforts to tap into renewable energy.

Fourth, renewable energies such as wind and solar are **not available 24 hours a day, 7 days a week, unlike fossil fuels.** Renewable energy technologies often require some means of storage so surpluses can be stockpiled for later use. Storing renewable energy can be difficult and costly. That said, it is not difficult to imagine an energy system consisting of a combination of renewable technologies — such as wind, hydropower, and solar — with backup energy from nonrenewable technologies such as coal, that provides us with a steady supply of energy. In addition, deficiencies in one part of the country can be offset by surpluses generated in others, as is common in the electric-generating industry today.

Fifth, another downside of renewable energy is that there are **far fewer experts and local suppliers of renewable energy technologies**. Open the Yellow Pages and check listings on solar hot water installers, then compare them to the list of companies that will install conventional water heaters.

Yet another disadvantage of some renewable technologies is cost. Some technologies are **quite expensive and not yet competitive with conventional fuels at current prices**, although this could change with rising oil and natural gas prices.

Seventh, **converting to renewable energy technologies may need to be done on a house-by-house basis**, which will require the efforts of millions of informed homeowners.

With this list of pros and cons in mind, let's move forward. As we explore various technologies that are available to homeowners, you'll learn more about the specific pros and cons of each energy source/technology. Along the way, we will even shatter a few myths that are holding back this important revolution in home energy production.

PROSPECTS FOR THE FUTURE

I run my entire house almost 100 percent off renewable energy — sunlight, wind, and firewood — with only a small amount of natural gas for heating water and cooking meals.

You can live independently, too.

As you will see throughout this book, energy independence is almost always more easily attained by those building anew than when retrofitting a home for self-sufficiency. When building a new home, simply orienting it to the south can cut one's heating and cooling bills by ten percent. By concentrating windows on the south side of the home, a homeowner can cut heating and cooling bills by up to 30 percent.

But like many readers you probably don't have the luxury of starting from scratch. You have a home that's firmly anchored to the ground and, most likely, not ideally situated for optimal solar gain. If you want to retrofit your home for greater energy self-sufficiency, you'll face a much bigger challenge than the lucky person who builds anew.

Don't be discouraged, however.

You can easily cut your energy demand by half, perhaps even more, with some simple, cost-effective measures that improve the energy efficiency of your home. A few more "aggressive" energy conservation steps could allow you to slash your fuel bill even more.

With these conservation measures in place, you can install some renewable energy technologies that bring your household much closer to full energy independence. In doing so, you'll not only reduce your current monthly fuel bill, you'll help protect yourself from the potentially devastating rise in fuel bills. And you make it easier for the United States and Canada — and all other nations — to meet their energy needs. The more of us that take these steps, the better our nations' futures. This stuff is national security at its best.

Fortunately, there are ample supplies of renewable energy in many areas. Many renewable energy technologies such as solar hot water and residential-scale solar electricity can be deployed by homeowners like yourself. Others like large-scale wind power will require the deep pockets of private industry and the far-sighted assistance of local, state, and federal governments.

In our quest for a better, brighter energy future, we should never lose sight of two facts. First, there's much we can do to improve energy efficiency in our homes. A huge amount. Moreover, we can improve energy efficiency without sacrificing services we've become accustomed to. We can live lightly and live well! Conservation isn't "freezing in the dark," as former President Ronald Reagan once proclaimed. Conservation is living comfortably at a fraction of the cost of our wasteful lifestyles. Conservation, if we're smart, means a better life for us.

Second, renewable energy resources are vast. They outshine the remaining nonrenewable energy resources by so much it would make your head spin. You may be surprised to learn that renewable energy, even sunlight, can be used to power nearly all of your family's needs — even in some of the gloomiest parts

Conservation isn't "freezing in the dark," as former President Ronald Reagan once proclaimed. Conservation is living comfortably at a fraction of the cost of our wasteful lifestyles.

Renewable energy and conservation are the key to a sustainable future, and you and millions of people like you hold the key.

of the United States! Renewable energy and conservation, then, are the key to a sustainable future, and you and millions of people like you hold the key.

I encourage you to think outside the energy box, too. Rather than think of energy in the conventional sense, I encourage you to look for other avenues that lead to considerable energy savings, for example, by growing more of your own food. Home gardens can save huge amounts of energy, and can help create a more independent and sustainable lifestyle (Figure 1-7). But what if you don't have room in your backyard, or don't even have a backyard?

You can be part of a community garden. Community gardens are often placed in vacant lots in cities and towns. They allow people to grow much of their own food. By growing your own food, you help reduce the need for the massive amounts of energy currently used to produce and ship food from farms all over the world to people like yourself.

So think beyond heating and cooling and lighting and you'll find yourself well on the path to energy independence and a better future.

What do you say, let's get started!

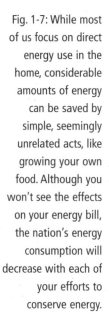

Fig. 1-7: While most of us focus on direct energy use in the home, considerable amounts of energy can be saved by simple, seemingly unrelated acts, like growing your own food. Although you won't see the effects on your energy bill, the nation's energy consumption will decrease with each of your efforts to conserve energy.

DAN CHIRAS

CHAPTER 2

CONSERVATION RULES

THE CORNERSTONE OF YOUR ENERGY FUTURE

A few years ago, one of my neighbors said, "I really admire what you do, Dan," referring to my energy-efficient home and lifestyle powered by wind, sun, and wood, "but I couldn't live like that."

I was puzzled by her response, and stood there speechless for a moment, wondering what to make of this comment. I finally offered up a response: "We have all of the conveniences of a modern home," I said, stretching the truth a bit. We've passed up opportunities to buy or receive (as gifts) various modern "conveniences," such as the electric can opener or electric carving knife. (The mechanical, non-electric options work just as well — or even better in my opinion — and require fewer materials to make and less energy to operate.)

Many other individuals I've run across in my travels throughout North America giving talks on renewable energy and green building have reacted similarly to the apparently odd notion of living on home-based renewable energy. Men sometimes say, "I like the idea of solar electricity, but I couldn't do it because I hear power tools won't work."

The fact is, you can live any way you want using solar electricity — or any other modern renewable energy technology. You can have a big screen TV, or two. You can run your lights 24 hours a day, and can use any power tool you'd like. If you choose to live this extremely energy-intensive (and wasteful) lifestyle, however, be forewarned: it's very likely going to cost you an arm and a leg to supply your needs with renewable energy!

Consider this true story. Many years ago I lived in a passive solar home that had been designed by a local, energy-conscious solar builder (Figure 2-1). After reading a book on solar electricity, I decided I wanted to install a solar electric system on the house. Unfortunately, this marvelous house — while designed to be heated passively — came with an electric stove, an appliance that eats electricity for dinner. As if that weren't bad enough, the home also came with an electric back-up heating system. It too had a voracious appetite for electricity.

Undaunted, I ran the calculations to determine exactly how much it would cost me to install a solar electric system to generate electricity for this otherwise energy-efficient home. When finished, I was aghast: by my estimations, the solar electric system would cost a whopping $50,000 in 1987 dollars!

Needless to say, I never installed a system on that home. Even with all of the energy-saving strategies in place, the cost was just too high.

Years later, I designed and built a home of equal size. Unlike the contractor who had built my previous home, I paid very close attention to energy efficiency at every step in the process. I installed energy-efficient lighting. I designed the house for day lighting — a technique that provides as much natural lighting as possible during daytime hours. I installed a super energy-efficient refrigerator and a top-of-the-line energy-efficient washing machine. I even purchased energy-efficient televisions. Rather than installing an electric stove, I put in a gas stove. And instead of installing an electric baseboard heating system for back-up, I installed an energy-efficient radiant floor heating system that I later replaced with a woodstove — because there's so much free firewood in our area. Someone's always thinning the trees on their property for fire safety or clearing a lot on which to build, so there are mountains of free firewood for the asking.

Through careful attention to detail, I was able to slash my projected electrical energy demands by 75 percent. I was also able to minimize heating demands, cutting them by 80 to 90 percent through a combination of renewable energy, notably passive solar design, and a host of energy-efficiency measures, among them superinsulation, air-tight construction, and earth sheltering.

Fig. 2-1: My first passive solar home, while heated by the sun, relied heavily on electricity for back-up heating and cooking. The demand was so high, despite energy conservation measures, it would have cost me $50,000 to install a solar electric system.

DAN CHIRAS

As a result of these and a host of other design ideas, my builder and I were able to dramatically reduce the size of the solar electric system. Instead of $50,000, my system cost around $15,000. Although it is a small system, it supplies *all* of our electrical energy needs (with a little help from a wind generator). The system allows my children and me to enjoy virtually all of the amenities of modern life we want, including two televisions, a stereo, a microwave oven, a blender, a computer, power tools, and others.

We don't leave lights on day and night like my neighbors, who complained about not being able to live the way I did, but bottom line: we live well using only a fraction of the energy of most households.

You can, too.

However, as this story suggests, the cornerstone of any sensible plan to switch to renewable energy is first and foremost to slash energy use through efficiency.

Let me point out, however, quite emphatically, that energy conservation doesn't mean living an austere life. It means eliminating massive amounts of waste in our homes, places of business, and most of our lifestyles. It means living well, staying warm in the winter and cool in the summer. Energy conservation also means saving money, enormous sums of money, that families can use for a host of other things, for example, financing their children's college educations, retirement plans, and vacations. (I'm pretty sure that most readers can find better ways to spend their hard-earned money than pay their utility companies!)

In sum, energy conservation means eliminating discomfort, slashing fuel bills, saving money, and, lest we forget, helping create a sustainable world — a brighter future for ourselves, our children, their children, and the millions of species that share this planet with us.

In this chapter, we'll explore ways you and your family can put a lid on energy consumption in your home (or office or cabin) while dramatically improving comfort. As you will soon see, saving energy can save you and your family tens, if not, hundreds of thousands of dollars over your lifetime.

It's no exaggeration.

I've run the math myself.

Using energy efficiently is like giving yourself a big fat raise. You should do it, even if you are not contemplating installing renewable energy technologies. Don't wait for your boss to open his checkbook. Go ahead and do it yourself!

If you are seriously thinking about installing renewable energy technologies on your home, even the most cost-effective options available today, energy conservation should be your first step. It will not only make the task easier (you'll need a smaller system which fits more easily on or in your existing home), it will be less costly. Why spend $50,000, for example, for a solar electric system when a $1,000–$2,000 investment in electrical energy efficiency enables you to install a much smaller

The cornerstone of any sensible plan to switch to renewable energy is first and foremost to slash energy use through efficiency.

Energy conservation means eliminating discomfort, slashing fuel bills; saving money; and helping to create a sustainable future for ourselves, our children, their children, and the millions of species that share this planet with us.

system costing, say, $15,000? Efficiency will not only pay huge dividends in the long run, it will dramatically reduce the initial capital outlay for a renewable energy system.

Before we begin our exploration of the ways you can cut energy demand in your home, let us take a look at energy conservation itself.

WHAT IS ENERGY CONSERVATION?

Energy conservation is the cornerstone of a renewable energy future, but what exactly is it?

Energy Frugality and Energy Efficiency

Energy conservation entails two separate but complementary strategies: frugality and efficiency. In the field of energy conservation, the frugality principle is all about using what we need — being frugal. Although waste is something of a North American religion, it's

Fig. 2-2: Compact fluorescent light bulbs like this one use one-fourth of the energy of standard incandescent light bulbs, produce much less heat, save big on energy bills, and dramatically reduce carbon dioxide emissions by using less electricity.

SUNWAVE

a habit we've got to discard. Frugality entails behaviors or actions that reduce energy use. Most are simple and painless. All offer amazing paybacks. You know the choices: turning off lights, televisions, and stereos in unoccupied rooms and taking shorter showers to reduce hot water use. The list goes on.

The efficiency principle, on the other hand, enjoins us to wring as much useful energy as is humanly and technologically possible from our energy supplies. Energy-efficient compact fluorescent light bulbs, for instance, convert 25 percent of the electricity flowing through them into light. A standard incandescent light bulb converts only five percent of the electricity flowing through it into light (Figure 2-2). Compact fluorescents are the hands-down favorites when it comes to energy efficiency.

Consider another example: water-efficient showerheads. These simple devices use one-half to one-third as much water as standard showerheads. Less hot water means less energy. Much less energy.

Both the compact fluorescent light bulb and the efficient showerhead perform their duties quite admirably while consuming only a fraction of the energy of their less energy-efficient counterparts found in many homes today. Bottom line: by switching to energy-efficient contraptions, you'll get the same services at a fraction of the cost.

Combined, frugality and efficiency can result in huge savings, making them indispensable components of our home (and office) energy conservation strategies. To understand the impact of such measures, consider first the impact of efficiency alone. Let's suppose that you have a security light on your front porch fitted with a 100-watt incandescent light bulb. The light operates 24 hours per day, 365 days a year because, well, you forget to turn it off most days when leaving for work. Let's suppose you decided to replace the 100-watt incandescent light bulb with an energy-efficient compact fluorescent light bulb. What's this going to save you?

A 100-watt incandescent light bulb left on 24 hours a day, 365 days a year will operate 8,760 hours each year. If you multiply the wattage of the bulb (its power demand) by the number of hours it operates, you'll find that the bulb consumes 876,000 watt hours of electricity. One thousand watt hours is a kilowatt hour and is the unit of measurement utilities use to charge you for electricity. So in this case, the bulb uses 876 kilowatt hours (kwh) per year.

The compact fluorescent light bulb you install instead uses one-fourth of the electricity of the incandescent light bulb in your porch light. By changing the bulb, your monthly electrical use plummets from 876 to 219 kwh per year. If you pay 10 cents per kwh of electricity your annual bill for this single bulb will drop from $87.60 to $21.90, a savings of $65.70 per year. Efficiency clearly pays!

Now, let's suppose that you also decide to remember to shut the compact fluorescent light bulb off each morning on your way out the door so the porch light only operates 12

hours a day. In other words, let's suppose you want to practice a little frugality, too.

By combining efficiency (use of the more efficient bulb) with frugality (turning the light off during the day), you'll reduce electrical consumption by around 110 kilowatt hours per year. The annual cost of running the light bulb 12 hours per day will be $11.00 per year, a $10.90 savings. The grand total of your savings from frugality and efficiency will be $76.60 per year!

But that's not all. To compare the economic cost of your current energy use plan to the proposed energy efficiency/frugality plan, you also need to factor in the costs of the light bulbs themselves. To do this, you have to determine how long each bulb lasts. Standard 100-watt incandescent light bulbs sold at my local hardware store are rated at 860 hours each. That means that each bulb in a packet will last, on average, about 860 hours. A typical compact fluorescent for sale on the same aisle, however, is rated at 10,000 hours. How does this affect the cost?

A compact fluorescent installed in your porch light and left on 12 hours per day will last a little over 2 years (2.2 years to be exact). An incandescent light bulb, which has a much shorter lifespan, will burn out approximately every two and a half months.

Over the lifespan of one compact fluorescent (2.2 years in this situation), then, you'd need to purchase and install 10 regular light bulbs.

Compact fluorescent light bulbs cost more, typically about $8–$10, while incandescent

Table 2.1 Energy Savings from Conservation Per Year			
Type of bulb	100 watt incandescent light bulb	25 watt compact fluorescent	25 watt compact fluorescent
Hours on per day	24	24	12
Electrical consumption	876 kWh	219 kWh	110 kWh
Cost at 10 cents per kWh	$87.60	$21.90	$11.00
Annual Savings in electrical bill	--	$65.70	$76.60

light bulbs might cost 33.5 cents each. Because in this example, the homeowner would need 10 bulbs to equal one compact fluorescent light bulb, the total cost will come to $3.35. Even so, the compact fluorescent light bulbs end up costing $4.65 more over two years. So why do it?

Because over two years, you'll save $153.20!

Not a bad return on investment. If only my mutual funds would perform half as well! As this example shows, although installing an energy-efficient compact fluorescent light bulb may cost a little more up front, it will save you a huge amount of money in the long run.

As you think about reshaping your energy future, bear in mind that you can tap into both efficiency *and* frugality measures. With a little thought, you can find many ways to reduce energy demand by being more energy conscious and more efficient, and you'll most likely need to enlist the rest of your family in the process as well. Pitching in together, your family can make tremendous strides in reducing overall energy use in your home — and the impact you have on the environment.

Energy Conservation as a Renewable Source of Energy

In most discussions on energy, energy conservation is highly praised but mischaracterized.

Most see it as a way of simply saving energy. To me, however, energy conservation also represents a way of producing energy, and producing it renewably.

To understand what I mean, let's suppose that you add insulation to the attic of your home. Then you shore up the leaks in the building envelope. Next you install storm windows to prevent heat loss from leaky single-pane windows. All of these activities cut down on your family's annual bill — that is, they help save energy.

The energy you save, however, can be used by others — say, the occupants of a brand new home in another part of your city or town. Your savings become their energy source. Although you haven't actually created new energy, the net effect is just the same. Why?

Let's suppose you had watched a baseball game on TV or gone shopping instead of investing time and energy into making your home more energy-miserly. Had you lazed around, the local utility company would have had to procure more energy from some other source to meet the demands placed on their system by their new customer. In other words, they would have had to procure more coal or natural gas to meet the newcomer's electrical and heating needs. By simply cutting back on your use, you've saved them the work. You supplied the energy they needed.

The energy conservation sources you've tapped into are also renewable. Insulation in the walls and ceilings of a home, for example, operates year after year after year, saving energy in those bone-chilling winter months as well as the hot muggy days of summer. Like renewable solar energy, energy conservation measures continue to deliver their services dutifully year after year.

Caulk applied to seal cracks in the building envelope of your home, say around windows or doors, also saves energy that is available to others. And it keeps on yielding its savings year after year.

Many local utilities understand the importance of energy efficiency in meeting future energy demands. And many of them even encourage their customers to conserve energy. What is more, some utilities offer fairly sizeable financial incentives to customers for energy conservation measures they undertake, like adding insulation to their attics or purchasing energy-efficient appliances. Why?

By promoting energy conservation, power companies can reduce their need for additional capacity. As a result of your efforts, and efforts of other citizens like you, local utilities avoid having to purchase additional energy on the spot market, which can be costly. Or they may avoid the need to build costly new power plants to service a small number of new customers. The savings can be quite significant.

In sum, then, while energy conservation is not, semantically speaking, a "new source of energy," it certainly acts like one, and it is renewable, providing benefits year after year.

While energy conservation is not, semantically speaking, a "new source of energy," it certainly acts like one, and it is renewable, providing benefits year after year.

Energy conservation is a reliable alternative to the stock market.

"If your vision of energy conservation is candles instead of lights, turning off the heat in the winter, and ignoring the air conditioner in the summer, think again. Comfort may be the most over-looked benefit from improving energy efficiency."
Corliss Karasov, *"Making the Case: The Benefits of Home Energy Efficiency," in* Smart Energy Living, *produced by the Colorado Energy Science Center.*

BENEFITS OF ENERGY CONSERVATION

Before we begin our exploration of home energy conservation, let's take a few minutes to ponder the benefits of conservation.

- Energy conservation measures **reduce fuel use and save homeowners money** — often lots of money. For every dollar you spend on energy conservation, you can easily reap five dollars per year in savings, according to the US Department of Energy. You can think of energy conservation as a reliable alternative to the stock market.

- Many energy conservation measures **increase comfort** in our homes by reducing cold spots, hot spots, and chilly drafts. Rather than turning up the heat to overcome a cold, drafty home, a homeowner can simply seal up the many leaks in the building envelope to create a cozier interior while saving hundreds of dollars a year. A tube of caulk costs a lot less than the energy required to pump heat out through the many leaks in the ceilings and walls of our homes day after day after day. (Interestingly, comfort is a major factor when deciding to upgrade the homes of many elderly individuals.)

- By reducing household utility bills, energy conservation can **free up money for other important activities** — such as bolstering sagging savings accounts, financing college educations, funding family vacations, and building retirement accounts.

- Energy efficiency measures in our homes may also **qualify homeowners for larger loans** and, occasionally, for lower mortgage rates. Some lenders, for example, FHA, Countrywide Home loans, and Chase offer such benefits for qualifying energy-efficient homes. Check them out when buying or building a new, energy-efficient home.

- Energy efficiency can also **reduce maintenance**. A well-insulated home, for instance, reduces the need for backup heating and air conditioning. This puts less strain on furnaces, boilers, air conditioners, and evaporative coolers, meaning they last longer and require less maintenance.

- Energy conservation measures are often **easy to implement**. In fact, it requires very little skill or training to make a home more energy efficient.

- Energy conservation measures can be **brought on line quickly**. A trip to the hardware store and a few afternoons working around the house can make significant inroads into your annual energy consumption.

- Energy conservation measures are often **free or quite inexpensive**. Turning off lights when rooms are unoccupied incurs no expense whatsoever, just a little extra effort on your part. Installing compact fluorescent light bulbs costs a little upfront, but as you have just seen it saves enormous amounts of money over the long haul.

+ Energy conservation could **increase the value of your home**. In a study that appeared in 1998 in *The Appraisal Journal*, a publication read by house appraisers, the authors report that the selling price of homes increased by nearly $21 for every $1 decrease in fuel bills the home-owners had achieved through energy efficiency. With the average American home currently (2004) using about $1,300 worth of energy per year, a reduction in the utility bill by one half could increase the home value by over $13,650. As energy prices escalate, this figure could go higher!

+ In an energy-tight world, energy conservation could make your home much **easier to sell**.

+ Energy conservation reduces fuel use and thus **reduces environmental damage** resulting from the production and consumption of conventional fuels (see sidebar).

HOME ENERGY USE

In North America, homes are huge energy consumers; in fact, they account for about one-fifth of the United States' total annual energy demand. The energy used in our homes meets our needs for heating, cooling, and lighting. It also powers a mind-boggling list of appliances and electronic gadgets. While homes vary considerably in their annual use, the average cost comes to about $1,300 per year in 2004, a figure that's bound to increase over the coming years. Before we can determine where we can apply conservation measures, however, we need to know exactly where all of this energy is going.

As you can see in Figure 2-3, heating and cooling the interior of our homes consumes the largest portion of the energy pie — about 44 percent. Lighting, cooking, and appliances (other than the fridge) consume one-third of our energy. Water heating consumes 14 percent and the refrigerator consumes about 9 percent of the energy pie.

Bear in mind, however, that these numbers represent the "average" American home.

The Impact of Electrical Use

On average, American homes use about 700 kilowatt hours of electricity each month. Each kilowatt hour of electricity from a coal-fired power plant results in the production of two pounds of carbon dioxide. Electrical consumption in the average American home, therefore, produces about 1,400 pounds of carbon dioxide a year. Cutting grid power electrical consumption through conservation by 50 percent reduces carbon dioxide emissions by 700 pounds per year.

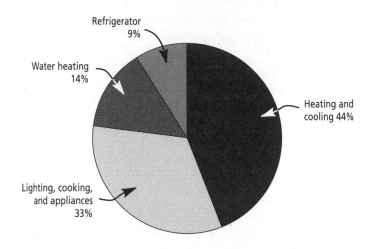

Refrigerator
9%

Water heating
14%

Heating and
cooling 44%

Lighting, cooking,
and appliances
33%

Fig. 2-3: Average U.S. home energy consumption by end use.

Your home may deviate considerably from the average. You may, for instance, live in the far northern tip of Idaho, where cooling bills in the summer are something you only wish you'd have to worry about. Or you may own an extra refrigerator and a freezer in your garage. Unfortunately, during the hot days of summer these appliances must work overtime to keep their contents cold. This drives up your energy bills. Or you may have a terribly inefficient heating system or a leaky house that requires lots more heat than the mythical "average home."

Although each home is different, this pie chart alerts us to the big energy consumers. In so doing, it can help us target the greatest potential gains. Valuable as this information is, it is still wise to contact your local utility to see if they can provide an energy pie chart of the "average" home in your area. If your local utility can't provide this information, your state's energy conservation office may offer some assistance.

Obviously, the closer the energy use data you rely on is to homes in your area, the more valuable it will be. Even so, houses range dramatically within a region. Newer homes are often much more energy efficient than older homes. In fact, many homes built prior to the 1970s in the United States are terribly leaky and horribly underinsulated — so much so, it would make your head spin! My students at Colorado College and I, for example, perform energy analyses on older homes near the campus in Colorado Springs. As part of this analysis, we measure how leaky the houses are (a procedure I'll explain shortly). The test we use simulates a 20 mile-per-hour wind. The houses we test often leak at a rate of 8,500 cubic feet per minute. (Just to put this in perspective, my new home comes in at 500 cfm.) The typical rate of 8,500 cfm constitutes a huge leakage problem. Cold air drafts in the winter chill off the interior of the home on windy days. It also results in excessive heat loss at all other times as warm interior air leaks out through the Swiss cheese exterior of these homes.

Leaky doors and windows can increase the cost of heating or cooling a home substantially, by up to 30 percent, according to Pat Keegan, executive director of Colorado Energy Science Center, an organization dedicated to promoting residential energy efficiency. "If you think of a house as a boat, a leaky one would sink in an hour," adds Keegan.

RETROFITTING YOUR HOME FOR ENERGY EFFICIENCY

Retrofitting a home for energy efficiency will save you money, lots of money. However, it will require some effort on your part. To begin this process you should start with an energy audit.

Start with an Energy Audit

When retrofitting homes for energy efficiency, as part of the community service component of my classes at Colorado College, we begin with a walk-through, a simple visual inspection of a home. Professional energy auditors do the same.

Starting at the top of the house, we examine the attic insulation, and then take a look at the windows: are they single- or double-paned windows, air-tight or leaky? We then search for obvious holes or gaps in the building envelope, for example, broken windows in the basement, gaps around pipes or electrical lines that penetrate the structure, and so on. You'd be amazed how many we find and how many you will find in your home. Don't forget to check fireplaces; open dampers result in incredible leakage.

After checking out insulation and potential leaks in the building envelope, we turn our attention to appliances. Our goal is to determine if there are any old, energy-inefficient models that need replacement. We then turn our attention to the water heater. If it appears to be in good operating condition, we note whether it is equipped with an insulation blanket. We then examine furnaces and boilers and take a look at the ducts or pipes that deliver heat to the house to see if they are insulated. We also look for potential leaks in heating and air conditioning ducts. Finally, we examine lighting, noting how many lights are in the house and the type of bulb in each one.

These simple visual inspections often turn up huge opportunities for saving massive amounts of energy. In one elderly lady's home we retrofitted in the winter of 2004, for instance, the class discovered that a heating duct coursing through her crawl space had never been connected to the heat register in a living room addition. The builder had forgotten to install a register, so the furnace installer simply left the job unfinished. When the furnace was running, however, hot air from the orphaned duct simply poured into the uninsulated crawl space, heating the great outdoors. Aghast, my students sealed it off and recommended that the owner hire a handyman to install a heat register in the living room, so the duct could be connected and heat could be delivered to the room.

We make numerous recommendations solely on the basis of our visual inspection, which you can do, too. Just take a pen and paper along with you to record your findings, room by room. Take your time and do a thorough job, especially in the basement, where energy leaks are common.

Visual inspections reveal the most obvious problems and help us determine the materials and supplies we'll need to retrofit

Simple visual inspections often turn up huge opportunities for saving large amounts of energy.

the home. Once this phase of the home energy audit is complete, we get a bit more scientific. We install a device known as a blower door on the front or back door of the house to determine how leaky the house is.

The blower door unit, shown in Figure 2-4, mounts snugly in most doorways in an adjustable aluminum frame. Nylon fabric is attached to the frame to make it airtight. Once the frame and fabric are in place, a large electric fan and an air-flow meter are installed. After the fan is in place, the house is sealed up as it would be in the winter. Doors and windows are shut; attic accesses, if any, are closed, etc.

When the house is buttoned up, the fan on the blower door test device is switched on. It immediately begins siphoning air from the interior of the house, pushing it outside. The air expelled in this manner, however, is replaced by air drawn in from the great outdoors through small cracks and large openings, if any, in the building envelope (Figure 2-5).

Once the fan is cranked up, the operator measures the total air flow through the building envelope on the air-flow meter. This measurement tells us how leaky the house we are testing is. A really good measurement

Fig. 2-4: A blower door test device like this one allows home energy auditors to determine how leaky a house is and to pinpoint the actual leaks so they can be sealed.

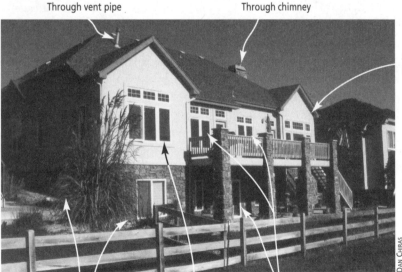

Through vent pipe   Through chimney   At juncture of roof and walls

Fig. 2-5: Air moves in and out of houses through a myriad of cracks, gaps, and holes in the building envelope, as shown here.

Between wall and foundation   Around windows   Around doors

is around 500 to 1,500 cubic feet per minute. The older houses we work on typically fall in the 6,500 to 8,500 cubic-feet-per-minute range, but they're ancient structures, often built in the late 1800s, seemingly without regard for insulation or concern over air leakage. (What hardy souls our ancestors must have been!)

Each time we run this test on an old home, we're shocked at how much like Swiss cheese these old homes are. However, I quickly remind my students that there's a silver lining to this black cloud. It is, quite simply, that waste = opportunity. Translated: while our homes are amazingly leaky, embarrassingly leaky, with a little time and money we can seal the leaks. With a little effort, we can dramatically reduce air infiltration and exfiltration (movement in and out). It doesn't take much to slice air flow through a building envelope by half, sometimes more. The good news, then, is that with a few hundred dollars worth of materials and a couple of afternoons of work, anyone with a lick of sense can dramatically reduce air leakage.

But how do we pinpoint the leaks?

We locate many large cracks and openings during the initial visual inspection, described above. Obvious cracks and "cat-sized openings" in the foundation — those holes big enough for a cat or a small dog to gain entrance — show up because they let in a lot of light (and cats).

Leaks can also be detected when the fan in the blower door test device is running by feel — that is, by slowly running your hands around window frames, at the juncture of walls and floors or walls and ceilings, at the openings of attic access doors, at outlets and wall switches, and so on.

Or you can pinpoint leaks by using incense or a smoke stick purchased from a local hardware store. A smoke stick is a device that produces fake smoke. When held near a leak, the smoke is blown into the room. (We usually reverse the fan so the smoke is blown out of the building through the cracks.) By carefully going over the entire house from top to bottom, a homeowner can locate the myriad of leaks in the building envelope that have been conspiring to make his or her life miserable — and much more costly than necessary. Take notes so you can come back later to seal up the leaks.

Hiring a Professional Energy Auditor

Most homeowners can't invest the $3,000 required to purchase a blower door test, nor can they rent the test device — they're not available for rent.

The best place to start, then, is with a simple visual inspection to locate the most obvious leaks — gaping openings between doors and door frames, or large openings in the building envelope that let cold air in when the wind's blowing and hot air out when the furnace is running. These can be sealed immediately and will often yield enormous benefits. Then, on a windy day, perform a search and destroy mission for smaller, less obvious leaks, using incense, a smoke stick, or your hand to detect leakage in the building envelope.

If this is more work than you'd like to undertake or if you are feeling uncertain, you can always hire a qualified professional energy auditor to perform the inspection/analysis for you. You'll find them in the business pages under "Energy Conservation and Management Services" or "Home Inspection."

Energy auditors perform visual inspections for around $75 – $100, at this writing, but can also perform more sophisticated tests on your home, like those my students and I do. These include a blower door test, duct leakage tests, and comprehensive computer energy analysis. Some inspectors even take infrared images of homes to help them pinpoint areas where heat is escaping. They then take this data, along with measurements of the house, and plug it into a computer program. This determines how much energy a home is currently losing and presents a variety of options for saving energy.

Home energy auditors provide a written report that lists potential energy improvements. The report will almost certainly include recommendations for sealing cracks and openings in the building envelope — that is, weatherizing a home. It's also likely to call for additional insulation in walls, ceilings, and perhaps floors, especially over crawl spaces or unheated basements. The report may also recommend an insulated blanket for your water heater and pipe insulation for hot water lines from the water heater to various faucets in the house. In addition, the report will very likely call for efforts to seal and insulate ducts that transport hot and cold air from heaters and air conditioners to the rooms of a house. If your home has a boiler that provides heat for a radiant floor or baseboard water heating system, the auditor's recommendations may call for pipe insulation between the boiler and the various baseboard heaters or heating zones. Lastly, home energy auditors may make recommendations for replacement of old, inefficient appliances. I recommend that once the report is done you ask for a quick tour of your home so the inspector can show you what needs to be done.

The cost of the complete energy analysis is typically $300 to $400, give or take a little. Although that seems like a lot of

Energy Leakage: Trouble Spots

- Windows and doors: check for leaks around the frames of doors and windows; also check for leaks between the door and the door jamb. Note that many older double-hung windows also leak.
- Penetrations of the building envelop where water and gas pipes and electrical wires enter or where dryer vents or vents from kitchen and bathroom fans exhaust to the outside.
- Recessed ceiling lights.
- Attic doors or hatches.
- Electrical switches and outlets.
- The junction of walls and floors along the trim.

Source: US EPA, Energy Star Program

money, this analysis is well worth the expense — provided you follow up on the auditor's recommendations.

Who Does the Work?

After reviewing the options outlined in your energy audit, it's time to do something. At this stage in the game, you have two options: you can roll up your sleeves and do the work yourself, or you can hire an energy retrofitter to perform the necessary work for you. Most auditors, by the way, are qualified to do the energy retrofitting.

Although hiring a professional will cost substantially more than doing the work yourself, a qualified expert is often worth the extra expense. They perform the work quickly and efficiently with a minimum of mistakes commonly made by many homeowners. In addition, a trained energy retrofitter will know the products that need to be used, saving you time in the hardware store anguishing over which caulk is best for cracks and which sealant is best for leaky duct work. A professional energy retrofitter can even access high-quality materials that aren't often sold in local hardware stores or building supply outlets, such as duct mastic, a paste used to seal leaky air ducts in heating and air conditioning systems. High-quality products mean a long-lasting job.

Other Options for Energy Audits and Upgrades

Rather than hire a professional to perform tests and retrofit your home, you may want to contact your local utility to see if they can help you out. Many efficiency-conscious utilities offer free or low-cost energy audits. Years ago, for example, my utility company performed a free energy audit on a rental house I was living in while building my new home. In addition to the free blower door test, they gave me two high-efficiency showerheads, three faucet aerators to save water, and three compact fluorescent light bulbs — all for free! The auditor even caulked the major cracks in the building envelope at no charge.

Yet another option is to contact non-profit organizations in your area that offer free or low-cost energy audits and retrofits. In Denver, the non-profit group, Sun Power Inc., offers a wide range of services, including energy audits, insulation, and weatherization (sealing leaks), They even repair heating and air conditioning systems and install new, energy-efficient heating and air conditioning equipment. Check around. There may be a similar non-profit group in your area; many of them focus on the residences of low-income families who can't afford high utility bills yet are unable to afford professional energy retrofitting.

Sealing Cracks in the Building Envelope

Sealing cracks in the building envelope is one of the easiest and most cost-effective measures a homeowner can take. For those who want to do the work themselves, I strongly recommend that you purchase the best caulk you can find. Don't skimp on caulk just to save a few bucks per tube. High-quality caulks can last for 20 years and are worth it in the long run. So ask a knowledgeable worker in the store which products are the best and then spend the extra money.

For small gaps, for example, around windows, I use a high-quality silicon paintable caulk made from latex and silicon. Larger gaps can be filled with expandable foam, which comes in spray cans. I use Great Stuff insulating foam sealant (red can) for smaller openings — those too large for silicon caulk — and Great Stuff insulating foam sealant (blue can) for the largest openings. Very large openings can also be filled with backer rod, a flexible material that is stuffed into openings.

In your quest to tighten up your home, you will also very likely need to seal wall switches and electrical outlets. You'd be amazed how much air leaks into wall cavities and out through attics through wall switches and electrical outlets.

Fig. 2-6: Foam gaskets like these are used to seal electrical switches and electrical outlets in walls, which can leak quite a lot of air to attic spaces.

DAN CHIRAS

Wall switches and electrical outlets are sealed by installing small foam gaskets available in local hardware stores and larger building outlets (Figure 2-6). To seal a switch or electrical outlet, even on inside walls, remove the cover plate, then insert the foam gasket and screw the cover plate back in place.

Installing Insulation

In your quest for comfort and energy savings, you will also very likely need to add insulation, boosting what's already in place. As a rule, the older your home, the more insulation you'll need to add. If your home was built in the late 1880s or early 1900s, you may find that it has no insulation whatsoever in wall cavities and barely enough insulation in the attic to make a difference.

How much insulation should you add?

Professional energy auditors will very likely recommend a boost in insulation to meet local building codes. Although such changes will increase the energy performance of your home and sharply decrease utility bills, I strongly recommend that homeowners go beyond the insulation standards in most jurisdictions.

Even if your local building department has adopted the Model Energy Code (and very few of them have), the best energy efficiency is achieved when builders and homeowners exceed the recommended levels by at least 30 to 40 percent. (That's what top-notch solar builders are using in their homes.) Super-insulating strategies such as this will help you achieve huge energy savings and dramatically improve comfort.

Insulating well above the Model Energy Code will cost a few hundred dollars more than merely meeting code, to be sure, but is worth it in the long run. Remember: energy costs are, very likely, going to continue to climb for a long, long time.

Insulating Wall Cavities. As noted above, many really older homes have no insulation at all in their exterior walls. Filling these cavities with insulation is, therefore, vital to achieving comfort and savings. Fortunately, there are several ways to do this. Most often, installers drill large holes in the siding from the outside or in the drywall from the inside, accessing each stud cavity (the space between adjacent studs) individually. They then either blow in cellulose insulation (made from recycled newspapers) or apply a liquid foam product that expands to fill the stud cavity. The holes used to access the interior of the walls are then repaired and repainted and the job is done.

Wall insulation retrofits can be difficult and are often best left to well-trained professionals with lots of experience in the area. There are many reasons for hiring a professional. First, if your home is two or more stories high, wall insulation retrofits may require a lot of potentially dangerous ladder work. Second, cellulose or liquid foam insulation may hang up on wires and pipes in stud cavities or on lath in older plastered walls. This, in turn, may result in large air pockets

in the wall cavities that provide no protection against heat loss.

Hiring a professional will cost more, as you would expect, but a highly qualified crew can do the job in a fraction of the time it takes most homeowners to complete the task. If the crew is experienced and conscientious, they will also probably do a much better job than the average homeowner.

Although cellulose is a popular product for insulating walls, there are some good alternatives that perform well and are good for people and the environment. One relatively new product is Icynene. Icynene is water-soluble, environmentally friendly liquid foam insulation. It contains no formaldehyde. It also contains no CFCs or HCFCs, both ozone-depleting chemicals, as do other foam products. Bear in mind, however, that Icynene must be applied by licensed applicators. You can't buy the stuff at a local building supply outlet and apply it yourself.

Another option, rarely pursued unless a complete remodeling is in the works, is to remove interior wall material — usually drywall or plaster — entirely, and then install the insulation in the exposed wall cavity. Wet-blown cellulose, liquid foam, and fiberglass insulation batts can be used in such instances. When the insulation is in place, new drywall is applied. The wall is then taped and painted.

After tearing off the drywall, you may want to deepen the wall cavity. If your home was framed in two-by-fours originally, and many are, and you want to provide adequate

Insulating well above the Model Energy Code will cost a few hundred dollars more than merely meeting code, to be sure, but is worth it in the long run. Remember: energy costs are, very likely, going to continue to climb for a long, long time.

insulation, a deeper cavity will allow you to beef up the insulation to levels that will make a difference in your comfort and energy savings.

To deepen a wall cavity, first remove the drywall, and then build a second two-by-four wall against the original two-by-four framing. Fill the wall cavity with insulation.

This double-wall technique dramatically increases the thickness of the insulation layer and dramatically improves the comfort of your home. However, as you can imagine, this retrofit is time-consuming, and a bit costly unless you do the work yourself. Note that in addition to building a second framed wall, you'll need to increase the depth of the window openings and bring wall switches and outlets out, too.

The double-wall technique allows for a dramatic increase in energy performance. However, it can be improved upon. Some builders, for instance, offset the second frame. That is, they place the new studs so that they don't align up with the original studs. This technique reduces bridging loss — the loss of heat that occurs through the framing members of a wall. Heat, it turns out, conducts fairly rapidly through studs in a wall, as they offer little resistance to heat flow by conduction.

When installing batt insulation into a stud cavity, be sure there are no air spaces between the insulation and the studs. Insulation needs to fit snugly in the stud cavities. If not, air currents can form in the stud cavities, circulating warm air between the inside and outside of the wall, dramatically reducing the R-value of the wall (R-value is a measure of a material's resistance to heat flow).

Another less time-consuming option, although rarely pursued, is to leave the existing uninsulated wall intact and then simply erect a new insulated wall against it. This technique requires the builder to first attach two-by-twos, two-by-fours, or even furring strips vertically to the existing wall. The spaces between the new studs are filled with insulation, either fiberglass, cellulose, liquid foam, or rigid foam. After the insulation is applied, a vapor barrier is laid down for fiberglass and cellulose insulation (see the textbox on page 54 for more on vapor barriers). Drywall or plaster is then applied to finish the wall.

A quicker way of rebuilding a wall is to apply foam insulation against existing drywall without erecting a two-by-two or two-by-four framework. Tape the sheets of foam together at the joints to reduce air infiltration. Once foam is in place, new drywall is attached using long drywall screws. Foam is advantageous because it offers a much higher R-value per inch than other forms of insulation (Table 2-2).

This technique, although relatively simple and fairly inexpensive, does have a few downsides. Like other similar techniques described above, it will require that window openings be deepened. Baseboards will also need to be removed and reapplied. Wall switches and electrical outlets will need to be remounted. It also slightly decreases interior floor space.

Insulating Ceilings. Ceiling insulation must also be fortified in both old and new homes. Even if your home was built in the 1990s, it may be worth adding more ceiling insulation.

Adding insulation is a breeze in homes with attics. You simply climb into the attic through an access hatch usually located in the ceiling of a hallway or a back room. Once in the attic, you can lay down fiberglass batts or blow fiberglass or cellulose over the existing insulation. Be sure to walk on the rafters so as not to fall through the ceiling when moving about in an attic.

Table 2-2 R-Values of Insulation		
Material	**R-Value Per Inch**	**Uses**
Loose-Fill and Batts		
Fiberglass (low density)	2.2	Walls and ceilings
Fiberglass (medium density)	2.6	Same
Fiberglass (high density)	3.0	Same
Cellulose (dry)	3.2	Same
Wet-Spray Cellulose	3.5	Same
Rock Wool	3.1	Same
Cotton	3.2	Same
Rigid Foam and Liquid Foam		
Expanded Polystyrene (Beadboard)	3.8 to 4.4	Foundations, walls ceilings, and roofs
Extruded Polystyrene (Pinkboard and blueboard)	5	Same
Polyisocyanurate	6.5 to 8	Same
Roxul (Rigid board made from mineral wool)	4.3	Foundations
Icynene	3.6	Walls and ceilings
Air Krete	3.9	Walls and ceilings

Protecting Insulation from Moisture

For optimal performance, many common forms of insulation, most notably cellulose and fiberglass, need to be kept dry. This can be achieved by applying a vapor barrier — a six mil layer of plastic applied to the studs after the insulation is put in place. Vapor barriers reduce moisture penetration through the walls of a home. This, in turn, helps to keep the insulation dry, as even a tiny amount of moisture can dramatically decrease its R-value.

By preventing moisture from entering wall cavities, vapor barriers also prevent water condensation inside the wall. This usually occurs against the exterior sheathing where the wall is coldest. Moisture condensing inside walls may promote the growth of mold and mildew in the stud cavities — on the framing members and in the insulation. Spores from mold and mildew may enter a home, causing obnoxious smells, discomfort, and even flu-like symptoms. As if that's not bad enough, moisture can cause wooden studs to rot and may lead to costly repair jobs.

So if you are retrofitting in a cold climate, and you are either tearing off the dry wall and installing insulation in existing stud cavities or simply building a double wall — install a vapor barrier against the framing members. To prevent moisture from entering the walls, it is also important to caulk and seal the inside wall switches and electrical outlets. This detail is often overlooked, even though the vast majority of moisture entering wall cavities from the interiors of our homes enters through such openings.

In cold climates, vapor barriers are applied to the framing members after the insulation is installed and before new drywall is put in place. In warm climates, however, moisture barriers need to be applied to the outside of walls. In new construction, they are applied on the framing members just beneath the exterior sheathing. But that's not possible in a retrofit unless you are planning on installing insulation from the outside — something rarely done. To apply insulation from the outside, you will need to tear off the old siding and then remove the exterior sheathing. You can then fill the wall cavity with insulation. When this has been completed, a moisture barrier is applied to the framing members. Exterior sheathing is then reapplied, followed by siding. Needless to say, that's quite a lot of work!

Why do builders install vapor barriers on the inside of walls in cold climates like Maine and North Dakota, but on the outside in warm climates like Florida and Georgia?

The reason's simple. In cold climates, the major source of moisture entering wall cavities is interior room air. This comes from cooking, washing machines, showers, plants and a variety of other sources. The occupants of a home even release considerable amounts of moisture through perspiration and respiration. In warm climates, moisture that enters walls tends to come from outside the home, from the moisture-laden atmosphere.

When retrofitting ceiling or attic insulation, I recommend bringing the R-value well above local building codes — to R 50 or R 60 — in most climates. In really cold climates, you may want to boost insulation even more.

When applying insulation in ceilings and attics in homes in hot climates, many builders fall into a trap set by conventional "wisdom." Conventional wisdom mistakenly holds that insulation's main value is in keeping houses warm in cold climates. That is to say, it is important in such climates because it helps to keep heat from escaping. (You don't need a heavy coat in a warm climate, after all, now do you?)

Although insulation is not needed as much in hot climates in the winters, it's absolutely vital in the summer. Why?

Because it acts just like the insulation in a thermos bottle. Pour a hot drink into a thermos bottle and it stays hot. Pour a cold drink in and it stays cold. Why is this?

Insulation in the thermos bottle prevents heat from moving in or out of a structure. If you pour hot liquid into a thermos, the insulation prevents heat from escaping. If you pour cold liquid into a thermos, the insulation keeps heat from entering. The same pertains to insulation in homes: in the winter, insulation keeps the interior of homes warm because it prevents heat from escaping. In the summer, it prevents heat from entering, keeping the interior cool despite sweltering hot temperatures outside, while reducing cooling bills. It may come to a surprise to many readers to

learn that, in many hot climates, utility bills for cooling often exceed winter time heating bills in colder climates.

If you don't have an attic, your home was probably built with a closed ceiling design and installing additional insulation can be very difficult, if not impossible. (Figure 2-7).

But all is not lost. You could, for instance, install additional insulation by framing in a second ceiling with two-by-fours and adding insulation to the cavities. Or you could apply large sheets of foam insulation. Once the insulation is in place, you'll need to attach a vapor barrier and new drywall.

Although feasible, this technique is costly and time-consuming, especially for homeowners with little experience in this area. Another option would be to apply rigid foam insulation on the roof. For example, if you need to reshingle your roof you can begin by tearing off the old shingles. When this is completed, lay down a two-to-three-inch thick layer of

Fig. 2-7: Two types of basic roof designs are commonly used in homes: (a) the attic design with a large, accessible space that can be easily retrofitted with additional insulation in most cases, and (b) the closed roof design that consists of an inaccessible insulated space.

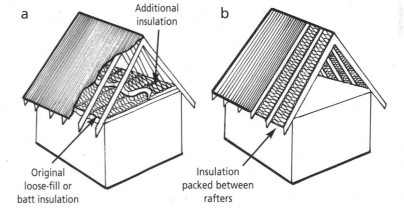

a

Additional insulation

b

Original loose-fill or batt insulation

Insulation packed between rafters

rigid foam insulation. New sheathing would then be applied to the foam. Shingles or metal roofing would then be attached to the decking.

Alternatively, you could leave the shingles in place, and attach two-by-four sleepers along the length of the roof at two- to four-foot intervals. Foam insulation could be applied between the sleepers. Next, metal roofing could be screwed into the sleepers. This method does not require a new roof deck.

Both of these techniques will greatly boost the R-value of your roof, although, as you can imagine, it is not going to be cheap, nor is it going to be easy. You'll need to pay attention to details like the fascia and overhang. I recommend that you hire a professional to do the work unless you're quite skilled at carpentry.

Upgrading Windows

Windows are a frequent target of energy efficiency upgrades, especially in homes built prior to the 1980s. Even in many newer homes, cheap energy-inefficient windows represent a huge source of energy loss. Not only are they poorly built and leaky, many windows are improperly installed. As a result, they'll almost always require improvements or outright replacement.

If your windows are old and leaky or were manufactured with aluminum or steel frames, or, God forbid, are the single pane variety, you should consider a complete upgrade. The cheapest and easiest upgrade for energy-wasteful windows is to install storm windows. Storm windows are installed on the outside of existing windows where they perform two vital functions. First, storm windows dramatically reduce air leakage. Second, they create a dead airspace that reduces heat loss. (Remember: air is a poor conductor of heat.) By reducing leakage and creating a dead air space between the existing window and the storm window, these simple, relatively inexpensive upgrades can dramatically decrease heat loss and increase interior comfort.

Another, more costly option, is to tear out existing windows and replace them with high-quality, energy-efficient models widely available throughout North America. Most people hire professionals to do this; it's not a job for the untrained occasional weekend handyman or handywoman.

Window replacements cost quite a lot — potentially $8,000 to $10,000, or even more for larger homes. The payback period, that is, the time in which this investment pays for itself in energy savings, is typically about 10 to 12 years at current energy costs. Although this upgrade is costly and pays back slowly, the gains in comfort are immediate. Moreover, rising fuel bills could help accelerate the payback.

Knowing what kind of windows to buy is a bit challenging. Window technology has advanced considerably in the past 20 years and because of this can be quite confusing. To help avoid confusion, here are some basic guidelines that will help you select an energy-efficient window to replace your old, leaky ones.

In most cases, existing windows should be replaced with double- or triple-pane assemblies. (Triple-pane glass is pretty expensive and should be used along the north side of homes in cold climates where heat loss is most pronounced during the winter months.)

To achieve the highest energy efficiency, select window assemblies whose glass is coated with a special clear, transparent low-e coating ("Low-e" stands for low-emissivity.) This thin coat of tin or silver oxide retards heat flow through windows. Low-e windows help hold heat inside your home in the winter but also retard heat flow into your home during the summer. As a result, they help maintain year-round comfort.

Also, be sure to select a window with warm edges. Warm edges are created by insulated spacers that are placed between the panes of glass along the edge of the window assembly. Spacers reduce conductive heat loss around the periphery of the window, which can be quite significant. This feature not only reduces heat loss, it reduces water condensation on windows on cold winter nights and that, in turn, leads to longer window life.

Finally, when shopping for windows, look for models that are as airtight as possible. Resist the temptation to save a few bucks by sacrificing air tightness. You'll be sorry you did.

Air leakage is measured in cubic feet of air per minute per square foot of window surface. Look for windows with certified air leakage rates of 0.3 cfm/square foot or less.

So how do you find out about all of these features? How do you know which window is best?

You'll be happy to find that manufacturers post all of this information on their products. Every window comes with a sticker that lists its vital stats such as the U-value and air infiltration rates. U-value is a measure of heat flow through a material and is the inverse of R-value, a measure of the resistance to heat flow. Thus, U-value is equal to 1/R-value. A window with a U-value of .25 has an R-value of 4 because one-quarter is equal to 0.25. Look for models with U values of 0.1 to 0.25.

U-value is a function of the number of panes of glass, the presence or absence of window spacers, and low-e coatings. It is also determined by the presence of inert gases between the panes of glass. As you shop for windows you will find that many manufacturers pump the inert gas argon into the air spaces between glass in their double- and triple-pane window assemblies. Argon gas further reduces heat flow, boosting the U-value.

The information on these stickers will help you select the most energy-efficient windows possible. You can also get a considerable amount of help from local knowledgeable window suppliers. (For more details on windows, you might want to check out several

Low-e windows help hold heat inside your home in the winter but also retard heat flow into our homes during the summer. As a result, they help maintain year-round comfort.

articles and books on windows in the Resource Guide or you can read the section on windows in my book, *The Solar House*.)

Instead of replacing windows or installing storm windows, many people tape plastic film over their windows each year as winter approaches. This effective but temporary answer to leaky, energy-inefficient windows, leaves much to be desired. Plastic tends to obscure views and looks … well, let's be honest … cheap, and it requires a lot of work.

Another simple solution to energy-wasteful windows is to install a second or third pane of glass in the existing window frame. While effective, this method is costly and time-consuming. To address the cost and potential safety issues resulting from the installation of another pane of glass, I've devised another option — one that is more aesthetically appealing than sheet plastic and much cheaper than installing additional panes of glass.

My solution is to install Plexiglas inserts along the inside surface of existing windows. Plexiglas is a clear, durable polycarbonate plastic. It can cost a tenth of the price of some window glass, and usually won't yellow in sunlight. It also conducts heat more slowly than glass, which results in a warmer surface and thus less heat loss than glass. Plexiglas is also a lot easier and much safer to handle than glass. You are less likely to cut yourself.

To begin, I measure the length and width of the interior window opening, then subtract about one quarter of an inch to allow for expansion and contraction of the Plexiglas. After measuring all of my windows and making the deductions for expansion and contraction, I call in the order. (I'd recommend you try one retrofit, before tackling all of your windows.)

Plexiglas can be purchased at hardware stores. (Ask, as they usually keep it in the back out of sight.) But for the best price and widest selection, I typically purchase it from a local plastic supplier, found in the Yellow Pages under "Plastics." I prefer three-eighth-inch or one-quarter-inch Plexiglas, not the cheaper on-eighth-inch variety carried by hardware stores. It is much too flimsy and difficult to work with. I've also found that that the one-eighth-inch Plexiglas bows when mounted in windows.

To mount the plastic insert, I use wood trim (one-half by one-half inch). I nail four pieces of stained or painted trim in the window opening (using finishing nails) about one half to one inch from the existing window. The trim creates an even base against which the Plexiglas will rest.

Next, peel the paper backing off the Plexiglas and place the plastic against the trim base. I then install four additional pieces of trim to hold the Plexiglas in place.

In some windows, I've used clear plastic mirror mounts to secure the Plexiglas, screwing the mounts directly to the sash — the wood that holds the glass in place in a window assembly. In some windows, I've found it necessary to screw the mirror mounts to the window frame, that is, the wood that attaches the sash to the rough window opening. (If these terms don't make sense, go take a look at one of your windows. You'll see that the glass is held in place by wood, known as the sash, and that the sash is mounted inside the wood frame. It fits into a rough opening created by framing lumber, which you won't be able to see.)

Although windows retrofitted in this manner do not look as nice as those I've retrofitted with wood trim and Plexiglas, this technique is much less expensive and much easier. You won't have to buy, cut, stain or paint, and mount the wood trim. Moreover, this technique makes it easy to remove the Plexiglas, for example on windows you may want to open in the spring, summer, and early fall.

Magnetic tape can also be used to mount Plexiglas in windows that you would like to open in the warmer months of the year. I begin by securing a trim base, as described above. Next, I strip the plastic backing off a piece of magnetic tape cut to fit the length of the trim. I then stick the magnetic tape to the trim base and nail it to the trim using finishing nails. (This gives it a more secure anchorage than the glue on the back of the magnetic strip.)

Once the base pieces are fitted with magnetic strips, I attach a second piece of magnetic tape along the perimeter of the Plexiglas insert. When this is in place, I insert the Plexiglas into the window opening against the base trim.

That's it. The Plexiglas can be removed in the summer so the window can be opened for natural ventilation.

Existing skylights can also be retrofitted with Plexiglas to boost their energy efficiency.

Replacing Energy-Inefficient Heating Systems

Sealing leaks in the building envelope, boosting insulation in walls and ceilings, and replacing or retrofitting windows can substantially increase the comfort of your home. It will also dramatically reduce your dependence on costly fossil fuels and even costlier nuclear energy (for homes heated with electricity from nuclear plants). You can also achieve huge reductions in energy consumption by replacing energy-consuming appliances and other devices — especially heating and cooling equipment, water heaters, refrigerators, and washing machines — with newer, energy-efficient models. (Be sure to recycle your old appliance, if possible.)

When buying replacements for inefficient appliances, seek out the most energy-efficient alternatives on the market. Take furnaces and boilers as an example. In recent years, manufacturers have introduced numerous state-of-the-art energy-efficient furnaces (for forced hot air heating systems) and boilers (for radiant floor and baseboard hot water systems). Furnaces and boilers use fossil fuels (usually either natural gas or oil) or electricity. The newest furnaces achieve efficiencies in the 80 percent range, while energy-efficient boilers

Fig. 2-8: Heat pumps like the one on the left in (a) strip heat from the ground via pipes (b) buried below the frost line.

achieve efficiencies in the 90 percent range. Efficiencies for new models are posted on a sticker as AFUE , the annual fuel utilization efficiency.

If your boiler or furnace is old and rickety and begging to be replaced, you'd be wise to retire the dinosaur and purchase a new, energy-efficient model to take over. Another option is to replace your furnace or boiler with a heat pump.

Heat pumps are devices used to heat *and* cool buildings (Figure 2-8). As explained shortly, heat pumps remove heat from the environment — from either the air or the ground or a nearby pond, depending on the model — concentrate it and then transfer it to our homes during the winter. Heat pumps deliver heat to existing heat distribution systems in our homes, for example, forced-air, or radiant-floor heat, or baseboard hot water.

Heat pumps come in two basic varieties: air-source and ground-source. Air-source heat pumps are used in warmer climates, for example, the southern United States, where freezing temperatures are a rarity. In an air-source heat pump, heat is drawn from ambient air, concentrated, and then used to heat our homes. Yes, you've read that correctly: cold outside air is used to heat a home on chilly winter days. These seemingly magical devices achieve this amazing feat by using refrigeration technology. In the summer, air-source heat pumps operate in reverse, that is, they draw heat out of a house, cooling it down.

Ground-source heat pumps capture and concentrate heat from the earth. In this system, shown in Figure 2-9, water is pumped through pipes laid in the ground well below the frost line. The water circulating through the tubing picks up heat, which the heat pump concentrates and then delivers to the house.

Heat pumps are remarkably energy efficient. They use electricity, which can be generated from coal and nuclear fuels or a host of renewable energy sources and delivered to our homes via the existing electrical grid. Heat pumps produce 4.5 times more heat energy than the electrical energy they consume, so are amazingly efficient, too. Because of their efficiency and the continued wide availability of electrical energy, heat pumps may be one of the shining stars of our energy future. Not only do they heat and cool homes, they also can be used to heat water for domestic use.

Unfortunately, ground-source heat pumps are fairly expensive. Boring vertical holes or digging trenches to bury the pipe can be costly. Thus, although you'll save a lot in heating costs, you'll pay more upfront.

Before you pursue this route, be sure to attend to the changes required to make your home energy-efficient. Pay special attention to the modifications that will reduce your heating and cooling loads (that is, how much energy you need to heat and cool your home).

You may also want to consider adding passive solar, described in Chapter 4, before contemplating a heat pump. If you live in an area with abundant wood supplies, you may want to consider installing a super-efficient woodstove instead of a heat pump.

Energy efficiency measures, passive solar, and a backup woodstove might be all you need to heat your home. If so, you won't have to install an expensive heat pump. We'll talk more about heating options in Chapters 4 and 5.

As a final note, if your furnace or boiler doesn't need replacement or you can't justify the costs, you should call your local utility — or a local heating contractor — to check the efficiency of your system. They may be able to adjust it to burn more efficiently. Also, be sure to replace the filters in forced-air

Fig. 2-9: Ground-source heat pumps, while energy efficient, can be costly because they require extensive excavation. This technology may help us make a transition to a more efficient, renewable energy system, but it won't be cheap.

heating systems frequently to maintain efficient operation.

Replacing Energy-Inefficient Cooling Systems

Cooling loads (the amount of energy required to cool our homes) are likely to increase in the near future in many places as the world grows warmer, thanks to global warming.

If you need to upgrade your cooling system, there are two things you should consider: first, be sure that you have made your home as efficient as humanly possible. Seal up the leaks and boost insulation levels. Upgrade windows. Then, read Chapter 6. In it, I discuss the many ways you can cool your home passively — at little or no additional cost. I also describe energy-efficient cooling equipment in that chapter.

What to do with Your Water Heater?

Water heaters consume a large chunk of the home energy pie. If your water heater is old and decrepit, replace it with an energy-efficient model. You should give strong consideration to an on-demand or instantaneous water heater, described in Chapter 3.

If your water heater still has a few good years left, you can cut fuel bills by making a few adjustments. The first thing you should do is check the water temperature. To do this, turn on the hot water and let it run for a minute or two. Next, hold a thermometer under a faucet. If the temperature is above 120°F (49°C), turn the water heater's temperature

down. Studies show that you don't need water to be hotter than 120°F (49°C) to wash dishes and clothes. This is sufficient to kill bacteria.

If you have a gas- or propane-powered water heater, simply turn the dial on the unit to a lower setting, then wait a day or two and check the temperature again. If the temperature is still too high, lower it again.

For electric water heaters, you'll need to remove the top and bottom covers on the side of the unit, one for each heating element, and turn the temperature settings down using a screwdriver.

Lowering temperature on a thermostat results in huge savings, but that's not all you can do. After lowering the water temperature setting, you should install an insulated water heater blanket over the tank. Water heater blankets come in several varieties and are available in all hardware stores. I like the bubble wrap plastic variety the best. My second favorite is made from aluminum and felt insulation material. My least favorite is the plastic water heater blanket with a fibrous insulation interior.

Water heater blankets wrap around the water heater and are secured by tape provided with the blanket. The instructions provide advice on how to install them. Be sure to follow them precisely, and be especially sure not to obstruct the flow of air to the top and bottom of gas- or propane-fired water heaters. Also take care not to cover the dials used to adjust water temperature.

Water heater blankets currently cost about $15, and pay for themselves in 3 to 6 months, depending on your family's hot water consumption. That means every year your water heater blanket is in operation, you'll save $30 to $60 on your annual energy bill. As energy costs go higher, you'll save even more!

After the water heater blanket has been installed, I strongly suggest that you insulate the hot water pipes in the crawl space or basement of your home. I like the foam insulation sleeves that fit over the copper pipe better than the type of insulation you wrap on the pipe. They're much quicker and easier to install.

You can also save hot water by installing water-efficient showerheads. Most showerheads in older homes consume 3.5 to 5 gallons of hot water a minute. Newer models use around 1.5 to 1.9 gallons per minute and cost about $8–$15, depending on the model.

Water-efficient showerheads reduce hot water use dramatically. One popular model reportedly saves a family of four up to $250 per year. As energy prices climb, this simple, inexpensive device could reap even higher dividends.

When purchasing a water-efficient showerhead, I strongly recommend you select one that comes with an on-off button or switch. This feature allows you to turn off the showerhead when lathering up, further cutting back on water and energy use.

You can also save energy and water by installing efficient appliances — notably washing machines and dishwashers, a topic discussed shortly.

Replacing Inefficient Lights

One of the easiest ways to reduce fuel bills in our homes is by installing compact fluorescent light bulbs in commonly used fixtures. Lighting in our homes is powered by electricity from nuclear power plants, coal-fired power plants, a few oil-fired power plants, hydropower in some parts of the world, or, increasingly, natural gas plants. Because most of these forms of electrical generation are either endangered — because of declining supplies — or are potentially perilous from an environmental standpoint, cutting down on electrical use is of great importance. Reducing electrical energy demand is doubly important for those who are planning on installing a wind generator or photovoltaics (PVs) to produce their own electricity.

I've made the case for compact fluorescent light bulbs (CFLs) earlier in this chapter, demonstrating how much energy and money they save. CFLs screw into ordinary sockets and can be used for a variety of applications, for example, in ordinary table lamps, ceiling lights, some chandeliers, recessed lighting, indoor spotlights, and even outdoor lights, for example, for patios, garages, and spotlights for lighting pathways and driveways. Some manufacturers even produce dimmable CFLs (most CFLs can't be used with dimmable or three-way switches).

CFLs use one-fourth as much energy as standard light bulbs, as noted earlier in the

DAN CHIRAS

Fig. 2-10: In compact fluorescent lights, a fluorescent tube is placed inside a glass globe, as shown here.

CFL Reading Lamps

At least one manufacturer (Sunwave) produces a line of CFLs designed for reading. Their CFLs emit light that is similar to the sunlight at noon, a cooler, bluer light than standard CFLs. I'm working under one right now and have used it for several years. The color of the light isn't as appealing as a standard CFL, but the bulbs do really make it much easier to read. According to the manufacturer, and several years of field testing in my home, these bulbs increase resolution — the ability of the eye to detect detail. According to the manufacturer, they also reduce eyestrain.

chapter, and give off much less heat, too. (They will help keep a home cooler in the summer as a result.) Each bulb is equipped with a ballast and a small tube, which is often coiled or looped inside a glass globe (Figure 2-10).

Unlike typical fluorescent lights, CFLs do not produce a spooky cool white light that would make even Jennifer Aniston or Brad Pitt look hideous when standing in front of a mirror. Rather, compact fluorescent light bulbs are coated with special chemicals (fluors) that produce a yellowish light, much like incandescent light bulbs.

You can purchase CFLs at hardware stores, building supply outlets, discount stores, drug stores, grocery stores, and even huge warehouses like Costco. A word to the wise, however: although the CFLs available through warehouse outlets are inexpensive, they also have a much shorter lifespan (about 6,000 hours) than higher quality CFLs found elsewhere (lifespans of 10,000 hours). I have also found through personal experience that they're not as well-made as the more expensive CFLs, and would recommend that you avoid going this route.

Also, be aware it doesn't make sense to install compact fluorescent light bulbs in every light fixture in your house. It's best to use them in lights that are on for at least three or four hours a day, such as kitchen or living room lamps. It such locations, they will earn their keep, saving you the most money.

If you haven't already installed CFLs in your home, I'd recommend that you buy a couple and give them a try. You may be pleasantly surprised by how well they work. I know I was!

CFLs come in several different shapes and sizes, so they fit into a wide variety of light fixtures and lamps. When selecting a bulb, you will notice that the manufacturers list the actual wattage of each bulb — how much energy each type consumes — and the wattage of the incandescent light bulb each model replaces. For example, the package of a 23-watt CFL may indicate that it replaces a 100-watt incandescent. In my experience, I've found that it is best to go up a step. That is, if you want to replace a 75-watt incandescent light bulb with a CFL, go to a CFL designed to replace a 100-watt incandescent bulb.

Replacing Inefficient Appliances. Dishwashers and washing machines may also need replacement. Once again, if your appliances are old and rickety and in dire need of replacement, you'd be wise to go with the most energy- and water-efficient models you can get.

As for washing machines, I strongly recommend the front loading (or horizontal axis machines) like Frigidaire's Gallery. I use this model and have been extremely pleased with it. It's quiet, and uses one-half the water and a third of the electricity of my old top-loading washer. It did cost more than a standard washing machine, but will pay back the extra cost in a couple of years in water and energy savings.

You should also consider replacing your old dishwasher with an energy- and water-efficient model if yours needs replacement.

Or, and don't e-mail in protest over this one, you could do the dishes by hand!

Dishwashing by hand saves a lot of energy and water. Although dishwashers can be just as efficient as washing by hand, most people rinse their dishes so thoroughly before they put them in their dishwashers that they're practically clean *before* they push the on button. In the process, they waste a lot of water and energy. In such instances, it would be hard to argue that a dishwasher actually uses less water than handwashing.

In our home, my boys and I wash and rinse dishes in two tubs, one in each half of the divided sink. Each tub holds about two gallons of water. When the dishes are done, we use the relatively soapless rinse water to water indoor plants. The net effect is that dishwashing consumed about two gallons per load.

End of sermon.

Where Do You Go for Information?

Buying energy-efficient appliances and heating and cooling equipment requires patience and perseverance. The job, however, is made a lot easier by consumer labels required by the US and Canadian governments. These labels list pertinent energy data on each model and are designed to help consumers make the wisest choices. EPA Energy Star labels will also help guide you to the best choices.

In the US, Energy Star labels, shown in Figure 2-11, are posted on a wide variety of electronic equipment and appliances. They don't list any pertinent data, but serve to

US EPA AND DAN CHIRAS

Fig. 2-11: The Energy Star label on appliances or electronics indicates that you are looking at one of the most energy-efficient models in its class.

Energy-Efficient Hot Tubs?

When many people think about making their homes energy efficient, they run into a stumbling block when it comes to one item: the hot tub. Electric heaters in hot tubs consume huge amounts of electricity. However, one company, Softub, has come up with an innovative new hot tub design that uses only a fraction of the energy of a standard hot tub. Instead of a standard resistance-type heater, the water is heated by waste heat from the water circulating pump. Water from the hot tub flows through pipes around the pump, drawing off waste heat that's used to bring the hot tub up to temperature. All in all, they use about $10 worth of electricity a month, compared to a standard hot tub that can use as much as $60. Moreover, their hot tubs are made of foam and are very lightweight. No need to hire a crane to lift it into your back yard. To learn more, log on to <www.softub.com>

indicate the most energy-efficient products in each category.

Another extremely useful tool when shopping for energy-efficient appliances is the *Consumer Guide to Home Energy Savings* written by Alex Wilson, Jennifer Thorne, and John Morrill. This handy, inexpensive guide is the Bible of energy efficiency. Worth its weight in gold, this book contains a wealth of information on windows, heating systems, cooling systems, water heaters, refrigerators, washing machines, and a whole lot more. Of even greater value to those on the prowl for energy-efficient replacement items, are the book's numerous tables that compare various models using a variety of measurements. For example, each table lists not only how much energy a particular model consumes, but also how much water it requires, if it indeed requires water, and other pertinent information that allows you to make a highly informed choice. It also contains model numbers so you can call around to see who sells the exact model you'd like to purchase.

I used this guide when I replaced my old, energy-guzzling water-hungry washing machine. It saved me an enormous amount of time and energy. Rather than having to shop around, asking ill-informed sales people about their most efficient models, I simply opened up the guide, found the model that interested me the most, then called around to see who carried it. A few phone calls later I was done and I've got an amazing washing machine to boot!

Ghost Busters

You probably don't know it, but your house is haunted.

Yes, haunted.

Not with spirits of people who have lived in your home before you, but by ghost loads, or, more commonly, phantom loads.

Phantom loads are the electricity used by appliances and an assortment of other electronic devices when they're not in active use. Your instant-on television, for example, is haunted by a phantom load. That is, it consumes electricity even when it's off. Why?

To keep the circuits buzzing, so that when you click the power button on the remote, the TV hums to life instantly.

Other examples include: the power transformers for cordless phones, answering machines, and keyboards; microwave ovens and coffee makers equipped with LED clocks; stereos, radios, audio receivers, satellite receivers, and power strips (Figure 2-12); even hard-wired smoke detectors and some GFIs (the electrical outlets with built-in circuit breakers). And don't forget your cell phone recharger; it may draw power even when the phone isn't hooked in to it.

Your home is full of phantom loads that, although tiny on their own, add up and collectively consume significant amounts of electricity over a year's time.

When I first moved into my solar home, I discovered that there were about 125 watts of cumulative ghost loads. That's the equivalent of over three 100-watt light bulbs running 24 hours a day, 365 days a year. In my case that came to 1,095 kilowatt hours per year that were putting a huge strain on my tiny solar electric system. Had I been buying power at the local rate, about 8.5 cents per kwh, it would have cost me $93 a year just to feed these annoying ghosts!

Needless to say, I set out to eliminate the ghosts from my life, and so can you. To do so, first look around you. You'll find them everywhere. Make a note of each ghost load, and then devise a strategy to get rid of them one by one. For example, you can plug televisions, stereos, microwaves, and the like into power strips that can be shut off when the electronic device or appliance is not in use (Figure 2-13).

Fig. 2-12: Ghost, or phantom, loads are everywhere in our homes, as in this stereo system. Finding ways to reduce them will help you save energy and make your home more suitable for a renewable energy system.

For appliances such as microwaves, you can replace the standard outlets they're plugged into with switch and receptacle outlets. These are electrical outlets, available at all hardware stores, that are controlled by a switch that is part of the unit. Turning the switch off, terminates the flow of power to the electrical outlet and thus ends the flow of energy that feeds the ghost load of the microwave or other devices plugged into the outlet. If you aren't skilled in electrical work, I would strongly suggest that you enlist the help of a qualified friend or hire a licensed electrician. Be sure to turn the power to the circuit off before you mess with any electrical switch or outlet.

Fig. 2-13: A power strip can be used to control phantom loads, but be sure to turn it off when the attached electronics are not in use; even the power strip comes with a phantom load.

DAN CHIRAS

Another source of ghost load are GFIs — those electrical outlets in bathrooms that have built-in circuit breakers to protect you from getting shocked if someone drops a hair dryer in the tub while you're taking a leisurely bath. (The GFI shorts out before you do.) Unfortunately, some GFIs draw power even though there's nothing plugged into them. To see if a GFI has a ghost load, plug in an amp meter. A trained electrician can do this for you. I replaced my GFIs with a no-ghost-load GFI from Leviton.

To reduce energy-draining ghost loads, you can also unplug power transformers or chargers when not in use. For example, if you have an electronic keyboard, unplug it when you're not using it. Unplug your cell phone charger when it's not in use, too.

To learn more about phantom loads, you may want to pick up a copy of my article, "Hunting Phantom Loads," which was published in *Home Power* magazine in May 2001.

THE SILVER LINING

Energy efficiency is vital to each of us and to our collective long-term future. So far, though, North Americans haven't taken energy conservation very seriously. Our wastefulness has actually hastened the depletion of oil and natural gas and seriously dimmed the lights along the path into our once illustrious future. Had we developed an energy efficiency ethic earlier in our history, or even heeded warnings about energy shortages in the 1970s and learned to use fossil fuels efficiently, this book probably wouldn't have been needed for another several decades.

But we didn't and there's no sense in crying over spilled oil.

The good news, of course, as I've stated earlier, is that our waste is the silver lining behind the cloud that darkens our future. Because we do waste so much energy, the easiest and most cost-effective way to meet our near-term energy demands is by practicing the lost art of energy conservation. In so doing, we could reduce potential hardship, making it easier on ourselves, our family, our neighbors, and very likely all of humanity.

You can do your part to help smooth the rocky road to a renewable energy future by spending some time energy retrofitting your home. The sooner the better.

You may find that the path has been made even smoother by financial assistance from your local utility or your state or local government. A quick phone call to your utility — or to your state energy office — may reveal that one or the other offers incentives, sometimes fairly sizable financial incentives, to help you become a model of energy efficiency. Federal subsidies and incentives may also be available. You can use your savings to implement other steps in this book, for instance, the installation of solar electric panels; local utilities may provide incentives for this, too.

I advise you to get moving now, though. Don't dally. The cost of energy retrofitting will very likely escalate in years to come, as more and more people see the need for it (increasing demand) and as energy prices themselves go up. Remember: it takes energy to create all the energy-efficient products I've been talking about, including energy-efficient appliances, so as the price of energy goes up, so will the cost of everything else, including the devices we buy to reduce our demand for energy.

Nancy Newhall once wrote that conservation is "humanity caring for the future," and she's right. Let's not forget that the future starts tomorrow. If we're to have a decent future, we need to get serious about energy conservation today.

Because we do waste so much energy, the easiest and most cost-effective way to meet our near-term energy demands is by practicing the lost art of energy conservation.

CHAPTER 3

SOLAR HOT WATER SYSTEMS

SATISFYING DOMESTIC HOT WATER NEEDS WITH RENEWABLE ENERGY

Solar energy is a gift from the sun, but one that's vastly underutilized by human society. As natural gas supplies dwindle and as prices skyrocket, however, more and more people will turn to the sun to meet their needs for energy. We'll use the sun's energy to heat our homes (Chapter 5) and to produce electricity (Chapter 7). And many will use the sun's massive outpouring of energy to heat water for a wide variety of domestic uses. This chapter explores this application.

Besides ensuring our comfort and promoting personal hygiene, hot water constitutes a huge portion of our annual fuel bill — about 20 percent of the average annual household fuel bill in the United States, according to the US Department of Energy. As natural gas production declines and prices climb, the cost of hot water is expected to rise dramatically. Those who retrofit their homes for solar hot water could save a sizeable amount of money.

Before we explore solar hot water systems and the options available to you, though, let's take a look at the most common hot water systems in use today. You'll need to understand how these systems operate because solar hot water systems are typically integrated with them.

CONVENTIONAL HOT WATER SYSTEMS

In most homes in North America, hot water is provided by a conventional gas or electric storage water heater — widely (and incorrectly) referred to as "hot water heaters." (We're not heating hot water!) The storage water heater consists of a free-standing water tank, a reservoir that holds 40 to 80 gallons of hot water (Figure 3-1). The tank itself consists of an internal storage vessel made from glass. It is encased in a steel envelope with a layer of insulation in between.

In electric storage water heaters, water is heated by two electric resistors, known as heating elements. The heating elements — one near the top and one near the bottom of the tank — generate heat when electricity flows through them, much like the electric heating elements of an electric stove. The heat produced by the resistors is transferred to the water in the tank.

Gas-powered storage water heaters have a single source of heat, a burner at the bottom of the water tank. The burner is connected to a thermostat and ignites when the temperature of the water inside the tank drops below a predetermined set point. When this occurs, the temperature sensor sends a signal to a valve that regulates the flow of natural gas or propane into the burner. When the valve opens, gas flows into the burner and is ignited, most often by a small pilot light that runs 24 hours a day, 7 days a week, 365 days a year.

Because the combustion of natural gas and propane produce carbon dioxide, carbon monoxide, and nitrogen dioxide, which are potentially poisonous to people and pets, gas-powered water heaters must be vented. Venting is accomplished by a flue pipe that directs hot combustion gases and pollutants though the ceiling. In most gas-fired water heaters, combustion air that feeds the burner comes from room air. For a discussion of newer, safer, and more efficient power-vented water heaters, see the accompanying sidebar on page 73.

Conventional storage water heaters maintain a large quantity of hot water day in and day out. This water can be used at any time. It's there at our command. Just open a hot water faucet or turn on an appliance like a clothes washer and you've got hot water in 10 to 30 seconds, depending on how far away they are from the tank.

Hot water drained from the tank is replaced by cold water from the main water line that supplies our homes. As it enters the

Fig. 3-1: Water heaters like this one (below) are popular in North America. They store 40 to 80 gallons of hot water, ready for use anytime of the day or night. Although they work well, they're not as efficient as other systems. Standby losses account for about 20 percent of the energy consumed by these units.

ECONAIR

tank, the cold water cools the water in the storage tank. When the temperature of the water in the tank drops below the desired setting, the gas burner ignites in a gas-fired water heater. Once the water reaches the desired setting, the flame turns off.

Pros and Cons of Storage Water Heaters

Conventional storage water heaters are widely available in North America, fairly inexpensive, and are about 80 percent efficient. However, they do have some drawbacks. For one, they generally don't last very long. You can count on replacing your water heater every seven to ten years, unless you take steps like those outlined in the sidebar on page 74 to ensure a longer life span.

Another problem with storage water heaters is that they use natural gas and propane, two fuels slipping toward extinction. Even electric water heaters have some problems. For one, they rely on an expensive source of energy:

Power Venting

Standard water heaters are popular in North America, but not as efficient or as safe as they could be. To address these issues, some companies sell power-vented water heaters. A power-vented water heater consists of a large storage tank and a burner, just like a conventional gas-powered storage water heater. However, that's where similarities end. This new and safer water heater also includes a fan. It draws outside air into the combustion chamber and forces combustion gases out through a vent. This is important for two reasons.

Bringing outside air in helps prevent leakage through cracks in the building envelope that reduces the overall energy-efficiency of a home. Power venting also actively expels combustion gases and the pollutants they contain. This ensures that pollutants produced by the combustion of natural gas or propane are vented to the outside and can't enter the room air, causing health problems.

Spillage is also prevented by a closed combustion chamber. It contains the fire and the combustion gases, unlike a standard water heater, making it impossible for them to escape into our homes.

Power-vented water heaters are not only safer, they're more efficient — usually at least ten percent more efficient than standard gas-fired storage water heaters. In fact, they're so much more efficient than standard storage water heaters that they can be vented with plastic flue pipes rather than the metal flue pipes of conventional water heaters.

While safer and more efficient, these models do cost more and they use electricity to run the fan. Your gas bills will go down, but your electric bill will go up a tiny bit. It's not a big deal, however. The increase will hardly be noticeable.

electricity. (Electricity is the most expensive means of heating water.)

Perhaps the most significant problem with storage water heaters is that they maintain a large quantity of hot water 24 hours a day, 7 days a week, 365 days a year. Heat invariably leaks out of tanks between uses. This is called standby loss. Standby heat loss must be replaced and one-fifth of the fuel consumed by a conventional storage water heater is used to offset the standby losses.

Many, myself included, believe this system wastes too much energy. It's a little like keeping your car running in the garage 24 hours a day so that it is ready to use anytime you want. A far better alternative is the tankless water heater.

TANKLESS WATER HEATERS

Travel through Europe and other parts of the world, like Japan, where energy is expensive and efficiency is a cultural norm and you won't find a storage water heater like the ones in North American homes.

In such regions, the tankless water heater is the technology of choice (Figure 3-2a). Why?

Because tankless water heaters outperform their conventional counterparts easily by 20 percent or more. Like storage water heaters, tankless water heaters provide hot water on demand but they do so without storing huge quantities of hot water. In fact, as their name suggests, they have no storage capacity at all.

Anatomy of a Tankless Water Heater

Tankless water heaters for household use are attractive, compact units that mount on the wall in a central location in our homes or near the main hot water demand centers (Figure 3-2a). The heart and soul of all tankless water heaters is a device called a heat exchanger — a combustion chamber in which cold water is quickly brought up to temperature (Figure 3-2b).

Water Heater Revival

Storage water heaters can be made to last much longer and operate more efficiently by draining sediment from the bottom of the tanks every year. Simply open the faucet at the bottom of the tank and drain off a couple of gallons of water containing sediment.

You can also extend their working life by replacing the anode in the tank. The anode is a long, slender metal rod that's usually attached to the cold water inlet pipe of the water tank. It extends down into the tank and prevents corrosion of the steel casing for reasons beyond the scope of this book. Periodic replacement can double the working life of a water tank, saving you lots of money.

For details on how to replace the anode, I refer you to Chuck Marken's article in issue 106 of *Home Power* magazine, "New Life for Your Old Water Heater."

The heat exchanger transfers heat from the burner to the water, heating it instantaneously. A flue pipe vents unburned gases and pollutants like carbon monoxide out of the house.

Here's how a tankless water heater works: when hot water is required — for example, when someone turns on a hot water faucet — a water flow sensor in the tankless water heater sends a signal to a central control module in the unit. This tiny computer, in turn, sends signals to an electronically controlled gas valve in the gas manifold. The valve opens and allows natural gas or propane to flow into the combustion chamber of the heat exchanger. The gas is ignited by a pilot light or by a spark from an electronic ignition device. Cold water flowing through the pipe in the heat exchanger is immediately brought up to the desired temperature. As soon as the hot water faucet is turned off, however, the water flow through the water

Under-the-Sink Water Heaters

Many tankless water heaters in use in Europe fit under the sinks of homes and apartments. They heat water for one sink only and are typically powered by electricity. The household-sized units described in this chapter are centrally located so they can service all hot water needs in a home. They are often powered by natural gas or propane, both of which are much more efficient fuel options than electricity.

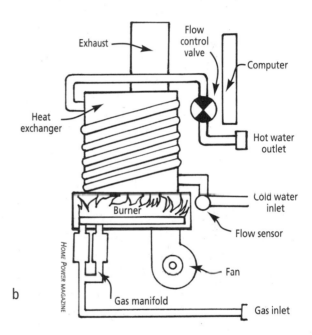

Fig. 3-2: (a) Tankless water heaters like this one heat water instantly (there's no need to store hot water for intermittent uses) and thus reduce the amount of energy required to supply a family with hot water by about 20 percent. These units are typically mounted on walls in a central location in the house. (b) Cutaway of a tankless water heater.

heater ceases and the flame goes out. The net result is that you heat only the water you need at any one time.

Pros and Cons of Tankless Water Heaters

Tankless water heaters cost more than their conventional counterparts and are a bit more challenging to install. (This isn't a job for most do-it-yourselfers.) However, they do provide significant advantages over storage water heaters. As just noted, they heat only the water needed at any one moment. As a result, they are usually at least 20 percent more efficient than standard water heaters. That means they provide the same amount of hot water as a storage water tank, but use 20 percent less fuel. Utility bills will be 20 percent lower, too.

Because there's no standby loss, they also produce less waste heat. In the summer, that means less internal heat gain and lower cooling bills, the topic of Chapter 6.

Another huge advantage of tankless water heaters is that they outlast conventional water heaters. They're typically designed to last as long as a conventional furnace or boiler — twenty years or more. Moreover, tankless water heaters are easy to repair. If a part goes bad, it can be replaced. You don't have to throw the unit out and replace it with a brand new water heater, as you do with a conventional storage water heater, when something goes wrong.

With this background in mind, let's turn our attention to solar hot water systems and how they are integrated with conventional or tankless water heaters. (If you want to learn more about tankless water heaters, I suggest you read Jennifer Weaver's piece on them in *Home Power*, Issue 105.)

WHAT IS A SOLAR HOT WATER SYSTEM?

Domestic solar hot water systems are probably familiar to most readers. They depend on solar collectors typically mounted on the roofs of homes. The solar collectors capture solar energy to heat water for use inside the home.

Most domestic solar hot water systems are designed to provide 40 percent to 80 percent of a household's annual hot water needs, although 100 percent is possible. (This requires using the most efficient solar panels and is typically achieved in the sunniest locations.)

Domestic solar hot water systems are usually integrated with conventional storage or tankless water heaters. (Be sure to purchase a tankless water heater that's designed to operate in conjunction with a solar hot water system.) As you shall soon see, when operating in conjunction with a solar hot water system, conventional storage or tankless water heaters become secondary heat sources. That is, they back up the solar hot water system.

Although this chapter deals with systems for domestic hot water, these systems can also be designed to provide space heat for homes. Solar hot water systems can also be designed to heat greenhouses and swimming pools. They can even provide hot water for hot tubs, saving homeowners tons of money and dramatically reducing the environmental impact of using conventional heat sources. I'll describe solar hot water systems for space heating in Chapter 5. (See Bob Owen's piece on solar hot water systems for hot tubs listed in the Resource Guide.)

But that's not all. Solar hot water systems are also installed for what may seem like an even more frivolous need — melting snow on driveways. In the upscale ski town of Aspen, Colorado, for example, many wealthy homeowners install solar hot water systems to de-ice their driveways.

A BRIEF HISTORY OF SOLAR HOT WATER

Solar hot water is not a new technology by any stretch of the imagination. In fact, solar systems were quite popular in the early 1900s in the United States, particularly in California and Florida. An estimated eight million systems were installed on the rooftops of homes in these areas.

But along came cheap natural gas, and the solar hot water industry took a nose dive. It wasn't until the oil embargoes of the 1970s that the solar industry got back on its feet again. To decrease our nation's dependence on foreign energy sources, in part by encouraging renewable energy, the federal government and many states offered generous financial incentives — tax credits and tax deductions — for homeowners who installed solar hot water systems. In my home state of Colorado, the combined federal and state

incentives covered 60 percent of the cost of a new system.

The domestic solar hot water (DSHW) industry boomed in the late 1970s and early 1980s, but during the Reagan Administration the incentives came to a screeching halt. Neither Congress nor the president even hinted at extending them. And so ended the second era of solar hot water. (Perhaps as a symbolic measure, President Reagan ordered the removal of the solar panels that President Jimmy Carter had installed on the White House during his brief tenure.)

As Greg Pahl writes in his book, *Natural Home Heating,* "The fall of the industry was as

Solar Driveway

In Aspen, Colorado, and other areas, solar hot water systems are often installed to keep driveways free of snow and ice. In these systems, pipes are installed beneath the driveway before the pavement is laid down. These pipes circulate a solar-heated fluid (a type of antifreeze) beneath the driveway. Even on cloudy days, the panels often produce enough heat to melt snow and ice, as the fluid circulating beneath the driveway doesn't have to be as hot as water in our homes. It has to be just hot enough to melt the snow.

This application may seem like a luxury to most of us, and it is, but it beats the alternative: using a gas-fired boiler or electrical wire to achieve the same result. And it does eliminate the need to plow driveways, an activity that uses a lot of energy!

sudden – and spectacular – as its rise." The second coming of solar hot water was not a complete bust, however. Its meteoric rise introduced many to a sensible and often economical alternative to natural gas. Even more importantly, it resulted in the installation of numerous systems, many of which are still operating today.

The rise and fall of the solar hot water industry in the late 1970s and early 1980s did create some lasting problems. One of those was that the generous tax incentives available to customers created an almost overnight industry. In their rush to deliver their products to market and tap into the generous governmental incentives for consumers, not all companies produced the highest quality systems. Moreover, some vendors and installers engaged in unscrupulous activities. Some overstated the economic benefits and many, it seems to me, engaged in price gouging. I fell victim to price gouging myself. I bought a system from a company (no longer in business), paying a premium price for the equipment and installation — a whopping $6,000. Like other customers, I was willing to pay what seemed like an outlandish price. Who cared what the sticker prices was? Federal and state incentives knocked the price back down into the ballpark — about $2,400, including installation.

Unfortunately, when the tax incentives withered away, so did most of the companies. Many homeowners, myself included, were abandoned. When systems needed repair we had no one to turn to. The service personnel were gone, and so were the parts we needed. Many systems fell into disrepair.

Since then, the solar hot water industry has been struggling to gain a foothold. But after years of struggle, solar hot water systems are gaining in popularity. I think they will become even more popular in the very near future as natural gas prices continue their upward spiral.

Today, their newfound popularity occurs primarily in areas where utility companies or state and local governments offer financial incentives to homeowners. Even without financial incentives, DSHW systems often make good sense, as you shall soon see.

Despite the resurgence in solar hot water, the solar industry still hasn't overcome the bad image lingering in the minds of many citizens. Today, many people still view this technology as too unreliable. "Happily, the industry has matured, the technology has improved," notes Pahl. Today's companies produce an excellent product. You can hardly go wrong. Making things better for homeowners, today there are performance standards for most of the components of active solar heating systems, which makes comparing different products much easier.

I believe that this time solar hot water is here to stay. Incentives offered at the federal and state levels could boost the industry dramatically, but they may not be needed. Market forces may drive the switch to solar hot water, creating a lasting energy source throughout the 21st century and beyond.

My recommendation to those thinking of installing a system is to go with companies like Thermomax and Heliodyne and a number of others who have struggled through the 1990s to fine-tune their products. You may also be wise to work with vendors and installers who did the same.

"Before you decide to buy an active solar heating system," notes Pahl, "be sure to check local zoning ordinances, land covenants, and any other possible local restrictions" that might apply to you. "Homeowner association rules, in particular, can be a real headache when it comes to solar collectors." Although such restrictions are not widespread, they can be insurmountable. If you do run into local restrictions, you may want to invest some time, energy, and money to combat them. As Pahl notes, "Most of these restrictions are absurd and deserve to be changed, so it's probably worth the effort if you are committed to solar heating." We need solar pioneers who will help pave the way for others.

SOLAR HOT WATER SYSTEMS

Domestic solar hot water systems consist of several basic components. The two most prominent are (1) the solar panels or collectors, as noted earlier, and (2) the water storage tank. The solar panels are usually located on the roof or on the ground next to a house. In both locations, they need to be positioned so they receive full sunlight year-round. The water storage tank is typically located next to the conventional water heater, often located in the basement of a home. Copper pipes connect the collectors with the storage tank, and various pumps, sensors, and controls ensure that the system works automatically (Figure 3-3). Because many DSHW systems utilize pumps, they are classified as "active systems." (As you shall soon see, though, there are a few DSHW systems that require no pumps at all.)

Solar hot water systems work in all climates, from the sunniest areas (the Sunbelt) to the dreariest of all climate zones (the so-called Gloom Belts). The type of system you install depends on the climate, as you shall soon see.

With this overview in mind, let's take a look at your options, starting with the simplest

SolReliant

Fig. 3-3: The most prominent part of a solar hot water system is the solar collector. Collectors are typically mounted on the roofs of houses or alongside homes to ensure year-round exposure to the sun from 9 a.m. to 3 p.m. each day. Heat energy gathered from sunlight is stored in a water tank, usually located in the basement, for use when needed. This model by SolReliant uses a PV panel to provide electricity to pump. No additional wiring is necessary.

of all systems. Table 3-1 provides a useful summary of the types of systems. Before we begin, though, permit me to make one more point vital to your understanding of domestic solar hot water systems.

As you shall soon see, domestic solar hot water systems fit into one of two broad categories: direct or indirect. Direct systems heat water that you use. Indirect systems heat a fluid that then heats the water you use. For reasons that will be clear shortly, direct systems are also referred to as open-loop systems; indirect systems are referred to as closed-loop systems.

Solar Batch Hot Water Systems

The simplest of all the solar hot water systems on the market is the solar batch hot water system. Solar batch water heaters are popular in many tropical countries such as Mexico. In such instances, solar batch water heaters consist of a single water tank mounted on the roofs of homes and other buildings. The tanks are often painted black to increase the absorption of solar energy.

Solar batch water tanks absorb sunlight all day long, heating the water inside. When hot water is required, it flows directly out of the top of the tank into the hot water supply line that feeds various hot water faucets inside the home. Cold water enters the bottom of the tank to replenish hot water drawn out of the tank with each use. Because the water used in the house is heated in the tank, the solar batch hot water system is considered a direct or open-loop solar hot water system.

Solar batch water heaters such as this are simple, economical, and reliable. However, they do have some shortcomings. One of those shortcomings is that the tanks are not insulated. As a result, they tend to lose much of their heat at night. Hot water is, therefore, typically available only in the afternoons and the early evenings.

But don't close the book on solar batch water heaters just yet. More efficient — and more attractive — models are available. One type, shown in Figure 3-4, consists of a large black water tank inside a glass-covered, insulated collector. Sometimes referred to as integrated collector and storage (ICS) water heaters because the collector and storage tank are one unit, these models are mounted on roofs, so long as they can support the additional weight, or alongside buildings.

For best results, batch heaters must face true south, not magnetic south. (True south corresponds to the lines of longitude and is not often the same as magnetic south, which is determined by magnetic fields. Magnetic fields don't always run true north and south.) Like all other solar collection devices you'll encounter in this and other chapters, solar batch water heaters need to be in a sunny location free from shade day in and day out, 12 months a year for optimal performance.

Fig. 3-4: The solar batch water heater is one of the simplest and most cost-effective solar hot water systems available on the market today. Unfortunately, it can only be used in warmer climates, where freezing rarely, if ever, occurs.

BOB BOWENS

As noted above, solar batch water heaters heat water during the day. In the United States and other more developed countries, however, solar batch water heaters are typically plumbed into a home's water heater. That is, they provide preheated water to a conventional water heater.

To understand how a solar batch water heater operates, let's trace the flow of water, beginning in the bathroom shower, say on a hot summer day (Figure 3-5). When a hot water faucet is turned on in the bathroom sink or shower, water is drawn from the conventional water heater. Replacement water flows directly into the water heater tank from the solar batch water heater. However, because solar batch water heaters often produce extremely hot water, over 160°F (71°C), installers must be sure to provide a means of reducing water temperature to prevent parboiling residents. This is achieved by placing a mixing or tempering valve in the hot water line leaving the water heater. This "smart valve" senses the temperature of the water leaving the tank. If it is too hot, the valve opens, permitting cold water to mix with the scalding hot water, achieving the desired temperature for showers and other domestic uses.

What happens on cooler, cloudy days when the temperature of the water in the batch heater only reaches 100°F (38°C), well below a comfortable setting for a shower? Will you end up taking a cold shower on those days?

No. In such instances, water temperature is maintained by the conventional water

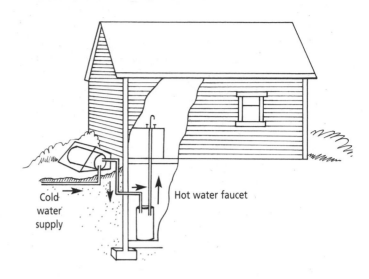

Fig. 3-5: In a solar batch hot water system, hot water for use inside the house is typically drawn from the storage water heater tank. The tank is replenished by water from the solar batch collector. Its tank is replenished by line water.

Turn Off Your Water Heater Entirely!

During really hot sunny weather, homeowners with solar batch water heaters — and other types of solar hot water systems — often turn off their conventional water heaters. During such periods, the batch heater provides 100 percent of their needs. This is accomplished by installing a bypass valve that allows water from the batch heater to be diverted past the water heater. When a hot water faucet is turned on, water flows directly from the batch heater into the hot water line. A mixing or tempering valve needs to be in the line, however, to prevent scalding.

heater. Cooler water flowing into the conventional water heater from the batch heater is boosted to the desired setting (usually around 120°F [49°C]). On such days, then, the batch heater only preheats the water that flows into the storage water heater tank or the tankless water heater.

The value of this arrangement is simple: On sunny days, the batch heater provides really hot water so that your storage water heater or tankless water heater doesn't have to do a thing. They just dole out hot water as needed. On cloudy days, though, the batch heater makes the water heater's job easier by providing preheated water. The water heater

Fig. 3-6: This modern progressive tube solar batch water heater (b) is much less obtrusive than older solar batch water heaters. It mounts on the roof (a).

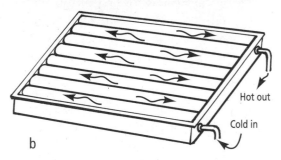

b

Hot out

Cold in

will operate, but it won't need to run very long to bring water up to a suitable temperature. As a result, a solar batch water heater can save energy and reduce utility bills even when not operating full tilt.

If the solar batch heater just described is too bulky for you, don't despair, there's a sleeker model that might fit the bill. It is known as a progressive tube solar water heater, and is shown in Figure 3-6b. This sleek four-foot by eight-foot collector mounts on the roof of a home and consists of long four-inch copper water pipes aligned horizontally (Figure 3-6a). The copper pipes are coated on the outside with a selective surface (sometimes called black chrome). Selective surface materials absorb sunlight (visible light) more efficiently than conventional black surfaces and convert it into heat. The heat is then transferred to the water inside the pipes. (Selective surfaces also reduce heat radiation back through the glass, and thus boost the efficiency of the water heater.)

The progressive tube solar water heater is glass-covered, like a batch heater, and highly insulated. The insulated metal box attaches to the roof via special metal roof mounts and can withstand winds up to 180 miles per hour, according to the manufacturer. How does this solar batch heater work?

As shown in Figure 3-6b, hot water is drawn off the top of the unit and is replaced by cold water that enters at the bottom of the collector. As water flows through the collector, it is heated by the sun.

Like other batch water heaters, the progressive tube solar water heater serves as a preheat tank on cooler, cloudy days, but can meet 100 percent of a family's hot water needs on warm, sunny days. Like other batch water heaters, this one requires no pumps, sensors, controls, or other moving or electronic parts. The progressive tube solar water heater comes in 30-, 40-, and 50- gallon sizes for different sized families or different levels of hot water consumption. When full, these units weigh upwards of 600 pounds — so be sure your roof can handle the load!

Pros and Cons of Batch Heaters

Batch heaters have no moving parts and are therefore the most reliable solar water heaters on the market today. They are available through solar suppliers such as Gaiam Real Goods but can also be manufactured at home using common building materials — an old water heater tank, wood, glass, and black paint.

Batch heaters are inexpensive and relatively easy to install, even by homeowners, although basic plumbing skills are required. Batch heaters don't require a pump, either, as noted above. Nor do they require temperature sensors. Because they're free of electronic controls, sensors, and pumps, they also require no electricity to run. They operate on line pressure — the water pressure in the pipes of your home.

Solar batch water heaters tied to domestic hot water systems provide year-round heat in areas where freezing temperatures rarely occur. However, they'll even work in areas that experience an occasional freeze, such as northern Florida. That's because of the large mass of heated water stored in the tanks. This makes batch heaters immune to an occasional freeze, so long as it doesn't last too long. (In such locations, though, the supply and return lines may be susceptible to freezing so it is wise to insulate them well and to keep pipe runs short.)

Solar batch water heaters are not without problems, however. Most notably, they're of no value in colder climates — places in which freezing temperatures are a more common occurrence. You can pretty much forget about installing a solar batch water heater for year-round hot water if you live in Minnesota, North Dakota, Maine, or even Kansas — or any other area with long, cold winters. If you live in a climate that freezes with any regularity, though, you may want to install a batch heater anyway but only use it during the spring, summer, and fall. You'll need to drain the system when freezing temperatures arrive. If you want year-round solar hot water, though, you should consider one of the other systems you'll learn about shortly.

Another issue to be aware of is that while batch heaters are cheap, shipping costs can be significant. These units are pretty heavy! Don't forget to add this expense when calculating the system cost. When filled with water, batch heaters are even heavier, so roofs need to be capable of supporting the additional weight. In older homes, installation of a solar batch heater may require additional framing. When contemplating this option, check your roof framing to be sure that it is up to the task. It would be wise to consult a structural engineer or contact your local building department to get their advice before you order a solar batch water heater.

Another potential disadvantage for many families is that solar batch water heaters may require a slight change in lifestyle. To get the most from a batch heater, you will need to synchronize your family's hot water use patterns with the batch heater's hot water production. Many homeowners who've installed these systems, for example, make an initial draw of hot water early in the afternoon, for example, to run a dishwasher or clothes washer because the water inside the tank is quite hot at this time.

After drawing off hot water, water temperature in the batch heater falls. If the sun is still shining, however, the batch heater will reheat so there's plenty of hot water by the end of the day. Showers can be taken in the early evening to utilize the hot water remaining in the tank. You can still take a shower in the morning, but remember that batch heaters cool down at night. Replacement water flowing into the storage water heater from the batch heater will be a tad cooler than it was at the end of the day, so your water heater will need to kick in to maintain a comfortable temperature for your morning shower. You won't notice any difference until you pay your utility bill — unless you cover the glass covering of the batch heater with a thick layer of insulation

each night to maintain water temperature. But this starts to get to be a lot of work.

To make the most of a batch heater, homeowners need to carefully manage water use. Such systems can work well for retirees or those of us who work at home. We can reschedule clothes washing and showers a little easier than those who dart off to work each day.

Another downside of solar batch water heaters is that they're designed for smaller households of two to four people. But like so many things, there are ways around this limitation. If you need more hot water, you can always install two (or more) batch heaters side-by-side (in series) to boost hot water production.

Separate Collection and Storage Systems

As you have just seen, batch solar hot water systems combine storage and collection in one unit. Because of this, the water storage tank is exposed to the cooler outdoor air at night or on cold days, with obvious disadvantages. For a system that performs year-round, solar designers have separated the collection and storage functions. They have placed the collection unit, the solar panels, on the outside of the house, usually on the roof, while sequestering the storage tank inside the house where it is much warmer. That way, hot water generated during the day isn't lost to the cold evening air. As a consequence, these systems can operate efficiently even in the coldest weather.

Separate collection and storage systems make up the bulk of the solar hot water systems in use today. The two most common types of collectors in use today are the standard flat plate collector and the evacuated tube collector. Let's take a look at each type of collector, before we explore the different types of DSHW systems.

Flat Plate Collectors

The flat plate collector consists of a glass-covered insulated box. Inside are copper pipes attached to a flat absorber plate, all painted black to optimize solar gain. (The black paint is usually a selective surface material described in the accompanying sidebar.) The pipes in a flat plate collector are typically arranged in series, which means that the water flows in one end and out the other end, as shown in Figure 3-7.

Sunlight entering a flat plate collector is absorbed by the dark-colored absorber plate where it is converted to heat. A heat transfer fluid flowing through the pipes absorbs much of the heat and transports it out of the collector.

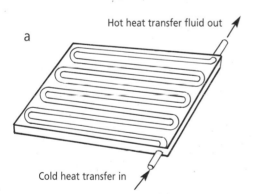

a

Hot heat transfer fluid out

Cold heat transfer in

Selective Surfaces

Researchers have discovered unique ways to capture solar energy and convert it to heat. One of them is a special coating applied to solar hot water panels, called selective surfaces. Although few of us have heard of them, selective surfaces have been around since the 1950s.

Selective surfaces are coatings that are much more efficient at absorbing sunlight (visible light) than a coating of black paint. (They're said to have a higher absorbance.) Not only do they absorb more light and convert it to heat, they also lose less heat than a black-painted material. That is, they don't re-radiate as much heat back into the surrounding environment. (They're said to have a lower emittance.)

Combined, these two features increase the efficiency of solar collectors. Although selective surfaces cost a bit more, they're well worth it, especially in colder climates where higher collector efficiencies dramatically boost solar hot water system performance.

b

HELIODYNE

Fig. 3-7: Flat plate collectors are the most popular models. Copper pipes in this collector form a continuous run.

This liquid delivers the heat to a well-insulated solar water tank. It stores hot water that is fed into a storage water-heater or tankless water heater.

Flat plate collectors are the most commonly used collector on the market today and are useful for lower temperature applications, that is, applications that require water temperatures under 140°F or 60°C, for example, domestic hot water. They're also useful in two space heating applications, notably radiant floor and forced-air heating systems, discussed in Chapter 4.

Evacuated Tube Collectors

Evacuated tube collectors, like those shown in Figure 3-8, are a relative newcomer on the solar hot water scene and a serious departure from conventional flat plate collectors. These revolutionary new solar collectors consist of numerous (20 to 30) long parallel glass or plastic tubes. Inside each tube is a copper pipe (absorber tube) coated with selective surface material. Air is pumped out of the glass or plastic tube, creating a vacuum, hence the name evacuated tube collectors. (Vacuums are poor conductors of heat.)

Inside each black copper pipe is a heat transfer fluid (methanol). It absorbs heat created when sunlight strikes the black selective surface of the absorber tube. Methanol flows upward (by convection) to a heat exchanger at the top of the unit. Here, heat is transferred to another heat transfer fluid. It carries the heat to a solar water tank where it is stored for later use. Cooled methanol returns to continue the cycle.

Evacuated or vacuum tube solar collectors perform well in all climates, and outperform standard flat plate collectors. Because they are so efficient, they work well in less-than-optimum regions — places that experience a lot of cold, cloudy weather. Manufacturers

Fig. 3-8 (a-c): Each evacuated glass tube in this collector houses a black absorber tube filled with methanol. Sunlight striking the absorber tube heats the methanol which rises inside the tube, releasing heat in the heat exchanger, and then returns to repeat the cycle.

of these devices note that there are several reasons for this superior performance. One is that the vacuum inside the tubes dramatically reduces heat loss. Heat produced inside the evacuated tube stays there. Consequently, evacuated tube collectors capture more solar heat than standard flat plate collectors from the same amount of sunlight, especially in cold climates.

The second reason for their superior performance has to do with geometry, notably the tubular nature of the glass collectors. This design is ideal for capturing diffuse radiant energy. During cloudy weather, the manufacturer claims, these collectors will capture around 80 percent of the available radiant energy.

Yet another advantage of this collector is that the vacuum eliminates moisture condensation inside the collector, a problem sometimes encountered in flat plate collectors, which often leads to early deterioration of collectors. This not only reduces performance but can lead to system failure.

Because they are so efficient, evacuated tube collectors are appropriate for high temperature applications — above 140°F or 60°C — such as domestic hot water and baseboard hot water heating.

Thermosiphon Systems

Now that you have familiarized yourself with the types of solar collectors in use today, it is time to explore solar hot water systems with separate collection and storage. We'll begin with the simplest of systems.

The most basic solar hot water system is the thermosiphon system, shown in Figure 3-9. As you can see, this system consists of a collector, a storage tank, and pipes connecting the two. Notice, however, that there are no pumps or sensors or controls in the system. There's no need for them. Water flows through the system by convection.

How does this work?

Convection is the movement of a hot fluid such as air or water. As you may recall from high school physics, air and water both expand when heated. When they expand, they become less dense. This causes them to rise. In the process, they carry heat with them.

But that's not the end of the story.

A liquid rising by convection creates a vacuum that draws fluid in; the result is a natural pump called a thermosiphon. Consider

Fig. 3-9: Convection drives the heat transfer fluid in this thermosiphon system, eliminating the need for a pump and electricity. Direct systems use water as the heat-transfer fluid. Indirect systems use antifreeze as the heat transfer medium. Note the absence of a heat exchanger in this system.

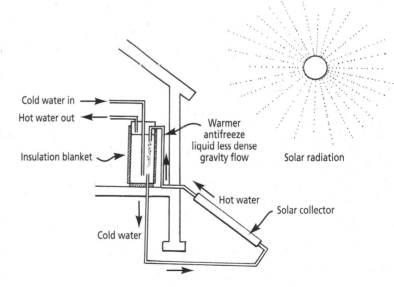

Cold water in →
Hot water out ←
Warmer antifreeze liquid less dense gravity flow
Insulation blanket
Solar radiation
Hot water
Solar collector
Cold water

an example: sunlight striking the Earth heats its surface. Heat is transferred to the air above it, causing it to expand and rise. Hot air rising, however, creates a vacuum that draws cooler air in from neighboring areas to fill the void.

In a thermosiphon solar hot water system, like that shown in Figure 3-9, water rises in the pipes inside the solar panels when it is heated, drawing cooler fluid in from elsewhere. The result is a natural pumping action, a convective loop. The convective loop propels the hot water into the house to a solar storage tank, where the heat is deposited. Cooler water from the bottom of the tank then flows back into the collector to be reheated.

The convective flow of liquid in this system is a simple, non-mechanical pump that operates throughout the daylight hours, stripping heat from the solar panels and depositing it in the storage tank in the house.

Thermosiphon systems are simple and elegant, and less expensive than more complicated pump-driven systems, discussed shortly. Like solar batch water heaters, thermosiphon systems are not, technically speaking, active systems. They have no mechanical pumps.

Before you race out to buy such a thermosiphon system, let's examine some crucial factors you'll need to know before laying down your hard-earned money. First, note that the hot water tank must be located *above* the solar collectors by about two feet. This is the only configuration that will allow natural thermosiphoning to occur. As a result, solar hot water panels are typically mounted on the

ground, slightly below the hot water tank, as shown in Figure 3-9.

Thermosiphon systems can also be mounted on roofs, so long as the water tanks are located slightly above the panels, for example, in an insulated space in the attic or in an upstairs room. Some tanks are even mounted on the roof themselves, although the tanks need to be very well insulated in most applications for this to work.

Thermosiphon systems use two types of heat transfer liquid: water, or a special nontoxic antifreeze, a food-grade propylene glycol. Water can be used as a heat-transfer liquid in systems installed on homes in warm climates where freezing is not expected. Food-grade antifreeze is used in systems installed in colder climates where freezing is expected.

As a rule, water systems are simple, cheaper, and a bit more efficient, as they require no heat exchanger. In this type of system, water heated by the panels flows directly into the solar hot water tank. It is then drawn into the storage water heater or tankless water heater and used directly any time a faucet is turned on. This configuration is referred to as a direct or open-loop system.

Antifreeze systems are more complicated, a bit more costly, and slightly less efficient than open-loop water systems. Efficiency suffers a bit and costs go up a bit because the antifreeze must travel through a heat exchanger in the first tank. The heat exchanger is typically a coil of copper pipe in the wall or in the base of, alongside, or inside the tank.

As the solar-heated liquid flows through the heat exchanger, heat is transferred from the propylene glycol to the water in the tank. Cooled antifreeze flows back to the panel to be reheated continuously during the day. This type of system is referred to as an indirect or closed-loop solar hot water system. (Because the heat transfer fluid does not mix with domestic hot water, it's in a closed loop.)

Pros and Cons of Thermosiphon Systems

Open-loop thermosiphon systems are relatively simple, inexpensive, and relatively trouble-free. Closed-loop systems are a bit more complicated, in large part because of the addition of the heat exchanger and the heat exchange fluid, propylene glycol.

One of the problems with propylene glycol is that it begins to deteriorate at high temperatures, turning into an acidic sludge that can gum up the pipes. When this occurs, it needs to be drained and replaced, a job best reserved for a professional.

Pump Circulation Systems: Open- and Closed-Loop

If a thermosiphon system isn't an option, your next choice is a pump circulation system. This system is pretty similar to the thermosiphon system except that the force that moves the heat transfer liquid is a small electric pump. Most systems use AC pumps that run off household current, but, as noted in the sidebar, another very smart option is a DC pump powered by a small solar electric (PV) panel.

Solar collectors in pump systems are usually mounted on roofs, but can also be mounted on wood or metal racks on the ground, so long as they are in full sunlight all year round. Solar hot water tanks are located inside homes, usually in basements or utility rooms next to the conventional water heater, soon to be relegated to the status of backup water heater.

PV-Powered Solar Hot Water Systems

If you are concerned about the electricity required to run the pump in a solar hot water system (to be honest, it's really not that much) or if you want to go totally solar and simplify your system, you can run a solar hot water system off a small solar electric or PV panel — a 30- or 50-watt PV. In such systems, a PV panel is mounted next to the solar hot water panels and is wired to a DC pump. (PVs produce direct current electricity.) When the sun rises, the PV panels begin to produce DC current. Electricity flows to the pump, waking it up from its evening snooze. The pump then begins to propel the heat transfer fluid in the system through the panels and through the pipes. Heat generated by the solar collectors therefore begins to flow from the panels to the storage tank. When the sun sets, the system shuts off.

PV direct systems are simple and cost-effective, and eliminate the need for sensors and controls that can break down. One manufacturer, Sol-Reliant, produces a sleek system with a built-in 35-watt PV panel. It is one of the easiest systems to install. You can learn more about it at <www.solreliant.com>.

The small electric pump, which is located inside, forces the heat transfer liquid up through the panels and then back down to the thermal storage tank.

Open-Loop Water Systems: Drainback Systems

Pump-driven systems may use water or propylene glycol as the heat transfer fluid. As in thermosiphon systems, discussed earlier, using water as the heat transfer fluid allows one to create an open-loop or direct system.

Although open-loop systems have their advantages and may, therefore, seem desirable, there is a major challenge that must be overcome in colder climates: freezing.

Freezing is a problem because when water freezes, it expands, and not just a little bit. It expands quite a lot. Water freezing inside a copper pipe can create enough force to crack it wide open.

Solar designers solved this problem in two ways. The first is a draindown system. This type of system is *not* recommended by most of the folks I've talked to, so I won't discuss it here.

There is a viable alternative to the draindown system, a simpler trustworthy cousin, the drainback system (Figure 3-10). "Although similar in name to the draindown system," writes Ken Olson, an expert on solar hot water systems, "the drainback system is far different and much more reliable."

Drainback systems rely on gravity to drain water from the pipes and panels when the circulating pump stops. When the sun stops warming the panels, a sensor signals the circulating pump to cease operation. Water flows out of the system into a storage tank.

Gravity drainback systems are simpler than draindown systems because they have no electronic sensors and motorized valves, which dramatically reduces the possibility of system failure and deep freeze. Remember: in active solar systems simplicity reigns supreme. The fewer the parts, the less likely the system is to malfunction — and the less maintenance will be required.

Fig. 3-10: This is a drainback system, generally recommended by solar installers over the draindown system.

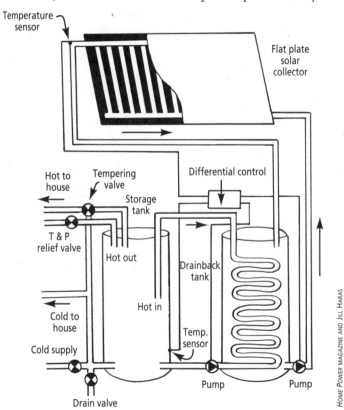

Home Power magazine and Jill Haras

Gravity drainback systems can be used in all climates and are less expensive and easier to maintain than other active systems. According to Greg Pahl, author of *Natural Home Heating*, direct-circulation, gravity-drainback systems are "considered by many people to be one of the simplest and best systems to install." They not only eliminate mechanical parts that can fail, they do not require a heat exchanger and propylene glycol heat exchange fluid which, as noted earlier, deteriorates over time and must be replaced every five years or so. Although a better option, these systems need to be designed and installed correctly to ensure complete drainage when the pump stops.

Pros and Cons of Drainback Systems

As just noted, drainback systems are not only simpler and more reliable than draindown systems, they're a little less costly. They can be used in cold climates and operate without propylene glycol. On the downside, these systems require the largest pumps of all solar hot water systems in use today.

Closed-Loop Antifreeze Systems

Although drainback systems work well in cold climates, most active systems in use today are pump-driven systems that employ polypropylene antifreeze as the heat transfer fluid. These systems are, therefore, indirect or closed-loop systems (Figure 3-11). In order to prevent

the mixing of the heat transfer fluid with domestic hot water, these systems require heat exchangers. They transfer heat from the antifreeze to the water in the solar hot water tank.

Closed-loop antifreeze systems require other components as well, some of which are not required in other SDHW systems. For

In active solar systems simplicity reigns supreme. The fewer the parts, the less likely the system is to malfunction — and the less maintenance will be required.

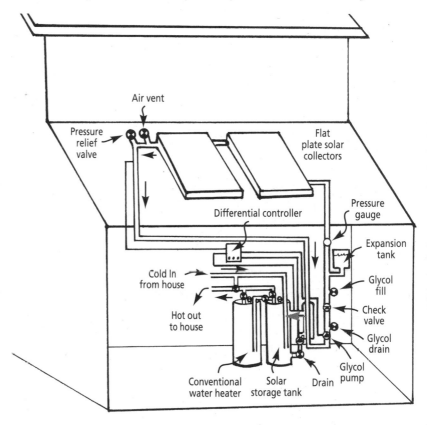

Fig. 3-11: This system uses a small electric pump to propel antifreeze (food grade propylene glycol) through a closed loop. Heat from the antifreeze solution is released at the heat exchanger, warming water in the solar hot water tank.

example, as shown in Figure 3-11, closed-looped antifreeze systems require an expansion tank. Located in the antifreeze loop, it accommodates the expansion of the antifreeze as it heats up during normal operation, preventing pressure from building to dangerous levels inside the closed-loop portion of the system. When the antifreeze heats up it expands, creating internal pressure. Rather than splitting the pipes open, excess is shunted into the expansion tank, reducing pressure. When pressure drops, the antifreeze empties from the expansion tank.

Closed-loop antifreeze systems also require a fill valve, a valve that allows service personnel to drain the antifreeze if it goes bad and then refill it.

Pros and Cons of Pump Systems with Antifreeze

Closed-loop antifreeze systems are popular, well understood by those who have been in the industry for a while, and reliable. They work well in all climates, hot or cold, and in cold climates provide excellent protection against freezing.

On the downside, closed-loop systems are the most complex of all hot water systems on the market today. They have more parts and, almost without exception, the more parts there are, the more chances there are for things to go wrong.

Another small downside of this system is that its use of a heat exchanger means that it functions slightly less efficiently than an open-loop pump-driven system in which water serves as the heat exchange fluid. In addition, propylene glycol needs to be replaced by a professional from time to time. This isn't a job for most homeowners.

WHICH SYSTEM IS BEST FOR YOU?

Although there are a lot of options, it's really not that difficult to select a system that will work for you. Get your felt tip marker out as Ken Olson summarizes the options: "If you live in a freeze-free climate, you should choose a batch heater or a small thermosiphon unit." Although these systems will only serve one to three people, you can always install a couple of batch heaters or thermosiphon solar panels side by side to boost your hot water production.

Or, says Olsen, you should consider "an open-loop direct pump system circulating water from the storage tank to the flat plate collector."

In colder climates or in regions with hard water, Olsen recommends "one of the closed-loop systems with antifreeze and a heat exchanger."

A closed-loop antifreeze system is recommended in regions with hard water because hard water contains minerals that can deposit on the inside of pipes of open-loop systems. Over time, these minerals accumulate, reducing flow rates and the efficiency of an SDHW system. The open-loop water systems just aren't worth it in such applications. Using water as a heat transfer medium in such instances, is going to cause you trouble.

SIZING YOUR SYSTEM

Sizing a SDHW system is pretty straightforward process. Before you get started, however, it is important to be sure you have a good solar site. That is, you need to be sure you can position solar collectors so that they're exposed to bright sunlight from 9 a.m. to 3 p.m. every day of the year. Fortunately, most homes, and even many apartments in cities, have good solar access somewhere on the site. Roofs are often free from obstructions that can shade solar panels.

If you have a good site, your next task is to scour your home for ways to make it more efficient with respect to hot water use. Remember: efficiency is the first rule of renewable energy system design! Make your home as efficient as possible, then size the system.

What do you do to make your home more efficient?

In his excellent article, "Solar Hot Water: A Primer," published in *Home Power* magazine Issue 84, Ken Olson recommends the following steps, all of which were mentioned in Chapter 2 on home energy conservation:

1. Turn down the thermostat on your water heater to 120° to 125°F (48° to 51°C). "Many water heaters," says Olsen, "are set between 140° and 180° F (60° and 82°C)," but much lower temperatures are just fine.

2. Wrap the water heater with an insulated water heater blanket.

3. Fix drips in faucets in the kitchen and bathrooms to prevent the waste of hot water.

4. Install water-efficient showerheads and faucet aerators to reduce hot water use.

5. Insulate hot water pipes in unconditioned space.

Once water and energy conservation measures are in place, it is time to size your solar hot water system. The size of a system depends on many factors, the most important of which are (1) your climate — how hot or cold it is and how sunny, and (2) your family's water consumption. It also depends, in part, on your solar exposure. Will your system have unobstructed access to the sun from at least 9 a.m. to 3 p.m. each day? If not, you'll need a larger system.

In the United States, most families consume 15 to 30 gallons of hot water per person per day for showers, baths, washing clothes, and dishwashing. By conserving water, you can easily slash daily water consumption to the low end of the range, about 15 to 20 gallons per day.

Knowing a family's daily water consumption, designers next turn their attention to daily storage capacity. If, for example, a family of 3 consumes 20 gallons per day per person, they'll need 60 gallons of hot water storage to meet their needs. For most households of 4, Olsen recommends an 80-gallon tank hot water tank, based on daily water use of 20 gallons per person.

Once you've determined storage capacity, you turn your attention to solar collectors. You will need to determine the number of square feet of solar collectors for your application.

Efficiency is the first rule of renewable energy system design. Simple, cost-effective measures to reduce your energy consumption pay huge dividends in the long run.

a

TOM LANE, ENERGY CONSERVATION SERVICES

Temperature sensor

Valve: Automatic bypass

Solar collector

Control: Automatic

Check valve   Filter   Pump

Hot water in

Cold water out

b

Solar Pool Heating

Got a swimming pool you'd like to heat with the sun?

No problem.

Solar hot water systems make great pool heaters.

Solar pool heaters circulate water from the swimming pool to the panels and back again during daylight hours (Figure 3-12). These systems are about as simple as you can get. There's no need for a heat exchanger, antifreeze, expansion tanks, or a hot water storage tank as in many SDHW systems. Sure, you will need sensors to switch the system on and off automatically each day and you'll need an electric pump. But you can avoid the sensors altogether by installing a PV panel that runs a DC pump, as mentioned earlier in this chapter. You'll also need a few more panels than you would if you were heating domestic water. ☞

Fig. 3-12: (a) Swimming pools can be heated by the sun. Such systems not only provide warmer water, they can extend the length of the swimming season. (b) Diagram of solar pool heating system.

HOME POWER AND JILL HARAS

Once again, this process is pretty straightforward and highly dependent on solar availability and local climate. Generally, the sunnier and warmer the climate, the fewer square feet of collector you'll need. The cloudier and cooler your region the more square feet of collector you'll need.

As a general rule, say the folks at AAA Solar in Albuquerque, New Mexico, in the sunniest locations like the desert Southwest and Florida, you'll need about one square foot of collector for two gallons of tank capacity. Thus, for or an 80-gallon tank, you'll need 40 square feet of collector. (A single 4- x 8-foot collector provides 32 square feet of collector surface.)

In the Southeast and the mountain states, which are a little less sunny and, in the case of

Solar hot water systems can warm our pools and lengthen the swim season substantially, as shown in Figure 3-13. And, if you like, you can even link the domestic solar hot water system with the pool heating system. Some homeowners have installed systems that heat their pools, their domestic hot water, and their homes. To learn more, I'd strongly urge you to read "Solar Pool Heating" Parts 1 and 2 by Tom Lane in *Home Power* magazine, issues 94 and 95. ■

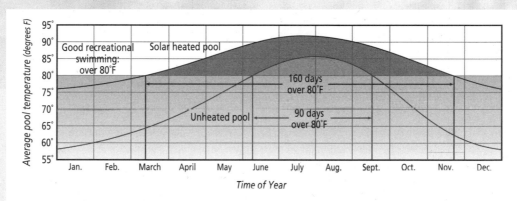

Conditions: 20-year average weather data for North Florida. 1,000 BTU per square foot per day of collector output for a pool in full sunlight; a screened-in pool would typically be 5°F lower year-round. Pool blanket used when night-time temperatures are below 60° F.

Fig. 3-13: This graph plots the water temperature in a swimming pool in northern Florida. As illustrated, solar pool heaters result in warmer water and also extend the length of the swimming season.

the mountain states, also a bit cooler, you will need one square foot of collector for 1.5 gallons of tank capacity. For an 80-gallon tank, then, you will need 53 square feet of collector.

In the Midwest and Atlantic states, you will need one square foot of collector per gallon of tank capacity. An 80-gallon tank will therefore require 80 square feet of collector.

In New England and the Northeast, which are the least sunny areas and pretty cold in the winter, you need one square foot per 0.75 gallons of tank capacity. An 80-gallon tank will then require 107 square feet of collector.

Solar systems designed to these general guidelines will provide approximately 100 percent of your domestic hot water needs in the summer, and about 40 percent in the winter, says Olson. If you want to obtain more hot water in the winter, you will need a larger system. But bear in mind that you will have a huge surplus in the summer.

Designers use these general guidelines to determine how many flat plate collectors are needed for a solar hot water system. Because all solar collectors differ with respect to their efficiency, be sure to consult with a local vendor or your supplier *before* you order panels. Remember, if you undersize your system, you can always add another panel later, if, that is, you have room for one.

FINDING A COMPETENT INSTALLER

Homeowners with considerable plumbing and electrical skills can build their own solar hot water systems, although I don't recommend this approach for any system other than the batch heater, the simplest of all solar systems. I don't mean to thwart creativity and independence, but as a general rule it is far better to purchase a reliable, well-built system and install it yourself or hire a professional to do the work for you than to build and install your own system.

Why not build your own solar hot water system?

Solar panels are exposed to extreme temperatures, wind, and hail. They live a pretty hard life up there on our rooftops. Over the years, manufacturers have made great strides in solar collector design and materials and are producing solar panels that can withstand the harsh treatment they'll receive. It is unlikely that you could come close to matching the solar collectors on the market today. One of the trickiest aspects of solar design is selecting black paint or coatings to paint the interior of the collector. Although store-bought black paint might work well for a few years, it is very likely going to vaporize. When paint turns to vapor, the vapor deposits on the inside of the collector glass, impeding solar gain and making the panel look pretty ugly.

Unless you're pretty good at plumbing and electrical work, you should probably also let a professional install your system. They're fast and experienced and will be done in the blink of an eye. For the homeowner, installation might take a full weekend interspersed with numerous trips to the hardware store to pick up plumbing supplies. A professional will have everything he or she needs in the truck.

For those who would like to install their own systems, I recommend an excellent series of articles published in one of my favorite resources, *Home Power* magazines. Issue 94 covers installation basics — information that applies to all pump-driven systems. Issues 85 and 95 cover closed-loop antifreeze systems and issues 86 and 97 describe the installation of drainback systems.

THE ECONOMICS OF SOLAR DOMESTIC HOT WATER

In "Solar Hot Water Primer," published in *Home Power*, Issue 84, Ken Olson writes, "An initial investment in a solar water heating system will beat the stock market any day, any decade, risk free. Initial return on investment is on the order of 15 percent, tax fee, and goes up as gas and electricity prices climb." Although I share Ken's enthusiasm for solar hot water, his endorsement is based on a comparison of a solar hot water system with a conventional electric storage water heater. Unfortunately, the economics don't always work out that well and homeowners need to be aware that the economics of the decision depend on many factors.

Let's start by comparing a solar hot water system with an electric storage water heater. Clearly, as Olsen indicates, a solar hot water system compares quite favorably with an electric storage water heater, especially if you are paying more than eight to ten cents per kilowatt hour. Here's how the math works out according to Olsen: a typical 80-gallon electric hot water tank serving a family of 4 consumes approximately 150 million BTUs over its 7-year lifetime. If your electricity costs 8 cents per kilowatt hour, hot water will cost approximately $3,600 in US dollars over that period. At the end of its short, useful lifetime, the water heater will need replacement, further adding to the cost. (To be fair, the water heater will very likely last a bit longer than Ken estimates and there are ways to ensure a much longer life span, as noted earlier in this chapter.)

In such instances, solar hot water systems make eminent sense. If you live in a warm climate, you can purchase and install a solar batch heater for much less than $3,600. If you live in a colder climate, you can purchase and install a pump-driven antifreeze system for $3,600 or slightly less — depending on the type of system you select (flat plate vs. an evacuated tube collector). From that point on, you will be getting hot water essentially free of charge.

The economics of a solar hot water system may be even better if you live in a state or city or are served by a utility company that offers financial incentives that offset the initial cost of the system. In many locations, homeowners can receive substantial financial incentives that dramatically reduce the initial cost of a solar hot water system. (I discuss financial incentives for solar hot water and solar electric systems in Chapter 8.)

Solar hot water systems also make economic sense compared to propane-fired water heaters. Propane is often used in rural settings to heat homes, provide cooking fuel, and to heat water. Although propane is not as expensive as electricity, it is still generally cheaper to generate hot water from a solar system than from a propane water heater, according to Alex Wilson, Jennifer Thorne, and John Morrill, authors of one of my favorite

Table 3-1
Solar Hot Water Systems

Type of System	Active or Passive	Heat transfer fluid	Propulsive force for heat transfer liquid	Open- or closed-loop	Suitable climate
Solar batch water heater	Passive	Water	Line pressure	Open	Warm, very infrequent freezing or cold weather
Thermosiphon	Passive	Water or propylene glycol	Convection	Open- or closed- with propylene glycol	Warm, infrequent freezing or shut off in winter
Pump circulation (Gravity drainback)	Active	Water	AC or DC Pump	Open	Any climate but designed for cold climates
Pump circulation (closed-loop antifreeze)	Active	Propylene glycol	AC or DC pump	Closed	Any climate

energy books, *Consumer Guide to Home Energy Savings*.

Because natural gas currently costs much less per BTU than electricity and a bit less than propane, solar hot water systems don't always make financial sense compared to natural gas-fired systems. (Although rising natural gas prices may render this judgment obsolete soon.) When contemplating a SDHW system in an home served by natural gas, contact a local installer who can run the numbers for you.

In closing, installing a solar hot water system is generally a smart move, and will very likely make more sense in more places as natural gas prices, propane, and electricity continue their upward spiral. With the information learned in this chapter, you can now proceed with confidence. I recommend that you select a solar system design that will work in your climate, and then shop around. Contact local suppliers/installers. See what they have to offer. Read up on each of their systems before you lay your money down. Talk to people for whom they've installed systems.

Good luck!

CHAPTER 4

FREE HEAT

PASSIVE SOLAR, ACTIVE SOLAR, AND HEAT PUMPS

I live in a cold climate, 8,500 feet above sea level nestled in the foothills of the Rocky Mountains. Our winters are long and cold, with evening temperatures falling well below freezing week after week. Our summers are short and cool, and spring occurs in a flash between the long cold winter and the short, cool summer. Fall passes quickly, too, morphing rapidly into winter long before many of us are willing to see it go.

Despite the chilly nature of our climate, I have no heating bill. Why?

My home is heated passively by the sun with a cord of free wood for backup heat to take the edge off those cold winter nights and to provide heat for long cloudy spells. Based on what my neighbors pay for heat, I estimate that I have saved $10,000 to $15,000 in the 10 years I have lived in my house — money I've tucked away for my retirement.

You too can rack up huge savings in fuel bills by tapping into the sun's generous supply of energy. And you don't have to live in the Sunbelt to take advantage of solar energy. Even if you live in a cold, cloudy region of North America — areas like Buffalo, NY or Portland, OR — places some of my colleagues in the solar industry refer to as the "gloom belt," you can supply up to half of your annual heat requirement from the sun, perhaps even more.

How? Through an active and passive solar retrofit, the subject of this chapter.

If you have a good southern exposure, you can discover what the ancient Greeks and the Anasazi Indians of North America learned

Passive solar heating is ideally suited to new home construction, where architects can design an entire house around this simple and effective concept, coordinating all features of the design to achieve maximum year-round performance and comfort.

thousands of years ago: the sun is an amazing source of free heat.

WHAT IS PASSIVE SOLAR HEATING?

Passive solar heating is a heating system with only one moving part: the sun. (Actually, the sun doesn't move; it's the Earth whose revolutions on its axis give rise to sunrises and sunsets.) Passive solar design provides space heat for all kinds of buildings from homes to offices to fire stations to airports to schools. You name it, passive solar can be used to warm the interior.

Passive solar design relies on ordinary visible light from the low-angled winter sun, which penetrates south-facing windows during the heating season. Inside our homes, the sun's visible light is absorbed by floors, walls, and other solid materials. Here it is converted

to heat that warms our homes and other buildings.

As just noted, passive solar design does not rely on complicated equipment and sensors as in active solar systems. It relies on ordinary building elements, such as south-facing glass, overhangs (eaves), and insulation. Competent designers incorporate several additional features too, for example, additional mass inside a home to absorb heat during the day. Absorbing excess daytime heat prevents overheating. However, thermal mass, as it is called, serves another important function. It releases its stored heat at night, helping to maintain comfortable conditions day and night.

Passive solar heating relies on the fact that the sun angle from the horizon (the altitude angle) varies during the year, as shown in Figure 4-1. In the summer, the sun is high in the sky.

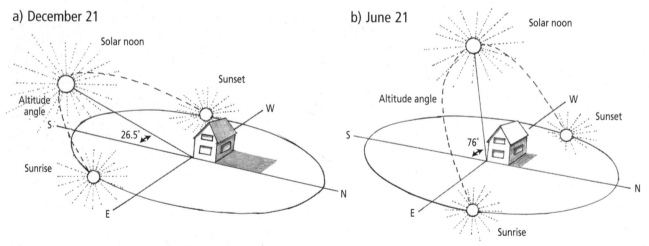

Fig. 4-1: In a passive solar home, the low-angled winter sun penetrates south-facing windows to heat the home. During the summer, the high-angled sun shines on the roofs of houses, reducing heat gain.

It beats down on the roofs of our homes, so very little penetrates windows. During the winter, the sun carves a low arc across the sky. The low-angled winter sun can therefore penetrate south-facing glass, warming the interiors of our homes. In between, the sun occupies a range of intermediate positions.

Passive solar heating is ideally suited to new home construction, situations where architects can design an entire house around this simple and effective concept, coordinating all features of the design to achieve maximum year-round performance and comfort.

One of the most important aspects of passive solar design is orientation. By orienting a new home properly, so that its long axis runs east and west, a solar designer can ensure maximal solar gain. But performance also hinges on the inclusion of thermal mass to absorb heat, as noted above. Performance also requires a designer to concentrate windows on the south side of the home while reducing the number of windows on the north, east, and west sides. Beefing up the insulation and sealing up the cracks in the building envelope are also essential to effective passive solar design. And no design would be complete without proper overhang, to shade walls and windows from the high-angled summer sun.

All these simple but effective measures add up. The net result is a house that acquires 50 to 100 percent of its heat naturally from the sun. Our concern in this book is primarily with passive solar retrofits — adding passive solar features to existing homes that have a decent solar exposure (Figure 4-2). For those who are building anew, I recommend my book, *The Solar House: Passive Heating and Cooling.*

Passive solar retrofits could help wean our society from its costly dependence on natural gas and fuel oil, whose production, you will recall, is entering terminal decline. Passive solar retrofits could also help many families reduce their electrical bills if their homes are heated with electricity. Passive solar design also increases natural light, or daylighting, further cutting household electrical demand.

But that's not all.

Much of what homeowners do to passively heat a home also reduces cooling loads (the amount of energy used to keep a home cool). Put another way, many of the design features of state-of-the-art passive solar homes

Fig. 4-2: This passive solar addition provides heat and additional living space. Although it looks nice, the two tiers of glass tend to cause overheating in the spring and fall because the lower tier of glass is not shaded. Two-story glass walls also provide an avenue for excessive heat loss. Be sure to insulate the glass at night with thermoshutters or quilted window shades.

DAN CHIRAS

help keep these buildings cooler — much cooler — in the summer.

Passive solar heating also provides many environmental benefits, all resulting from a decline in our use of fossil fuels and nuclear energy. In sum, passive solar creates a win-win situation for everyone, except for the big energy companies.

IS PASSIVE SOLAR FOR YOU?

To determine if a passive solar retrofit is feasible for your home, you'll need to begin by assessing your home's solar resource — specifically, how much sunlight strikes your home during the heating season (that part of the year that requires heat). Good solar exposure is essential from October through March or even April or May in some parts of North America. How much sunlight is needed to make passive solar heating work?

As a basic rule, your home needs to be in a location that ensures good solar exposure on its south-facing wall from around 9 a.m. each morning to 3 p.m. each afternoon. This time slot is the main "window of opportunity," that is, the main period during the day for collecting sunlight during the heating season (usually late fall, winter, and early to mid spring). Earlier and later hours, though they may be sunny, won't provide as much solar energy, so don't sweat if your house is shaded from sunrise to 8 or 9 a.m. or is shaded after 3 p.m.

Good solar exposure means that the south-facing wall, preferably the longest wall

of the building, needs to be exposed to the sun from 9 a.m. to 3 p.m., and not shaded by neighboring buildings, privacy fences, evergreen trees, or anything else. Without a good clean view of the sun during this period during the heating season, you can't retrofit for passive solar. (If your south-facing wall is shaded but your roof is exposed to the winter sun, however, you may be able to heat your home with one of two active solar systems — a solar hot water or solar hot air system — described shortly.)

As just noted, an ideal home from a passive solar perspective should be oriented so that its long axis runs from east to west. This orientation allows for the largest surface area of exposed wall and window to the low-angled winter sun, an orientation that permits maximum solar gain. Unfortunately, many streets in cities and towns run north and south and many home builders, over the years, oriented the homes they've constructed so that the long axis of the houses face the street and point east or west. Because many homes are rectangular, the south-facing walls are small compared to the east-and west-facing walls. Making matters worse, many homes are tightly packed like sardines in a tin, so there's not sufficient sunlight on south-facing walls to make a passive solar retrofit worthwhile.

If your house is oriented toward the street, all is not lost. You may still be able to retrofit it for solar heat, provided the south side is not shaded, for example, by a neighbor's home or fence or trees. Don't expect to achieve huge reductions in your annual heating bill, however. You may only be able to acquire 10 percent or so of your heat from the sun. If you have insulated your home well, dutifully sealed cracks, replaced energy-inefficient windows or added storm windows, and taken other conservation measures outlined in Chapter 2, the combination of the conservation and solar could easily slash your heating bills by half. As always, don't retrofit until you have made all of the vital improvements in energy conservation.

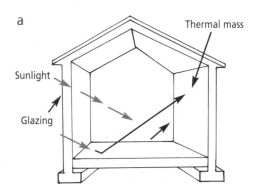

a

Thermal mass

Sunlight

Glazing

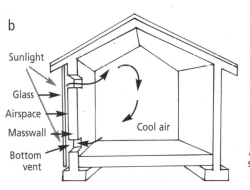

b

Sunlight

Glass

Airspace

Masswall

Bottom vent

Cool air

TYPES OF PASSIVE SOLAR DESIGN

If your home meets the criteria just described and you'd like to try passive solar, you will have three basic choices for a passive solar retrofit: direct gain, indirect gain, and isolated gain. Although that may sound mind-boggling, it's not. Let me explain each one.

Direct Gain Retrofits

Direct gain passive solar is probably the most common type of passive solar design for new construction (Figure 4-3). It has limited uses in retrofits, however.

In a direct gain design, the long axis of the home is oriented east and west, creating the largest possible southerly surface for solar gain. The designer concentrates windows on the south side to absorb the low-angled winter sun — but not too many! See the textbox on page 106, for recommendations. Sunlight enters the south-facing windows and, as noted above, is absorbed by solid surfaces in the house. It is then converted to heat. The

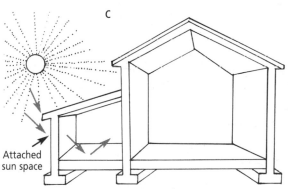

c

Attached sun space

An ideal home — from a passive solar perspective — should be oriented so that its long axis runs from east to west. This orientation allows for the largest surface area of exposed wall and window to the low-angled winter sun and thus permits maximum solar gain.

Fig. 4-3: Solar options: (a) direct gain, (b) indirect gain (Trombe wall or thermal storage wall), and (c) isolated gain attached sunspace). Homes can be retrofitted using all three designs, although adding a thermal storage wall can be difficult and costly.

Be sure that solar glazing in retrofits or additions can be insulated at night, either by rigid foam insulation, internal shutters, or by a quilted fabric like those used to make Warm Windows insulated shades. Good window insulation dramatically improves the performance of a passive solar home.

heat warms the room. In this design, heat is gained directly by the structure, hence the name, direct gain.

To retrofit a home for direct gain, you'll very likely need to add a few windows along the south side of the home or install larger windows to maximize solar gain. Adding windows is a job best reserved for professionals. It typically involves construction or reinforcement of rough window frames to ensure that windows won't crack and that the walls won't collapse. You may even need to obtain a building permit from your local building department for this work. They'll send an inspector to check out the work at various stages. A professional usually handles such details, pulling the permits and arranging for inspections.

Retrofitting for direct gain may also require you to increase the size of the overhang, or add overhang or some other kind of shade structure, if there is none. Overhangs shade windows and walls and protect a home

from overheating during the summer. In some cases, you may need to reduce the size of overhangs to optimize solar gain. A contractor can help you with this, too.

Direct gain retrofitting is a great way to invite the winter sun into a home and reduce the demand for fossil fuel energy. It does, however, involve careful planning to avoid sacrificing privacy. Also, be sure that you are not letting in so much sunlight that you decrease the utility of the rooms in your home. Bright sunlight streaming in during the daytime, for example, can render a home office where computers are used during the day almost useless. Too much light cause glares on computer screens that can lead to severe eyestrain. Even window shades won't help unless they completely block out the sun.

Solar direct gain retrofitting is tricky and presents many challenges. But there are ways to make the job easier. Rather than retrofit an existing wall, you can build an addition that incorporates direct gain passive solar design features as in Figure 4-2. The addition contributes heat to adjoining rooms. If you are thinking about adding a room or two to your existing home, and the room faces south, why not make it a passive solar addition?

No matter what you do, be sure that solar glazing (south-facing glass) in retrofits or additions can be insulated at night — either by rigid foam insulation internal shutters, as shown in Figure 4-4, or by a quilted fabric like those used to make Warm Windows insulated shades, available at fabric stores. Good window

Window Allocation for Passive Solar Homes

For new passive solar homes, south-facing glass should fall within the range of 7 to 12 percent of the total square footage of the home. A 1,000-square-foot home should have 70 to 120 square feet of south-facing glass. North- and east-facing glass should not exceed four percent of the total square footage, and west-facing should not exceed two percent.

insulation dramatically improves the performance of a passive solar home!

When retrofitting a home for passive solar, you'll want to be certain that you don't end up overheating it. Overheating can be prevented by several measures, for example, by installing overhangs. A two- to three-foot overhang works in many climates. Overheating can also be avoided by installing window shades and by installing additional thermal mass. (Thermal mass usually consists of masonry materials such as concrete, tile, or bricks that absorb sunlight and hold heat.) You can boost thermal mass in an existing home by removing wall-to-wall carpeting to expose wood floors. (Although wood is not as good as masonry material, it does provide thermal mass in a home.) Floors exposed to direct sunlight can be tiled to improve the performance of your retrofit.

When retrofitting your home for passive solar, it is important to proceed carefully. Work out a plan before you start adding new windows and think through the repercussions of each change you make in your home. Pay special attention to thermal mass. If the total square footage of the solar glazing will exceed seven percent of the floor space, you'll very likely need to add thermal mass. If not, the incidental mass, that is, the thermal mass in drywall, framing, floors, cabinets, and furniture, usually suffices to absorb heat and prevent overheating. To determine how much thermal mass your home will need, you may want to contact a local passive solar designer/architect or hire a solar consultant. Or, you

can pick up a copy of my book, *The Solar House*, for guidance on the subject, too.

Indirect Gain Retrofits: Thermal Storage Walls

Indirect gain passive solar is so named because it involves an intermediary structure that absorbs the sun's energy, converts it to heat, and then transfers the heat to the house (Figure 4-3b). That intermediary is a Trombe wall, pronounced "trom" and named after a French engineer who's the inventor of this innovative passive solar design feature. Trombe walls are also called thermal storage walls, a term I like to use.

KEN WOODS

If the total square footage of the solar glazing exceeds seven percent of the floor space, you'll very likely need to add thermal mass. If not, the incidental mass, that is, the thermal mass in drywall, framing, floors, cabinets, and furniture, usually suffices to absorb heat and prevent overheating.

Fig. 4-4: Thermoshutters like these are made of rigid foam insulation and plywood, covered with a decorative fabric. Closing the thermoshutters at night or on cold, cloudy days greatly reduces heat loss.

Thermal storage walls are built from solid materials such as poured concrete, cement blocks, bricks, adobe blocks, or even rammed earth (a natural building material). These materials store considerable amounts of heat.

Thermal storage walls are located along the south side of homes. The outside of the wall is fitted with glass — usually double-pane glass mounted three to six inches away from the thermal storage wall. Low-angled winter sun penetrates the glass and is absorbed by the surface of the mass wall. It is then converted into heat that warms the surface of the wall. The heat then begins to migrate slowly into the mass wall, eventually reaching the interior surface from which it radiates into the adjoining room.

Mass walls are generally designed so that the heat reaches the interior of the wall early in the evening, around sunset, and continues to radiate heat into the room throughout the night. For daytime heating, builders often install a window or two in the wall. This allows for direct gain, and permits views of the outside.

Daytime heating can also be achieved by placing openings in the thermal storage wall, as shown in Figure 4-3b. These openings allow room air to circulate through the space between the wall and the glass, drawing off heat.

Thermal storage walls work well in many climates, but because they are so massive, they're not an option for retrofitting most homes. That's because most foundations in existing homes are not designed to support the weight of the mass wall. If you want to retrofit your home to include this effective passive solar design, you'll very likely have to beef up the foundation, a procedure that is not only a bit tricky, but pretty costly.

So why mention the thermal storage wall at all?

If you are building a new home or building an addition, a thermal storage wall is a wise choice. It works well in a variety of climates from warm to extremely cold. For details, you may want to take a look at the section on thermal storage walls in my book *The Solar House*.

Isolated Gain Retrofits: Attached Sunspaces

The final option for passive solar design is the isolated gain system, more commonly referred to as the attached sunspace or solar greenhouse (Figure 4-3c). Attached sunspaces are passive solar heat collectors built on to the side of a building. They are heated by the sun and the heat is then transferred to adjoining rooms. Hence the term, isolated gain.

Attached sunspaces are relatively easy to build on to many homes, provided there's adequate solar exposure. All-glass attached sunspaces are available in kits and there is no shortage of installers who can put one in for you. Unfortunately, this design is fraught with problems. As I tell my passive solar design workshop audiences, there are many many ways to botch this design.

All-glass designs — that is, attached sunspaces with glass walls and glass roofs — tend to overheat in the summer and fall, causing severe discomfort in the home. They may even overheat in the winter. But isn't this structure designed to collect heat and transfer it to the house in the winter?

Absolutely, but don't expect to be able to use the space for much else. Overheating renders the sunspace much too hot to enjoy during wintertime daylight hours. Moreover, all but the hardiest of plants (cacti and succulents) find the intense heat overwhelming. Most plants need to be kept below 85°F (29°C) for optimal growth; photosynthesis grinds to a halt at 100°F (37°C).

Despite the fancy brochures and advertisements you receive in the mail touting the value of all-glass attached sunspaces from local vendors, you'll very likely be disappointed if you go this route. I recommend that you think long and hard about the downsides of this retrofit. You're basically buying a solar oven. To prevent overheating, you'll need to cover the glass much of the year in most climate zones. The results can be quite hideous, as Figure 4-5 demonstrates.

A more effective attached sunspace design is shown in Figure 4-6. This design with a solid roof permits solar gain during the later fall, winter, and early spring, when the sun is in an intermediate and low position in the southern sky. Sunlight penetrating the south-facing windows warms the interior of the attached sunspace; the warm air created in the sunspace can then be transferred to adjacent rooms. During the summer, the solid roof all but eliminates unwanted solar gain.

While attached sunspaces of this nature are the best option in new and existing homes, you still need to design them very carefully to ensure optimal performance, especially maximum heat transfer into the house; otherwise, they'll basically heat themselves and provide very little, if any, additional heat to your home.

Here's what you need to do to make an attached sunspace work optimally:

First, install openings in the wall between the sunspace and the adjoining rooms to permit warm air to flow into the house. To promote passive air movement, install openings near the floor and the ceiling of the wall between the sunspace and the adjoining room. This helps to create a convection current that circulates warm air into the house. (Note that a door opening into the space rarely suffices for heat transfer.)

Fig. 4-5: Attached sunspaces are an easy way to retrofit a home for passive solar, although they often don't perform well. This all-glass attached sunspace must be covered during the late spring, summer, and fall to prevent over-heating. All-glass attached sunspaces also tend to lose lots of heat at night and therefore must be isolated from living spaces by doors.

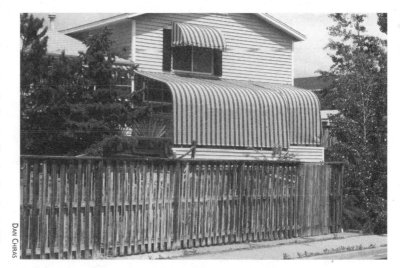

DAN CHIRAS

To improve heat transfer from the sunspace to the house, I recommend installing a thermostatically controlled fan in the window or in an opening between the sunspace and the house. (Be sure to install a quiet fan.) Fans can be powered by a 20- to 50-watt photovoltaic panel. When struck by sunlight it generates DC electricity, powering the fan. When the sun sets or is covered with clouds, the fan shuts off. You won't need any fancy switches or controllers of any sort with this sort of system.

Second, be sure that the wall between the attached sunspace and your home is insulated to prevent heat inside the house from escaping at night into the cold interior of the sunspace. You may also want to consider building a mass wall between the two as I did on a home office I retrofitted for passive solar (Figure 4-6). The mass wall will warm up during the day, and then radiate heat into the adjoining room at night.

Third, be sure the ceiling and foundation of the attached sunspace are well-insulated. Ceiling insulation should exceed the Model Energy Code by around 30 to 40 percent for best results. To make the floor, I'd recommend

Fig. 4-6: This mass wall in an attached sunspace I designed for my previous home heats up during the day and radiates heat into the adjoining room at night.

DAN CHIRAS

pouring a four- to six-inch concrete slab or excavating and backfilling with crushed rock. Insulate around the perimeter of the foundation and under the slab, if you go that route, to retain heat. Use rigid foam insulation rated for underground applications.

Fourth, for best performance, use low-e double-paned glass (described in Chapter 2). Be sure the glass has a high solar heat gain coefficient, which means that it permits lots of sunlight to enter the structure. Ratings of around 0.6 are ideal. Your glass supplier will know what you mean when you tell him this and should be able to help you select the best glass. If he or she doesn't know what you are talking about, call someone else.

Fifth, for the absolute best performance, insulate the glass at night. I recommend that you use rigid foam insulation panels that can be placed against the glass between the framing members to reduce heat loss. Or you may want to install insulated shades. (Of the two, rigid foam panels are better; they have a higher R-value.) Rigid foam insulation panels will require additional work on your part each day; you'll have to take them out in the morning and put them back at night. Raising and lowering shades will also require some extra effort, but it's less work than inserting foam insulation panels. Either way, the additional labor on your part is a small price to pay to keep the interior of an attached sunspace warm at night. The sunspace will also warm up much more quickly the next day, resulting in more heat gain for your home.

Sixth, be sure to install some openable windows in the attached sunspace to bleed off hot air during the summer and fall. To ventilate naturally, that is, without fans, you'll want to create a convection current by installing a couple of opening windows low in the structure and a couple opening windows up high — or include a roof vent. Because warm air rises, it will escape through the upper windows or a roof vent, drawing cooler air in through the lower windows.

As noted above, attached sunspaces are the "easy option" for solar retrofits. They're pretty easy to integrate into an existing home and relatively easy to build. They're not very expensive, either, and they go up quickly, providing instant savings and comfort.

Attached sunspaces also provide a space for a solar cooker like the one shown in Figure 4-7. A solar cooker is a remarkably simple device consisting of a box with reflectors that concentrate sunlight striking the device, a dark interior to convert sunlight to heat, a glass lid to hold in the heat, and a shelf to hold cooking pots or cookie sheets. You can purchase one online through Gaiam Real Goods or make your own. Numerous plans to build your own are available online at: <http://solarcooking.org/plans.htm>.

Attached sunspaces of the type I'm recommending generally perform much better than the all-glass variety. They stay cooler in the summer, provide more usable space, and provide adequate levels of heat during the winter. Still, they do have some downsides.

For one, they make lousy growing spaces. If you are hoping to grow year-round in an attached sunspace with a roof, forget it. You'll be disappointed by its performance. That's because many plants, especially vegetables, do best when the sunlight comes from above. A lack of summer sunlight often causes plants like tomatoes to become tall and thin. Spinach and lettuce like overhead light, too. Although such plants may thrive in the sunspace during the winter, especially if you can keep the temperature up at night via the insulation strategies I've mentioned, they'll languish in the shade inside the sunspace in the summer, because the sun is high in the sky, and very little sunlight will penetrate the structure.

To offset this problem, you can install a few standard skylights in the roof. Unfortunately, this could lead to summertime overheating. In addition, skylights lose huge amounts of

Fig. 4-7: Solar cookers like this one can be used to bake cookies or bread, and make a variety of one-pot meals. You can build your own inexpensively by using aluminum foil, glass, and a cardboard or wooden box.

DAN CHIRAS

heat on cold winter nights, causing the space to chill down, thwarting plant growth.

Another option for providing overhead light in the summer is the solar tube skylight, shown in Figure 4-8. Solar tube skylights consist of a small lens mounted on the roof that collects sun and directs it into a polished aluminum tube that extends from the roof to the ceiling. (The polished aluminum ensures maximum light transmission.) Light enters the room through a ceiling fixture, a diffuser that disperses light.

Solar tube skylights let in lots of light from a rather small opening — much smaller than standard skylights; as a result, they minimize unwanted heat gain caused by conventional skylights. This in turn considerably reduces the threat of overheating. Because they utilize a small opening, tubular skylights also minimize wintertime heat loss at night, a huge problem with conventional skylights.

Fig. 4-8: (a) Tubular skylights allow light into a home, thus reducing daytime lighting and electrical demand. They lose much less heat than conventional skylights at night. (b) Hallway before installing tubular skylight. (c) Hallway after installing tubular skylight.

Another problem that you may find with an attached sunspace is that it won't be habitable during the winter, except perhaps during the morning before the sun has warmed it. Once the sun begins beating in, however, you'll fry.

Like other forms of solar retrofitting, you will have to obtain a permit from the building department for an attached sunspace. They'll inspect the project at various stages and upon completion of the project.

GETTING THE HELP YOU NEED

Passive solar retrofits, combined with energy efficiency modifications, can help propel you and your loved ones toward energy independence. Although I've outlined many of the ideas and methods to achieve this laudable goal, don't be afraid to ask for help. Although it may cost you a bit, the assistance of a skilled and knowledgeable solar architect or builder can help you avoid costly mistakes. Don't assume that any architect can help you, however. Even ones who claim to be interested in doing more solar may not have the experience you need.

I strongly recommend that you work with an architect who can perform a computerized energy analysis of your home to determine how the changes you and he are proposing will affect energy consumption. Running an analysis on your home with the proposed efficiency and solar retrofits in mind will not only give you an idea of how the changes will improve the performance of

your home, they may enable you to discover more ways to save on fuel and increase comfort. Bear in mind, though, some of the more sophisticated energy analyses like Energy-10 can be costly.

To reiterate, whenever possible hire an architect or builder who has experience in passive solar design. I recommend working with designers and architects who actually live in passive solar homes, although, regrettably, not many that I've encountered practice what they preach.

Why hire someone who lives in a solar house?

Architects and designers who live in solar homes often develop a strong appreciation of the art of building comfortable, energy-efficient structures. Without this day-to-day experience, it's my belief that many designers miss key points. They may, for example, fail to include sun-free zones — areas where family members can relax, work, or watch TV without being blasted by bright sun. (Sun drenching has rendered many a new passive solar home almost unlivable.)

Bear in mind, too, that one design does not fit all. A passive solar design or a passive solar retrofit that works in Minnesota might overheat in Kansas or Tennessee. You and your architect need to design specifically for your region using computer software that allows you to assess the performance of a design — before you build it. Your job in retrofitting your home is to do the most for the least, but don't cut corners. Use high quality windows, for instance, and insulate, insulate, insulate. (For more on this subject, you might want to take a look at my book, *The Solar House*, especially if you are planning on building a new home or adding an addition to an existing home.)

SOME FINAL THOUGHTS ON PASSIVE SOLAR RETROFITS

Passive solar retrofits offer many advantages, as I've noted. For additions, direct gain systems are really quite economical. If you and your architect are smart, you can design and build a direct gain passive solar addition for little, if any, more than a conventional addition would cost. You will be blessed with totally free heat immediately with no worry over payback for your investment.

Retrofitting an existing home or office will always cost money, however. For direct gains systems, you'll need to tear out and replace existing windows. For isolated gain systems, you'll need to build an attached sunspace. Unfortunately, I've never seen any figures on the economics of various retrofits that determine costs and savings or determine payback periods for the investments. That leaves the task up to you. My suggestion is to compute the costs of the retrofit, then estimate your savings on fuel bills, being sure to take into account the rising cost of fuel. This may help to guide your decision. Bear in mind, however, when calculating the costs and benefits of a passive solar retrofit, that not only will increasing fuel costs make the economics more favorable, you will also benefit aesthetically

and increase your home's value. For example, adding windows will provide better views, create a roomier feel to your home, and provide natural daylighting. Of course, passive solar retrofits will also make your home warmer and more comfortable. In addition, a passive solar retrofit could add to the curb appeal of your home, making it more desirable should you decide to sell it. An attractive, energy-efficient passive solar home with much lower fuel costs than similar homes is likely to be much more attractive to potential buyers, especially if fuel prices continue to escalate. The resale value of your home could increase dramatically as a result of your lower fuel bills.

ACTIVE SOLAR RETROFITS

If your home can't be retrofitted for passive solar or if passive solar won't meet all of your heating needs, you may want to consider an active solar hot water system to provide space heat. Discussed at length in Chapter 3, active solar hot water systems consist of solar collectors, typically mounted on the roof of a house, and a water storage tank. While typically used to provide hot water for domestic uses, they can also be expanded to provide space heat. In such instances, though, you'll need two things: a much larger tank and a much larger solar array.

Unlike domestic solar hot water systems that typically require 60- to 80- gallon storage tanks, the tank of a solar hot water space heating system typically holds 1,000 to 1,500, perhaps even 2,000 gallons of hot water. The tank is usually extremely well-insulated to retain heat. Heat is drawn from the tank at night and fed into a radiant floor heating system or, less commonly, baseboard hot water systems (they require hotter water than most panels can provide). Heat can also be drawn off and fed into a forced-air heating system.

Pros and Cons of Solar Hot Water Heat

Solar hot water space heating systems, like virtually everything we've contemplated, have advantages and disadvantages, many of which were discussed in Chapter 3. For a quick recap, let's start with the positive aspects.

Solar hot water space heating systems mount on rooftops and can be angled to access sun on almost any roof. Thus, even though a house may not be easily retrofitted for passive solar, it may be possible to retrofit for active solar.

Active solar systems provide heat from a clean, renewable source and new models are well made and often backed by respectable warranties.

Yet another benefit of active solar systems is that they can be used to supply hot water for a variety of other purposes, such as dishwashing, showers, baths, and pool heating.

Despite their obvious appeal, solar hot water systems have some drawbacks. Systems designed to provide space heat, for instance, require many solar panels. Although costs have come down considerably since the late 1970s and early 1980s, systems tend to be fairly pricey, although local and state rebates and other financial incentives can drive the cost down considerably.

. Solar hot water systems may also require periodic repair. Sensors and controllers of active systems are the most common sources of breakdown. Motors may also require periodic replacement, and maintenance means fixing things yourself or hiring someone to perform the work for you.

ACTIVE HOT AIR SYSTEMS

Another option for supplying heat renewably is the active solar hot air system. These systems are simple and straightforward, with only one part: a solar hot air panel — that is, a flat plate-like solar collector (Figure 4-9). Room air is circulated through the panel, heated, then blown back into the room.

Solar hot air collectors are typically mounted on a south-facing roof or wall of a home. Two ducts connect the unit to the interior air. One draws cool room air into the panel; the other transports heated air from the panel back into the room. It's that simple.

As shown in Figure 4-10 a blower fan is used to propel air through the system. It's controlled by a thermostat that turns the fan on when the temperature in the solar collector reaches 110°F (43°C) and turns it off when it drops

Even though a house may not be easily retrofitted for passive solar, it may be possible to retrofit for active solar.

Fig. 4-9: Hot air panels like this one provide backup heat.

to 90°F (32°C). So why don't you see these units everywhere?

One reason is that they typically only provide daytime heat. All other active solar systems (discussed earlier) are able to provide heat day and night, and most homes need heat at night. (Most people are gone during the day at work.)

To address this problem, some designers have created hot air systems that blow solar-heated air into rock bins located in the basement of homes. The heat is stored during the day and released at night. (It's drawn out of the rock bin by circulating air through it.)

While this may seem like a good idea, those that have tried it have often met with failure. Truthfully, many of these systems failed miserably. As solar hot air system expert Chuck Marken points out in his article in *Home Power* magazine, Issue 98, "Rock storage

and air collectors don't mix well most of the time. Air is just too unpredictable. It's tough enough to try to predict the movement through a smooth duct or fairly smooth collectors — try it with a bunch of rocks. If it works, you're lucky."

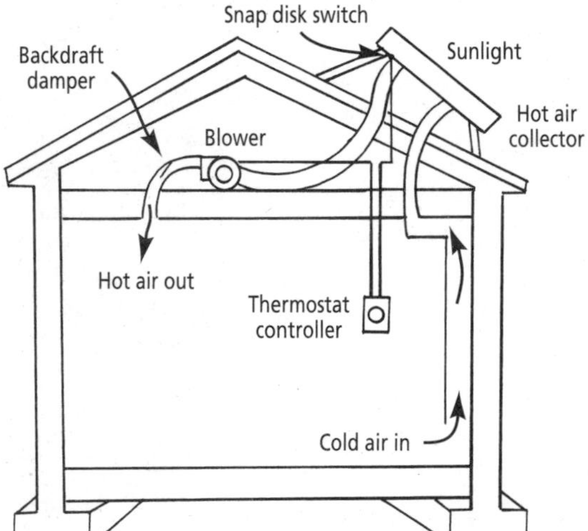

Hot air systems, however, can be used in applications where daytime heating is required, for example, in offices, shops, and small businesses. They can also be used to pump heat into floors built from cinder blocks turned on their side, creating a massive duct system. Concrete slabs are poured over the blocks. Heat absorbed by the blocks during the day, radiates upward through the slab into the house at night.

Hot air systems can also be used to pump air through ducts buried in concrete slabs, but both of these are suitable only for new buildings. To learn more, I encourage you to read Chuck Marken's articles in *Home Power* magazine, issues 98 and 99.

HEAT PUMPS

If a solar retrofit isn't in the cards, you may want to consider a heat pump. A heat pump is an ingenious device designed to extract heat from the ground or the air around a home in the winter, concentrate it, and then transfer the heat into the interior of the structure. Heat pumps can be used as the primary heat source for new or existing homes. They're ideal for sites that aren't conducive to solar energy retrofits.

What makes heat pumps so special is that they don't burn fossil fuel like many

Fig. 4-10: This diagram shows the anatomy of a solar hot air system. Note that room air is drawn into the device, heated, then pumped back into the room.

Snap disk switch

Backdraft damper

Sunlight

Blower

Hot air collector

Hot air out

Thermostat controller

Cold air in

conventional home heating systems. They operate entirely on electricity. (Electricity may be generated from fossil fuels, however, and usually is.) Moreover, heat pumps can be run in reverse during the summer to extract heat from our homes.

Heat pumps fit into two basic categories: air-source and ground-source. Let's begin with the ground-source heat pump.

Ground-Source Heat Pumps

Ground-source heat pumps (GSHPs), as shown in Figure 4-11, extract heat from the earth around a home and transfer the heat

into the house in the winter, providing space heat. Ground-source heat pumps consist of three parts: (1) pipes buried in the ground to draw heat from the earth, (2) the heat pump, and (3) a means of distributing heat in a house (a conventional heating system such as a radiant floor or forced-air heating system).

In the winter, ground-source heat pumps gather heat from the subsoil, well beneath the frost line where temperatures remain about 50°F (10°C) year round. Heat is collected from

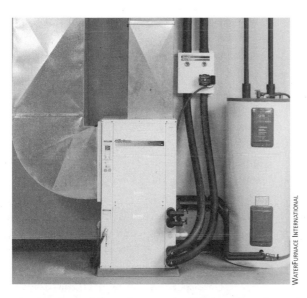

Fig. 4-11: Ground source heat pumps draw heat from the earth, concentrate it, using refrigeration technology, then pump the heat into the house. Pipes are laid horizontally in the ground 4 to 6 feet below the surface or vertically where they extend 100 to 400 feet below the surface. Water or a mixture of water and an environmentally benign antifreeze circulates through the pipe, gathering heat in the winter. A small electric pump provides the propulsive force.

this massive heat sink by water or propylene glycol pumped through the underground network of pipes. The heat is then concentrated by the heat pump and transferred into a home.

How do heat pumps turn 50°F ground heat into 80° or 90°F (27° or 32°C) space heat?

Ground-source heat pumps rely on refrigeration technology —refrigerants, gases, compressors, and pumps. Without getting too technical, the heat delivered to the heat pump causes the refrigerant in the unit to expand. The refrigerant is then sent to a compressor. Compressing the vaporized refrigerant releases heat. It is captured and transferred to the heating system while the refrigerant gas is recompressed and reused.

Heat pumps can also be used to draw heat from the groundwater or even surface waters, for example, a nearby lake or pond. These units are known as water-source heat pumps.

Pros and Cons of Ground-Source Heat Pumps

Ground-source heat pumps have many great features. Perhaps the most important is that they are extremely energy efficient. According to the United States Department of Energy (DOE) and Environmental Protection Agency (EPA), ground-source heat pumps are the most efficient, environmentally benign, and cost-effective space-heating and cooling system on the market today. These systems use relatively small amounts of electricity to power their pumps and compressors — about 25 to 50 percent less than conventional heating and

cooling systems. Moreover, ground-source heat pumps require no additional fuel other than the heat they extract from the earth, which is free. Because of this, ground-source heat pumps offer the lowest carbon dioxide emissions of any *conventional* heating and cooling system on the market today.

Yet another advantage of ground-source heat pumps is that they can be installed in virtually any climate. Although they're more expensive to install than conventional heating and cooling systems, efficiency gains pay for the additional costs in two to ten years. In addition, ground-source heat pumps carrying EPA's Energy Star label can be financed with special Energy Star loans from banks and other financial institutions. Some of these loans offer a lower interest rate than you'd be able to get for a conventional heating system. Others allow longer repayment. Some combine both features. (For information on Energy Star loans, call 1-888-STAR-YES).

Another advantage of ground-source heat pumps is that they are more compact than conventional heating and air conditioning systems. They also have relatively few moving parts and typically require less maintenance than conventional heating and cooling systems. Underground piping is often warranted for 25 to 50 years.

Yet another advantage of ground-source heat pumps is that they are much less likely to set your home on fire, as they contain no flames. The absence of combustion also eliminates indoor air pollution. And as if that's not enough, ground-source heat pumps operate fairly quietly.

Further adding to the list of advantages, residential ground-source heat pumps can be fitted with a device that transfers waste heat from the compressor pump to a family's hot water tank. In the summer, while the unit is cooling the house, waste heat from the ground-source heat pump provides 100 percent of a home's hot water; in the winter, it provides about 50 percent.

Ground-source heat pumps do have a few disadvantages, however. The main problem is that they use a refrigerant known as hydrofluorocarbon-22 or HCFC-22. Although this chemical is less stable than ozone-depleting CFCs and therefore tends to break up in the lower atmosphere, it does reach the ozone layer where it can destroy ozone molecules. As most readers will know, ozone provides a protective shield against ultraviolet-B radiation, which causes cataracts and cancer, and injures plants. Although HCFCs destroy far fewer ozone molecules than CFCs — 5,000 per molecule of HCFC compared to 100,000 per molecule of CFC — ozone loss is still significant. Fortunately, ground-source heat pumps come with factory-sealed refrigeration systems that, according to manufacturers, will seldom or never have to be recharged. This reduces leak potential and ozone destruction.

And then there's the issue of cost. As noted earlier, ground-source heat pumps cost more than conventional heating and cooling systems, largely due to the fact that they require extensive excavation, although bore holes can be drilled vertically to eliminate this problem.

Be sure to call your local utility to see if they offer any rebates or other incentives for installing a heat pump.

Air-Source Heat Pumps

Air-source heat pumps operate the same way as ground-source heat pumps, but capture heat from the air rather than the ground. In the summer, they operate in reverse. That is, they strip heat from the house and dump it outside. As illustrated in Figure 4-12, the air-source heat pump extracts heat from outside coils filled with refrigerant. The refrigerant absorbs heat from the air, even at very low temperatures.

How?

The refrigerant is cold, sometimes as cold as 0°F (−18°C). Because it is cooler than ambient air, the refrigerant can absorb heat from it. Figure 4-12 illustrates how this device actually operates.

Although air-source heat pump sales outstrip ground-source heat pump sales and installations, they are not as efficient as ground-source heat pumps. Nor can they be installed in as many places. As a rule, air-source heat pumps work best in warmer climates, such as that of the southeastern United States, where the cooling load exceeds the heating load. Of the two models, choose a ground-source heat pump. They use half as much HCFC as the air-source heat pumps and deliver more heat (or cooling) per unit of electricity consumed. If you'd like to learn more about heat pumps, I strongly recommend John Lynch's article, "Heat from the Earth" in *Home Power*, Issue 98.

In closing, although heating oil and natural gas are heading toward extinction, we have many options to heat our homes that make sense economically and environmentally. In the next chapter, we'll tackle one more option: wood heating technologies.

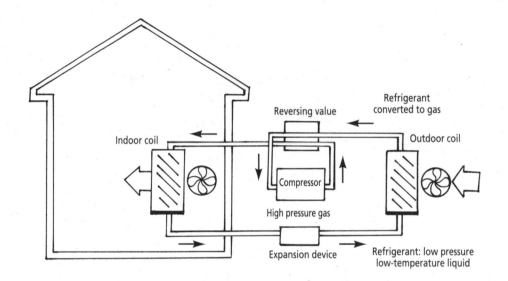

Fig. 4-12: An air-source heat pump consists of an indoor and an outdoor portion. After giving off its heat inside a house, the cool refrigerant passes from the house to the outside. Here the pressurized liquid enters an expansion device and is converted to a low-pressure, low-temperature liquid, which then enters the outside coil. A fan blows outside air over the cold coils. Heat is transferred from the outside air into the coils where it warms the refrigerant, causing it to transform from liquid to a gas. As the gas expands, it absorbs heat. Next, the heated refrigerant gas passes through a compressor, reducing its volume. The heated, high-pressure refrigerant then enters the house. Because it is hotter than the inside air, it gives off heat in the inside coil. A fan blows across the coils, stripping the heat away. When cooling a house in the summer, the process is identical, except the heat is obtained from inside the house and transferred to the outside.

CHAPTER 5

WOOD HEAT

Many people currently heat their homes with wood. With the decline of two vital home heating fuels, natural gas and oil, on the near horizon, wood is very likely to become even more popular, especially in rural areas. Surprisingly, however, many city and suburban homeowners may also find wood to be an economical source of primary or secondary heat — backing up conventional fuels or renewable home heat sources such as those discussed in the last chapter.

Although this may seem like an outlandish claim, you'd be amazed at how much wood is available in and around cities from tree removal, packing crates, and discarded skids. You may even be able to grow some of your own wood for heat if your lot is big enough and you plant fast-growing trees such as cottonwoods.

This chapter offers some guidance on wood heat, a source I've used as a backup and primary heat source for decades. In this chapter, I will outline options and provide information that will help you make sound economic and environmental choices

RETROFITTING FIREPLACES FOR EFFICIENCY

Many homes in North America have fireplaces and many homeowners may be inclined to use them to provide heat. Before you stoke up the fire, though, hear me out. Fireplaces are attractive, and a fire burning in a fireplace can indeed be a comforting sight. There's nothing more soothing than a crackling fire on a cold winter night. Unfortunately, fireplaces are one of the least efficient heating technologies humans have ever invented. Most of them achieve efficiencies of only 10 to 20 percent. In other words, only 10 to 20 percent of the heat generated by the fire actually makes its way into adjoining rooms. Unfortunately,

Fig. 5-1: Fireplace inserts are wood stoves that fit into fireplaces and dramatically increase their efficiency.

most of the heat is lost up the chimney. Some fireplaces may even lose more heat than they generate.

Unless you've got an extremely efficient fireplace, either close it up or install a fireplace insert in the opening (Figure 5-1). Fireplace inserts are steel boxes that fit into fireplace openings. Most models are about 70 percent efficient.

Fireplace inserts cost as much as woodstoves, but don't require the purchase and installation of a flue pipe because they rely on the existing chimney — provided it is in good shape — to vent combustion gases. Models vary considerably in their heat output, ranging from 30,000 BTUs per hour to nearly 85,000 BTUs per hour. The difference is related to size and construction.

When purchasing a fireplace insert, be sure to select a model that comes with a blower fan. Fans circulate room air around the insert's combustion chamber, then propel it into the adjoining room, boosting the efficiency of the stove very nicely.

For more information, you may want to consult John Gulland's piece, "Woodstove Buyer's Guide," published in one of my favorite magazines, *Mother Earth News*.

FUEL-EFFICIENT WOOD-BURNING STOVES

Free-standing wood stoves are another option for home heating. Wood stoves are widely available and come in a wide variety of shapes, sizes, colors, and materials. Let's begin by looking

When Building a New Home

Although most old fireplaces are pretty inefficient, many newer ones can achieve efficiencies similar to those offered by fireplace inserts. Why? Because they *are* essentially fireplace inserts. The builder constructs a conventional fireplace using conventional masonry materials, and then installs a fireplace insert with a blower in the opening of the fireplace. This boots the efficiency. RSF Energy's Opel AP is rated at 75 percent efficiency.

at the three basic types: radiant, circulating, and combustion.

Radiant Wood Stoves

Radiant wood stoves are constructed of a single layer of metal — either sheet metal, cast iron, or welded steel (Figure 5-2). To protect the metal from heat damage and prolong the life of the stove, manufacturers typically line the combustion chamber with fire brick.

Radiant stoves are so named because they warm rooms primarily via radiation: heat energy produced by the fire radiates off the hot metal surface of the stove. But heat is also stripped from the hot stove and circulated throughout the room by convection. Convection currents are created by the heat released from a wood stove. It warms room air near the stove. The hot air then rises. Cooler room air flows in to fill the gap. As the cooler room air flows near the stove, it strips off additional heat that then rises, continuing the convection loop that circulates heat through the room. Because heat may accumulate near the ceiling, some homeowners install ceiling fans to assist the natural convection current.

Radiant stoves constitute the bulk of the wood stove market because they are simpler than the next major type, the circulating stove, and use less material. Their sparing use of material makes them less expensive to manufacture and hence less expensive to buy. Some cast iron radiant stoves are an exception; they can be quite costly due to more extravagant design (Figure 5-3).

Fig. 5-2: Radiant wood stoves like this model from Travis Industries are made from cast iron or welded steel.

Fig. 5-3: This cast iron radiant wood stove from CFM Majestic is attractive and efficient.

Creosote and Other Considerations

Many stove operators like to turn their wood stoves down once they've gotten sufficiently hot. Unfortunately, reducing the flow of air into the combustion chamber reduces the combustion efficiency of the stove. Restricting the air supply may cause a fire to smolder and produce more air pollution, especially particulates and carbon monoxide. In addition, volatile gases from the wood escape up the chimney unburned. These organic chemicals are often deposited on the walls of the flue pipe, forming dreaded creosote. If not periodically removed from the flue pipe, creosote may catch on fire, burning at a searing 2100°F (1150°C). These extremely hot fires can spread to the house.

Fig. 5-4: Circulating wood stoves feature double-wall construction. They're a bit more expensive than radiant wood stoves.

Besides being fairly economical, radiant wood stoves are fairly efficient. As you shop, you'll see combustion efficiencies in the range of 70 to 80 percent.

When shopping for a radiant wood stove, look for models that allow you to control the flow of air into the combustion chamber. Controlling the amount of air entering the combustion chamber allows the operator to regulate the rate of combustion. The more air that's allowed into the combustion chamber, the hotter the fire. Because hotter fires also burn out more quickly and often generate more heat than is necessary at any one moment, many homeowners restrict the air flow to the combustion chamber once the fire has been started and is going strong. This ensures a good long steady burn and helps prevent a room from overheating.

As you shop, you will find that some wood stoves come with automatic controls. They allow the operator to set the desired room temperature; the stove then regulates air flow into the fire to maintain it. Vermont Castings' Encore wood stove is an example. This stove is also designed for smokeless top loading and has a removable ash pan for ease of cleaning, convenience features many homeowners find appealing.

Circulating Wood Stoves

The second type of wood stove is the circulating wood stove (Figure 5-4). Circulating wood stoves look like ordinary wood stoves. However, upon closer examination you will notice one striking difference that affects both price and performance.

Circulating stoves are double-walled. The combustion chamber is constructed of cast iron or welded steel and is typically lined with fire brick. The outer shell, however, is typically made from a light-weight sheet metal. Separating the two is a small air space.

When the fire burns inside the stove, heat is transferred to the inner shell. This heat is removed by room air that circulates through the air space either passively (by convection) or actively (by a fan). The hot air is then vented into the room.

Heat also radiates off the outer shell, but the double-walled construction prevents the outer metal layer from getting as hot as the surface of a radiant stove. This is important for safety — although circulating stoves cost more, they provide a greater measure of safety. This is especially important for families with young children who might be inclined to touch a hot stove out of curiosity or who might stumble and fall against the stove. (Note that all wood stoves should be "fenced off" from young children.)

Like radiant wood stoves, circulating stoves achieve efficiencies in the range of 70 to 80 percent, depending on the design.

Combustion Wood Stoves

Last, and certainly least, is the combustion wood stove. The old-fashioned Ben Franklin stove is a good example. Combustion stoves are radiant wood stoves with one significant difference: the doors can be opened when the fire is burning. Opening the doors converts the combustion wood stove into a fireplace, albeit a bit more efficient.

Open doors provide a view of the fire, which many people find desirable, but allow a huge amount of air to enter the combustion chamber. As a consequence, the fires tend to burn much hotter. Also, and perhaps more importantly, much of the heat generated in the combustion chamber is lost up the flue pipe. Therefore, combustion stoves achieve efficiencies in the range of 50 to 60 percent, depending on the amount of time the stove is burned with the door open.

In an energy-short world, combustion stoves should be given little consideration. If you want to see the fire, purchase a radiant or circulating wood stove with a glass door, a feature offered by most wood stove manufacturers.

Where's the Heat?

You may be surprised to know that half to two-thirds of the fuel value of wood is locked up in gases and volatile liquids. When a piece of wood is burned, for example, only 30 to 50 percent of the heat comes from combustion of the solid woody fibers. The rest comes from the combustion of hydrocarbons, if your stove burns hot enough to ignite them.

From *The Solar House: Passive Solar Heating and Cooling*, by the author.

SHOPPING FOR AN EFFICIENT, CLEAN-BURNING WOOD STOVE

If you live in a rural setting and have a ready supply of wood, or if you live in an urban or suburban setting and have access to wood, a wood stove may be a very wise investment. As is the case with all renewable technologies discussed in this book, you will need to shop carefully. There are a lot of models on the market. So what do you look for?

I strongly recommend that you shop for efficiency. The higher the efficiency the better. You should also select a clean-burning stove. Efficiency and cleanliness go hand in hand when it comes to a wood stove. A stove that wrestles as many BTUs out of the wood as possible also typically produces the least amount of pollution.

Be patient and research your options carefully. Visit as many dealers as you can and ask lots of questions. Which questions? Let me answer that by telling you a little more about your options.

Wood Stoves with Catalytic Converters

One of the first hurdles you will encounter when shopping for a wood stove is whether or not you should purchase a stove with a catalytic converter. To meet the clean air requirements of many cities, wood stove and fireplace insert manufacturers have equipped their products with catalytic burners (Figure 5-5). Catalytic burners contain a ceramic honey-comb structure coated in palladium or platinum, the catalyst. Like the catalytic converter in a car, the catalytic burner completes the combustion of unburned hydrocarbons, that is, the gases escaping from the wood. (Remember, these gases ignite at a higher temperature than most wood stove fires provide, so unless there's a catalytic burner or combuster, the energy in these gases will be wasted.)

Catalytic converters can improve wood stove efficiency by 10 to 25 percent. Wrestling more heat from the wood by burning these gases boosts a stove's efficiency. Increasing efficiency not only means you get more heat from the wood you buy or collect, it means

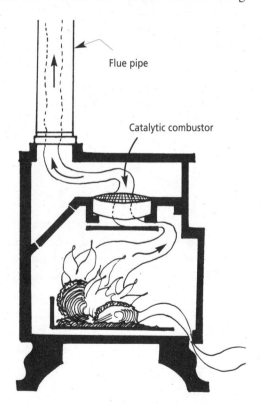

Fig. 5-5: Catalytic converters in wood stoves increase their efficiency and reduce air pollution.

Flue pipe

Catalytic combustor

you will burn less wood and spend less time and money heating your home. It also reduces creosote buildup and the problems it creates. According to several sources, catalytic burners pay for themselves in two years, give or take a little.

Catalytic burners are located in chambers above, behind, or below the main combustion chamber. Because catalytic burners burn the gases and liquids that escape from firewood, these devices reduce creosote deposits on flue pipes by 80 percent or more, reducing the risk of house fires. Less creosote buildup also reduces cleaning costs. Many sources recommend that you clean your chimney or flue pipe every year.

Although catalysts are a great idea, they do have some drawbacks. One of them is that they don't last long. The life expectancy of new catalytic burners is only about three to six years. Yet another disadvantage is that they don't work well at higher elevations, according to my local wood stove dealer.

Catalyst-Free Stoves

Fortunately, many wood stove manufacturers have found an alternative to the catalytic converter, one that's cheaper in the short term *and* long term. These designs utilize a baffle that forces combustion gases — including unburned hydrocarbons — escaping from the fire back over the flames, causing them to ignite and

How Wood Stove Catalytic Converters Work

Catalysts speed up the rate of chemical reactions by lowering the temperature at which they occur. Combustion, believe it or not, is a chemical reaction between oxygen and organic materials triggered by heat.

Combustion temperatures inside a wood stove are normally only around 400° to 900°F (204° to 482°C), well below the normal combustion temperature of hydrocarbons. Wood stove catalytic converters dramatically lower the ignition temperature of hydrocarbons released from the fire from 1100°–1300°F (593°–704°C) to around 600°F (315°C). Without a catalyst, much of the wood's heat would be lost.

Although catalytic burners start out burning at low temperatures, internal temperatures climb to 1700°F (926°C) or more, well over the temperature required to burn the gases and liquids released by firewood. Once the catalyst reaches these temperatures, it generates its own heat and will maintain temperatures sufficient to burn off hydrocarbons, even when the air supply to the stove air is restricted to prolong the burn time. Thus, even though a reduction in air flow creates a less efficient, cooler fire that releases more unburned hydrocarbons than a high-temperature fire, you don't need to worry about losing energy from your wood or polluting the atmosphere. Once the catalyst reaches temperature it remains very hot.

Fig. 5-6: Baffles in wood stoves increase their efficiency and reduce air pollution.

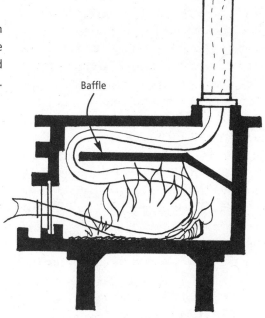

Baffle

burn (Figure 5-6). This process is typically referred to as secondary burning.

Baffles increase combustion efficiency, in part, by increasing air turbulence. Greater air turbulence puts unburned hydrocarbon gases in contact with air and heat. The greater the mixing of these "elements," the greater the efficiency.

Baffled wood stoves burn cleanly and achieve high efficiencies — on par with wood stoves equipped with catalytic combusters — and they're usually a bit cheaper.

What Else to Look for when Shopping for a Wood Stove?

When shopping for a high-quality, clean-burning, energy-efficient wood stove, there are a number of features to look for besides those just mentioned — features that help you obtain the most efficient, safest wood-stove on the market.

First on the list is durability. Durability is a function of the material from which a stove is made. Cast iron and welded steel are your best bet. Stay away from stoves made from sheet metal. They are inexpensive, but won't last long.

Stoves built entirely out of sheet metal are typically designed only for occasional use. Extensive use of a sheet metal stove leads to its early demise. Let me make this perfectly clear: a sheet metal stove is a very bad investment for those who want to heat their homes with wood.

Stoves made from one quarter-inch thick or thicker steel plates are welded together and

Should You Buy a Used Wood Stove?

Those inclined to save a little money may think about buying a used wood stove. Is this a good idea?

Not usually.

Although a used wood stove may be inexpensive, older models are often pretty inefficient. Being inefficient, they also produce a lot more pollution than newer models. Older models, for instance, produce 30 to 80 grams of particulate matter per hour. Newer models produce 90 percent less, or about 3 to 6 grams per hour.

Even though you may save upfront, you'll burn more wood, spend more time tending the fire, and pollute more. You'll also need to clean your flue pipe more often.

last a lifetime. Although the steel may warp a bit over time, steel stoves are durable and function year in and year out without a problem.

Cast iron stoves, as just noted, are also a great choice. Some people consider them the best wood stoves on the market.

Cast iron stoves do not warp like steel stoves and may last longer. However, despite its greater fire tolerance, cast iron is more brittle than steel. What this means to you is that a cast iron stove may crack if it is not shipped and installed with care. (For this reason, you should inspect a cast iron stove carefully for damage before firing it up the first time.)

Cast iron stoves can be coated with a durable, lustrous porcelain finish, adding beauty. A word of warning, though: cast iron stoves are typically the most expensive of all your options.

When shopping for a wood stove for your home, you should be sure to look for models that come with firebrick or ceramic tile linings. These materials shield the metal casings of wood stoves from high combustion temperatures, increasing their life span. Firebrick or ceramic liners may also increase the temperature of the fire, which can increase combustion efficiency.

You should also consider buying a wood stove that preheats the air delivered to the combustion chamber. Preheating usually occurs in pipes or channels inside the stove. They transport incoming air in such a way that it can be warmed before it reaches the fire. The advantage of this is that preheated air helps to maintain a hotter fire, and results in higher combustion efficiency. Cold outside air can cool a fire and reduce its efficiency.

Another highly desirable feature is a tight door seal. Good door seals help to prevent pollutants such as carbon monoxide from escaping from the combustion chamber and poisoning you and your family. A leaky door lets too much air in to the combustion chamber, making it harder to regulate the combustion temperature and burn time.

How Big Should Your Stove Be?

When shopping for a stove, you will also need to consider its size. This depends on the size of your home and its energy efficiency, notably the level of insulation and air leakage. (Be sure to make your home as energy efficient as possible upfront.)

Fortunately, wood stove manufacturers offer a fair amount of information on their products that can help you make an intelligent choice. Unfortunately, many manufacturers use different methods to rate their stoves. That is to say, there's no set standard.

Some wood stove manufacturers provide data on the heat output of their stoves, measured in BTUs per hour, while others list the number of rooms or the number of square feet each of their models is designed to heat. Still others list the cubic feet of room space a stove will heat.

Although this may seem pretty straightforward, there's a problem. Unless you know the precise conditions under which the stoves were tested, for example, the type of wood and the insulation levels in the test facility, data such as these may not be relevant to your home.

Personally, I think that your best bet is to ask a reputable local supplier who is familiar with the heating requirements in your area. However, be sure he or she visits your home. If you have upgraded the insulation in your walls and ceilings, sealed your house, and taken other measures to reduce heat demand, be certain the supplier knows this. If not, you

Installing a Stove for Optimal Performance and Safety

Wood stoves need to be strategically placed for optimal performance and safe operation. Here are some general guidelines for installing a stove.

Choose a Central Location

When selecting a location for a wood stove, it's best to avoid placement against an exterior wall. That's because heat from the stove will warm up the interior surface of the wall, causing heat to flow out of the house. (Remember: heat flows from hot to cold.) Warming the inside wall increases the temperature difference across the exterior wall; the greater the difference, the greater the heat loss.

The best spot for a wood stove is in the center of the space you're trying to heat. A central location ensures that heat from the stove spreads naturally throughout the house by convection and radiation. If you are concerned that heat won't flow well, you can always install a ceiling fan or two to move heat around.

Of course, you'll need to locate a wood stove so that it can be easily and economically vented to the outside.

Protecting Against House Fires

Although it goes without saying that you should install a wood stove in a way that protects against house fires, I'll say it anyway. Be careful. Safe installation requires placement of the stove and flue pipe the proper distance from combustible materials in floors, walls, and ceilings. Your local building department offers guidelines. Be sure to consult them.

Safe installation also requires the use of various materials that shield the floor and the walls from the intense heat of the stove. Most stoves are installed on a tile base, either purchased or installed specifically for the stove. Tile, metal, or other noncombustible materials are often placed on the wall behind the stove.

Details of safe installation are beyond the scope of this book, so be sure to check your local building code and recommendations from your insurance company. Professional installers know the codes and can save you the trouble of having to learn them.

may end up buying a model that is larger than you really need.

Pros and Cons of Wood Stoves

Wood stoves are widely available and are easy to use. They are also relatively easy to install, although professional installation by a competent crew is highly recommended (see textbox on page 130).

Many people choose wood stoves because they are one of the least expensive heating systems. You won't need the extensive and costly heat distribution systems required for conventional heating systems like forced hot air or radiant floor systems. Because there are so many suppliers and retail outlets in most locations, careful shoppers can usually get a pretty good deal on a wood stove, especially if they buy during the much slower summer season.

Wood stoves are available in many different models, with many shapes, styles, and sizes to choose from. They can be used to heat a room or an entire home. The larger the home, of course, the larger the wood stove you'll need.

Further adding to their appeal, wood stoves require very little cleaning or maintenance. For an older model, a good hot cardboard fire once a month or an annual cleaning of the stove pipe usually suffices to remove all creosote, greatly reducing the chance of a chimney fire that could spread to the home. New models require less cleaning because they burn so much cleaner, but don't get lazy.

Flue pipes still need to be cleaned from time to time.

Many modern wood stoves are nice looking. Some models with glass doors allow you to view the fire, further adding to their appeal.

If you are concerned about air quality, remember that new wood stoves manufactured in the United States, Canada, and other countries burn pretty clean. In fact, all new wood-burning stoves, except cook stoves, currently sold in the United States and Canada must comply with government regulations aimed at reducing air pollution. In the United States, the EPA sets standards for wood stoves. In Canada, the Canadian Standards Association has developed emission standards for wood stoves, fireplace inserts, and small fireplaces. Stoves certified by these agencies reduce smoke pollution by as much as 90 percent when compared to older models.

And if you live in an area that imposes wood-burning bans on high-pollution days, you may be surprised to learn that EPA-approved stoves burn so cleanly that they are exempt from these bans. EPA Phase II stoves produce almost no smoke at all.

But what about carbon dioxide emissions from wood stoves and global warming?

Burning wood in a wood stove produces carbon dioxide to be sure. It's unavoidable. All organic matter that burns produces this greenhouse gas.

However, unlike coal or natural gas or oil, wood is a renewable resource. As long as we plant trees to replace those that we cut down and burn, wood burning should not increase global carbon dioxide levels. (Cutting wood with a chain saw and transporting wood in a vehicle powered by gasoline or some other fossil fuel will produce carbon dioxide.) If you are cutting your own wood, replant trees. If you are buying from a local supplier, be sure to purchase from those who are good stewards of their forests and are involved in replanting efforts, too.

Outside Combustion Air

Some states, like the state of Washington, require that all new wood stoves draw their combustion air from outside the home. This is designed to prevent backdraft —air being drawn down the chimney into the wood-stove and then into the house when vent fans are being used inside a house. Vent fans create negative pressure inside the house that draws air in from any source it can. The flue pipe of a wood stove is a good source of replacement air. Backdraft of this nature may cause smoke and other pollutants from a smoldering fire to enter the home, creating a potentially dangerous situation.

Air can be brought in from the outside by creating an opening in the building envelope that delivers cool outside air to the wood stove via a pipe. To be effective and safe a system to supply outside air must be carefully designed. Powered make-up air systems are probably your best bet. They only operate when the stove is in operation, and thus help prevent cold air from entering your home. Be sure to get professional help on this aspect of installation.

Another benefit of wood stoves is that they're fueled by a renewable resource. If sustainably managed, wood lots can provide a lifetime of fuel to a family without damaging the environment. (To learn ways to harvest safely and sustainably, you may want to read *The Good Woodcutter's Guide* by Dave Johnson.)

Harvesting woodlots can even benefit forests. For example, thinning woodlots reduces crowding and competition among trees for limited water supplies. Trees that are less crowded are healthier and better able to resist insects and other pests.

Wood burning is also economical. A cord of wood yields the same amount of useable heat as 200 gallons of heating oil, a ton of hard coal, or about 4,000 kilowatts of electricity. A cord of wood costs about $120 to $150, depending on your location and the type of wood. With home heating oil running $2.10 a gallon at this writing (March 2005), 200 gallons of heating oil will run about $420. At 8 to 10 cents per kilowatt hour, 4,000 kilowatts of electricity will cost $320–$400.

Wood burning does have some downsides. First and foremost, heating with wood may require a lot of work, especially if you are cutting from your own woodlot. You'll have to fell dead trees, trim off limbs, cut up the wood, haul it to the house, split it, and stack it. Even if you purchase unsplit logs that are delivered to your home, you'll be spending a lot of time cutting and splitting firewood. And don't forget, you'll be hauling wood into the house on cold winter nights, lighting fires, and tending to them. You'll be cleaning up bark and debris deposited on the floor and cleaning the ashes out of the wood stove every few days, and then disposing of them.

Although hard work is good for the body and soul, and many people enjoy it, especially if it helps increase self-reliance, wood heat is more than many people want to deal with. You may want to consider purchasing firewood. Many companies will deliver it to your home and some will even stack it for you — for a price, of course. Or you may want to consider a pellet stove, discussed shortly.

But those are not the only downsides of wood burning you should be aware of before you set off on this venture. As environmentally benign as wood is, it can cause indoor air pollution. As noted earlier, smoke may escape from a wood stove as a result of backdraft. Smoke may also escape when a stove is improperly opened, or from leaks, and can result in unhealthy indoor air. In recent field tests of Canadian homes, varying degrees of combustion spillage in assorted furnaces, fireplaces, and wood stoves were detected in an alarming percentage of the homes tested. Soot deposits on walls, ceilings, and drapes is not only a nuisance, it is a sign that the air is polluted with potentially harmful particulates. Wood stoves, even clean-burning models, contribute to ambient air pollution.

Yet another potential problem is that wood stoves tend to produce really hot, dry heat that may lead to uncomfortable interiors. This can be rough on sinuses and nasal passages.

Wood heat also tends to occur in a gradient. The hottest room is the one in which the stove is located. Outlying rooms are typically much cooler. Because most wood stoves don't come with fans to force air out and away from the stove, you may need to make some provision to achieve better heat distribution. Many homeowners use ceiling fans to distribute heat.

Wood heat may also be problematic in homes with cathedral or vaulted ceilings, a feature in many newer homes. This is a problem because heat from a wood stove tends to rise and accumulate near ceilings — far away from the occupants. Although ceiling fans help to force the warm air back down, you will very likely end up burning more wood to achieve a comfortable room temperature. The more wood you burn, the more it costs, and the more outdoor pollution you produce. Second-story rooms or lofts may overheat, too, as a result of this phenomenon.

Remember, too, that because wood stoves require tending, they can't supply back-up heat when you are away from home. Only the automated pellet stoves will keep a home warm when you're away, so long as the pellet supply in the hopper lasts. (More on this shortly.)

In new construction, building departments rarely approve a wood stove as a source of back-up heat. You will most likely need to install an automatic wall heater or a furnace or some other conventional heat source controlled by a thermostat in new construction.

In existing homes, that's not a big deal. You probably already have a conventional heat source that you're trying to marginalize by using wood heat. Your furnace or boiler can be relegated to a back-up heat source.

Wood stoves can also be a fire hazard if improperly installed and maintained. Unfortunately, many houses go up in flames each year as a result of either poor installation or improper stove maintenance.

Another important consideration is that wood stoves are not as efficient as other forms of back-up heat. A wood stove isn't as efficient as a high-efficiency furnace or boiler. That said, wood is a renewable resource while oil and natural gas, two conventional home heating fuels, are not. Even though wood stoves may not be as efficient as conventional heat sources, they are still cheaper. To learn more, you may want to read John Gulland's piece, "Responsible Wood Heating" in *Home Power* magazine, Issue 99.

WOOD FURNACES

Another renewable option for home heating is a wood furnace. Wood furnaces are typically installed in basements, garages, or even, as you will soon see, outdoors. Wood furnaces can be used in conjunction with a conventional home heating system, for example, radiant floor heat, baseboard, or forced-air heating systems. The Lynndale and Yukon Eagle wood furnaces, for instance, contain blower fans that move air through the ductwork of forced-air heating systems (Figure 5-7). Some companies also design their furnaces to pre-heat domestic hot water. During the winter, these units not only heat the home, they provide hot water for washing dishes and other household tasks, greatly reducing natural gas or electricity consumption.

When shopping for a wood-burning furnace, be on the lookout for various features that improve combustion efficiency. Combustion air blowers, for instance, are fans that force a stream of air into the fire, increasing combustion efficiency. Secondary combustion chambers, like those found in wood stoves, also increase efficiency. A secondary combustion chamber increases efficiency by burning

Fig. 5-7: The Lynndale wood furnace.

YUKON-EAGLE FURNACES, ALPHA AMERICAN CO.

gases released from wood during combustion. In some furnaces, secondary combustion chambers are designed so that they have their own air supply, that is, a supply of air in addition to that provided to the main combustion chamber. This feature also promotes greater combustion efficiency.

Increased efficiency, of course, means you'll need less wood to heat your home. It also means your furnace will produce less pollution. Cutting down on pollution (soot and unburned hydrocarbons) helps keep the air in our cities and towns cleaner, and also has a very direct benefit to homeowners: it reduces creosote buildup in the chimney, reducing fire potential. This, in turn, reduces the need to clean the chimney as often, saving you money in the long run.

Some wood furnaces are designed to be used in conjunction with conventional fuels, ensuring that your home will be heated when you are gone for extended periods of time. Summeraire, a company in Peterborough, Ontario, Canada, for instance, manufactures a wood furnace that can be used in conjunction with home heating oil, natural gas, and propane. This dual-fuel furnace helps to prevent pipes from freezing when a homeowner is gone for extended periods.

Wood furnaces offer many advantages. They are pretty efficient and clean-burning. They also use a renewable resource and are fairly easy to operate. On the downside, wood furnaces are much more costly than wood stoves and more difficult to install. They also require large fans to distribute hot air through the duct work of a home. Fans consume electricity, though not that much, and are often pretty noisy. And don't forget, you will need to periodically load wood and remove ashes from the furnace. Wood furnaces, like many home heating technologies, also present some fire hazard if not properly installed and maintained.

Those who like the idea of a wood furnace but don't have room to install one in their home — or don't like the idea of hauling wood to the basement during the winter — may want to consider an outdoor wood furnace.

Yes, your eyes aren't deceiving you. A handful of companies are now producing outdoor wood-burning furnaces. Central Boiler in Greenbush, Minnesota, for instance, manufacturers a line of high-efficiency outdoor furnaces. They're made from heavy-gauge carbon steel and titanium-enhanced steel (Figure 5-8). These furnaces look like a shed and can be placed as far as 500 feet away from a home. They burn wood to heat water, which is then pumped to the home through buried insulated pipe.

Outdoor furnaces are typically used in conjunction with radiant floor, baseboard hot water, and forced-air systems. However, they can also be used to supply domestic hot water in the winter, when they're running day in and day out.

Another well-made outdoor wood furnace is manufactured by HEATMOR in Warroad,

CENTRAL BOILER

Fig. 5-8: Central Boiler's outdoor wood furnace supplies hot water to the house that can be used in conjunction with radiant floor, baseboard hot water, and even forced-air heating systems.

SHANE KELLY AND DELL-POINT

Fig. 5-9: Pellet stoves are the lazy person's wood stove. They're clean burning and operate automatically.

Minnesota. These furnaces come in a variety of colors to match your house or to blend with the environment. Their furnaces are easy to load and maintain, and efficient to operate. They use a heavy-gauge steel that the manufacturer claims long outlasts its competitors.

PELLET STOVES

If cutting firewood and hauling wood into your house all winter long isn't your cup of tea, you may want to consider a pellet stove. I like to think of pellet stoves as the lazy man's — or lazy woman's — wood stove (Figure 5-9).

Pellet stoves are much like wood stoves. They are free-standing stoves that provide space heat. They also burn wood, but not bulky pieces of firewood. Rather, they are fueled by dry, compressed wood pellets. Wood pellets, in turn, are made from sawdust, a waste product of the timber industry.

Sawdust, from milling trees to produce finished lumber, was once burned at local wood mills throughout North America in huge incinerators. They produced lots of smoke that smeared the skies of small rural towns. Today, many of these facilities convert their waste into small pellets, resembling rabbit feed, and sell it to eager customers throughout the nation. This trade has not only helped bolster local economies, it has provided a clean-burning fuel source for millions of people across the continent.

Pellets are packaged in 40-pound bags and are sold in hardware stores and many large discount stores. You can purchase a single bag or buy pellets by the ton to save money. At home, pellets are typically stored in a dry place, either in the garage or basement or under a waterproof tarp in the back yard. Pellets are loaded into a hopper in the pellet stove which automatically feeds them into the combustion chamber by a screw auger powered by electricity.

Because pellets are dry, and because they are fed into the combustion chamber at a controlled rate with plenty of air, these stoves burn very cleanly; they're cleaner than most wood stoves.

Pellet stoves offer many of the advantages of a wood stove with fewer downsides. As just noted, they burn a renewable fuel, which is actually a waste product. By burning wood pellets, you're helping reduce pollution in rural areas where mills are located. You're also helping to support the wood products industry.

Another advantage of pellet stoves is that the operator can set the rate at which pellets are fed into the combustion chamber. This regulates the heat output of the stove.

Yet another advantage of pellet stoves is that they come equipped with fans that blow hot air from their surface into the room. This helps distribute heat throughout the house.

Two other advantages is that they are easier to load and not as messy as wood stoves. Another huge advantage is that they operate automatically, providing heat while you are gone, although usually no longer than a day or two. Many pellet stoves can be ther-

mostatically controlled. And pellet stoves also allow for more precise control over heat production than your standard wood stove.

On the downside, pellet stoves require electrical energy to operate, for both the auger and the blower fans that come standard on many models. In addition, pellet stoves usually cost more than similarly sized wood stoves and require more service. Wood pellets cost more than firewood, too. You'll also generate a lot of plastic waste from the empty bags. You can use these for trash bags, though, if you like.

MASONRY HEATERS

Between 1550 and 1850, Europe was gripped by an intense cold spell. Historians, in fact, often refer to this period as the Little Ice Age. At the beginning of the Little Ice Age, homes and buildings in Europe were primarily heated by wood. However, wood was burned in inefficient fireplaces, simple stoves, and braziers. Inefficient wood-burning, in turn, led to widespread shortages of wood. But like many problems, this one led to a happy ending. Shortages led to the development of masonry heaters, highly efficient wood-burning stoves that allowed people to use a fraction of the wood once required to heat their homes. Not only did masonry heaters use less wood, they also produced greater comfort. Masonry heaters were so successful that, by the end of the Little Ice Age, nearly every building in Europe was heated by one (Figure 5-10).

Masonry stoves are still in use in northern Europe. Not just in old buildings, either; they're often installed in many new buildings. In Finland, for example, 90 percent of all new homes are heated with masonry stoves thanks, in part, to generous tax incentives offered by the forward-thinking and conservation-minded government. Masonry heaters are also very popular in Norway, Sweden, Denmark, and Germany, where they are highly regarded for their excellent efficiency, reduced pollution output, and safety. Because they offer so many benefits, masonry heaters are even starting to make their way into more and more new homes in North America as primary and secondary heat sources. I think they could be an essential element of our transition to a renewable energy future, especially in new housing stock, for reasons you'll soon understand.

Fig. 5-10: Masonry heaters burn wood efficiently and provide a steady supply of heat. The masonry heater is an ideal heating system for homes, though difficult to install in existing homes.

ALBERT BARDEN

What is a Masonry Heater?

Masonry heaters are massive wood stoves typically made from bricks and mortar, rather than welded steel or cast iron like modern wood stoves (Figure 5-11). Many masonry stoves are free-standing structures that are located in the center of the heated space from which they radiate heat outward in all directions. In some homes, masonry stoves serve as room dividers, providing heat to rooms on either side of them. Although many masonry stoves are free-standing (this installation is the most efficient), some stoves are built against outside walls.

As you shall soon see, masonry heaters are designed to burn much hotter than ordinary wood stoves, so they are able to wring even more heat from wood than the most efficient wood stoves. They therefore require much less wood than a standard wood stove. Masonry heaters are also designed to emit a lower temperature heat, and release it steadily over many hours. To understand how all of this is possible, let's peer inside a masonry heater to see how it works.

The main reason masonry heaters operate so efficiently is that their fireboxes are designed to burn at extremely high temperatures by ensuring ample air flow. Most designs also maximize turbulence in the firebox, which also increases combustion efficiency.

Like wood stoves, the combustion chambers are lined by firebrick. Firebrick protects the rest of the masonry heater from the intense interior temperatures but also provides a greater level of insulation. This, in turn, holds heat in the firebox. By preventing heat from dissipating from the combustion chamber, internal temperatures can get quite high — in the range of 1200° to 2000°F (650° to 1095°C).

High-temperature combustion in a masonry heater results in the complete, or nearly complete, combustion of wood, including all of the gases and liquids driven out of a piece of wood after it catches fire. Masonry heaters, in fact, achieve efficiencies ranging from 88 percent to nearly 95 percent. (Remember wood stoves achieve efficiencies in the range of 70 to 80 percent.)

A hot-burning fire not only results in greater efficiency, it also eliminates creosote buildup in the flue system. And it reduces air pollution. Like Phase II wood stoves, masonry stoves burn so cleanly they're approved for use when wood-burning bans are in effect, even in several areas in the United States known for tough wood-stove standards, like Colorado, Washington, and San Luis Obispo County, California.

Another important feature of masonry heaters is the often huge amounts of mass provided by the masonry materials from which they're built. These stoves are the leviathans of the heating world and range from one to eight tons.

What good is all of this mass?

Mass absorbs heat produced in the firebox and slowly radiates it into the neighboring rooms. In fact, a masonry stove will emit heat from a single load of wood for 6 to 24 hours, depending on the mass of the stove.

That's right, a single load of wood will heat a room, or a small open house, for 6 to 24 hours!

Fig. 5-11: The super-efficient masonry heater relies on three features: a well-insulated combustion chamber, a labyrinth flue, and high mass.

How Clean Are They?

Masonry stoves are in the super-low emissions category of wood-burning devices because they release only 1 to 2 grams of particulates per hour. Many wood-burning stoves release 3 to 6 grams per hour, although some of the best models achieve emissions of 1.5 to 3 grams per hour.

Mass is not all that's required to make this happen. Masonry heaters are also designed so that hot combustion gases escape through a labyrinth flue system that courses through the mass, as shown in Figure 5-11. In this design, hot gases from the firebox rise, but unlike a wood stove in which the gases escape through a fairly straight piece of flue pipe, in the masonry heater the hot gases are directed downward through the mass into channels on either side of the combustion chamber. As the gases flow through these channels, heat is absorbed by the masonry material. The heat slowly migrates through this mass, eventually reaching the surface of the stove.

Unlike a wood stove, with surface temperatures in the 500°–700°F (260°–370°C) range, the surface temperature of a masonry heater is 155° to 175°F (68° to 80°C). The brick radiates heat slowly into the room, creating long-lasting comfort with very little fuel. As the folks at Temp-Cast, a leading manufacturer of masonry heaters note, the masonry heater is "cherished for its gentle heating nature."

Masonry heaters wring lots of heat from wood by virtue of their super-efficient combustion chambers. They trap that heat in their mass, then slowly release it into the room, providing long-lasting heat. Another secret of the exceptional performance of a masonry heater lies in the way they heat rooms through their release of radiant energy. That is to say, the heat given off by the stove radiates from its surface outward like heat from the glowing embers of a fire, warming the walls, floors, furniture, pets, and people. All solid objects and living beings in the vicinity are heated.

What's in a Name?

Masonry stoves or masonry heaters go by several different names, reflecting either the origin of their design or the type of stove. Those of Russian origin are often called Russian fireplaces or Russian stoves. Swedish masonry stoves are ... you guessed it ... called Swedish stoves. Those originally made in Finland are Finnish stoves. Some lighter-weight units are known as tile stoves because of the use of decorative tile as a facing material. Austrian, German, and Swiss tile stoves can be quite ornate.

From *The Solar House*, by the author.

Should You Consider a Masonry Heater?

Masonry heaters are ideal for new home construction, but not so good for retrofitting. As noted earlier, masonry heaters weigh considerably more than wood stoves — an awful lot more!   In order to retrofit a home, then, you will very likely need to fortify the floor structure to support the mass of the stove. For models placed on wood floors, for instance, homeowners will need to install additional floor joists and very likely even additional support posts in underlying rooms. Of course, beefing up the framing may require the expertise of a structural engineer and the efforts of a skilled framer. Both add to the cost of a retrofit.

If you are installing a masonry heater over a concrete floor, you'd think you'd be all set.

Think again.

Fact is, you may need to dig it up and pour a deeper slab to support the weight of the structure. Most concrete floors aren't strong enough to support a masonry heater.

For these reasons very few masonry heaters are installed in existing homes. Most are installed in new homes designed specifically to accommodate the additional mass.

How Big a Stove Do You Need?

As a general rule, the colder the climate, the greater the stove's mass. The reason for this is that the more thermal mass a stove has, the longer it will heat. As I note in my book, *The Solar House*, which contains a more extensive section on masonry heaters, in extremely cold climates five-ton stoves would not be uncommon. Bill Eckert of Friendly Fire in Fort Collins, Colorado, sells Temp-Cast stoves. The modular kits alone weigh 2,800 pounds. When facing is added, the finished Temp-Cast stoves range from 4,000 to 8,000 pounds" — 2 to 4 tons.

When considering this option remember that lower-mass models tend to cool down more quickly and therefore require more frequent fires or longer burns. In warmer climates, lower-mass models work well. In colder climates, higher-mass stoves are your best bet.

Those interested in masonry heaters can learn more about them and view some their options by logging on to the Masonry Heater Association's web page, <www.mha-net.org>. Be sure to check out their photo gallery; it showcases a variety of beautiful masonry heaters from different installers. While you are visiting this site, be sure to check out the various dealers' websites for photos of custom-made masonry stoves and kits.

Can You Install a Masonry Heater Yourself?

Homeowners can purchase and install masonry heaters themselves, but it's not a route I'd recommend. Masonry stoves require considerable knowledge of masonry materials and considerable expertise. Most stoves are built

Operating a Masonry Heater

Most masonry stoves are fired once or twice a day, using 35 to 50 pounds of wood, depending on the stove design, for each firing. Because there's a lag time between the time you start a fire in the stove and the time the heat reaches the surface of the stove, masonry stoves are not considered a fast source of heat. Hence, operators must anticipate their heat demand and plan accordingly. Firing mid-to-late afternoon, for example, will begin to provide heat for a family within a few hours, depending on the mass of the stove, and will keep a house warm throughout the night and into the next day.

From *The Solar House*, by the author.

by skilled masons with years of experience in masonry stove construction. (To learn more about masonry heaters, I highly recommend David Lyle's book, *The Book of Masonry Stoves*. Kate Mink has also published an excellent article on masonry heaters titled "Living with a Masonry Stove", in *Home Power*, Issue 103.)

Pros and Cons of Masonry Stoves

As you can probably tell, I'm a big fan of masonry heaters. That said, I do recognize that they have some negatives. Let's take a look at both the pros and cons so you enter this adventure with eyes wide open.

To begin, as noted above, masonry heaters are efficient and clean-burning. They produce a great deal of heat from a single load of firewood. The heat is radiated into the house over a long period, providing hours of comfort from a relatively small amount of fuel. In addition, because masonry stoves burn cleanly, creosote buildup in their chimneys is not a problem, nor are creosote fires.

Masonry stoves are also pretty attractive. Facings of brick, stone, adobe, tile, and stucco give them a distinctive look. In fact, masonry heaters can be blended very nicely with almost any architectural style and décor. As I like to point out, there aren't many heating systems that you'd want to prominently display in your living room. This is one of them.

Many masonry stoves can be constructed with built-in bread or pizza ovens, so you can bake in them at the same time you are heating your home. Glass doors can also be installed so you and your family can watch the fire. Note also that some designers build stoves that also heat water for radiant floor heat and hot water for showers and other domestic uses.

Masonry stoves require very little maintenance. An annual chimney cleaning is advised, although very likely a waste of time. Creosote should never be a problem, unless the stove has been improperly designed and built or the user isn't operating it correctly. The most common mistake occurs when users build small smoldering fires instead of hot, intense ones. Smoldering fires produce a lot of smoke, as do fires that burn green wood. Inefficient combustion, in turn, leads to creosote buildup. If you want less heat, build a small, hot fire that burns fewer minutes.

Small amounts of fly ash may need to be removed periodically from the masonry flues. Accordingly, a masonry stove should have a clean-out that permits access to the smoke channels.

On the downside, masonry heaters are not widely available. To find a dealer near you, contact the Masonry Heater Association of North America's web page listed above or ask around. A local wood stove retailer may be able to help you out. They may even sell masonry heater kits that they can install for you.

Like wood stoves, masonry heaters aren't generally controlled automatically. Thus, they don't provide heat when you are away from your home for any length of time, although some models can be equipped with a thermo-statically controlled natural gas burner for such times.

Masonry stoves are not cheap, either. Building a masonry heater yourself could cost $5,000 or more. Tulikivi stove kits cost between $7,500 and $10,000. Their high cost is largely due to the fact that they're imported to North America from Finland. Temp-Cast stoves, which you can also assemble yourself, cost about $3,500 but will very likely require the services of a skilled stove mason to apply a stone facade. Bill Eckert, a distributor of Temp-Cast stoves in Colorado mentioned earlier, recommends against owner installations of his stoves. "Even with a kit," he says, "there are too many places for error." His stoves typically run $6,000 to $8,000 installed, but can run as high as $8,000 to $10,000 with options like a bread oven and a glass door for viewing the fire. A custom-made stove can cost $11,000 to $15,000 or more, depending on size and details.

In closing, although it may seem out of step with the times to heat a house with a 16th century wood-burning technology, don't forget that we descend from generations of people who have heated their homes with wood.

Building Your Own Masonry Heater

You may be tempted to build your own masonry heater. Although this is possible, as noted in this chapter, it takes a lot of skill. Stoves need to be airtight and the materials must be capable of withstanding extremely high combustion temperatures. Perhaps even more importantly, masonry heaters need to be built to accommodate the expansion and contraction of the mass as it heats and cools. An owner-builder is unlikely to have the kind of skill and expertise to pull this off. Only the most experienced stone masons should be used, and even then only those with experience building masonry heaters.

When facing material such as tile or brick is installed, it must be spaced properly so it doesn't crack as the stove expands and contracts. Temp-Cast masonry heaters incorporate a "floating firebox" in their products. It isolates the heater core from the external masonry facing, which prevents the expansion and contraction of the firebox from damaging the facing. If not built correctly or not built from the right materials, severe cracking can occur, leading to the collapse of the heater.

As also noted earlier, masonry stoves require additional framing of wood floors and additional reinforcement of concrete slabs, which add to the cost of new construction and make it difficult to add a masonry heater to existing homes.

In airtight homes, make-up air needs to be supplied to masonry stoves. This also makes it difficult to retrofit a home for a masonry stove. It adds a little expense when building a new home.

Wood is a renewable resource, too, that we can count on from year to year if we manage our forests sustainably. And, as I like to remind audiences, many old ways of doing things are still the best ways.

CHAPTER 6

PASSIVE COOLING

STAYING COOL ALL SUMMER LONG, NATURALLY

One hot July day, shortly after I'd moved into my new energy-efficient home in the foothills of the Rocky Mountains, a white car pulled into my driveway and parked. Two women emerged, then walked to the front door. Dressed in business suits and carrying clipboards, I guessed that they were representatives of some branch of local or state government.

I greeted them at the door and quickly learned that they were from the county tax assessor's office. They had arrived unannounced to look over my newly-built home to take measurements and to enumerate its various features so they could determine my property tax.

After stepping out of the 95-degree summer heat into my naturally cooled home, one of the women glanced at the checklist on her clipboard and said, "You must have central air."

"No," I said, "this house is naturally cooled."

She shot me a suspicious look.

"Really," I said, "it's super-insulated and earth-sheltered. Together, they keep it pretty cool in the summer. There's no need for air conditioning."

She gave me another look, this one a little more impatient. Her impatience, no doubt, stemmed from frequent conniving of members of the general public who want to dodge their duty to provide taxes needed to maintain our roads, pay for schools, and provide a host of other vital services. I don't particularly like taxes, but I realize that if we're going to have a decent education, snow-free roads, police protection, fire protection, and other vital services we're got to pay for them.

Undaunted, I repeated my earlier statement, then added, "Look around, there's no air conditioner."

With that, the ladies went about their business, measuring rooms and checking off various features of the home and secretly searching for ducts or vents that might deliver cool air to my home. Outside, I'm sure they scoured the landscape for some sign of a central air conditioner.

Cooling the various homes I've owned or rented over the years has been a challenge until I built my current house. This house, designed to be passively cooled, doesn't have an air conditioner despite some pretty hot summer days.

You may face a summer cooling challenge, too, one that is only bound to get worse in the many parts of the world suffering from the ravages of global warming that is causing record-breaking heat waves with record-breaking frequency. Fortunately, you don't have to build a new home to solve the puzzle. With time-tested techniques outlined in this chapter, you can single-handedly retrofit your home to greatly reduce — perhaps even eliminate — your need for mechanical cooling. All you need to do is to apply the principles and practices of the lost art of passive cooling.

WHAT IS PASSIVE COOLING?

Passive cooling is a key element of a larger strategy known as natural conditioning —

providing heating, cooling, ventilation, and lighting naturally, without mechanical or electronic devices and without outside energy.

Like passive solar heating, passive cooling may require some backup from time to time. The goal, however, is to reduce our reliance on mechanical cooling and ventilation systems and the outside energy needed to run them, and to slash energy bills. In the process, we increase our level of independence, and dramatically reduce our impact on the environment, the life-support system of the planet and, lest we forget, the source of all our wealth.

How Does it Work?

Passive cooling taps into natural forces, such as cool breezes, shade, and cool nighttime air, and ordinary building components, such as insulation, overhangs, and energy-efficient windows, to cool homes or any other buildings. As you may recall from Chapter 4, many of the steps taken to heat a home passively also contribute to passive cooling. When building a new home, for instance, the simple act of orienting the building to the south increases wintertime passive solar gain while greatly reducing summertime heat gain. The net effect of this simple measure is that the house stays warm in the winter and cool in the summer, naturally. Other passive heating strategies like insulating homes well, installing energy-efficient windows, and building with sufficient overhangs also contribute to year-round comfort. But there's a lot more you can do to passively cool a new home, and there's much you can do to an existing home to reduce its reliance on mechanical cooling and the costly, environmentally damaging energy supplies that power them.

Moreover, it doesn't matter where you live. Passive cooling techniques work well in all climate zones from hot, humid regions like the midwestern and southeastern United States to hot, arid climates like the western and southwestern US, although humid climates pose greater challenges, as you shall soon see.

Why is Passive Cooling Important?

As you may recall from Chapter 1, one of the main challenges of the coming decades will be finding substitutes for oil and natural gas supplies that are rapidly declining. Fortunately, most homes in the United States are cooled by air conditioners powered by electricity derived from the combustion of coal. Nonetheless, some of the oil and natural gas we consume each year is used to generate electricity. Passive cooling will therefore help ease our demand on these fuels, allowing their diversion to other uses for which there are fewer alternatives (for example, natural gas can be used for cooking and making fertilizer; oil can be used for generating transportation fuel, plastics, and chemicals used to make medicines).

Passive cooling not only frees up natural gas and oil for other vital activities, it also reduces our reliance on coal-fired electricity, reducing environmental damage from the entire fuel cycle, from exploration and mining to the combustion of coal and the disposal of wastes from power plants. Increasing our reliance on passive cooling techniques will also reduce the growing strain on North America's already-taxed electrical supply system. This, in turn, will help to reduce the potential for annoying, costly, and sometimes highly disruptive summer brownouts and blackouts.

TOOLS IN THE PASSIVE COOLING TOOLBOX

Passive cooling relies on numerous seemingly insignificant measures that, when combined, dramatically reduce cooling loads in a building. Home designers group these measures in four general categories: (1) reducing internal heat gain (2) reducing external heat gain, (3) purging built-up heat, and (4) cooling people directly. Let's take a look at each one and explore the strategies at our disposal.

Reducing Internal Heat Gain

All homes contain numerous sources of heat within their walls. These, in turn, result in a phenomenon called internal heat gain.

Passive cooling taps into natural forces, such as cool breezes, shade, and cool nighttime air, and ordinary building components, such as insulation, overhangs, and energy-efficient windows, to cool homes.

Power outages can be costly, according to the Arthur D. Little Company. They can cost brokerage operations nearly $6.5 million an hour. They can cost credit card companies over $2.5 million per hour and airlines $90,000 per hour in lost reservations.

Common sources of internal heat gain include people, pets, electronic devices, and lights, which all generate varying amounts of heat. Even small transformers for answering machines produce a small amount of waste heat. The most significant sources of heat include conventional stoves and ovens, clothes dryers, dishwashers, water heaters, conventional incandescent lights, aquarium lights and heaters, television sets, and computers. Even microwave ovens produce waste heat, though much less than conventional stoves and ovens.

When added up, these numerous small and seemingly insignificant internal heat sources collectively generate a substantial amount of heat. In the winter, internal heat sources help keep buildings warmer; in fact, in some super smart, energy-efficient office buildings, internal heat sources from copy machines, computers, lights, people, and other sources satisfy much of the wintertime heat load. At times internal heat sources are an asset.

In the summer, however, internal heat sources become a liability; they make our homes and offices warmer and less comfortable, and they contribute to higher fuel bills. Although ridding a home of internal heat sources could increase heating costs, cooling costs generally outweigh heating costs. It makes economic sense in the long run to eliminate internal heat sources.

Eliminating internal heat gain is the first step to passively cooling your home. I recommend that you start by systematically locating all sources of internal heat gain in your home. To begin, take out a piece of paper and make a list of all appliances, electronic devices, and lights in your home. Which ones are used most frequently? Star those items and focus your attention on them.

With this list completed, your next task is to jot down a strategy or two for reducing or eliminating the heat generated by each item on your list. For example, next to the most commonly used incandescent lights you could write "replace with compact fluorescent light bulbs." Next to the stove and oven, you can write "use the microwave during the summer more than the stove," as microwaves produce much less heat to do the same job. You could also consider cooking more meals outdoors on a grill or a solar oven. Or, you could eat meals that require less cook time, for example, salads with chicken or boiled eggs for protein. Next to the water heater, write "install an insulated water heater blanket." Next to the clothes dryer, you could write "hang clothes on outside line."

As you work through the list, you will find that most heat-reducing solutions are fairly easy and inexpensive. Bear in mind, however, that some of the more costly responses

When You're Hot You're Hot

An adult produces as much heat as a 50 to 70 watt light bulb, depending on his or her age, metabolic activity, and level of physical activity.

make sense over the long term, for example, replacing an old, inefficient water heater with an on-demand model, especially a model without a pilot light (Chapter 2). More costly solutions such as this often make good sense, especially if the appliance needs replacement anyway.

Table 6-1 lists major heat producers in a typical North American home and ways to reduce their contribution to internal heat gain — both inexpensive options and more costly ones.

Reducing External Heat Gain

Strategies to reduce internal heat gain are, for the most part, relatively painless and economical. Unfortunately, the most significant source of heat in most homes during the summer is external heat gain — heat that enters your home from the outside.

Heat enters our homes in a variety of ways. For instance, light striking the roof of a house is absorbed by the shingles and converted to heat (Figure 6-1). Much of this heat is conducted through the roof into the attic. It then passes through the insulation or, more likely, through the wood framing of the ceiling and radiates into our homes. (Attics are typically 30° to 40°F [17° to 22°C] hotter than

ambient air.) In homes built without attics, heat passes directly from the roof through the ceiling cavity into the living space.

Sunlight striking windows and walls also heats up our homes, as shown in Figure 6-1. But that's not all. Warm air surrounding our homes also contributes to external heat gain. Warm air is generated when sunlight strikes driveways, streets, sidewalks, patios, and decks. Warm air surrounding our homes heats up the walls and windows, much the same way a pie is heated in an oven. External heat is then conducted through walls into our homes. Warm air can also enter our homes through open doors and windows and through cracks in the building envelope, as explained in Chapter 2.

The most significant source of heat in most homes during the summer is external heat gain — heat entering a home from the outside.

Fig. 6-1: This drawing of a typical house shows all of the potential sources of external heat gain.

Sunlight strikes pavement and ground

Sunlight striking roof, walls, and windows flows into a house by conduction and radiation

Warms walls and windows

Warms air

Warm air leaks into home through openings in building envelope

DAN CHIRAS

Heat conducted to interior

Table 6-1
REDUCING INTERNAL HEAT GAIN

Heat Source	Contribution to Internal Heat Gain	Cheap Option	More Costly Option
Incandescent lights	Major	Use lights more sparingly. Turn lights off when not in use. Unscrew light bulbs in areas where they are not needed.	Replace with compact fluorescents. Install occupancy sensors that switch lights off when rooms are unoccupied.
Water heater	Major	Turn temperature down to 120°F (49°C). Install insulation: water heater blanket. Insulate hot water pipes.	Replace old models with on-demand (tankless) water heaters.
Stove and oven	Major	Eat more cold meals during the summer. Cook outside as much as possible. Use the microwave more during the summer Bake at night. Run the exhaust fan when cooking.	Replace old, worn-out gas stoves (with pilot lights) with models that have electronic ignition switches.
Clothes washer	Minor	Use the cold or warm water settings. Wash clothes at night.	
Computer	Minor	Turn the computer off when not in use.	Replace old, outdated computers with energy-efficient models. ☞

Heat Source	Contribution to Internal Heat Gain	Cheap Option	More Costly Option
Clothes dryer	Major	Hang clothes on outside line. Dry larger loads. Close off utility room to rest of the house. Open window to utility room when clothes dryer is in use.	Replace with a more energy-efficient model.
Television	Minor	Watch TV more sparingly. Unplug TV when not in use. Plug TV into power strip and turn off when not in use.	Purchase the most energy-efficient model possible, when buying a replacement TV set.
Furnace (pilot light)	Minor	Turn off pilot during the cooling season; reignite during the heating season.	When replacing furnace, purchase an efficient model that does not have a pilot light.
Pets	Minor	Let pets spend more time outside, but be sure to provide shade and water for them.	
People	Minor	Spend more time outdoors on porches or patios or on shaded lawns.	☞

Heat Source	Contribution to Internal Heat Gain	Cheap Option	More Costly Option
Shower	Major	Turn water heater temperature down. Take shorter showers. Open window when showering. Run exhaust fan when showering. Replace showerhead with a more efficient model.	
Stereo	Minor	Turn stereo off when not in use. Unplug components of stereo system that are not frequently used, for example, tape players. Plug stereo into power strip and turn off when not in use.	
Dishwasher	Major	Hand-wash dishes. If it is not already turned off, switch off the drying option.	■

Stopping the flow of heat into a home from the outside requires a new set of tools. One of the most important is to cool the external environment by providing shade, for example, by planting shade trees.

Reducing External Heat Gain Through Natural Shade

Shade trees cool in two ways. They block sunlight directly, reducing heat absorption by roofs, walls, driveways, walkways, and nearby streets (Figure 6-2). They also cool evaporatively. That is, shade trees remove heat from the air surrounding a home by evaporation. Evaporation occurs in the leaves of a tree. Just like perspiration that cools our bodies on a hot summer day, evaporation from the surface of leaves removes heat from the environment, creating a cooler atmosphere.

How does this work?

Evaporation requires energy to propel water molecules into the air around them. That energy is supplied by heat. (Scientists call this the latent heat of vaporization, just in case you wondered.)

Evaporation occurring in trees and vegetation is one reason why it is typically three or four degrees cooler in rural areas surrounding cities than in the cities themselves. (Cities typically have much less vegetation than the surrounding countryside.) The other reason is that cities contain lots of unshaded, heat-absorbing surfaces such as sidewalks, parking lots, streets, and massive concrete buildings.

Carefully placed shade trees can block sunlight striking the house. They can also be used to shade heat-absorbing streets, sidewalks, driveways, patios, and other sun-absorbing, heat-producing surfaces, even sheds and nearby vacant lots. If you want shade now, however, plant fast-growing trees. Also, buy the largest trees you can afford. Don't plant tiny seedlings to save a few bucks. Young trees are more likely to perish, and take many years to reach full size. You may be in the retirement home — or in the nearby cemetery — before they begin producing significant shade. Bite the bullet and purchase large trees or, at the very least, fast-growing trees like cottonless cottonwoods. (Consult your local nursery for advice on the hardiest, fastest-growing shade trees.)

I recommend planting deciduous as well as non-deciduous trees (evergreens) on the north, west, and east sides of home to provide shade. If you are going to retrofit your home for passive solar to provide space heat, keep the south side tree-free. If you want to plant trees on the south side, be sure to minimize the number and then plant only high-crowned deciduous trees; they'll lose their leaves in the fall which will still allow some solar gain. (Consult with a local nursery on the best type of tree.) Whatever you do, don't plant evergreen trees on the south side of your home (Figure 6-3). Evergreens dramatically reduce, even eliminate, the potential for passive solar gain.

If you are planning on adding a solar hot water system or solar electric system, be certain that the roof is unshaded year-round. As you will learn in Chapter 7, even a small amount of shade on a solar electric panel will cripple it.

Fig. 6-2: Shade trees cool homes by blocking sunlight and through evaporative cooling.

DAN CHIRAS

Fig. 6-3: Evergreens on the south side of homes block the low-angled winter sun and dramatically reduce, even eliminate, potential passive solar gain.

Fig. 6-4: Vine-draped arbors such as this provide many benefits and are a great passive cooling measure.

If the roof is shaded, you can still install a solar hot water system or a solar electric system but you'll need to have access to a sunny space near your home, for example, the roof of your garage or a section of your lawn where you can mount solar panels on a pole, tracking device, or rack (Chapter 7). They need to be shade-free year-round, too, for optimal production.

Reducing External Heat Gain by Shade Structures

Shade can also be provided by structures such as an arbor. As shown in Figure 6-4, an arbor is a wooden frame for growing grapes, ivy, or other forms of vegetation (even squash and cucumbers) in the spring and summer. The vegetation provides edible fruit, lovely flowers, and habitat for birds and butterflies, but also intercepts the sun, creating delightful shade. Shade provided by an arbor reduces heat gain through the windows and walls of a home. The vegetation adorning an arbor, however, also cools the air around a home (via evaporation), reducing external heat gain. Arbors create lovely spots for you to relax on a hot summer day, too.

Vines can also be grown on trellises or directly on the exterior walls of a home. Ivy adds a touch of beauty to a home, and also shades the walls and provides evaporative cooling.

Appropriate overhangs also reduce external heat gain (Figure 6-5). Unfortunately, many homes in North America were built without overhangs to save money. It's even offered as a suggestion to cut costs today, for example, in *Building an Affordable House* by Fernando Pagés Ruiz. And some designs, for example, traditional southwestern-style homes, come without overhangs.

Although it is possible to retrofit a home that lacks sufficient overhangs, it is not easy, nor is it cheap. It may also detract from its aesthetics. Don't despair, though; there are ways to compensate for the builder's cost-saving measure, for example, awnings and external shades. We'll examine these options in the next section.

Reducing External Heat Gain via Mechanical Shading Devices

One way to provide shade to walls is by installing awnings like those shown in Figure 6-6. Properly installed awnings can reduce heat gain through windows by as much as 65 percent on south-facing walls and 77 percent on east-facing walls. Select light-colored awnings to reduce heat buildup around the house.

Awnings may be fixed or retractable. I recommend retractable acrylic awnings whenever possible, especially on the south side of a home, so you can have maximum solar gain in the winter. You may even want to consider motor-driven awnings with wind sensors that retract in high winds to prevent damage. For more information on retractable awnings go to <www.retractableawnings.com>. This website contains 3-D rendering software that allows

Fig. 6-5: Overhangs protect windows and walls from the high- and intermediate summer sun.

Fig. 6-6: Awnings can dramatically reduce heat gain through windows in the summer.

you to enter a picture of your home so that you can see what different retractable awnings will look like before you lay your money down.

Window shades also help to reduce external heat gain. Window shades come in a variety of forms and are especially useful on west-facing windows during the summer as the sun makes its long, slow descent. Window shades are also useful on the hot days of spring and especially the fall, times when heat is not required, yet the sun is beginning to descend in the sky. It's at such times that the sun is beginning to provide a little unwanted solar heat.

For best year-round performance in colder regions, you should give strong consideration to insulated window shades, for example, cellular shades made from quilted

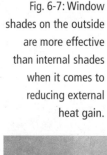

Fig. 6-7: Window shades on the outside are more effective than internal shades when it comes to reducing external heat gain.

DAN CHIRAS

fabrics or, best of all, shades made from Warm Window material. (Warm Window fabric comes with two layers of insulation to reduce heat flow and a layer of silver mylar to reflect heat.) Insulated window shades will help to keep the sun out during the late summer, and will help hold heat in your home in the winter.

Window shades may be installed inside or outside (Figure 6-7). In the vast majority of homes, window shades are installed inside for practical reasons: they are accessible, easy to operate, and protected from the weather. But while most window shading devices are internal, external shades are preferable.

Why?

Unless shades are coated with a reflective material, internal shades still allow considerable amounts of sunlight to penetrate windows. Sunlight is then converted into heat that leaks into rooms.

External shades, on the other hand, block or nearly completely block sun from entering homes, greatly reducing external heat gain. Don't worry about having to live in a dark cave; shades can be drawn only when sunlight penetration is greatest, for example, in the late afternoon. As you will soon see, some types of external window shades permit certain light to enter your home.

In recent years, manufacturers have devised some rather innovative internal and external window shades to which you should also give strong consideration. One is the solar screen. Solar screens consist of a fine mesh that blocks sun much like the solar screen used in greenhouses. They're installed in frames that are usually mounted in window frames from the outside.

Another is the solar shade, a tinted acrylic shade typically installed inside homes. Although the solar shade blocks sunlight, it is also clear enough that one can see outside.

Another ingenious invention is cellular shades that raise from the bottom up. They can be used to block the sun penetrating the lower parts of windows in late spring and early fall. For more on window shade options, you may want to check out the chapter on passive cooling in my book, *The Solar House*.

Reducing External Heat Gain by Upgrading Insulation, Sealing Cracks, and Replacing Windows

Insulation in ceilings, walls, and around foundations also helps to thwart external heat gain. Because I listed many options for upgrading insulation in Chapter 4 on passive solar heating, I'll simply refer you to that section now, if you haven't already read it.

Suffice it to say that any step taken to improve the heat resistance of the building envelope will help keep the home warmer in the winter and cooler in the summer. Because of this, insulation is one of our greatest allies in reducing external heat gain.

The same can be said for efforts that make our homes more airtight. Sealing up cracks and various openings goes a long way toward making a house more comfortable all year long. It's one of the least expensive, easiest, and most profitable steps you can take to make your home cooler in the summer and warmer in the winter. For more details, see Chapter 4.

Yet another dual-function measure — that is, a measure that helps make a home warmer in the winter and cooler in the summer — is window replacement. Replacing old, leaky, and energy-inefficient windows with modern, airtight, energy-efficient models can make a world of difference. As noted in a publication on home energy efficiency published by the US Department of Energy, about 40 percent of summertime external heat gain enters a home through its windows. If you want to save energy and achieve a greater level of energy independence, low-e windows are a must! Even if you can't afford to replace your windows, other upgrades, such as those discussed in Chapter 4, can go a long way toward eliminating external heat gain and making your summers much more comfortable.

Reducing External Gain by Repainting Your Home

Several studies over the past 20 years have shown that light-colored paints dramatically reduce heat gain in urban homes. Combined with other measures, like improving shade, upgrading insulation, and sealing a house against leaks, light-colored paints can dramatically reduce a family's cooling needs.

Light-colored walls help reduce heat gain because they reflect more sunlight off a home

Insulation is one of our greatest allies in reducing external heat gain. The same can be said for efforts that make our homes more airtight.

than darker colored walls. Lighter siding also lasts longer and saves you money, too.

Combined with other measures, light-colored walls can take a significant chunk out of your annual fuel bill. One study in a residential neighborhood in Phoenix, Arizona, for example, showed that three trees planted near light-colored houses could cut cooling costs by 18 percent per year. In Sacramento and Los Angeles, the savings were even greater: 34 and 44 percent, respectively.

Certain colors and types of roof shingles can also reduce external heat gain. If your home is in need of re-roofing, consider lighter-colored shingles, metal roofing, or Spanish tile, if they fit in with your home design and color schemes. Lighter-colored shingles reflect more sunlight back into the atmosphere, reducing heat gain through ceilings. Metal roofing tends to be installed in ways that creates a small airspace between the roofing material and the decking that retards heat gain. Spanish tiles create even larger airspaces that reduce heat absorption.

Reducing Heat Gain by Installing Radiant Barriers

Radiant barriers are relatively new products that are becoming more and more popular each year in new construction as well as in homes being retrofitted for energy efficiency, especially in hot climates like that of the southeastern United States (Figure 6-8). Radiant barriers are durable aluminum foils (with a sturdy backing material) that are stapled to roof rafters or attached to roof decking. Radiant barriers block heat from entering the attic. According to the Florida Solar Energy Center, a radiant barrier can cut cooling costs by 8 to 12 percent per year in hot climates like Florida's. This small but significant reduction, when combined with other measures described in this chapter, can nudge your home much closer to energy independence and cheap, low-impact comfort.

Purging Heat

In my house, I've succeeded in eliminating enough external and internal heat gain that I am 100 percent passively cooled. Much to the

Fig. 6-8: Radiant barriers help reduce external heat gain through roofs and are becoming much more popular in modern construction. This drawing shows three locations in which radiant barrier are installed.

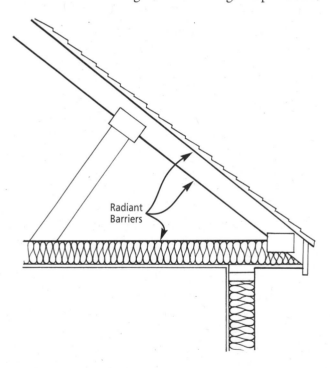

Radiant Barriers

dismay of the tax assessor's office, I have no cooling system, yet stay cool all summer long, even when outside temperatures are in the mid to high 90s.

In most existing homes, built with less exacting energy standards, it is nearly impossible to achieve this goal. No matter how hard you try to eliminate internal and external heat sources in your home, you will still be left with some heat. It must be eliminated to achieve optimum comfort.

Getting rid of that heat is the third line of attack in achieving passive cooling. What you do to address this problem depends on the climate in which you live.

Purging Heat via Natural Ventilation

In temperate climates, heat can be purged naturally by establishing some good old-fashioned cross ventilation — that is, by allowing air to flow through your home during the day. For this strategy to work, you must have a cool air reservoir. That is, you must have a cooler area, for example, a well-shaded back yard on the north side of the home, from which you draw cool air into your home. Cool air entering through windows on the north side flows naturally through a house, purging heat. It then exits through windows on the warmer side, for example, the south, east, or west sides, on the same level.

Air can also be encouraged to flow vertically from windows on lower levels to windows in upper stories. Creating air flow from lower to upper levels occurs because of a phenomenon known as the stack (or chimney) effect. This results from a phenomenon we're all familiar with: hot air rises. When hot air in a home rises, it draws cooler air in through open windows on lower levels. If those windows open to much cooler outdoor air, you should be in for a treat. Natural convection currents should naturally purge heat from your home, helping to maintain internal comfort.

The natural flow of cool air through a home performs a second function as well: it helps to cool people down much like a fan blowing air across your face. (I'll discuss this in a moment.)

Natural cross-ventilation and the stack effect produce a soothing flow of cool air that removes heat from your home. To enhance the effect, you may want to draw outside air into your home through your basement, provided the basement is not too musty smelling.

Why?

Basements tend to stay cool in the summer. By drawing outside air through a basement, cool outside air can be funneled through an even-cooler basement. Outside air, cooled by the basement, then flows up through the stairwell into the first level — and even into the second level of two-story homes — where it exits via a few open windows.

Natural ventilation works in virtually all climates early and late in the cooling season. There's generally no need to run air conditioners during this time. In some climates, though, natural ventilation can work throughout most, if not all, of the cooling season, especially if you have insulated your home well, planted trees for shade, painted your home a light color, sealed cracks, and pursued other measures described in this chapter to reduce your cooling load. Hot, arid climates are one such place where passive cooling works well.

Nighttime Heat Purging

In desert climates, daytime cross ventilation strategies work well early and late in the cooling season. For most of the rest of the summer and fall, however, daytime temperatures are too high for this strategy to work. Natural ventilation must occur during the night.

Why?

In deserts, air cools dramatically at night because of the lack of moisture in the atmosphere. (Moisture in the atmosphere is a greenhouse gas, retaining heat like a huge blanket over such areas.) Thus, even though temperatures may climb to 105°F (40°C) or more during the day, evening temperatures in the desert typically fall into the 50s and 60s (10°–15°C).

The sudden and significant drop in evening temperature provides conditions optimal for nighttime heat purging. Opening a few windows to encourage cross ventilation, or to promote the stack effect in two-story homes, allows cool air to circulate through a home. The cool nighttime air scours heat that has accumulated inside the structure from internal and external sources. By morning the home is cool as a cucumber and ready to repeat the cycle once again.

Homes that contain significant amounts of thermal mass, such as tile floors or adobe walls, work even better. That's because these forms of thermal mass absorb heat during the day, helping to maintain cooler interior temperatures. At night, cool outside air flowing through the house strips the heat from the mass, rejuvenating it for another day's cooling cycle.

Not only are cool evenings in desert climates ideal for passive cooling, they're amazingly comfortable for sleeping. Unless you're in a highly developed area with so many homes that evening breezes are thwarted and so much heat-absorbing pavement that it takes a long time to cool down, nighttime purging, when combined with all of the other measures I've been discussing, could provide your ticket to energy independence.

A Little Active Boost

In some areas, you may have to rely on some active measures to provide a little boost to passive cooling measures and achieve comfort levels you and your family find desirable. Three of the least expensive and most effective measures are window fans, attic fans, and whole-house fans.

Box fans mounted in windows can dramatically increase air circulation; they're an inexpensive and simple way to boost natural ventilation.

Attic fans are usually mounted on the roof, like the solar attic fan in Figure 6-9. Attic fans typically operate during the day to purge heat that seeps in from the roof.

Purging heat with a fan reduces heat buildup in attics and thus reduces the amount of heat that enters our homes through ceilings.

Whole-house fans mount in the ceilings, usually in a central location (Figure 6-10). They draw air in through open windows, then vent it out through the attic. (Openings in the gable ends of homes allow air to escape from the attic.)

Whole-house fans not only help to cool attics to reduce external heat gain, they also cool the interior of homes by drawing cool air into the structure.

"Whole-house fans are ideal for homes in climates that don't require air conditioning. However, they are also a perfect solution for homeowners who wish to run their air conditioning less often," says Marianne Methven, vice-president of marketing for Air Vent, Inc., a company that manufactures amazingly quiet whole-house fans. Some homeowners use whole-house fans early and late in the cooling season — or early and late in the day — when daytime temperatures are below the temperature inside their homes; others use them at

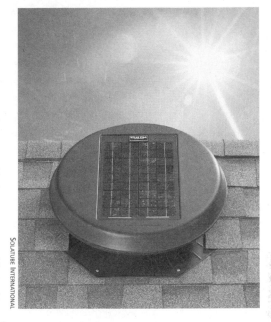

SOLATUBE INTERNATIONAL

Fig. 6-9: Solar attic fans purge heat from attics, reducing external heat gain through ceilings.

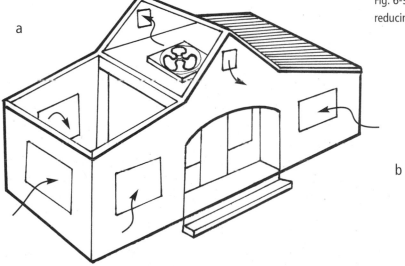

a

AIR VENT, INC.

b

Fig. 6-10: Whole-house fans create cross ventilation and also purge heat from attics.

night to encourage nighttime purging. This strategy, however, won't work if outside temperatures remain high during the evening, as in hot, humid climates like Georgia and Louisiana.

Whole-house fans can be noisy and clunky looking; they appear rather industrial. Responding to this criticism, Air Vent, Inc. created Whisper Aire, a sleek, attractive model, shown in Figure 6-10b. According to Methven, homeowners also said they liked the benefits of whole-house fans (energy efficiency, fresh air), but that they were too difficult for the average do-it-yourselfer to install. To simplify the installation process, the unit is designed so that it can be located between ceiling joists spaced at either 16 or 24 inches on-center, which means the fan will fit between the joists without having to cut and reinforce ceiling joists, which is difficult and time-consuming. Because it's smaller and lighter than traditional whole-house fans, it's easier to handle during installation too.

Another advantage of the Whisper Aire whole-house fan is its insulated automatic shutter. Providing an R-value of 25, the shutter minimizes the heat transfer between attic and living spaces. Whisper Aire is operated via remote control. This eliminates the need to drop wires down an interior wall to a switch, which makes this model even less complicated for the typical homeowner to install. The remote has five speeds and four timer settings that can be set to circulate for one-half, two, four or six hours.

Air Conditioners and Evaporative Coolers

Heat can also be purged at night — or on days when passive cooling measures can't keep up with internal and external heat gains — by air conditioners or, in arid climates, evaporative coolers (once commonly referred to as swamp coolers).

If your home is equipped with an air conditioner or evaporative cooler, you should notice a dramatic decline in usage and electrical bills after implementing the suggestions in this chapter. Don't rest on your laurels. There are additional ways to cut the use of these devices, for example, by improving their operating efficiency. For central air conditioners, you can begin by replacing dirty filters. This simple, cost-effective step will make the units work more efficiently and cut energy bills.

If your air conditioner is located in a sunny location, find a way to shade it. Air conditioners work a lot more efficiently if they're not baking in the hot sun all day long. Even an artificial shade structure over an air conditioner will help it function more efficiently — and will cut down on energy use.

Next, be sure that the air ducts that distribute cool air in your central air conditioning system are well sealed. Poorly sealed ducts can leak a considerable amount of cool air into unconditioned spaces, for example, attics. Leaks of this nature can easily waste a quarter of the energy your air conditioner uses to keep your home cool. Leaks dramatically increase run time and overall energy use.

To seal ducts, use mastic. It is a gooey, long-lasting adhesive that's painted on with a paint brush. Do not use duct tape or aluminized duct tape. Mastic will last much longer than either of these products.

You may also want to insulate cooling ducts that run through unconditioned space. Most local hardware stores carry a couple of different products for insulating large ducts.

Finally, you may also want to call your local utility company or contact a local air conditioning specialist to take a look at your air conditioner to make sure that it is running efficiently.

If you need to replace your air conditioner, purchase a super-energy-efficient model. Don't call around to local suppliers or installers, though. Look first in the *Consumer Guide to Home Energy Savings*. It lists the most efficient air conditioners on the market today, and should help you select a model that will work for you.

On a related issue, be sure that whoever sells and installs your new air conditioner doesn't oversize it. Be certain they know all you have done to reduce the cooling load in your home. Give the installer a list of your energy upgrades so he or she can size the system correctly. The energy efficiency improvements you've made should reduce the size of the air conditioner, easily paying off most, if not all, of the costs of your upgrade.

Alternatively, you may want to consider installing an energy-efficient heat pump "air conditioner." One common type used largely in warmer or moderate climates like that of the southern United States is the air-source heat pump, discussed in Chapter 4. Air-source heat pumps suck heat out of our homes in the summer and release it into the outside environment. They are generally much more energy-efficient than air conditioners. In fact, they are used in a lot of new homes right now.

As you may recall from Chapter 4, heat pumps can also be used for wintertime heating. During the winter, a heat pump extracts heat from the outside air. Using refrigeration technology, the heat pump concentrates the heat and then transfers it into the home. (If you want to learn more about them, you might want to pick up a copy of *The Consumer Guide to Home Energy Savings*.)

Evaporative coolers are also widely used in many areas, notably hot dry regions, to cool homes, stores, restaurants, shops, and other buildings. Evaporative coolers draw dry outside air through a wet porous mat, kept moist by water dripping down from the top of the mat. Dry air passing through the mat evaporates the moisture and is therefore

Size Matters

Contrary to common belief, an oversized air conditioner is extremely inefficient. It cycles on and off very frequently, which is inherently inefficient, and in so doing, doesn't effectively dehumidify the air, either.

cooled. (Remember, evaporation sucks heat out of air.) The cooled air is then blown into the building, providing economical comfort on the hottest of days.

Evaporative coolers use much less energy than air conditioners, but as noted above are only appropriate in dry climates. They do use a considerable amount of water.

Cooling People

The fourth tool in the passive cooling toolbox falls under the category of cooling people directly.

One of the most economical ways to cool people off is the fan. Any fan will do as long as it creates air movement that strips heat from our bodies. You can test this idea by fanning your face with a piece of paper or this book.

You feel immediately cooler without lowering the air temperature. Why does this make you feel cooler?

Heat tends to accumulate in a zone immediately surrounding our bodies called the boundary layer. Pushing that warm air aside immediately makes a person feel cooler.

How much?

Operating a ceiling fan has the same effect as lowering room temperature by 4°F (2°C), and ceiling fans use much less energy than air conditioners or evaporative coolers!

Fans can be used in any climate in conjunction with air conditioners or evaporative coolers. They are especially useful in hot, muggy climates. Using a ceiling fan in conjunction with an air conditioner allows us to raise thermostat temperature settings, saving considerable amounts of energy. In fact, each degree of increase in your thermostat setting cuts cooling costs by about eight percent, according to the authors of the *Consumer Guide to Solar Energy*.

The Trickiest Climates

Passive cooling is a pretty straightforward process that requires incremental application of many small, seemingly inconsequential measures, that collectively make huge dents in our cooling bill (Tables 6-1 and 6-2). The hardest of all climates to cool in, though, are those with hot, humid weather. In such areas, hot, humid days turn into hot, humid nights. Heat trying to escape from the Earth's surface in a hot, dry climate can't — it is trapped by atmospheric moisture.

In hot humid regions, the passive cooling measures outlined in this chapter often work well early and late in the cooling season when combined with natural ventilation (to purge heat from homes) and fans (to cool people). During the hottest days of the year, however, passive cooling measures will very likely require a little assistance from a ceiling fan or two and perhaps even an air conditioner. If interior daytime temperatures are sufficiently comfortable, an air conditioner can be used to purge heat at night. If that doesn't work, you'll need to run the air conditioner during the day, but run time should be dramatically reduced.

BUILDING A BETTER FUTURE

Table 6-2 lists the ideas presented in this chapter. By conscientiously applying these measures, you can achieve greater energy independence. In so doing, you can help slash your energy bills. You can also help foster a transition away from natural gas and oil, both of which are declining rapidly. Your efforts will, in a small but important way, help build a stronger and brighter future for ourselves and our children.

Table 6-2 STEPS TO PASSIVE COOLING		
Strategy	**Ideas Presented in Chapter**	**Ideas of Your Own**
Reduce Internal Heat Gain	Use lights sparingly. Turn lights off when not in use. Remove light bulbs in areas where they're not needed to avoid overlighting. Turn water heater temperature down to 120°F (49°C). Install water heater insulation blanket. Insulate hot water pipes. Eat more cold meals in the summer. Cook outside. Use the microwave in the summer. Bake at night. Run exhaust fan when cooking. Use the cold or warm water settings on washing machine. Wash clothes at night. Hang clothes on outside line. Dry larger loads. Close off utility room. Open window to utility room when the clothes dryer is in use during summer. ☞	

Strategy	Ideas Presented in Chapter	Ideas of Your Own
	Turn computers and other electronic devices off when not in use. Watch TV more sparingly. Unplug TV and stereo when not in use. Plug TV and stereo into power strip and turn off when not in use. Turn off furnace pilot light during the cooling season. Let pets spend more time outside in the summer. Spend more time outdoors on porches and patios. Take shorter showers. Open window when showering. Run exhaust fan when showering. Install an efficient showerhead. Hand-wash dishes. Switch off drying option on dishwasher.	
Reduce External Heat Gain	Plant shade trees. Build artificial shade structures such as arbors and trellises. Install awnings. Install and use window shades. Seal cracks in building envelope. Upgrade insulation. Replace energy-inefficient windows. Repaint with a lighter color. Replace roof shingles with lighter-colored ones or metal roofing or Spanish tiles. Install radiant barriers. ☞	

Strategy	Ideas Presented in Chapter	Ideas of Your Own
Purge Heat	Use natural ventilation early and late in cooling season and as much as possible during the height of the cooling season, if your climate permits. Purge heat at night in dry climates. Install and use window fans. Install attic fan. Install whole house fan. Improve efficiency of air conditioning system (seal ducts, replace dirty filters, shade air conditioner, etc.). Replace inefficient air conditioners with more efficient models or evaporative coolers if you are in a dry climate. Install an air-source heat pump.	
Cool People	Use fans Install and use ceiling fans. ■	

CHAPTER 7

SOLAR ELECTRICITY

POWERING YOUR HOME WITH SOLAR ENERGY

Solar electricity is something of a paradox: it is by far the most expensive means by which we humans generate electricity, yet is it one of the most popular choices of the poorest people in the poorest nations, for example, villagers in remote villages in India.

The reason for this is simple: although solar electricity costs quite a lot, in rural areas in less developed countries it's cheaper to install solar electric panels than to string electric lines to villages hundreds of miles from central power plants.

Far cheaper.

Solar electricity is also much cheaper than conventional electricity in certain areas in the United States. For example, when building a new home more than a couple tenths of a mile away from a power line it is often cheaper to install a solar system — especially if your home is energy efficient and the local utility won't foot the bill for grid connection. Contact your local utility to determine their line extension policy and pricing. Some companies don't charge much to connect.

If you are building a home more than half a mile from a power line, it often makes more sense to install a solar electric system than to connect to grid power. Although some local utilities have generous line extension policies, many typically charge $50,000 or more to run a line to your home. That $50,000 investment to hook up your home to the grid will buy you an enormous solar system, nearly double what you will need. Moreover, the $50,000 or higher fee to connect to the grid doesn't pay for a penny's worth of electricity.

It just gets you utility poles, an electric line, a meter, and a connection to the grid. You'll be charged for electricity on top of the hookup fee. In contrast, a $25,000 to $50,000 solar electric system provides you a lifetime of electricity (although you will need to replace batteries every 7 to 15 years, depending on how you maintain them).

Solar electric systems also make sense in states or countries in which electrical costs are extremely high. In California and Germany, for instance, conventionally produced electricity goes for premium prices. Solar electric systems also often make sense in states in which utilities offer generous financial incentives to install them. In California, for example, customers can receive rebates from various local and state agencies, totaling about half the cost of the system. Such generous incentives dramatically reduce the cost of solar electricity, driving it down to about 12 cents per kilowatt hour. By the way, Californians are currently paying about 30 cents a kilowatt hour for electricity from the grid.

Illinois also offers generous incentives totaling about 50 percent of the cost of a solar electric system. New York State provides a 25 percent tax credit. The state of Florida currently exempts solar electric systems from certain taxes, and some areas like Colorado's Roaring Fork Valley, home to the prosperous town of Aspen, offer zero-interest loans for homeowners who install solar electric systems.

If you live in a state like Arizona, Illinois, New York, Colorado, or New Jersey, or a solar-friendly municipality, or are served by a progressive utility that offers generous financial incentives that slash the initial costs of a solar electric system, you may want to do it right now. (I predict that many states and local utilities will be offering rebates as the energy picture becomes more grim.) To determine whether you are qualified to receive a rebate, call your local utility. Better yet, check out incentives on the Database for State Incentives for Renewable Energy Incentives (<www.ies.ncsu.edu/dsire>).

But what if there aren't any incentives available in your area?

You may want to install a solar electric system as a hedge against rising prices. Or you may, like me, want to install a system to achieve energy independence and reduce your environmental impact. Because solar systems can be expanded, you may simply want to invest in a few panels at a time and build your system over a period of five to ten years. For more on financing a renewable energy system, see Allan Sindelar and Phil Campbell-Graves's article on the subject in *Home Power* magazine, Issue 103.

WHAT IS A SOLAR ELECTRIC SYSTEM?

Solar electric systems fall into three main categories: grid-connected, grid-connected with battery backup, and stand-alone, a distinction that will become clear shortly. Figures 7-1a – 7-1c show all three options and their main components.

Grid-Connected PV Systems

To gain a deeper understanding of the anatomy of solar electric systems, we will begin with the grid-connected system, the simplest of all three. We begin with a basic schematic, shown in Figure 7-1. As you can see, this system consists of three main parts: a solar module, an inverter, and the main service panel. Let's begin with the solar array.

Like all other solar systems, the grid-connected system consists of one or more solar electric modules also known as photovoltaic or PV modules (Figure 7-1). Each solar module consists of numerous smaller solar cells, usually round, square, or rectangular cells about $1/100^{th}$ of an inch thick and made from silicon dioxide (Figure 7-2a). Silicon dioxide comes from a highly ubiquitous material, high-grade sand, and quartz rock. The solar cells most widely used today typically consist of two thin layers of silicon. As illustrated in Figure 7-1b, each cell in a module has numerous thin metal electrical connections (metal contacts) on the surface that gather up electricity generated by the cell.

A solar or photovoltaic cell is a solid state device that absorbs visible light and converts its energy to electricity. How that works is fascinating, but beyond the scope of this book. Suffice it to say that when sunlight strikes a PV cell it liberates electrons from silicon atoms. Thanks to some ingenious chemistry (boron and phosphorus are added to different layers of the PV cell), these electrons are forced to migrate from one side of the cell to the other, where they are drawn away by the metal contacts on the cell's surface, as shown in Figure 7-2b. Flowing electrons form an electrical current.

Because silicon reflects about 35 percent of the light striking it, the cells are coated with a thin, anti-reflective layer of silicon monoxide or titanium dioxide; it is applied after the metal contacts have been put in place. The back of the cell is made of a thin layer of metal that completes the electrical circuit, as shown in Figure 7-2.

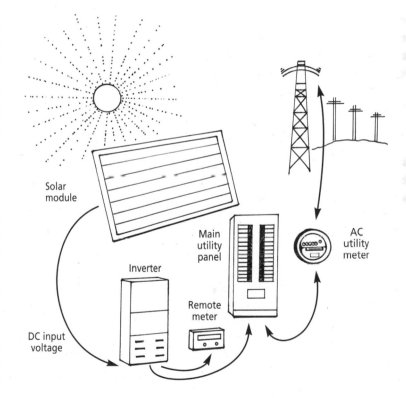

Fig. 7-1: The anatomy of a grid-connected solar electric system.

Solar module

DC input voltage

Inverter

Remote meter

Main utility panel

AC utility meter

Silicon cells are mounted in the metal-backed module casing and wired in series to boost the voltage. The unit is sealed by a clear layer of glass or, in some cases, durable sun-resistant plastic. Glass and plastic prevent moisture from reaching the cells and also resist the pounding force of hail stones. Typical modules produce between 40 and 200 watts of electrical power under peak sunlight conditions, although some manufacturers are producing larger modules that produce 300 watts. Numerous modules together form a solar array.

PV modules are typically mounted on a durable metal rack. The rack may be located on a roof of a home or on the ground in a sunny location with good access to the sun year round. In some installations, the modules are mounted on a rack attached to a pole. In others, the racks are part of a more elaborate tracking device that enables the panels to follow the sun from sunrise to sunset each day. (Be sure

to install your solar electric panels so they are out of the reach of vandals or livestock.)

Solar arrays produce direct current (DC) electricity when the cells are struck by sunlight. Direct current electricity consists of electrons flowing in wires in a single, fixed direction. The energy they contain can be used to power motors, lights, home appliances, and a host of other electronic devices.

The DC electricity produced by a solar array is carried away by wires that lead into the home. As you may know, however, virtually all of our homes use another type of electricity, known as alternating current (AC). AC electricity consists of electrons that cycle very rapidly back and forth through a wire. In North America, standard household current is 60 hertz, or 60 cycles per second. That means that in standard household electrical current, the electrons cycle back and forth 60 times per second. The energy these electrons carry is used to power a wide range of 120- and

Fig. 7-2: (a) Two solar cells. (b) Note that solar cells consist of two layers. Light striking the layers liberates electrons from the silicon atoms. These atoms flow from the deeper layer to the more superficial layer and then are drawn off by the metal contacts on the surface, creating direct current electricity.

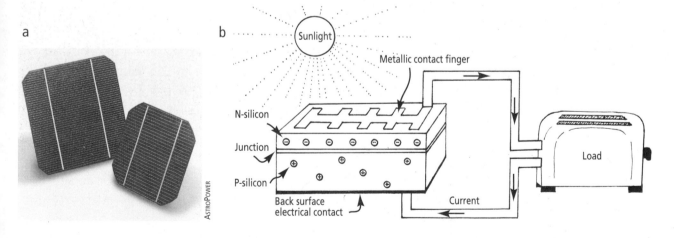

a

b

240-volt appliances and electronic devices in our homes.

In order for the DC current produced by PV cells to power our homes, then, it must be converted into AC current. This task is relegated to a component of the solar electric system known as an inverter, shown in Figure 7-3. The inverter converts DC electricity into AC electricity. It also boosts the voltage from 12, 24, or 48 volts to 120 volts or 240 volts (for some appliances like electric clothes dryers). The 120-volt or 240-volt AC current then travels to the main electrical service box of your home which routes the electricity to the circuits in your home.

In grid-connected systems, electricity from the solar array powers a wide range of devices. Excess electricity is diverted automatically into the electrical grid. Surplus power simply flows out through the main service panel to the electrical wires that connect your home to the grid.

In many grid-connected solar electric systems, electricity flowing to the grid runs through the very same meter that keeps track of electricity delivered to your home from the grid. Electricity you are sending to the grid, however, runs the meter backwards, so you are credited for the electricity you are supplying to the grid. (More on this shortly.)

Additional Components: Meters and Disconnects

All code-compliant solar systems include two additional components: meters and disconnect switches.

Meters are used to measure electrical production and consumption. The meters that measure electrical production by a PV system and consumption by you and your family

AC Devices Run on DC

Even though we plug all electronic devices and appliances into wall sockets that deliver alternating current, many of them actually run on DC current. The small black transformer of a laptop computer, for instance, converts the AC to DC and decreases the voltage.

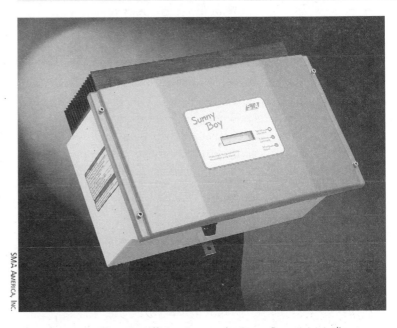

SMA America, Inc.

Fig. 7-3: Inverter. This quiet, efficient inverter by Sunny Boy converts direct current produced by PVs (or a wind generator) into alternating current and boosts the voltage to 120. Inverters also typically contain battery chargers for stand-alone solar electric systems.

at any given time, providing an instantaneous picture of energy production and consumption. They are typically located on the inverter itself or in a separate location, situated in a convenient place for ease of monitoring.

Meters typically track electrical production and consumption in amps or amperes. More sophisticated meters, however, measure long-term electrical production — that is, the total energy produced and consumed over long periods of time. As a result, they typically keep track of production and consumption in kilowatt hours.

If an inverter doesn't come with a built-in meter, you can buy a separate unit and connect it to your system.

Grid-connected PV systems also require one — sometimes two — standard utility electrical meters. These large, tamper-proof glass-encased meters are installed by the utility company. They keep track of monthly energy production and consumption so the utility can bill you at the end of each month.

Grid-connected solar electric systems also contain a couple of safety switches, called disconnects. Disconnects enable homeowners or service personnel to shut power down to prevent electrical shock when working on the system.

As shown in Figure 7-4, the DC disconnect is located between the solar array and the inverter. It is used to terminate the flow of electricity to the inverter. The other disconnect, the utility-accessible AC disconnect, is located between the inverter and main service panel. It is used to shut off the flow of electricity from the inverter to the household circuits and the grid. The AC disconnect is a safety switch utility workers shut off if they need to work on the electric lines to your home or in the neighborhood.

How Utilities Meter Electricity in Grid-Connected Systems

Before we explore the two other types of solar systems, let's take a moment to see how a grid-connected system works. Let's also see how utilities keep track of electrical production and consumption.

Unlike stand-alone systems, grid-connected PV systems have no physical on-site electrical storage capacity. That is, they have no means of storing electricity for later use, for example, at night when the PV modules are inactive. Solar homeowners, however, use the electrical grid as their "storage battery." That is to say, the electrical grid can be used to accept excess electricity when a solar electric system is producing more electricity than a home is using. Excess electricity that's transferred onto the grid is used by one's neighbors. At night, when a system is no longer producing electricity — or during the day when a home requires more electricity than the PV system is producing — electricity is drawn from the grid.

To keep track of this, many utilities simplify matters by installing one electrical meter. It contains a flat disk that runs forward when electricity is being drawn from the grid.

Each rotation of the disk represents a certain amount of electricity consumed by a household. Rotations of the disk are converted to kilowatt hours by the meter.

When electricity is flowing in the opposite direction, the meter runs backwards subtracting from the amount of electricity your home has consumed previously. The kilowatt-hour reading on the meter decreases.

This simple arrangement is called net metering. What it means to you, the producer and consumer of utility power, is that you are charged for net electrical usage (production of electricity – consumption = net use).

If, at the end of the month, your system has delivered 400 kilowatt hours of electricity to the grid and your household consumed 400 kilowatt hours at night, your cost will be zero — although the utility will very likely charge you a fee (around $10– $20 per month)

More on Net Metering

To view some frequently asked questions on net metering, you can log on to this website sponsored by *Home Power* magazine, a leader in home renewable energy: <www.homepower.com/resources/net_metering_faq.cfm>.

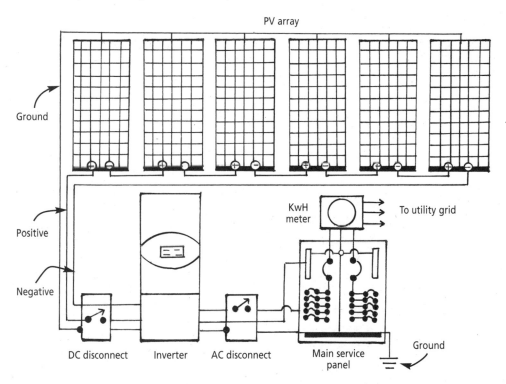

Fig. 7-4: This schematic shows all of the components of a grid-connected solar electric system, including charge controllers and disconnects.

to read the meter. If your system delivers 800 kilowatt hours of electricity during a month, but only draws 600 kilowatt hours of electrical power from the grid, you won't be charged for any electricity. But don't expect a check for the excess you sold to the utility. From the research I've done, utilities don't reimburse customers for surpluses. They may credit it to offset future bills when customers consume more electricity than they produce.

As of December 2004, 23 states had net metering laws in place requiring utilities to credit customers for the electricity they deliver to the utilities at the same rate they charge for the electricity they deliver to a home. See the sidebar for a website that will help you determine if the state you live in requires utilities to use net metering.

In states where net metering is not required by law, utilities can make the lives of those with grid-connected PV systems rather difficult. They typically require the installation of two electric meters on houses, one to measure how much electricity is delivered to the grid, and another to determine how much the customer buys from them. This allows the utility to monitor the electricity they sell to the homeowner, for which they charge the

full retail price, usually around eight to ten cents per kilowatt hour. The second meter in the system allows the utility to monitor the electricity customers "sell" to them. By law, however, the utility is only required to pay what it costs them to generate electricity, usually only two to three cents per kilowatt hour. In addition, solar home owners will very likely also have to pay for the second meter, and the utility may charge more to read two meters.

To understand how this works, let's suppose that you consume 400 kilowatt hours of electricity from the grid one month but generate twice as much, 800 kilowatt hours of surplus electricity, that you deliver to the grid. How much will the utility charge you?

Under this plan, the utility will charge you $32 for the 400 kilowatt hours of electricity that you purchased from them (400 kwh x 8 cents per kwh) *plus* a fee to read your meter. However, they will only credit your account $16.00 (800 kwh x 2 cents per kwh = $16.00). You'll owe them $16 plus a meter reading fee of $10 to $20. You lose; they win.

Had your home been in an area that permitted net metering, the utility would have

Does Your State Net Meter?

To see if your state offers net metering and to learn the specifics of your state's program, log on to this website, maintained by the US Department of Energy:
<www.eere.energy.gov/state_energy/policy_content.cfm?policyid=26>.

credited you for the excess. In other words, you would have been $36 dollars ahead of the game, minus a meter-reading and billing fee.

Grid-Connected Systems with Battery Backup

Some homeowners elect to install batteries in their grid-connected systems to provide backup power in case grid power goes down, for example, if a tree branch falls on a utility line and shuts down the electrical power system supplying you and 65 million other people. A typical grid-connected system with batteries is shown in Figure 7-5.

In grid-connected systems equipped with battery banks for backup power, the solar array produces electricity that feeds live circuits in the house during the day. Excess electricity is shunted to the batteries. When the batteries are full, excess electricity is diverted onto the electrical grid. At night, power required for household use is typically delivered by the

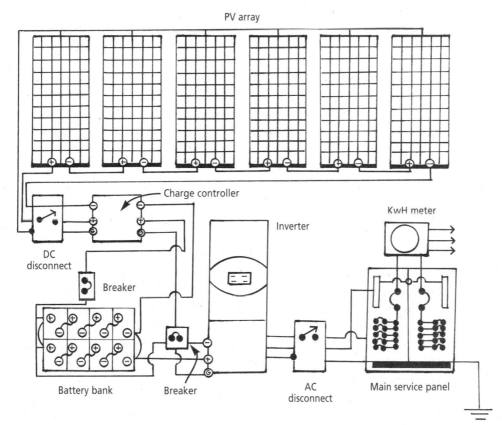

Fig. 7-5: This schematic shows all of the components of a grid-connected solar electric system with a battery bank to store back-up electricity. Note the presence of controllers and disconnects whose functions are explained in the text.

grid. The batteries are called into action only when grid power fails. (Batteries can also be charged by grid power when voltage runs low.)

A grid-connected system with battery backup includes all of the components of a grid-connected system, including disconnects for safety and meters to track electrical production and consumption, and to monitor the condition of the battery bank.

Grid-connected solar electric systems with battery backup, however, also require an additional component, one we haven't discussed yet. That is a charge controller, as shown in the schematic in Figure 7-5.

Charge controllers are electrical devices that monitor battery voltage and then utilize the information to protect the batteries. The charge controller is typically housed in a metal box.

The charge controller protects batteries against overcharging and is also known as a high-voltage disconnector. When the device detects high battery voltage, indicating batteries are full and in danger of overcharging, the charge controller interrupts the flow of electricity from the PV array into the batteries, protecting them from overcharging. Overcharging can damage the metal plates in batteries, reducing battery life.

Grid-connected systems with battery backup also contain meters to monitor electrical production and consumption and battery voltage. Battery voltage provides a measure of the state of charge of a battery bank — that is, how much electricity batteries are holding at any one time. Other more sophisticated ways to keep track of your batteries are discussed in the accompanying sidebar.

Stand-Alone Systems

Next on our list is the stand-alone system. Figure 7-6 is a schematic of a stand-alone solar electric system. As you can see, it is very similar to the grid-connected system with battery backup. You will notice two distinct differences, however. First, there is no connection to the grid. Thus, no power is shunted to the utility grid. This system, which must have batteries, "stands alone." Second, this system usually includes a backup generator. It can be run to charge the batteries when they run low. Some people install wind turbines to serve as a second charging source, according to Johnny Weiss, Director of Solar Energy International.

As illustrated in Figure 7-6, the main power source of a stand-alone system is the PV array. Electricity flowing from the array into the house first travels to the charge controller,

Checking Your Batteries

Most sophisticated solar electric homeowners monitor battery performance with an ampere-hour meter. Besides supplying information on battery voltage, this device keeps track of how many amp-hours of electricity are stored in the battery bank at any one time. They also typically monitor how many amps are going into and how many are being drawn from the batteries at any given point in time.

then to the inverter. The inverter converts the low-voltage DC solar electricity to high-voltage AC current. It is then delivered to open (active) circuits in the house via the main service panel.

Excess electricity is shunted to the batteries via the inverter, which doubles as a battery charger. The inverter battery charger converts the AC back to DC power, and sends it on its way to the batteries where it will be stored until needed. If the batteries are full the system merely shuts down temporarily so the batteries don't overcharge and fry. This task is managed by the charge controller with its high-voltage disconnect.

Stand-alone systems shunt additional power into the batteries during daylight hours for use at night. But batteries can also be called into duty during the day, for example, when clouds cover the sky.

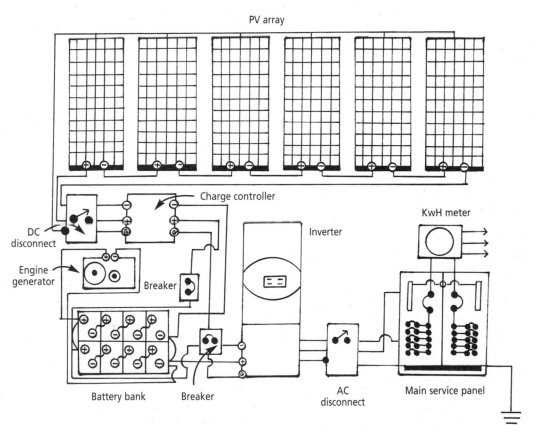

PV array

Charge controller

DC disconnect

Engine generator

Breaker

Inverter

KwH meter

Battery bank

Breaker

AC disconnect

Main service panel

Fig. 7-6: This schematic shows all the components of a stand-alone solar electric system including charge controllers and disconnects.

Like other solar electric systems, stand-alone systems require a couple of disconnects, to enable you or a repairman to service your system without being electrocuted.

Stand-alone solar electric systems like the one shown in Figure 7-6 also include another charge controller, known as a low-voltage disconnect. This device monitors battery voltage. When it senses low voltage, the low-voltage disconnect temporarily terminates the flow of electricity from the batteries to the inverter. This prevents over-discharging — that is, draining the batteries too far. Over-discharging can permanently damage a battery bank.

Fig. 7-7: For stand-alone systems, the power center is a helpful organizer of components. It contains meters, charge controllers, and disconnects.

Power Centers

Stand-alone solar electric systems can seem pretty complex with enough connections to frustrate the far more complex neuronal pathways in the human brain. There is, however, a way to avoid some of the confusion: install a power center (Figure 7-7).

A power center is the grand central station of a stand-alone solar electric system. All of the components of the system connect here. For example, there are busses (connection points) to which the electrical wires leading to the battery bank, the inverter, and the solar array all connect. The power center houses the disconnects, the charge controller, and the meters required by a system, too, making it relatively easy for someone with a few million functional brain cells to hook up a system.

I love my power center and strongly recommend that you consider one, too, if you are going to install a stand-alone system. It may cost you a bit more than buying the components separately, but it is well worth it when

KYOCERA SOLAR, INC.

you take into account the reductions in cerebral hemorrhaging that will result from attempts to buy all of the components separately and wire them in some meaningful and functional manner that meets all of the safety requirements of the National Electrical Code.

Another good reason to consider buying a power center is that they are very popular among electrical inspectors who typically know very little about solar electric systems. When an inspector sees a power center, he or she knows that all of the essential safety circuitry and all of the vital components required in a solar electric system are present and accounted for, housed as it were within that outwardly simple box. Rather than have to go through the system with a fine-toothed comb, they'll take one look at your system, find the UL (Underwriter's Laboratory) sticker, and then check it off on their inspection sheet and move on to their next home inspection.

DC Circuits

So far, the discussion of solar electric systems has focused on converting the DC power they produce into the AC power used in our homes. I'd be remiss to leave the discussion there. Solar electric systems can be designed to use DC power directly for all circuits or a few. In my home, for instance, I run a small DC electric pump to pump water from my cistern to the house. This pump uses 24-volt DC current.

I did this for one simple reason: to bypass the inverter both to save energy and to simplify the system. How does bypassing the inverter save energy?

Inverters consume energy when they're operating. For example, when my inverter converts 24-volt DC electricity from my batteries or my solar electric arrays to 120-volt AC current, it loses about 10 percent of the energy that goes through it. By bypassing the inverter with a DC circuit to the water pump, I raise the efficiency of my system.

Other appliances and consumer electronics can also be run on DC power. For example, SunFrost refrigerators, which are one of the most efficient refrigerators on the market today, can be ordered with DC motors at no extra cost. Because refrigerators account for about one tenth of your daily electrical consumption, you can save substantially by purchasing a DC refrigerator and bypassing the inverter.

Ceiling fans can also be ordered in DC models. Here, though, you need to think carefully. I was planning on doing this until I found out that DC ceiling fans cost $200 each, compared to $40 each for standard AC ceiling fans. I couldn't justify spending $480 more for three ceiling fans to bypass the inverter.

Many other DC appliances are available, but they tend to cost more and are typically designed for use in RVs or cabins. They're not ideal for household use, unless you've pared down your demands.

As a rule, then, DC circuits aren't of much value in most homes. But don't close the book on them. Johnny Weiss recommends installation of at least one DC circuit to power a light bulb in the utility room (where the inverter is located) in case of emergency.

Which System is Best for You?

As you have just seen, you've got three choices when it comes to installing a solar electric system. You can install a grid-connected system, which is by far your cheapest and easiest option. Or you can install a grid-connected system with a battery bank. Or you can go off-grid entirely, by installing a stand-alone system.

When consulting on this matter, I suggest that clients start simple with a grid-connected system. Use the grid as your battery bank and suffer through power outages like the rest of us. Or install a battery bank for backup, and invite your neighbors to stay with you when grid power crashes.

Using the grid as a battery bank obviously poses potential problems. Most notably, it is going to cost you some money. In new construction, for example, you'll have to pay to run electrical lines to your home and to install a meter or two. (When I was building my home, the local utility wanted about $2,000 to run an electrical line to my house from the buried electrical line near the road 150 feet away from the house and to install a meter.)

In new and existing homes, you will also very likely be required to install a safety switch (an AC disconnect) so firefighters can shut your solar system off in case of a fire or

so that utility company employees can shut off your system if they're working on the lines in the neighborhood. (They don't want electricity flowing onto the grid from your system while they're working on nearby lines for fear of electrocution. What some building code officials don't seem to realize or accept is that modern inverters automatically terminate the flow of electricity from solar electric homes when they sense a drop in line voltage in the grid.)

If you are installing a system on an existing home, be sure to contact the local utility company and inform them of your plans. You'll need to work out an arrangement with the company: either a single-meter net metering deal or a more cumbersome two-meter system, where they pay you for the electricity they buy from you at a discounted rate.

Despite these problems, grid-connected systems have some serious advantages. They eliminate costly batteries. A single battery bank may contain one to two dozen batteries costing $200 to $300 each. The battery bank needs a home, too, that is, some safe place where batteries can be kept warm but not hot. That's because the lead acid batteries typically used in solar electric systems function optimally at around 70°F (21°C).

Many people house their batteries in sheds or in garages, often inside a sealed battery box. The battery room or battery box needs to be vented to the outside so that hydrogen gas produced when batteries are charging can be safely vented outdoors. (Hydrogen is explosive at certain concentrations.) Building a battery box and a place to keep it costs money. And don't forget that your battery bank needs to be wired into your solar electric system, which also requires a bit of money. In addition, batteries require periodic maintenance that is going to take some time on your part (battery maintenance is discussed below).

Optimistically, lead acid batteries only last five to ten years, according to Weiss, depending on how you take care of them, and how heavily you draw on them. Replacing batteries costs money.

In sum, then, even though a grid-connected system may cost you a bit more upfront (to hook up to the grid and install meters) and may cost you a bit each month (for meter reading), it will avoid hefty battery costs. As such, it is usually cheaper to install a grid-connected solar electric system (provided you live near the grid). You may grumble about the monthly meter reading bills and the fact that the utility doesn't pay for the surplus you generate, but remember how much your batteries would have cost you and how much you would have spent replacing them every five to ten years.

A Few More Considerations: Battery Maintenance

Before you make up your mind what kind of solar system you want, you should consider system maintenance. A grid-connected system is virtually maintenance-free. If you live in a dry dusty area or a polluted city, you may need to periodically clean your PV modules; for example, you may need to wipe or rinse dust off your modules from time to time. In most locations, however, rain does the job free of charge. (I've never cleaned mine and we only get about 20 inches of precipitation per year.)

In snowy climates, you may also need to periodically sweep snow off your panels, being careful not to damage the modules. Even a tiny amount of snow blocking the bottom of a PV panel can reduce its power production by more than 90 percent, although several manufacturers (like Sharp) have produced modules that minimize the power drop caused by shade (they've installed bypass diodes in their modules). If you live in a snowy climate, be sure to install PVs in a place that's easy to reach so you can remove snow easily.

Stand-alone solar electric systems are a bit more complicated than grid-connected systems and require a lot more maintenance. Why do I recommend against them?

As noted earlier, lead acid batteries used in stand-alone systems require babying. Batteries function optimally at 70°F (21°C).

Battery Room Safety Equipment

A battery room should be equipped with a smoke detector, an appropriate fire extinguisher, and a case of baking soda to neutralize acid in case of a fire or spill. Rubber gloves and safety glasses are also essential for dealing with batteries.

At higher or lower temperatures, their performance plummets. To ensure optimal performance and long life, you'll need to be certain that you have a location to house batteries at their preferred temperature.

Batteries also naturally lose water when being charged, either by electricity from the PV panels or the generator. To keep the lead plates from drying out, which can ruin them, you will need to periodically refill your batteries, one cell at a time, with distilled (de-ionized) water. Batteries should be checked every month and topped off if necessary (be sure not to overfill), according to Richard Perez who publishes *Home Power* magazine. Refilling takes a half-hour or so, depending on the size of your battery bank and how accessible the batteries are.

To reduce water loss and battery maintenance, two companies have produced special

Reducing Battery Maintenance

When batteries are being charged, they give off hydrogen and oxygen, both gases derived from the breakdown of water. (Electricity passing through water breaks it down into hydrogen and oxygen. Thus some of the recharging energy is being wasted by splitting water molecules, a process called electrolysis.) Hydrogen and oxygen enter the catalyst-filled reservoir in the Hydrocap where they recombine to form water. It drips back down into the battery. This not only reduces watering, but reduces the danger of hydrogen gas emissions from battery banks.

battery caps: Hydrocaps and Water Miser caps. Both caps are designed to replace standard cell caps that come with lead acid batteries.

Hydrocaps contain a small catalyst-filled reservoir (Figure 7-8). The platinum catalyst converts hydrogen and oxygen released by batteries when being charged into water (see sidebar for explanation). Hydrocaps reduce water losses by around 90 percent. (As noted in the sidebar, you can also install automatic and manual battery filling systems to reduce battery maintenance.)

Water Miser caps can also be used, but they reduce water loss by only 30 to 75 percent. They also function differently. Rather than trapping hydrogen and oxygen and converting it back to water, Water Miser caps trap water vapor and fine acid particles evaporating from the battery fluid. Water and acid drip back into the batteries. Of the two, I prefer Hydrocaps. They cost more than Water Miser caps but do a better job at reducing water losses.

Another way to reduce maintenance is to install a battery filling system, shown in Figure 7-9. Battery filling systems automatically fill batteries from a central reservoir filled with distilled water, totally eliminating this time-consuming chore. Battery filling systems consist of a series of plastic tubes connected to a central reservoir in the battery room. Each battery cell is fitted with a special cap equipped with a float valve. When the water level drops in a cell (there are usually three cells per battery), the valve opens and allows enough water to fill the battery to the proper level. Unfortunately, the unit costs about $16 per cell or $48 per battery. A battery bank with 12 batteries would cost $575.

Another disadvantage of the stand-alone system is that batteries need to be equalized from time to time — usually, every three or four months. Equalization is a controlled overcharge of the batteries. Batteries are typically equalized by running a generator. The process is pretty simple: to equalize batteries, a homeowner starts up the generator, which is connected to the inverter/battery charger, then flips on the circuit breaker in the line connecting the generator to the inverter/battery charger. At this point, the inverter/battery charger takes over. When equalizing batteries, electricity is fed into the battery bank very rapidly at first. As the batteries are charged, however, the flow of electricity gradually slows. At the end of the process, electrical current trickles into the batteries. When the batteries are fully charged and equalized, the inverter shuts off, and you're done.

Equalization achieves two important goals. It raises the voltage of each cell to the same level for optimal function, hence the name equalization. (A battery bank performs only as well as the lowest-voltage cell in the array.)

Equalization also cleans the plates in your batteries; that is, it drives the lead sulfate off your plates. Lead sulfate forms on the lead plates of batteries when they discharge —

JOE SCHWARTZ

Fig. 7-8: Hydrocaps. These battery caps replace standard caps that come with lead acid batteries. The catalyst in the reservoir captures hydrogen and oxygen given off by the breakdown of water and recombines them, reducing water loss by 90 percent, thus cutting down on routine maintenance.

BATTERY FILLING SYSTEM OF THE AMERICAS

Fig. 7-9: Battery Filling System. This product is designed for those who don't want to have to top off their batteries every three or four months. Float valves in the caps tell when a cell needs replenishment. Distilled water flows into the cells and keeps them at optimum operating levels.

that is, give off electricity. (For those who know a bit about batteries and lead acid battery chemistry: lead sulfate forms on the lead plates that feed into the anode [the negatively charged pole] as well as those that feed into the cathode [the positively charged pole]).

Lead sulfate accumulating on the plates inside a battery reduces the amount of electricity a battery can store, greatly hindering a system. Periodic equalization helps restore the batteries and increases their lifespan.

Making Sense of Generators

Stand-alone systems typically require a generator for backup power, but also to perform routine battery maintenance, notably periodic equalization. How often homeowners need to run a generator depends on many factors, among them the size of the PV system, household energy use, and the amount of available sunshine.

Generators are expensive and burn costly fossil fuels (gasoline, diesel, propane, or natural gas). They're also prone to breakdown and many models are quite noisy. In addition, some units may not last more than 500 hours, according to some sources. Because of these factors, I recommend that homeowners oversize their solar electric systems — that is, that they install a larger PV array and a larger battery bank than they might ordinarily consider. This way, they won't need to supply backup power so often. A larger battery bank means that batteries aren't deep discharged as often, which reduces the need for periodic equalization.

Which Way to Go?

If you are considering installing a solar electric system, you obviously have to think this through very carefully. To hold costs down, you might want to begin with a small, grid-connected system. You can install 10 50-watt panels, giving you a 500-watt system, which would cost around $5,000. (Modules will cost $200 to $300 each, a rack will cost a few hundred dollars, a disconnect will cost a little over $100, and an inverter will cost $2,000 to $3,000. Installation by a professional might cost $2,000 or more. Total system cost will be $5,000 to $10,000.)

At this point, you've got the main components of a full-fledged solar electric system. That is, you've got all of the expensive hardware in place. You can then add modules as your finances permit, so long as you have sized your inverter properly. (I recommend oversizing the inverter initially to match your projected future demand.) You can even add a battery bank at a later date, if you want. And you could eventually disconnect from the electrical grid entirely if you feel comfortable that a stand-alone system will work for you.

Efficiency First!

If you decide you are going to join the growing legion of solar electric homeowners, the first thing you need to do is to make your home as efficient in its use of electricity as humanly possible. You'll save a fortune on your solar electric system if you do. As a general rule of thumb, every dollar you invest in efficiency will save you $3 to $5 in system cost. Thus, a thousand dollars invested in measures that cut electrical demand by 25–50 percent can save you $3,000 to $5,000 in system cost. Chapter 2 outlines efficiency measures that will help reduce electrical demand.

While you are at it, be sure to eliminate or reduce phantom (ghost) loads. Although individual phantom loads are small, remember that they're on 24 hours per day. Many tiny loads in a house add up and can add substantially to the cost of your system.

How to Size a System?

Sizing a solar electric system can be tricky, especially if you are installing a system on a house you're just moving into or a house you are building. In such cases, how do you know how much electricity you'll need?

What most people do is make a list of all the appliances and electronic devices that will be used in the house. Once this is complete, they estimate how long each appliance or device is used each day. They then multiply the power consumption of each device. Power consumption is listed on all electronic devices on a small plate or sticker on the back of the unit. Go check your microwave or TV right now.

Another way is to consult a table that lists typical wattages of all household appliances and electronic devices. Figure 7-10a shows a typical appliance wattage chart. It gives the electrical consumption for each device.

Multiplying wattage of each appliance by the estimated time it is used each day gives you the daily electrical consumption.

From this analysis, you should be able to calculate your total daily energy requirement in watt-hours. Note, however, that some appliances or electric devices may be used more during some parts of the year than others. Lights, for example, are on more often during the winter than the summer because the days are shorter in the winter. The television may run less frequently during the summer while kids are outside playing. Try to take such differences into account when computing energy consumption (Figure 7-10b).

Once you know how much electricity you consume, you need to run through some additional calculations. These are typically in a worksheet form. You can also complete this process using computer software.

The worksheets available through Solar Energy International's book *Photovoltaics: Design and Installation Manual*, first allows you to determine electric load (demand for electricity) as just described. It then leads you through a few computations necessary to determine the size of the inverter you'll need. After this, you determine the size of the battery bank you'll need if you are designing an off-grid home. It then leads you through calculations to size the array – that is, to determine the number of PV modules you'll need. This calculation takes into account your demand, the efficiency of the entire system, and solar availability.

Before installing a solar electric system, make your home as efficient in its use of electricity as humanly possible. You'll save a fortune by making your home efficient.

Figure 7-10a
Typical Wattage Requirements for Common Appliances

General household

Air conditioner (1 ton) 1500
Alarm/Security system 3
Blow dryer...........................1000
Ceiling fan 10-50
Central vacuum.....................750
Clock radio 5
Clothes washer 1450
Dryer (gas)............................300
Electric blanket.....................200
Electric clock 4
Furnace fan...........................500
Garage door opener 350
Heater (portable)................1500
Iron (electric).......................1500
Radio/phone transmit 40-150
Sewing machine 100
Table fan 10-25
Waterpik 100

Refrigeration

Refrigerator/freezer 540
  22 ft³ (14 hrs/day)
Refrigerator/freezer 475
  16 ft³ (13 hrs/day)
Sun Frost refrigerator 112
  16 ft³ (7 hrs/day)
Vestfrost refrigerator/ 60
  freezer 10.5 ft³
Standard freezer....................440
  14 ft³ (15 hrs/day)
Sun Frost freezer 112
  19 ft³ (10 hrs/day)

Kitchen appliances

Blender 350
Can opener (electric).............100
Coffee grinder 100
Coffee pot (electric) 1200
Dishwasher..........................1500
Exhaust fans (3) 144
Food dehydrator....................600
Food processor......................400
Microwave (.5 ft³) 750
Microwave (.8 to 1.5 ft³) 1400
Mixer 120
Popcorn popper.....................250
Range (large burner)..........2100
Range (small burner)..........1250
Trash compactor 1500
Waffle iron...........................1200

Lighting

Incandescent (100 watt)........100
Incandescent light 60
  (60 watt)
Compact fluorescent 16
  (60 watt equivalent)
Incandescent (40 watt)...........40
Compact fluorescent 11
  (40 watt equivalent)

Water Pumping

AC Jet pump (¼ hp) 500
  165 gal per day, 20 ft. well
DC pump for house................60
  pressure system (1-2 hrs/day)

DC submersible pump 50
  (6 hours/day)

Entertainment

CB radio.................................10
CD player................................35
Cellular telephone..................24
Computer printer 100
Computer (desktop).........80-150
Computer (laptop) 20-50
Electric player piano...............30
Radio telephone 10
Satellite system (12 ft dish).....45
Stereo (avg. volume) 15
TV (12-inch black & white) 15
TV (19-inch color) 60
TV (25-inch color) 130
VCR.......................................40

Tools

Band saw (14") 1100
Chain saw (12") 1100
Circular saw (7¼") 900
Disc sander (9") 1200
Drill (¼") 250
Drill (½") 750
Drill (1") 1000
Electric mower.....................1500
Hedge trimmer 450
Weed eater 500

Figure 7-10b
Stand-Alone Electric Load Worksheet

Individual Loads	Qty	X	Volts	X	Amps	=	Watts AC	DC	X Use Hrs/day	X Use days/wk	+ 7 = days	Watts AC	Hours DC
											7		
											7		
											7		
											7		
											7		
											7		
											7		
											7		
											7		
											7		
											7		
											7		
											7		
											7		
											7		
											7		

AC Total Connected Watts: _____   AC Average Daily Load: _____

DC Total Connected Watts: _____   DC Average Daily Load: _____

SOLAR ENERGY INTERNATIONAL

Fig. 7-10: Sizing a Solar Electric System. (a) This table provides typical wattage (power consumption) readings for major appliances and household electronics. (b) This table can be used to list all of your appliances and to determine how much power they use each day.

As a general rule of thumb, if your home is a normal, inefficient North American residence, you will need about two watts of solar electric power per square foot of home. If you are efficient, you could cut this by half. If you are super-efficient, you could cut this by half again.

If your eyes are starting to glaze over, don't despair. A local installer can run the numbers for you. Even if you are planning on installing the system yourself, you might want to hire a local installer to consult with you at this stage. (Be careful, warns Weiss, if you install a system yourself. You'll be dealing with high-voltage DC and AC current that can be dangerous!)

PV systems should be sized for the season with the highest energy demand and the lowest insolation. You can determine this with a little simple math: simply divide each season's electrical energy requirements by the corresponding insolation values.

Bear in mind that solar systems, like any energy systems, are not 100 percent efficient. That is, you won't obtain 100 percent of the electricity solar electric panels generate. As a rule, you should size your system about 35 percent bigger than you'd expect to need based on electrical demand and solar modules production. This takes into account the efficiency losses of batteries and inverters. (Batteries give you only 70 percent of the electricity that goes into them and inverters lose about 5 to 10 percent of the energy flowing through them — it takes a little energy to convert DC to AC and to boost the voltage of electrical current in an inverter).

Bear in mind that many people grossly underestimate how much electricity they and their families use. For instance, you might estimate that you run your TV only a few hours a night when, in reality, you and your family watch four hours per night on weeknights and eight hours per day on the weekends.

If you are feeling a bit dismayed, don't be.

As noted earlier, solar installers (catalog suppliers and installers alike) provide worksheets like the one shown in Figure 7-10b that will make this process much easier. You can also find one in *Solar Living Sourcebook* and Solar Energy International's *Photovoltaics: Design and Installation Manual*, an absolute must for those who are thinking of installing their own system. (You can learn more about this book and contact SEI on the web at <www.solarenergy.org>.) You can also log on to <www.realgoods.com/renew/sizing/index.cfm> for assistance. *Home Power* magazine offers a free downloadable spreadsheet (called Energy Master) to analyze loads at <www.homepower.com> under Resources. Suppliers and installers will even lend you a hand with the process if you are buying a system from them.

If you are installing a solar electric system on an existing home for which you have electrical consumption data, use that information; it's much more reliable than the guesswork required to size a system for a new home. But remember: reduce your demand first! Be sure to apply energy conservation measures vigorously before you estimate how much electricity you will be using. Again, solar suppliers and installers will help you size your system.

As a general rule of thumb, if your home is a normal, inefficient North American residence, you will need about two watts of solar electric power per square foot of home. If you are efficient, you could cut this by half. If you are super-efficient, you could cut this by half again.

This means that if your home is 2,000 square feet, you'll need a system whose capacity is about 4 kilowatts. This rating is determined by multiplying the number of square feet by the maximum output of the modules. In this instance, 2,000 square feet x 2 watts per square foot = 4,000 watts or 4 kilowatts). If the modules produce 100 watts each at peak power, you'll need 40 of them. If they cost $500 each, your cost for PV modules will be $20,000. You'll also need batteries, which could run you $10,000, and an inverter, that might cost $3,000 to $4,000, and charge controllers and disconnects, which cost $600, and then there's the installation cost of $4,000 to $6,000 or more. Your system could run you $42,000 to $45,000, or more.

If your home is pretty efficient, however, you could get by with a two-kilowatt system, costing nearly half as much. If your home is super-efficient, you will need only a one-kilowatt system, costing one-fourth as much as the system you'd need if you hadn't invested the time, energy, and money to make your home energy efficient.

Once you have sized your system, you will also need to determine the system voltage. As a general rule, most installations that require fewer than 2,000 watt-hours of electricity per day are designed as 12-volt systems, according to Richard Perez in *Storage Batteries for Renewable Energy Systems*. The 2,000 to 6,000 watt-hour per day range is a gray zone, says Perez, but most are probably 24 volt. Over 6,000 to 8,000 watt-hour per day systems are 24 volt or higher (48 volt). SEI's Johnny Weiss notes that "high-voltage systems are more desirable because they save on wire size, fuse, and circuit breaker size."

BUYING A SOLAR ELECTRIC SYSTEM

When it comes to buying a solar system, many people wisely turn to a local PV dealer/installer who can select the components and ensure that all of them work well together. Although this option may cost a bit more than those I'll explain shortly, it's a good approach. A competent local installer can answer all of your questions and take care of problems that may arise. (Be sure they really know what they're doing.)

Unless you're mechanically inclined and pretty knowledgeable, embarking on this process yourself can put you on a steep and treacherous uphill climb! "Even licensed electricians often need help from experienced PV installers," notes Weiss. You can find a list of local installers at <www.homepower.com.> Also, be sure to check out the local business directory your phone company provides.

Another approach is to buy a system from an Internet supplier. This approach can save you a substantial amount of money, as deep discounts are available through the Internet. Once the system arrives, you will have to install it yourself, or try to hire a local installer to do it for you. Bear in mind, local installers may not be happy that you cut them out of the first part of the deal!

If you do buy through an Internet supplier, you'll need to know quite a bit more about PV modules, racks, inverters, charge controllers, disconnects, and batteries than when purchasing a system from a local supplier/installer. If you decide to take this route, you should read one of the books on solar electricity in the Resource Guide to deepen your knowledge. I've provided a lot of information in this chapter, but there's much more to know. As Weiss points out, "PV systems are not plug and play."

For years, my favorite book on solar electric systems has been *The New Solar Electric Home* by Joel Davidson. It presents a lot of technical information in a way that is amazingly comprehensible and was recently updated. Unfortunately, most of the rest of the books on solar electricity seem to have been penned by engineers or tech-heads for whom writing is not their strength. There is at least one exception, though, a book from Johnny Weiss and his colleagues at the nonprofit organization Solar Energy International in Carbondale, Colorado, that might be useful to you: *Photovoltaics: Design and Installation Manual*. This book is a manual for individuals who want to size, design, and install solar electric systems. It is very well-written and full of good information. It should bring you up to speed on the subject so that you can size and design your own system and purchase its components with confidence. Who knows, after

reading it — and taking a workshop on the subject from SEI, the Solar Living Institute in California, or the Midwest Renewable Energy Association in Wisconsin — you might want to install the system yourself!

After studying solar electricity in more detail to learn your options, you can move to the next step: specifying the components of your system and ordering them. Be very careful when buying system components yourself. Be certain that you are working with a very knowledgeable dealer who really knows what he or she is talking about and offers solid technical support. Look for a supplier who's been around for a long time. And look for one who will sell you what you need, not what they have in surplus.

In recent years, there's been an onslaught of Internet renewable energy suppliers. Some of them apparently operate from remote sites; they have no inventory, so everything must be shipped from the manufacturers. They typically offer little, if any, technical support, lack expertise, and may have lousy return policies. They may even charge you to replace items that they shouldn't have sold you in the first place.

As a starter, I recommend that you log on to Solatron Technologies' website (<www.solaronsale.com>) and read their piece titled "Six Important Questions to Ask before Choosing an Alternative Energy Dealer." (As a side note, I've purchased PV modules, Water Miser battery caps, and an inverter through this company — and even sold a used inverter through their website — and have found their service and products to be exceptional. Moreover, their website is one of the most secure sites from which you can order. End of free advertisement.)

Another highly reputable supplier is Real Goods. They've got excellent, highly knowledgeable people who can help you size and select components.

Other online suppliers provide top-notch service and products, too, but you need to be careful when shopping for an online supplier. Look through *Home Power* and *Solar Today* magazines. Check out each company's website, its return policies, its expertise and level of technical support, and other aspects of their business. Does the company actually have a location or are they operating from someone's home? Ask friends who may have dealt with online dealers for recommendations.

Buying Solar Panels

When buying PV modules, you'll find that you have quite a lot of options; over a half-dozen manufacturers produce several different sizes of modules. Fortunately, they're all pretty good, so it is hard to go wrong.

Given this, what criteria do you use to select a PV module?

If you are working with a local installer, he or she may have a favorite company he or she has had good luck with. In fact, most local installers are distributors for one or two of the major PV manufacturers. Call several local suppliers to see what each one offers.

If you want more options and want to save some money, you can contact a reputable online source. Experienced and knowledgeable sales people may be able to give you sound advice on which panels will work best for you. Be sure to ask for sale items, too. You can often obtain some amazing deals this way. Also, be sure to ask if their companies offer any solar kits. Solar kits are complete packages that include the modules, racks, inverters, controllers, and everything else you'll need. Kits usually include whatever type of module the supplier can order in bulk at a deep discount, which they pass on to you.

When it comes to studying your options, I found ETA Engineering's website (<www.engineering.com>) very useful. They provide information on modules from six different manufacturers (although there are a few important manufacturers like BP Solar missing from the list). ETA's descriptions of the various PV modules that they sell include tables that list key information you need to know when purchasing one, including power output, maximum power voltage, maximum power current, cell efficiency, and physical dimensions. You can use this information to compare modules from different manufacturers. (I'll fill you in on this shortly.)

One criterion many solar buyers use when comparing modules from different manufacturers is the cost per watt. To determine this, simply divide the cost of a module by its maximum power output. The maximum power output is the maximum wattage under standard test conditions (1,000 watts per square meter of irradiance at 25°C or 77°F cell temperature). Sharp's 165-watt panel, for instance, produces 165 watts under standard test conditions and costs $639 through ETA

A Short History of PV Cells

Although PVs are generally thought of as a modern invention, they were discovered a long time ago. In fact, they've been around for more than 100 years, according to John Perlin author of several excellent books on the history of solar energy, including *From Space to Earth: The Story of Solar Electricity.*

The very first cell was made by an American inventor, E. E. Fritts, from selenium with a transparent gold foil layer on top and a metal backing. When struck by light, this primitive cell produced a tiny electrical current. Fritts called his device a "solar battery." This mysterious invention stirred considerable controversy, though. Many prominent engineers and scientists at the time proclaimed that it violated the laws of physics. How could it make energy without burning a fuel?

Although Fritts is credited with developing the first solar cell, it turns out that a Frenchman, the experimental physicist Edmond Becquerel, had made one in 1839 out of two brass plates immersed in a liquid. When exposed to sunlight, this unusual contraption produced an electrical current.

Today, most commercial PV modules are made from silicon, though new and more efficient designs made from materials with space-age sounding names are in the works.

at this writing (December, 2004). The cost per watt is $3.87. Kyocera's 125-watt PV module sells for $489 or about $3.91 per watt. These are good prices, by the way, although you can sometimes purchase PV modules on the Internet for as low as $2.08 per peak watt — so shop around!

While you're shopping around, be sure to check out the manufacturers' warranties. The ETA site lists this for the modules they sell. Sharp and Kyocera offer a 25-year warranty on their modules; Astropower offers a 20-year warranty. Most manufacturer warranties fall within this range.

Finally, I recommend that you also check out peak voltage very carefully, especially if you live in a hot, sunny area. PV modules that operate below 16.5 peak operating volts tend not to perform as well in hot climates as higher voltage panels. "Be wary of suppliers who do not post a solar module's peak operating voltage," write the folks at <www.solaronsale.com.> "Before buying any panel," they add, "be sure to ask what the peak or maximum power voltage (not the open circuit voltage) is for each panel." Always look for panels that operate at 16.5 or higher (for 12 volt panels) or 33 volts or higher (for 24 volt panels) for best performance in hot weather.

Types of PV Modules

To help you in your selection of PV modules, let me tell you a bit about the types of silicon cells that are on the market today and the pros and cons of each. Solar electric cells come in three basic varieties, all made from silicon.

The first commercial solar cell produced was the single crystal cell. These are made from a pure ingot of silicon — a long solid cylinder that was then sliced into thin wafers.

Unfortunately, producing pure silicon ingots required lots of energy and cutting the ingot into thin wafers produced lots of waste. The process was not only expensive; but wasteful; however, single crystal solar cells boast the highest efficiency of all three solar cells on the market today. They are about 15 percent efficient — that is, they convert about 15 percent of the sunlight energy striking them into electricity.

Single crystal cells are still manufactured today, but they're not as commonly used in

Fig. 7-11: Polycrystalline Solar Electric cells: (a) in production, (b) finished cell, and (c) modules in solar array.

commercial PV production as their newer, less pure cousin, the polycrystalline cell (Figure 7-11). Polycrystalline cells are so named because they consist of numerous silicon crystals of varying size. They're beautiful to behold, but slightly less efficient than single crystal models, about 12 percent, compared to 15 percent. However, because they require less energy to manufacture, they are cheaper. Lower production costs easily outweigh their lower efficiency. By and large, they're the main type of solar cell in use today.

Silicon solar cells can also be produced by depositing thin layers of silicon on a thin metal backing, producing long ribbons. This technology is known as amorphous silicon. It uses less energy, less silicon, and is less expensive than either the single crystal or polycrystalline cells.

Amorphous or thin film silicon technology was first used to create tiny solar cells for calculators and watches. Although this technique is less expensive than crystalline cell production techniques, the very first thin film materials were damaged by direct sunlight and had very low conversion efficiencies — only about five percent.

In the years that followed the introduction of thin film solar materials, however, manufacturers have found ways to layer thin film materials to boost efficiency to about eight percent and to make this material resistant to photodegradation. Today, thanks to this research, amorphous silicon is being used to produce solar cells and solar modules by a company called UniSolar. UniSolar produces amorphous silicon in long rolls with sticky backing that can be applied to metal roofing (Figure 7-12a). UniSolar is also using its thin-film process to create solar cells incorporated in roof shingles, as in 7-12b, although

a

b

Fig. 7-12: Solar Roofing. Amorphous silicon ribbons can be used to make (a) long rolls of material that can be applied to standing seam metal roofing and (b) solar shingles. Both are forms of building-integrated photovoltaics.

this product is not ready for prime time, according to SEI's Johnny Weiss. When perfected, this amazing product will protect homes from the weather while generating electrical energy (Figure 7-12b).

In recent years, thin coats of amorphous silicon have even been sprayed on glass, creating solar electric window glass that produces electricity from sunlight. This application is ideal for skylights and glass canopies, for example, over gas pumps at gas stations. It is being used in large commercial buildings, too. British Petroleum, the third largest oil company in the world, which has made a major commitment to renewable energy and currently manufactures BP solar modules, has installed solar electricity canopies in numerous gas stations throughout the world.

Thin film glass and solar roofing materials are called building-integrated photovoltaics. Although you may want to consider solar roof materials, if you are thinking about installing solar electricity and reroofing your home, a coated glass skylight is probably not going to be an affordable option just yet.

Buying an Inverter

Inverters are a key component of virtually all residential solar electric systems. They come in many shapes, sizes, and prices. When purchasing an inverter from a local supplier who's also going to install the system, your choices may be relatively limited. They typically have inverters they like and therefore will probably make a recommendation that fits your needs.

Even though a local supplier/installer will do the thinking for you, you should still understand something about inverters, so they don't supply you with a model that doesn't work for you.

First and foremost, you need to determine whether you need an inverter for a grid-connected or stand-alone system.

Second, when selecting an inverter, be sure that its voltage corresponds to the voltage of your system. As noted earlier, solar electric systems are either 12-, 24-, or 48-volts (the most common are 24- and 48-volt systems; 12-volt systems are common in small applications such as cabins or summer cottages). This means that the panels produce 12-, 24-, or 48-volt electricity; the inverter boosts the voltage to 120 standard household current. So remember, the inverter you buy must fit your system voltage. A 12-volt inverter won't work in a 24-volt system.

The next selection criterion is the wave output form. Here, you will find two basic options: modified sine wave or pure sine wave model. Basically, output wave form tells you how pure the electricity is. Sine wave is purer than modified sine wave. It is equivalent to the electricity you buy from the electrical grid, without the hassles of blackouts, brownouts, and dangerous power surges!

Sine wave is also more expensive.

Unless money is a problem, I strongly recommend that you purchase a sine wave inverter, not a modified sine wave inverter. Sine wave inverters produce "cleaner" AC electricity, so they tend to work much better with modern electronic equipment. In fact, some of the newest electronic equipment — like most of the energy- and water-efficient front-loading washing machines — won't operate on modified sine wave electricity. The sensitive computers that run these washing machine just plain won't work! Some laser printers apparently also have a problem with modified sine wave electricity, as do some cheaper battery tool chargers. Furthermore, and here's an important thing, I found that electronic equipment like TVs and stereos give off a rather annoying high-pitched buzz when they're operating on modified sine wave electricity.

When selecting an inverter, you will also need to check out three additional factors: output power, surge rating, and efficiency. Let's start with output power.

Output power is a measure that tells you how many watts the unit can produce on a continuous basis. The Xantrex RS3000 inverter, for instance, produces 3,000 watts of continuous power, which means it will be able

Modified Sine Wave Inverters

Modified sine wave inverters are much cheaper than true sine wave inverters, and work in many applications. If your electronic arsenal is minimal and your bank account is low, a modified sine wave inverter will probably work just fine. As noted in the text, most electronic devices and appliances, including TVs, lights, stereos, computers, inkjet printers, power tools, and standard washing machines run well on modified sine wave electricity.

Modified sine wave inverters come in two varieties: high-frequency conversion units and low-frequency (60 hertz) conversion units. High-frequency units are much cheaper and much lighter than low-frequency models. A typical 2,000-watt high frequency inverter, for example, will cost 2 to 5 times less than a low-frequency model and may weigh 13 pounds versus 50 pounds.

But don't be fooled by cost and weight into buying a high-frequency inverter for your home. You get what you pay for. High-frequency inverters are generally manufactured overseas in Taiwan, China, and other countries. They're sometimes dumped on the US market by companies going bankrupt, so servicing a defective model can be difficult.

Low-frequency modified sine wave inverters are typically produced in North America by fairly reliable manufacturers like Xantrex (formerly Trace Engineering). These inverters cost more and weigh a lot more, but they are a much better product. In addition, these inverters typically have a much higher surge capacity, meaning they can produce greater surges of power needed to start power tools, dishwashers, washing machines, and the like.

to power a microwave using 1,200 watts, an electric hair dryer using 1,200 watts, and many other smaller loads simultaneously without problem. The Sunny Boy 2500U, made in Germany but available in the US, produces 2,500 watts of continuous power, still quite a lot for most households (that's the size inverter I have in my house and we rarely, if ever, reach this level).

Surge rating is the wattage an inverter can put out over a short period, usually around five seconds. The Xantrex RS3000 inverter has a 7,500-watt surge power rating (60 amps). That means it can produce a surge of power up to 7,500 watts. Why is this important?

Many appliances like washing machines, refrigerators, and power tools like table saws require a surge of power when first turned on. It's required to get the ball rolling, so to speak — to start parts moving, overcoming inertia. Typically, these devices only need this surge power for a tiny fraction of a second, but without it, the tool won't start! (Kind of like many people who need their morning coffee to get going.)

Next is efficiency.

Inverters consume energy to change DC to AC and to boost voltage. Look for models with the highest efficiency possible. The Xantrex RS3000 has a peak efficiency of 90 percent. The Sunny Boy 2500U is 93 to 94.4 percent efficient.

If you are going to have a battery bank you also need to see whether the unit you are interested in contains a battery charger. Not all sine wave and modified sine wave inverters have the additional circuitry needed to charge batteries from an external AC source (a generator or utility power, for example). Even if you are not planning on installing a battery bank, you may want to purchase an inverter with a battery charger just in case you decide to add battery backup or go off-grid.

You should also check into noise, especially if the inverter is going to be installed inside your home. Be sure to ask about this feature upfront, and, if possible, ask to see a model you are considering in operation to be sure it's quiet. My Trace inverter, now manufactured by Xantrex, is located inside my home. The manufacturer describes it as quiet, but the unit emits a loud and annoying buzz. (If that's their notion of quiet, they must be deaf.) The first six months after I moved in, it drove me nuts, though now I'm used to it. The Sunny Boy inverters define the word quiet.

There are other things to look for as well, for example, ease of programming, the type of cooling system in the inverter, and search mode power consumption. My first Trace inverter (DR2424, modified sine wave) was a dream when it came to programming: all of the controls were manual. I simply adjusted a dial to change the settings and I was done. My new Trace PS2524, a sine wave inverter that works wonderfully in all respects except for programming, is a nightmare. I have found the digital programming to be virtually impenetrable; the instructions don't help a whole lot, either. You pretty much have to be a genius to figure them out! So find out in advance, how easy it is to change settings, and don't rely on the biased view of a salesperson or knowledgeable tech person. Ask friends or dealers/installers for their opinions or, better yet, have them show you.

Inverters produce heat and need to be cooled. Ideally, you want an inverter that cools itself passively rather than an inverter that requires a fan, which consumes energy.

Last, but certainly not least, is the power consumption under search mode. Search mode is an operation that lets your inverter turn off completely when there are no active loads in your home — no devices or appliances drawing power. To stay on the alert, though, inverters send out tiny pulses of electricity that search for a load (an open circuit). If you switch on an appliance, the system immediately kicks into gear and starts supplying electricity to meet the demand.

The search mode saves energy because it allows the inverter to shut down and go to sleep. During the day that means that all of the electricity you are producing either goes on the grid, as in a grid-connected system, or goes into your batteries, in a stand-alone system. Search mode consumption of under 0.5 amps is good.

Be sure when buying an inverter that the supplier, be it an Internet supplier or a local supplier, takes the time to determine which inverter is the correct choice for you. Ask lots of questions. According to the folks at <www.solaronsale.com>, "Too many inverters are sold to customers by dealers that fail to ask the customer what the inverter is being used for, which is no different than selling someone a pair of shoes without asking what size he wears." They add, "Four of ten inverters sold in the United States are returned to the vendor due to poor manufacturing quality or due to a lack of technical support before or after the sale!" (Solaronsale.com tests each inverter before it is shipped to avoid this problem.) Furthermore, "a full 20 percent of inverters that are purchased on the Internet without pre-sale technical support will actually cause irreversible damage to the appliance that is plugged into it."

Supplying 240-Volt Electricity

Many homes require 240-volt electricity, for example, to operate appliances such as electric clothes dryers and electric stoves. As a general rule, you should try to avoid such appliances, not because a solar system cannot be designed to take care of them, but because they use lots of electricity and you'll need many PV modules to supply them.

If you must have 240-volt AC electricity, don't despair. All you need to do is purchase and install a step-up transformer such as the Xantrex/Trace T-240. This unit takes 120-volt AC electricity in and steps it up to 240-volt AC electricity. Whatever you do, don't wire two 120-volt inverters together in series to double your voltage. You'll burn out both units instantaneously!

Buying Batteries

If you are going to install a grid-connected solar electric system with a battery bank or a stand-alone system you'll need batteries. The more energy your home consumes and the longer the cloudy spells, the more batteries you'll need. (As a friendly reminder: because batteries are expensive and require periodic maintenance, be sure to cut your electrical demand through efficiency and other measures first. Efficiency will save you a fortune on panels and batteries!)

Most batteries used in solar electric systems are 6-volt, deep-cycle lead acid batteries. Trojan L-16s have been the mainstay of the solar electric industry for years, but their dominance in the battery market has been challenged in recent years by Surrette Batteries, among others (Figure 7-13).

Batteries are wired in a combination of series and parallel circuits to produce 12-, 24-, and 48- volt systems. As you will soon see, batteries are rated by their capacity to store electricity. The common measure for battery storage is amp-hours. An amp-hour is one amp of current flowing for one hour. Just to give you an idea of what you will be looking for, a battery in a solar electric system should probably store over 350 amp-hours of electricity to be useful.

When shopping for batteries, it's hard to go wrong. Most deep-cycle lead acid batteries manufactured for solar systems are pretty good. But be sure to check out the storage capacity and manufacturer warranties first.

Surrette S460s come with a seven-year warranty. The manufacturer will replace the battery free of charge for the first two years if it fails during that period. After that time period, the manufacturer will replace it at a pro-rated value.

Although lead acid batteries are less efficient than some of the newer battery technologies on the market today, old batteries are recycled. In fact, nearly 100 percent of the lead from used batteries makes its way back into the production cycle.

Fig. 7-13: Lead Acid Batteries. The Surrette battery shown here is an excellent choice for a solar electric system.

Solar electric systems can run on ordinary car batteries, but not for long. Car batteries are not designed for deep discharging — drawing off lots of power. They're designed to crank out tons of amps to start a car, but they're the rabbits of the battery world. What you need is a tortoise, a battery that can give you all it has for long periods of time. No sprinters need apply.

So be sure not to make the mistake of running a solar electric system on car batteries. It is a waste of your time and money.

Also, be sure not to purchase marine deep-cycle batteries. They are only slightly better than car batteries. You'd be lucky to get more than a year or two of service out of this type of battery in a stand-alone solar electric system. Both car and marine batteries are manufactured to optimize cranking power, that is, they are manufactured with thin plates to provide a surge of power to start engines. Thin plates, however, are damaged by the deep discharges that typically occur in solar electric systems.

Golf cart and forklift batteries make a better choice, as they contain many thick lead plates capable of undergoing deep discharges day after day. (Remember: they need to be recharged at night!) A properly maintained golf cart battery could last three to five years in a stand-alone solar electric system. If you can get them and get them cheaply, this might be a viable option. Bear in mind, however, that the typical golf cart battery only stores about two-thirds of the electricity of a standard deep-cycle battery designed for solar electric systems.

Far better are the batteries manufactured specifically for renewable energy (RE) systems by companies like Surrette and Trojan. These batteries have thicker plates that can withstand deeper and more frequent deep discharges than the standard golf cart battery. As a result, they have longer life expectancies — they'll last 6 to 20 years.

How long an RE system battery can last depends on how often it is deep discharged and how well you take care of it. Generally, the more often a battery is deep discharged, the shorter its lifespan. (They'll typically withstand 750 to 1,000 deep discharges before needing replacement.) If battery acid levels are not maintained by periodically adding distilled water or if the batteries are not periodically equalized, expect a much shorter lifespan. Also, if batteries are kept in a cold place, they'll not function optimally. They lose capacity when cold, according to Johnny Weiss.

Battery terminals need to be cleaned at least once a year, too. If they're not kept free of corrosion, they'll not perform well. While you are at it, you should also be certain to keep the batteries clean. Wipe them off regularly for optimal performance. I like to spray the terminals with a corrosion-resisting product like Permatex's Battery Protector and Sealer, sold in the automotive department of hardware stores.

Lead acid batteries designed for solar systems are your best bet. Lead acid batteries contain sulfuric acid (a 30 percent solution). Although they work well if well taken care of, lead acid batteries produce hydrogen gas when they're being charged, whether by a solar array, a back-up generator, or grid power. They also produce a corrosive acid mist. They need to be installed in a well-ventilated area away from people and sources of combustion.

Whatever you do, don't buy used batteries. According to Richard Perez of *Home Power* magazine, used batteries are probably abused. Most of the people he knows who have installed used batteries ended up being sorry they did. To learn more about battery maintenance, I strongly recommend that you check out the video *An Introduction to Storage Batteries for Renewable Energy Systems with Richard Perez* produced by Scott Andrews.

Sizing Your Battery Bank

Most professional installers design stand-alone solar electric systems with about three to five days' backup. That is to say, they size the battery bank so that it can supply your needs for three to five cloudy days. Generally, the sunnier climate, the fewer batteries you will need. That said, I think a three-to-five cloudy-day storage capacity is best for most climates. While creating a more substantial storage capacity may give homeowners greater peace of mind, few beginners realize that PV modules produce electricity in cloudy weather, although at a reduced rate. The system doesn't go dead the minute a few clouds block the sun.

To determine how many batteries are needed to provide sufficient backup, you'll need to run through some fairly complicated calculations that require computing your household's average daily consumption of electricity in amp-hours.

Suppliers should be able to help you determine your needs, especially if they have worked with you to size your solar electric system. They'll also help you determine how many amp-hours of electricity you'll need to store in your battery system to ensure that you can achieve the desired number of days of autonomy.

Once you determine the number of amp-hours, all you have to do is to select a battery you like. Next, divide its storage capacity in amp-hours (minus its discharge limit — how deeply it can be discharged) into the total amp-hours of electricity you need to get by for three days. This tells you the number of batteries you'll need in your system. For example, let's say you need 3,500 amp-hours of electricity to provide three days of back-up power. The Surrette S460 batteries you are thinking about buying store 350 amp-hours of electricity each (at 6-volt DC). If they can be discharged by 80 percent, they effectively supply about 280 amp-hours each. To determine how many Surrette S460s you will need, simply divide 3,500 amp-hours by 280 amp-hours, which gives you 12.5 batteries.

Other Types of Batteries

Most batteries used in solar electric systems are 6-volt, deep-cycle lead acid batteries.

However, they're not the only batteries in use today. Nickel cadmium and nickel iron batteries can also be used. These batteries can be deep discharged many more times than lead acid batteries and therefore last a lot longer. Unfortunately, they don't store as much electricity as the standard lead acid battery and cost a heck of lot more. They're also not widely available.

Another type of battery that is useful in certain applications is the sealed battery. (They're also called captive electrolyte batteries for reasons that will be clear shortly.) To learn more about them, you may want to read the sidebar on this page.

Two types of "sealed" batteries are currently available: absorbent glass mat (AGM) batteries and gel cell batteries.

In absorbent glass mat batteries, thin absorbent fiberglass mats are placed between the lead plates to immobilize the acid. Furthermore, the mat is a microporous meshwork that creates tiny pockets that capture hydrogen and oxygen gases given off by the battery during charging. The gases recombine in these pockets, forming water. (As a side note, AGM batteries tend to tolerate overcharging a bit more than gel cell batteries.)

In gel batteries, the lead plates are separated by cavities, as they are in a standard lead acid battery. However, the electrolyte (sulfuric acid) is in a gel state, not a liquid. The electrolyte is gelled by the addition of a small amount of silica gel, which turns the electrolyte into a material much like hardened Jell-O.

Sealed batteries are maintenance-free, which means they don't need to be filled with water or equalized. This saves lots of time and hassle and makes them a good choice for very remote locations where routine maintenance is unlikely, according to *Photovoltaics: Design and Installation Manual* by Solar Energy International.

Sealed batteries are also spill-proof. The gel cell batteries won't even leak if the battery casing is broken (a rare occurrence).

Because of their design, sealed batteries charge faster than standard lead acid batteries.

Sealed Battery — A Misnomer?

Sealed batteries are so labeled because they have no caps and you never have to fill them or fuss with the electrolyte. They also release no explosive or toxic gases like conventional lead acid batteries. Basically, a sealed battery is filled with electrolyte at the factory, fully charged, sealed, and then shipped. Because they are sealed, they're easy to handle and ship without fear of spillage. A typical lead acid battery, on the other hand, must be shipped dry and filled with electrolyte (30 percent sulfuric acid) on arrival.

The truth be known, sealed batteries are not totally sealed. Each battery contains a pressure relief valve that blows if a battery is accidentally overcharged. A better term for sealed batteries would therefore be valve regulated lead acid batteries (VRLA). The valve keeps the battery from exploding. Once the valve has blown, though, the battery is done for, shot, kaput, dead.

Sealed batteries also release no explosive or toxic gases like conventional lead acid batteries. In addition, sealed batteries are much more tolerant of low temperatures than lead acid batteries. They can even tolerate occasional freezing, although this is not recommended.

Sealed batteries are commonly used for storing electricity in solar electric and wind generating systems on sailboats and RVs where the rocking motion would spill the sulfuric acid of flooded lead acid batteries, and lose electricity where space is limited and batteries are frequently crammed into out-of-the way locations. They also have a lower rate of self-discharge, which means they discharge more slowly than conventional lead acid batteries.

Sealed batteries can be used for grid-tied systems with battery backup. In such instances, the batteries are typically kept at a full state of charge (they're regularly recharged by the solar array and the electrical grid). Unfortunately, sealed gel batteries are much more expensive than flooded lead acid batteries. They also typically store less electricity and have a shorter lifespan than the more commonly used lead acid battery. Steven Strong, solar electricity expert and author of *The Solar Electric House*, says, "They should be considered for all photovoltaic applications, especially those where site access for regular periodic maintenance is impractical." Frankly, I'm no expert in this area, but I wouldn't recommend them for most home systems.

Buying a Solar Electric Kit

If all of this seems like too much work, you might consider buying a system package. As noted earlier, many suppliers offer packages that include all of the components you will need for grid-connected and stand-alone systems. Solatron Technologies (<www.solaronsale.com>), mentioned earlier, for instance, offers seven different grid-connected systems that provide different amounts of energy. The kits include PV modules, an inverter, disconnect switches, and rack and mounting hardware. Their 1.9 kilowatt system purchased separately would cost nearly $15,000. The kit runs for a little over $10,000!

LOCATING A RELIABLE CONTRACTOR

To install a solar electric system you will need equipment, but also a permit in many locations. It's a good idea to check out permit requirements *before* you order any equipment. A local supplier/installer should be able to help you with this.

While you are at it, be sure to check out financial incentives, too, before you order your equipment. They may come with some restrictions imposed by local utilities or by the state government that will affect the size of the system you can install, the type of equipment, and the installer.

To locate a reliable installer, it's always good to ask around. Talk to people who have had systems installed recently. Get their advice on companies listed in the phone book or ask for references when talking to local suppliers/installers.

Professional credentials are one indication of a PV dealer's knowledge and qualifications, so be sure to ask what courses they've taken, what certifications they've earned, and what licenses they've received.

Experience is also important. Be sure to find out how long they've been in the business and how many systems like yours they've installed. Ask to see the systems and talk to the owners.

Service is important, too. Be sure they will be there to take care of your system if you have any problems with it. Find out what services your supplier/installer will provide. Also, will your installer provide any perform-ance guarantees? What are the warranties offered by the manufacturers of the compo-nents of your system?

Finally, be sure to get a cost estimate up front, and ask that the dealer itemize all aspects so there are no surprises. "Consider having a dealer supply, install, and warrant your sys-tem. Go for the full-service approach," advises Johnny Weiss.

WHY INSTALL SOLAR ELECTRICITY?

Solar electric systems are a great source of clean, reliable electricity. Solar electricity can be stored in battery banks for use at night or on cloudy days. Or it can be "stored" on the electrical grid. Remember, even though initial costs may be high, running from $5,000 to $20,000 or more, the fuel (sunlight) is free and abundant and clean and it's not under the control of some powerful multinational cor-poration.

Solar electric systems require minimal maintenance, too, unless batteries are included in the mix. And solar electric systems are a relatively environmentally benign source of energy. In addition, they operate quietly, unless you need considerable backup from a generator.

Solar electric systems are modular, which means that you can install them incremen-tally. You can start small and expand as your finances permit.

Solar electricity, like other technologies discussed in this book, provides energy inde-pendence. No matter whether you live in a busy city or a sleepy town or a remote rural area, solar electricity can meet your needs, and help replace waning supplies of oil and natural gas.

CHAPTER 8

WIND POWER

MEETING YOUR NEEDS FOR ELECTRICITY

In November 2004, I took a group of students in my "Introduction to Sustainable Development" course at Colorado College to a coal-fired power plant in Denver, Colorado. After trudging through the hot, noisy, and dangerous facility, listening to the spiel on the benefits of coal, we hopped in our vans and drove north to Wyoming to visit a wind farm.

The wind farm was perched on a plateau visible from the interstate. As we drove onto the property, the giant white wind machines came into full view. Buffalo grazed around the base of their massive towers, munching on the dried grasses (Figure 8-1). My students were awestruck when we got out of the vans and stood at the base of these massive, quiet machines towering 260 feet above our heads.

MATT REUER

Fig. 8-1: These contented bison graze around the base of the gigantic wind machines at the Ponnequin Wind Farm in southern Wyoming, demonstrating that wind energy can be coupled with other commercial activities, notably farming and ranching, providing dual income for landowners.

As I looked around, I could see smiles on my students' faces. The contrast between the noisy, dirty coal-fired power plant fed by huge piles of coal shipped in from hundreds of miles away, and the hushed efficiency of the wind farm fed by an abundant, clean, and free renewable resource was just too much for them. "Wow," was about all they could say. "This is amazing!"

I was pretty amazed, too. It was my first up-close encounter with gargantuan commercial wind generators. Watching the shadows of the turning blades was indescribable — "way cool," as one of my young students remarked. I don't know how I could improve on his assessment.

This chapter is not about large commercial wind systems, but rather about smaller systems, those that generate electricity for individual homes, businesses, farms, and ranches. This chapter should help you decide whether wind is for you and if you have sufficient resources to make it work.

IS WIND POWER IN YOUR FUTURE?

Wind isn't for everyone. In fact, if you live in a city or town, chances are wind power is very likely not going to be an option for you. Although the wind blows in cities and suburbs, and sometimes blows quite fiercely, in heavily populated built-up environments, wind flows are often pretty turbulent at the heights where wind generators are located. That is to say, although the wind blows, it doesn't flow smoothly. It can't. There are too many obstructions — trees and buildings — that cause wind turbulence. Turbulence is pure hell on wind machines, viciously tearing many of the lighter-weight models.

Even if turbulence wasn't a problem, there's often not enough room in urban and suburban neighborhoods to install wind generators. And even if there is room, chances are neighbors would complain, saying the wind machine is unsightly. Or city officials might tell you that wind machines violate height ordinances.

Wind power is primarily useful as a source of electrical energy in rural areas on lots of one acre or more, but only in places where there are no ordinances prohibiting installation of a wind machine. Even though that limits the potential for residential wind energy, there are still plenty of suitable sites. According to *Small Wind Electric Systems* published by the US Department of Energy, "Twenty-one million homes in the United States are built on one-acre and larger sites." About ten percent of the US population could theoretically take advantage of wind energy. But that number may be a little smaller. Wind power will work only for those who live in rural areas with sufficient wind resources. (Be sure to check with local authorities and neighbors, if any, to be certain you're not going to have a problem.)

If you live in a city or town, though, don't be dismayed. You can still power your home with wind energy by buying wind power from your local utility. I'll explain how at the end of this chapter.

WIND POWER: A BRIEF HISTORY

Unbeknownst to many, winds are generated by solar energy. For example, in coastal areas offshore winds are created by sunlight warming nearby land masses. Hot air, created when sunlight strikes the land, rises. Cool air from nearby water bodies — large lakes or the oceans — rushes in to fill the gap, creating winds.

Even large air movements across entire continents are driven by the differential heating of the Earth's surface. During the winter, for instance, the poles are cooler than the equator. Hot air rises in the equator and cooler air from the poles moves down to replace it. The result is that huge Arctic air masses (storms) sweep across the continent, bringing cold air as far south as southern Florida.

Humans have tapped the power of wind energy for centuries, first to power sailing vessels and later to grind grain and pump water. The very first wind generators were believed to be used in Persia in the 5th century AD. Wind machines spread from the Middle East to Europe in the 12th century AD. From Europe wind technology spread to North America; by the late 1800s, there were thousands of wind machines in Europe and North America in rural settings. From the late 1880s to the early 1900s, more than eight million windmills, most of which were used to pump water for livestock, were installed in the United States, according to

the National Renewable Energy Laboratory (Figure 8-2).

In the 1920s, however, American cities began to electrify thanks to the pioneering work of Nikola Tesla, the brilliant scientist who "invented" alternating current electricity. At first, the electricity that powered cities came from centralized power plants that burned coal. Electric lines strung here and there like spider webs throughout cities delivered electricity to homes, offices, and factories. By the

DAN CHIRAS

Fig. 8 2: This old wind machine, which is still functional today, was once a common sight on the plains of North America, where it was used to pump water for livestock. Its larger cousin, which produces electricity in the background, is now becoming a much more common sight.

From the late 1880s to the early 1900s, more than eight million wind turbines were installed in the United States, most of which were used to pump water for livestock.

end of the 1920s, North American cities were completely electrified. Oil lamps were a thing of the past. But things were quite different in rural areas. There were no central power plants to deliver electricity. Small wind turbines were the sole source of electricity on farms.

The US government then set its sights on rural areas, launching the Rural Electrification Program. With this ambitious program, wind power entered into a period of steady decline. It did not die out completely, though. Many small windmills continued to pump water to fill stock tanks on the Great Plains, and some are even working today. (Some areas of the Midwest weren't electrified until the 1970s.)

Then came the 1970s and oil shortages. Although the crises were artificial, they fueled tremendous interest in energy self-sufficiency, conservation, and renewable energy. Wind benefited greatly, even though it was largely liquid fuel supplies that were threatened by the oil embargoes of the 1970s. By the early 1980s, there were 80 companies manufacturing wind machines in the United States, including large commercial generators and smaller household-sized units. During this exciting period, several utility companies in California built large wind farms to provide electricity to residents in San Francisco.

Unfortunately, early wind machines were plagued with mechanical problems and frequent breakdowns. Large commercial wind machines, for example, could only be counted on 60 percent of the time. They were broken down and out of service the rest of the time.

The early models were also fairly inefficient. These technological problems, combined with a growing lack of concern over achieving energy independence, caused wind power to decline. Sullied by wind energy's bad reputation, many people lost interest in this important technology, and many people today continue to view wind power with undeserved skepticism.

Convinced of wind's importance, several manufacturers began to tackle the technological problems that arose in the 1970s and early 1980s and greatly improved their products. Thanks to their efforts, and the work of the National Renewable Energy Lab in Golden, Colorado, the efficiency of large commercial wind machines increased, climbing two or three times above efficiencies achieved in the 1970s and early 1980s. Reliability increased as well, climbing from 60 percent to an astounding 97 to 99 percent. Small wind generator manufacturers also improved the design of their machines, simplifying them and getting rid of parts, like the brushes, that required frequent replacement. These improvements have created a resurgence in wind power production. Today, wind power is the fastest growing source of energy in the world!

UNDERSTANDING WIND GENERATORS

Wind generators go by several names: wind turbines, wind machines, and wind plants. All residential wind generators large and small have the same three basic components: (1) a blade assembly, commonly referred to as a rotor, that turns in the wind; (2) a shaft that connects to the rotor and rotates when the blades turn; and (3) a generator, a device that produces electricity (Figure 8-3).

Wind machines exist in two basic varieties: horizontal axis units and vertical axis units, as shown in Figure 8-4. Horizontal axis units are the most widely used in household-sized wind turbines. Vertical axis wind machines, now making a slow comeback, have blades that resemble a big egg beater. When wind strikes the blades, they turn around a vertical shaft.

Because horizontal-axis wind machines are the main players in home wind energy systems, we'll focus our attention on them. From this point on, when I use the term wind machine, I'll be referring to horizontal-axis

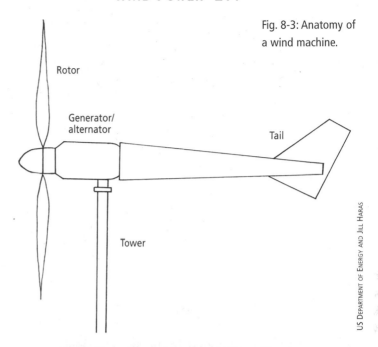

Fig. 8-3: Anatomy of a wind machine.

Rotor

Generator/ alternator

Tail

Tower

US DEPARTMENT OF ENERGY AND JILL HARAS

AFRICAN WIND POWER

DAVID SIEDBAND

Fig. 8-4: Two types of wind machine are in use today: the horizontal axis machine shown on the left, and the much less common vertical axis machine on the right.

machines. The machines we'll be studying are typically used to provide back-up power or to supply enough electrical energy to power an entire home, small business, or farm.

A horizontal-axis wind machine is equipped with two or three blades, three being the most widely used and most desirable: the use of three blades results in less wear and tear on the generator in shifting winds and results in more reliable wind turbines. Blades are typically made of a highly durable plastic, fiberglass, or wood with a urethane coating and polyurethane tape to protect the leading edge of the blade from wear.

AC Wind Machine

DC electricity is generated by many household wind machines. But DC electricity doesn't travel well. Voltage drops quickly over distance, rendering a source ineffective. Unfortunately, the electricity generated by wind machines mounted on tall towers must travel long distances to reach battery banks. To avoid line loss, installers use costly, large diameter (low gauge) electrical cable.

Several manufacturers also produce wind machines that generate 120-volt or 240-volt AC electricity. The higher voltage AC current they produce is able to travel over great distances without losing power. AC power can be used to power household appliances, but excess AC electricity can be diverted to the grid. Excess can also be stored in batteries. However, to be stored in batteries, AC electricity must first be converted to DC power. This is achieved by installing a bank of diodes in the system.

The blades of a wind machine and the central hub to which they are attached are called the rotor. This is the "collector" of the wind machine.

The rotors of wind machines capture kinetic energy from the wind and convert it into rotating mechanical energy, notably a spinning shaft. The spinning shaft is attached to the generator. It converts mechanical energy into electrical energy.

Several types of generators are found in household-sized wind machines. The most common is the permanent magnet alternator. When the shaft of a wind machine with a permanent alternator spins, it causes a component called the armature inside the generator to spin. The armature consists of a mass of tightly coiled copper wire. It spins inside a magnetic field. If you remember your high school physics, moving an electrical coil through a magnetic field creates an electrical current in the wires.

DC current produced by a wind generator is carried away by electrical wires. They deliver the electricity to a device known as an inverter. Inverters convert DC current to AC current. They also boost the voltage from 12, 24, or 48 volts, produced by wind generators to 120 volts, the required voltage for most household appliances and electronic devices. (You can read more about inverters in Chapter 7.)

WIND SYSTEMS: THREE BASIC OPTIONS

Like solar electric systems, wind systems fall into three basic categories: (1) grid-connected,

(2) grid-connected with battery storage, or (3) stand-alone.

As you may recall from Chapter 7, a grid-connected system consists of three main components: (1) a renewable energy source, in this case, a wind machine, (2) an inverter, and (3) a main service panel. DC electricity produced by the wind machine is converted to AC by the inverter, and then travels to the main service panel. From here it travels to various open circuits (loads). Excess power goes on to the grid, and may be "banked" as a credit on your utility bill. When the wind isn't blowing, electricity you need to power your home comes from the grid. Because the grid is your "storage battery," a grid outage will result in a power outage in your home even if the wind is blowing. This is due to the design of the inverters. (For more details, be sure to read the section on grid-connected solar electric systems in Chapter 7.)

If you want to store electricity for emergency use — for example, to protect your home, office, or farm from an occasional grid failure — you may want to install a battery bank for back-up power. In these systems, the wind generator supplies electricity to active circuits in the house. Excess electricity is fed into the batteries. When the batteries are full, excess electricity is diverted to the grid. If a blackout occurs, the batteries kick in, supplying electricity to your home to keep the refrigerators running and lights burning. (For more details, check out the section on grid-connected systems with battery backup in Chapter 7.)

Your third option is a stand-alone system, that is, a system that provides 100 percent of your electricity. Stand-alone systems are not connected to the electrical grid. Because of this, you cannot send surplus to the grid in times of excess production, nor can you draw from the grid in times of need. In stand-alone systems, surplus electricity is stored in a bank of batteries, usually lead acid batteries. (This battery bank is much larger than in the previous system.) Electrical demand during windless periods is satisfied by electricity stored in the batteries, as in a stand-alone solar electric system. A back-up electrical generator may also be required. (Again, you can refer to Chapter 7 if you need to brush up on stand-alone systems.)

Hybrid Systems

Because winds don't blow all of the time, even in windy locations, many homeowners and businesses who want to be off the grid turn to hybrid systems. A hybrid system is a renewable energy system that combines a wind machine with solar electricity (PVs) or some other renewable energy technology. PVs and wind work particularly well together in many parts of the world.

In many locations, during the winter (actually November through March), winds blow frequently and fiercely. Because of this, wind can supply a large portion of a family's, business's, or farm's electrical needs. During this time, the PV array supplements wind-generated electricity. During the rest of the year, however, winds continue to blow, but they are often less frequent and milder than winter winds. However, because sunshine is now more abundant, it provides the bulk of one's electrical power. Wind-generated electricity serves as the backup.

Although wind and solar electricity work well together and can provide nearly all of your electricity, you may still need to install a backup generator. It will supply electrical energy in periods of low wind and low sunshine. You also need to maintain batteries in peak condition, a topic discussed in Chapter 7.

A Final Note: DC Electricity

As in solar electric systems, wind systems can be designed so that some of the DC electricity bypasses the inverter. Thus, homes and businesses powered by wind energy can utilize

DC power directly to pump water, run refrigerators, and even operate household items like ceiling fans. Homeowners can even go entirely DC, although that's not very practical or economical for most applications.

As you may recall from Chapter 7, bypassing the inverter is an energy-saving measure. Inverters require energy to convert DC current into AC current. As alluded to above, this strategy does have some downsides. Because I covered this subject in Chapter 7, I'll refer you to that material. It's a topic you should thoroughly understand before designing your system.

IS WIND ENERGY APPROPRIATE WHERE YOU LIVE?

Before you invest too much time learning about wind generators and wind energy systems, it is important to ask a key question: is a wind generator a worthwhile investment? In other words, do you have enough wind energy in your location to make it worth the money?

Assessing Your Wind Resource

Wind is the clean, free fuel that powers wind generators. In order for a system to make sense economically, you'll need a site with sufficient wind. Most systems for homes and farms require an average annual wind speed at ground level of about seven to nine miles per hour, according to the American Wind Energy Association. Although that sounds like a lot of wind, it doesn't mean that the wind has to blow constantly at seven to nine

---

Sizing a Hybrid System

Because PVs supplement wind power in the winter and because wind supplements PVs the remainder of the year, homeowners will very likely be able to pare both systems down a bit. That is, they will need a smaller PV array and a smaller wind generator than if either were used as the sole source of electrical production. In a hybrid system, size the PV array for summer production and size the wind system for winter production. That's because PVs will be your main source of electricity in the summer and wind will generally be your main source of electricity in the winter.

miles per hour year-round in order for this energy source to make sense.

Not at all.

It means that wind speeds need to *average* seven to nine miles per hour year-round. Remember, however, that wind machines are not mounted at ground level. They're typically mounted on sturdy poles or towers 60 to 120 feet tall. At these heights, wind also blows at a higher speeds. For example, a wind blowing at 8 miles per hour at ground level could be blowing at about 14 miles per hour at 100 feet above ground. It also blows more smoothly — that is, it is less turbulent. Slight increases in wind speed dramatically increase electrical generation. (For example, increasing wind speed from just 8 to 10 miles per hour will increase electrical output by 100 percent!)

As a rule, the areas with the best wind resources in North America tend to be along seacoasts, on ridgelines, on the Great Plains, and along the Great Lakes. The northeastern United States and the deserts of the southwest are also excellent wind sites. That said, many other areas also have sufficient wind resources to make a wind system a viable option.

Before even considering installing a wind system, homeowners need to assess their sites very carefully. To assess the suitability of your location, you can begin by taking a look at a wind map. You'll find several online examples by visiting http://rredc.nrel.gov/wind/pubs/atlas/ or www.awea.org/faq/usresource.html.

These maps show average wind speeds. As you can see, the entire United States appears to be suitable for small wind generators. This map is a bit deceiving, however, for the estimates shown here generally apply to terrain that is well exposed to the wind, for example, hill tops, ridge crests, or plains. So, whatever you do, *don't* make a decision based on a map of the entire United States. "Local terrain features may cause the wind resource at a specific site to differ considerably from these estimates," note the authors of *Small Wind Electric Systems*. In fact: "The wind resource can vary significantly over an area of just a few miles because of local terrain influences on the wind flow."

For a more accurate picture of the wind resource in your area, you should access a map of wind resources in your state. You can obtain a copy on the Internet at <www.awea.org>. Or you can locate a map at the National Wind Technology Center's website at <www.nrel.gov/wind>. In Canada, you may want to contact the Canadian Wind Energy Association.

State maps provide a closer look at potential wind resources by region. Even so, you need to assess the resource at your home *before* buying a wind generator.

One of the easiest ways to assess local wind resources is to obtain average wind speed data from a nearby airport, again being careful to take into account factors at your site such as the terrain or tree cover that could increase or decrease wind speed.

To obtain data on wind speed at your local airport, you can contact them directly.

Even small increases in wind speed can result in huge increases in electrical output.

Or, in the United States, you can contact the National Climatic Data Center. They publish a book titled, *Wind Energy Resource Atlas of the United States*, that provides a wealth of information. This data is available online at <www.ncdc.noaa.gov>. In Canada, check out the Canadian Wind Atlas at <www.cmc.ec.gc.ca/rpn/modcom/eole/CanadianAtlas.html>. While you are studying the data in your locale, be sure to examine average wind speed by month, so you know how much wind is available during different parts of the year. This is especially important if you are planning on installing a wind/PV hybrid system.

When assessing your wind resources using this data, bear in mind that airport wind data are collected by a device called an anemometer, mounted 20 to 33 feet above ground. However, household-sized wind machines are typically mounted higher, usually 60 to 120 feet above ground. Remember also that wind speed increases with height. Wind speed, for example, may be 15 to 25 percent higher at a typical wind turbine height of 80 feet (24 meters) than measurements closer to the ground. As you will soon see, even small increases in wind speed can result in huge increases in electrical output. Finally, as Johnny Weiss at Solar Energy International points out, bear in mind that airports are frequently sited in the least windy places to make takeoff and landing safer.

If your wind resource seems adequate, based on assessments of maps, local airport data, and personal observations, some people, like wind expert Mick Sagrillo of Sagrillo Power and Light, recommend buying a small, inexpensive wind generator — for example, a 400-watt wind machine — and installing it without further assessment. You can then determine how well it works over a period of a year or two.

Although this may seem like a waste of money, it isn't. The cost of a tower and a small wind machine is typically only slightly higher than that of an anemometer and a tower. If it turns out that your site merits a larger investment, you can easily sell the wind machine and use the proceeds to help purchase a larger model.

Relying on the Fickle Wind?

Michael Hackleman, a wind expert, and writer/editor Claire Anderson, write in an article in the June/July 2002 issue of *Mother Earth News*, "The idea of relying on the wind as an energy source may strike you as risky, since wind seems to be so variable from day to day. But wind actually acts in fairly predictable ways. Analysis of more than a half-century's recorded data, from thousands of sites, shows distinct patterns in both wind direction and speed through the season. The windiest months occur in winter, while the calmest winds are during summer." (This fact is often used to justify hybrid PV/wind systems, as noted earlier.)

Hackleman and Anderson go on to say, "Two distinct kinds of wind can be found at most locations." They are prevalent winds and energy winds. "Prevalent winds blow frequently and reliably. Energy winds are storm winds or gusts that piggyback the prevalent winds and vary in velocity and duration." In a two-week period, the authors note, there are an average of "seven days of prevalent winds and three days of energy winds." Oddly enough, while energy winds blow only 3 of every 14 days, they contain about 70 percent of the potential energy that can be harvested by a wind generator. That's because power output increases dramatically at higher wind speeds. For those who are mathematically inclined, the power output of a wind generator increases with the cube of the wind velocity. Here's an example for everyone to drive home the point. Imagine that wind speed increased from 10 to 12.6 miles per hour, a mere 2.6 miles per hour increment, or 26 percent. That's hardly noticeable to you or me.

But not to your wind machine.

This modest increase in wind speed will increase power production by 100 percent! That is, it will double power production. Imagine what a 30-to-70- mile-per-hour increase in wind speed during a storm can create!

Storms that create strong winds cause wind generators to produce enormous amounts of electricity. Hackleman and Anderson note, "While your region of the country might not be ranked as ideally suited for wind power, your individual microclimate paired with energy winds might yield enough energy to justify a wind system." You'll need a battery bank or an electrical grid to store the excess electricity for later use.

SELECTING A WIND GENERATOR AND TOWER

If wind is a viable option for you, you'll next need to determine which machine and tower to buy. You've got lots of choices. This decision typically hinges on two basic considerations: how much electricity you want to generate from the wind and how much money you have to spend. As you shall soon see, there are hidden traps for those who don't shop carefully. I'll explain how you can avoid these traps in this section.

Choosing a Wind Generator

As just noted, choosing a wind generator can be tricky. Soon you'll discover that there are numerous manufacturers and numerous models to choose from, ranging from 400-watt to 20,000-watt units (see sidebar). Moreover, there are many different factors to consider when making a decision, among them rotor size, cut-in wind speed, rated output, peak output, swept area, weight, and price. There's also the issue of noise and reliability. Finding information on the latter may be difficult.

As you shall soon discover, not all of the information provided on wind machines by manufacturers and retailers is useful. To help avoid confusion, let's see what factors are the most important to consider. Bear in mind, though, if you are dealing with local wind energy suppliers/installers, they can often ease the pain a bit. A reliable supplier/installer, for example, typically recommends a few models with which he or she has had success. Be sure to hire someone whose opinions are based on experience and not what they've read in the product literature or been told by company sales staff.

Wind machines can also be purchased through national suppliers like Gaiam Real Goods or online suppliers. Although such sources typically carry models that work well for them, you should know as much as you can about wind machines before putting your money down.

In this section, I'll provide a great deal of information in an effort to help you understand the most important factors you'll need to consider when shopping for a reliable wind machine. If you want to do a detailed analysis of your options before talking to a local dealer/installer or before perusing catalogs of various online suppliers, I strongly recommend that you read and digest Mick Sagrillo's article on choosing a home-sized wind generator. It is published in the August/September 2002 issue of *Home Power* magazine. This piece, titled "Apples and Oranges, Choosing a Home-Sized Wind Generator," is Mick's fourth article on the subject in *Home Power* over a period of ten years. (Mick regularly updates the piece every few years.) Reading and studying this excellent piece will provide a very solid understanding of wind machines and what to look for. That said, let's take a look at the most important criteria you'll need to assess when shopping for a wind generator.

Wind Machine: Which Size is Right for Your Home?

Wind generators for use in homes, on farms and ranches, and in small businesses, come in many sizes, ranging from 400 watts to 20,000 watts. This measurement is their output at a certain wind speed, and serves as a rough guide for selecting a machine. Generally, the 400- to 1,000-watt machines only supply 40 to 200 kwh of electricity per month, and only in areas with good solid 12-mile-per-hour average wind speeds. Most homes in America consume around 750 to 1,000 kilowatt hours per month. All-electric homes could easily consume 1,500 to 2,500 kwh per month, as would a small business or a farm or ranch operation.

Unless your home or business is super-efficient, you will need a larger wind machine, around 2,500 to 6,000 watts. Even then, you'll need to use electricity efficiently unless you install one of the largest and costliest models with rated power values of 10,000 kwh. Or you could install a hybrid system: a smaller wind generator with a PV array.

Swept Area

As you may recall, the spinning blade assembly is known as the rotor. It is the collector of wind. As noted earlier, the rotor converts the movement of air passing through the blades into mechanical energy. It, in turn, is converted into electrical energy by the generator. As a general rule, the larger the rotor, the more electricity it will produce. As Mick Sagrillo points out in his piece in *Home Power*, a wind generator's rotor size "is a pretty good measure of how much electricity a wind generator can produce." Although other features such as the efficiency of the generator and the design of the blades can influence efficiency, Sagrillo argues that "they pale when compared to the overall influence of the size of the rotor." With wind machines, size does matter.

Rotor size can be measured by the diameter of the circle described by the spinning blades — the area of wind the turning rotors intercept. This is known as the swept area.

The swept area is measured in square feet or square meters. Figure 8-6 illustrates the differences in swept area of three household-sized wind machines. You can quickly pick out the high-energy models just by looking at the swept area.

Hugh Piggot of Scoraig Wind Electric in Scotland points out that "Swept area is easier to measure and harder to lie about than performance." This is the one factor that allows for easy comparison of different models.

Cut-In Speed

Household-sized wind machines start producing useful amounts of electricity at wind speeds in the range of six to eight miles per hour. This is known as the cut-in speed. Because the cut-in speeds of most models fall within a narrow range, this generally won't be a feature that will influence your decision.

Rated Output

As you may recall, PVs are compared by their output — the amount of electricity they produce under standard conditions. Wind machine manufacturers, perhaps wanting to assist customers in making a decision, also rate the output of their products. They provide rated output data on various models in watts. Bergey Windpower's BWC XL.1, for instance, has a rated power output of 1,000 watts. So does Southwest Windpower's Whisper 200 and Abundant Renewable Energy's ARE 110.

The trouble is, there are no set standards in the wind industry, as there are in the solar electric industry, for determining rated output. All three manufacturers rate their wind machines at different wind speeds (called rated wind speeds). Bergey rates their machine at 24.6 mph, while Southwest Windpower rates theirs at 26 mph, and ARE rates theirs at 25 mph. So which one would be better?

Because they are all rated at different wind speeds, you can't really say. You would think

Fig. 8-6: The swept area varies dramatically from one wind machine to the next. By and large, you should choose the model with the greatest swept area. It will produce the most electricity at your site.

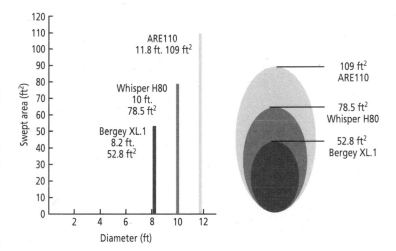

that the wind machine that produces 1,000 watts at the lowest wind speed would be the best buy. But not so. Not in this case.

To make a decision, you'd be better off looking at the swept area. In this case, the swept area of the Bergey is 52.8 square feet, the Whisper is 78.5 square feet, and the ARE is 110 square feet. Which one will produce the most electricity for you?

The model with the largest swept area. Let's let Mick Sagrillo have the last word on this subject: "While comparing PVs based on rated wattage makes for great cost comparisons, comparing rated outputs is a poor way to compare wind generators. You are far better off comparing swept areas or the kwh per month of electricity the different systems will produce at different average wind speeds." In the example just given, the Bergey produces 115 kwh per month in an area with 10 mph wind, while the Whisper produces 125 kwh per month and the ARE 110 produces 130 kwh — a clear reflection of the swept area.

Governing System

All wind machines come with a mechanism to prevent the generator from burning out in high winds. Why?

High winds increase the rpms of a wind machine, producing more power. However, really high rpms can lead to overheating and burnout. They can also literally tear a wind machine apart, causing parts to break, just like a car engine that revs too high.

Manufacturers install two basic types of governor. One type simply turns the blades out of the wind so they stop spinning or, for one model, slow down. The blades, for instance, may tilt up and out of the wind. Although this type of governing mechanism protects wind machines from damage, it does greatly reduce, even halt, power production.

The other governing system changes the blade pitch, that is, the angle of the blades, so they no longer intercept as efficiently. This causes the rotor to spin at a slower rate. Although blade pitch governing systems allow wind machines to continue to produce power, they require more moving parts. The more moving parts you have, the more maintenance. Talk to local installers for their recommendations.

Shut-Down Mechanism

Some wind machine manufacturers include a shut-down mechanism — a mechanical or electrical device that allows an operator to shut a wind generator off. This is important because it allows the owner to repair or maintain the wind machine without fear of injury. It also provides a means to shut the wind machine down when a violent storm is approaching.

Shut-down mechanisms come in many varieties from disc and dynamic brakes to folding tails — that's right, tails that fold in such a way that the wind machine is forced out of the wind and the blades stop rotating.

Mick Sagrillo believes that the shut-down mechanism of a wind turbine is another key factor to consider when shopping for a wind machine. Unfortunately, he notes, "very few turbines have reliable shut-down mechanisms." The most effective seem to be those systems that allow the operator to crank the tail out of the wind or engage a disc brake. They are usually attached to a cable attached to a winch located at the base of the tower.

Some Less Meaningful Measures

Manufacturers provide a host of other, relatively useless (at least to most buyers) measurements such as peak output and maximum design wind speed. Peak output is how much electricity the wind machine can produce at maximum power output; this is usually above the rated wind speed. While this figure may be of interest, it is of little relevance to buyers. The question you should be asking, according to wind energy engineer Eric Eggleston is "What will this wind generator do at my site in my average wind speed?"

Maximum design wind speed is another number sales people throw around. It's meant to signal to the buyer the sturdiness of the machine. However, according to Sagrillo, "it has little bearing on the expected life of a wind generator."

Sagrillo points out that wind generators are designed to survive wind speeds of 120 mph or more, but they are not necessarily tested at these speeds — or repeatedly tested at these speeds — to see if the claims really hold up over time. The fact is, more machines are damaged by turbulence than high winds.

Even in high wind situations, says Sagrillo, it is not the wind that damages wind generators, it is flying debris.

Sagrillo argues that the best criterion for durability is tower top weight: how much the unit weighs. "My experience," says Sagrillo, "is that heavy duty wind generators survive, and light duty turbines do not." Therefore, even though most wind machines are rated for 120 mph or greater maximum wind speeds, "experience indicates that many of the lighter turbines cannot handle sites with heavier winds or turbulence." Of the three models we

Noise

Wind machines are not, by their very nature, quiet, although some models are significantly quieter than others, and some of these are so quiet you have to look to see if they are actually spinning. Noise is primarily generated by the blades cutting through the air.

As a general rule, the blades of light-weight wind generators spin faster than heavy-weight units. As a result, the high rpm light-weight models tend to be noisier than their powerful heavy-weight cousins. One light-weight model in particular, the Air-X, turns into a monster at high speeds, growling fiercely in the wind.

Fortunately for all concerned, the greatest noise levels occur at high wind speeds, when background noise increases as well — for example, when the leaves and branches of trees are being blown by the wind. Also, fortunately for us, sound drops off fairly quickly with distance. Thus, the taller the tower, the less noise you will hear.

are examining, the Bergey XL.1 weighs 75 pounds, the Whisper H80 weighs a mere 65 pounds, and the ARE 110 weighs 250 pounds. Sagrillo goes on to say, "Be forewarned! Weight … will be reflected in the price." The heavier the unit, the more you will pay. However, you will definitely get what you pay for.

Another common but fairly useless tool for evaluating wind machines is their power curve, like the one shown in Figure 8-7. This graph plots the power production in watts at different wind speeds. While it is nice to look at, it doesn't really help you very much in making a decision. Again, the more valuable measures are swept area, kwh per month in different wind speeds, and weight.

Fig. 8-7: This power curve shows the output of an ARE110 wind machine at various wind speeds

Cost Factors

You'll learn a lot more about other measurements in Sagrillo's article, but by now you've gotten the main points: weight and swept area should be the primary criteria for selecting a

wind machine. Cost comes into play, too. That is to say, comparing costs on the basis of weight and swept area can help you decide. Sagrillo recommends calculating the cost per unit of weight and cost per unit of swept area. Table 8-1 shows the cost of the three models we examined earlier based on weight and swept area.

Purchasing a Tower

Wind machines constitute a major expense in any wind system, but these costs are often rivaled by tower costs. Before we talk about costs, let's take a look at your options.

Towers come in two basic varieties: free-standing and guyed. Each type has a couple of subtypes.

Free-Standing Towers

Free-standing towers are those that require no additional support: they are self-supporting. Because they have a relatively small footprint, they are ideal for applications where space is limited.

The most common free-standing tower is the lattice or truss tower, shown in Figure 8-8. Lattice towers resemble the latticework of arbors. The Eiffel Tower in Paris is an example of a lattice structure.

Lattice towers are secured to a massive foundation and are engineered to withstand powerful winds. Because of the large amount of metal that goes into them and because of the need for a sturdy anchoring foundation, they are the most expensive tower option.

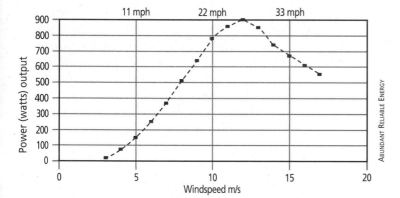

	Table 8-1 Comparison of Three Wind Generators					
Model	Swept Area (square feet)	kWh per month at 10 mph	Weight (pounds)	Cost	Cost/square foot swept area	Cost per pound
Bergey XL.1	52.8	115	75	$2,450	$46.40	$32.66
Southwest Windpower Whisper 200	78.5	125	65	$2,602	$33.15	$40.03
ARE 110	110	130	250	$8,700	$79.10	$34.80

Free-standing lattice towers are typically installed in 20-foot sections. Paul Gipe, an internationally recognized wind expert and author of several popular books on wind power for residential use, describes the process like this: "For small wind machines, the sections are typically preassembled and welded together prior to delivery. For larger machines, the tower is shipped 'knocked-down' or in parts and must be assembled on the site." Large towers are typically assembled on the ground, then erected with a crane and bolted to the foundation. Some installers assemble towers in the upright position piece by piece, which Gipe considers a risky and time-consuming venture. Yet another method

BERGEY WINDPOWER

Fig. 8-8: The lattice or truss tower is strong and durable and an excellent choice for mounting larger wind machines. It can be supported by guy wires, if necessary.

is to install a tower that's hinged at the base. The tower is then assembled on the ground, the wind generator is attached, and the assembly is tilted up using a variety of different techniques.

Rigid metal poles can also be used to create free-standing towers for wind machines. Most poles or masts are made from steel, although other materials are sometimes used.

Pole towers are usually installed with a crane, though they can be hinged at the base and tipped into place as well. (I'll describe how this is accomplished momentarily.) Pole towers are anchored in a concrete foundation that is even more hefty than that required for a truss tower.

Poles are more expensive than lattice-style free-standing towers, according to Mick Sagrillo. Whatever choice you make, you need to be sure that the tower is strong enough to withstand the winds in your area and strong enough to support the weight of the wind machine, both of which can be quite substantial. Several of the largest home-sized wind machines weigh around 1,000 pounds. The Jacobs 31-20, admittedly the heavyweight of the residential- or business-sized units, weighs an amazing 2,500 pounds!

The Mathematics of Wind Power

The electrical output of a wind energy system depends on many factors: the most important are air density, swept area, and wind velocity. This relationship is expressed in the mathematical equation $P = \frac{1}{2} d \times A \times V^3$.

What this equation tells us is that the greater the density of the air, the greater the swept area, and the greater the velocity, the higher the power output (measured in watts). Air density varies with elevation above sea level and humidity. Although we have no control over air density, there are a few things one should know. First of all, if you live in the mountains where air is less dense, you'll need to lower your wind machine's rating accordingly. Don't expect it to produce as much electricity as it would at a lower elevation at any given wind speed. Second, you can expect greater output from a wind machine in the winter — about 13 percent greater — because the air is a bit denser in the winter than the summer. This is great for those who are installing a hybrid wind/PV system.

While you can't control air density, you can control swept area and wind velocity. Swept area, as explained earlier, is determined by rotor size. The bigger the rotor, the greater the swept area. Select a wind generator with the largest possible swept area.

You can also affect wind speed by choosing the best site and installing your wind generator on the tallest tower possible. This allows you to raise the wind machine into the fastest winds and will have an enormous effect on power production. For example, by doubling the wind speed from 8 miles per hour to 16 miles per hour, power production increases by 800 percent!

Guyed Towers

Guyed towers typically consist of steel pipe or lattice uprights supported by cables called guy wires that run from the tower to anchors in the ground. (Figure 8-9). Guyed towers are cheaper than free-standing towers and are therefore the most commonly used towers for household-sized wind machines.

Steel pipe can be used for the masts of all household-sized wind machines. The steel pipes are assembled section by section, secured by bolts or slipped together, then erected using a crane or a gin pole. A gin pole is a pole anchored to the bottom of the mast that allows the assembly to be tilted up using a tractor, truck, or heavy-duty winch (Figure 8-10).

For the largest wind machines, the lattice tower is the tower of choice. They're strong, mass-produced for the telecommunications industry and therefore widely available, and cheaper than other options. They're also available in different strengths. Like free-standing lattice towers, they can be assembled in the horizontal position on the ground then tilted into place, or can be assembled upright, one section at a time or in their entirety, using a crane.

In all guyed towers, strong steel cable is attached to the tower and anchored in the ground using an assortment of anchoring mechanisms, depending on the soil type. Smaller towers require an extra-high-strength stranded-steel cable. Large towers may use aircraft cable, which is even stronger. Installers use three guy wires for each section of the tower, while tilt-up towers have four. Manufacturers typically specify guy radius — that is, how far out the anchors for the guy wires need to be for optimal strength.

Tower Kits

If all of this seems a bit daunting, don't be dismayed. A professional installer will design a system for you, order the components, assemble the tower, mount your wind machine, and raise the tower ... for a price, of course. If you'd like to try your hand at this, you'll be

Fig. 8-9: Guy wires help hold many towers in place. Wires are installed in groups of three to four. Typically, each segment of the tower is guyed.

BERGEY WINDPOWER

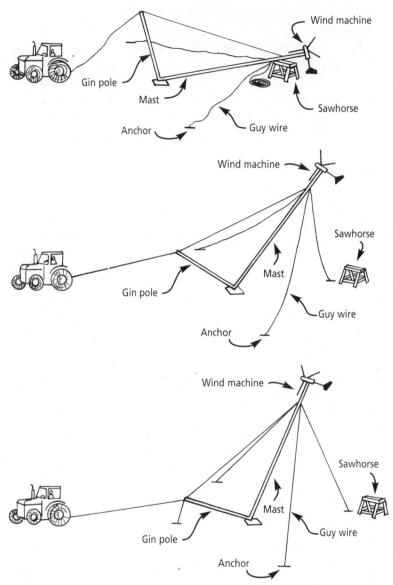

Fig. 8-10: The gin pole shown here allows an installer to tip a large tower into place without an expensive crane.

happy to know that several manufacturers sell tower kits designed and engineered for their wind machines. Southwest Windpower, Lake Michigan Wind and Sun, Abundant Renewable Energy, and Bergey, for instance, all provide affordable tower kits. Because it doesn't make sense to ship fairly inexpensive, but very heavy and bulky steel tubing long distances, Southwest Windpower kits provide all of the materials you need *except* the poles. Their kits don't include the anchors, either, because the type of anchor varies from one location to another, depending on the soil type. You can purchase steel pipe locally at a building supply outlet or steel fence supplier. You can purchase the anchors from Southwest Windpower separately, or from a local wind energy supplier/installer, or directly from the manufacturer (the last option is usually the least expensive). To learn more about towers, you may want to read Ian Woofenden's piece, "Wind Generator Tower Basics" in *Home Power*, Issue 105.

Tips on Finding a Supplier or Installer

If wind seems like a viable option to you — that is, you have enough wind in your area and can afford to buy and install a machine — you have two obvious options for proceeding. You can purchase and install the equipment yourself or you can hire a professional. If you select the first route, you'll need to do a lot more in-depth research. You'll also need to read up on installation. You'd also be wise to take a course on wind energy that includes hands-on installation work. Be careful. Installation can be dangerous to people and equipment. You don't want a $5,000 to $25,000 wind machine to come crashing down because you made a mistake during installation.

When purchasing a wind machine, be sure to check out warranties and read the fine print. Warranties run from one to five years. Also check out how long companies you are considering have been in business.

The second option is to go with a local supplier/installer. Their expertise can be highly valuable. A local expert can also help you troubleshoot problems once the system is up and running and can repair and maintain your system, if need be. Yes, I did say maintain.

Wind energy systems need periodic maintenance like any mechanical and electrical system. Batteries require maintenance, which is described in Chapter 7. Wind machines and towers also require periodic inspection and maintenance. Larger units may, for instance, need grease or oil changes. As Mick Sagrillo points out, "All towers and wind turbines require annual inspections at the very least. If you are not into maintenance, don't buy a wind turbine."

Although manufacturers have made tremendous strides in improving the quality of their wind generators since the early 1980s, mostly by simplifying their machines and using stronger, more durable materials such as carbon-reinforced blades and new metal alloys, don't forget: wind machines are exposed to extreme weather (heat and cold, snow, ice,

and fierce wind) and amazing stresses. Fortunately, many problems that arise are simple ones, like loose bolts, that can be fixed in seconds. If left unattended, though, small problems can lead to catastrophic failures!

Blades may require maintenance, too. For example, some blades may need a new coat of paint from time to time. Wooden blades may have protective tape on their leading edges to protect them against grit in the air. The tape may need to be replaced from time to time. And, of course, bearings may wear out and need replacement.

To maintain a wind generator, you'll either need to periodically ascend the lattice tower using a climbing harness —very carefully so as not to fall — or lower the machine to ground level if you have a tilt-up tower. After 20 years of successful operation, the guts of the wind machine may even have to be ripped out and replaced.

As Mick Sagrillo points out, "The life of a wind generator is directly related to the owner's involvement with the system and its maintenance." If you expect a wind machine to work doggedly in its harsh environment without maintenance, wind power might not be for you. That's a pretty unrealistic expectation.

Some Tips on Installing a Wind Machine

To be effective, wind machines need to be installed in a good windy site, usually upwind of buildings and other obstructions. If installed downwind, they need to be significantly past the wind shadow — the relatively windless eddy created by obstructions. The best wind, as you've already learned, is the smoothest and strongest wind located 60 feet or more above the ground. The higher the better.

To access the best wind, wind turbines for household, farm, business, and ranch use are erected on poles or towers ranging from about 60 to 120 feet above ground level. Most serious installations are 80 to 120 feet above ground.

Also, wind machines need to be placed on towers so that the entire rotor is at least 30 feet above the closest obstruction or treeline within 500 feet. Whatever you do, do not mount a wind machine on a roof or against a building — even if a supplier provides special mounts for such applications. The vibrations will be conducted into the building and can be very annoying. I know, I tried this … just to test it, of course. (Yeah, right!) Moreover, buildings create air turbulence that lowers performance and increases wear and tear on the machine.

While we're on this topic, be sure to mount your DC wind generator as close to the inverter as possible. This is important for two reasons: to reduce line loss and to reduce the need for larger (and more costly) electrical wire. (The larger the wire, the lower the electrical resistance. The lower the electrical resistance, the lower the line loss.) Installation manuals will help you determine the gauge wire you will need.

Before you decide to install your own wind generator, be sure to read more on the subject.

Paul Gipe's more advanced books on wind power are a good start. You may also want to check out the superb video *An Introduction to Residential Wind Power with Mick Sagrillo*, produced by Scott Andrews. You can order it online through Real Goods and other suppliers.

If you feel comfortable with the installation process, be sure to study instruction manuals from the manufacturer. It wouldn't be a bad idea to sign up for a course on wind energy through the Midwest Renewable Energy Association, Solar Energy International, the Solar Living Institute, or some other organization.

FINANCIAL MATTERS

Like a good sales person, I've given you the scoop on wind power before I drop the cost bomb. How much does it cost to install a wind machine?

As noted earlier, wind generators for household use vary from the smallest 1,000-watt machines to the largest 20,000-watt unit. If you simply want to supplement your electrical energy from the grid, a wind machine of 1,000- to 3000-watt rated output might be ideal. When buying, look for models in this range, then compare them using swept area, weight, kwh per month at different wind speeds, and costs — notably, cost per square foot of swept area and cost per unit of weight. A 1,000- to 3,000-watt wind generator might also work if you live in a tiny cabin or you are extremely efficient. And it might suffice if you are installing a hybrid system — a combination of wind and PVs — or some other renewable resource such as microhydro (Chapter 9).

If you want to go off-grid completely and are hoping to supply electricity solely from a wind machine, you'll very likely need a larger wind generator — a machine with a rated power output of more than 3,000 watts but more likely 6,000 watts or higher. Again, whatever you do, be sure to make your home as efficient as possible in its use of electricity first. As I've said before, small investments in electrical efficiency pay huge dividends by reducing system size and costs.

Also, remember that you get what you pay for. Heavy-duty wind machines cost more but are more durable and will very likely outlast their cheaper, lighter, high-speed cousins. A good heavyweight wind turbine will very likely last 20 years or more. Its light-weight cousin will last half that time, maybe even only one-fourth as long, according to Sagrillo. So savings on a less expensive model are eaten up by replacement costs.

Another important consideration when designing a wind system is that tower height makes a huge difference in power output. Because power increases dramatically with wind speed and because wind speed increases with height, raising the tower a bit can greatly boost a system's output. So rather than paying twice as much to purchase a more powerful wind machine, consider a smaller investment in tower height to increase energy production.

Wind machines cost about $1.50 to $2.50 per watt of rated output. Smaller wind machines around 1,000 watts rated output cost about $1,600 to $2,200. Larger units around 2,500 – 6,000 watts will run about $7,000 to $13,000. The largest wind machines rated at 8,500 to 20,000 watts will run about $20,000 to $25,000.

But don't forget the tower, another big expense. Guyed towers cost about $30 to $40 per foot, so a 100-foot tower will cost about $3,000 to $4,000. Tilt-up towers cost about $30 to $50 per foot, while free-standing towers cost about $40 to $50 per foot.

But that's not all. You will need to install a concrete base for your tower. Electric wiring and supplies need to be added to the cost. And then there's installation costs if you're hiring a professional installer. Remember, too, that tall towers need to be grounded to protect them against lightning strikes. This will add a little expense, too.

You will also very likely need an inverter, unless you're buying an AC wind machine, in which case the inverter comes with the turbine. And if you are installing a grid-connected system with battery backup or a stand-alone system, you'll also need a battery bank. An inverter could run you $2,000 to $3,000 and a battery bank could easily cost $2,000 or more, depending on its size. See Table 8-2 for the total cost of installing several different wind systems.

When calculating costs and trying to determine whether wind makes financial sense, remember that a number of states and utilities and even some local municipalities offer financial incentives to cut initial costs. These include tax credits, property tax exemptions, low-interest loans, and rebates. They are discussed in Chapter 7.

Remember, too, that on grid-connected systems surplus electrical energy can be sold back to power companies. Again, rather than repeat what I've said in Chapter 7, I refer you to that material.

WIND POWER WITHOUT INSTALLING A WIND GENERATOR

If a wind generator is not right for you, don't despair. Many utilities offer green power to their customers. Green power is electricity generated from renewable sources, mostly gigantic wind machines on commercial wind farms, like those shown in Figure 8-11. Green power

Table 8-2 Typical Prices for Installed Systems (July, 2005)								
Model	**Swept Area**	**"Rated output"**	**Turbine Cost**	**Tower**	**Tower Cost**	**Installed Cost**	**kWh @ 10 mph**	**kWh @ 12 mph**
Lakota	36.9	1 kW	$1,699	84' T	$3,935	$14,700	96	155
Whisper 100	40	900 W	$2,085	84' T	$3,935	$14,986	63	105
XL .1	58	1 kW	$2,450	80' T	$1,890	$12,734	91	147
Cyclone	65	1 kW	$2,148	85' T	$3,600	$15,137	163	260
Whisper 200	80	1 kW	$2,602	84' T	$3,935	$14,981	124	193
Proven 2.5	97	2.5 kW	$13,665	105' T	$7,364	$35,774	231	351
ARE 110	110	2.5 kW	$8,700	85' T	$3,600	$20,784	117	175
Jake Long	154	3.6 kW	$9,200	100' G	$5,000	$28,063	350	520
Whisper 500	175	3 kW	$7,095	105' T	$7,364	$31,079	341	538
Proven 6.0	254	6 kW	$22,439	120' G	$10,850	$59,596	618	931
XL-S	398	10 kW	$24,750	120' G	$10,850	$52,117	520	900
31-20	754	20 kW	$21,255	120' F	$14,887	$54,056	1644	2691
V-15-35	1963	35 kW	included	110' F	included	$105,000	3354	5371
V-15-65	1963	65 kW	included	140' F	included	$115,000	3675	5992

may be produced by other renewable sources as well, but wind is the dominant source. It's the cheapest and most widely developed renewable energy source in the world, other than hydropower from hydroelectric plants on rivers.

In my area, the local utility offers its customers an option to purchase blocks of wind energy from their ever-expanding wind farms in northern Colorado and southern Wyoming. Currently, customers pay an additional $2.50 per 200 kilowatt hours of electricity. Customers can opt to buy as many blocks as they want, provided the company has enough to sell. (Interestingly, without telling its customers, the company also deducts some of the other charges related to coal-fired production, so the final cost is a bit lower than $2.50.)

Even if the utility company in your area does not have its own wind farm, it may currently be purchasing power from renewable producers and can offer you green energy just the same. At this writing, 80 utilities in 28 states are offering some form of green power. What that means is that more than a third of all US households could choose some type of green power directly from their local utility or through the competitive marketplace, according to Blair Sweezy and Lori Bird, authors of "Businesses Lead the Green Power Charge" in *Solar Today*. California and Pennsylvania have been the most active markets for green power, they add.

Chances are you've heard about green power and already know whether it is available.

Fig. 8-11: This large wind machine in northeastern Colorado is used to create green power for a local municipality.

DAN CHIRAS

If not, ask your local utility. As the markets for electricity deregulate, meaning more and more companies can provide power on electrical grids owned by others, you may be able to purchase green power from one of these competitors. Even if it costs a few bucks more each month, and it usually will, it's well worth it.

If there are no utilities in your area that sell green power, you can still play an active role in this growing industry by purchasing a green tag. A green tag is a small subsidy to power companies producing green power. It supports their green power programs. Bear in mind, however, that you won't actually receive the electricity. Someone else will, but you will help make it happen.

Green tags are sold by a number of companies and go by different names. The Los Angeles Department of Water and Power, for example, calls their green tags Green Power Certificates. Pacific Gas and Electric sells Pure Wind Certificates. Waverly Light and Power in Iowa sells Iowa Energy Tags.

With city governments such as those of Salem, Oregon, Chicago, Illinois, and San Francisco, California, and federal agencies such as the US Environmental Protection Agency,

US Department of Energy, and the US Postal Service making substantial commitments to buy green power, homeowners are very likely going to have even greater opportunities to purchase it.

At the present time, electricity from clean, reliable sources costs a little more, but some service charges may be deducted from your bill, reducing the costs. In addition, the cost of wind power is likely to fall in the very near future as more wind machines go on line and more improvements are made in wind generator technology. Furthermore, we've recently seen that while prices for electricity from coal have increased, wind-produced electricity has remained the same.

In closing, as I like to remind audiences: good planets are mighty hard to come by. A small investment in environmentally friendly electricity is a small price to pay to create a sustainable way of life and a better future. Investments in renewable energy will also help build stronger economies that resist the potential turmoil caused by declining supplies of conventional fuels.

The Cost of Green Power

Over time, as wind becomes more widespread, the price is bound to plummet. Newer machines are already producing electricity more cheaply than natural gas and at a price only slightly higher than coal.

CHAPTER 9

MICROHYDRO

GENERATING ELECTRICITY FROM RUNNING WATER

Humans have been tapping the power of flowing water for centuries. In the early history of North America, for instance, New Englanders tapped the power of water flowing in the streams that ran through their towns by installing small dams and water wheels. The water wheels, in turn, powered the machinery of textile factories, even grain mills where wheat was ground to flour used to make bread, a staple of early American life.

Hydropower continues to play a pivotal role throughout the world today. Its primary value, however, is as a source of electricity. Today, hydroelectricity constitutes 7 percent of the total electrical generation in the United States and 21 percent in Canada.

But that's not hydropower's only claim to fame.

Hydropower is not only a significant source of energy, it also has the distinction of ranking number one among *all renewable energy resources*. That is, of all renewable energy sources in the world, it's the "top dog." Large-scale hydropower projects, however, are not the main topic of this chapter. Rather, we'll focus our attention on microhydro, small-scale facilities — those that provide electricity to power homes, small farms, and small businesses.

Yes, even small businesses.

One of the best examples of a business application is the shop run by Don Harris in Santa Cruz, California. Fittingly, this pioneer in renewable energy manufactures turbines for microhydro systems.

According to Scott Davis, author of *Microhydro: Clean Power from Water*, "Even at

Fig. 9-1: Don Harris, a pioneer in microhydro power in North America, manufacture microhydro turbines/generators in his shop in the hills outside of Santa Cruz, quite fittingly powered by hydropower.

DON HARRIS

The Renewable Energy of Choice

For those who are fortunate enough to have a good site, hydro is really the renewable energy of choice. System component costs are much lower and watts per dollar return is much greater for hydro than for any other renewable source.

Microhydro, given the right site, can cost as little as a tenth of a PV system of comparable output. Moreover, hydropower users often are able to run energy-consumptive appliances that would bankrupt a PV system owner like large side-by-side refrigerators and electric space heaters.

John Schaeffer, *Solar Living Source Book*

the smallest of scales, water power continues to be a reliable and cost-effective way to generate electrical power with renewable technology." Although microhydro is a reliable and economical source of electricity for those wishing to go part way or entirely off-grid, it does have its limitations. First and foremost, you need a stream or river nearby — one that has sufficient flow and offers sufficient water pressure (more on this shortly) to produce enough power to make the investment worthwhile.

Unfortunately, there aren't that many microhydro sites available worldwide into which homeowners can tap. For this reason, microhydro is of limited use in most countries. However, for those who are lucky enough to live near a suitable stream, usually those living in mountainous or hilly terrain, microhydro offers great promise. Even people in the flatlands can tap the power of moving water if a stream nearby flows at a sufficient rate of speed. It is for these lucky individuals — and for folks who just want to learn more about this fascinating energy source — that this chapter was written.

AN INTRODUCTION TO HYDROELECTRIC SYSTEMS

Hydroelectricity is based on some pretty simple concepts. If you have read the wind power chapter in this book or have studied conventional electrical production by coal, nuclear, or geothermal energy you'll see the similarities instantly. In a microhydro system, moving water turns a turbine. The turbine spins a generator. The generator (or alternator) produces electricity. These components are common to all of the electrical generating equipment discussed in this book, except PV modules.

"Many other components may be in a system, but it all begins with the energy ... within the moving water," says Dan New, author of "Intro to Hydropower" published in *Home Power* magazine, Issues 103–105. (This information can also be found on Dan New's website <www.canyonhydro.com> under "Residential Systems." Click on the "Guide to Hydropower.") The energy of moving water, in turn, is produced by gravity, that magical force that propels water down the slightest of gradients, causing it to flow from high to lower ground. It is important, however, to point out that water reached the heights from which it flows downward thanks to two other natural forces — evaporation and precipitation. Water evaporation, we mustn't forget, is triggered by solar energy. Sunlight striking the Earth and various water bodies causes moisture to evaporate, and that is where the flow of water through the hydrological cycle begins. You might say that it is all downhill from that point on. Because of this, hydropower is just another form of good old-fashioned solar energy coupled with that mysterious force, gravity.

As in other renewable energy systems, microhydro systems fall into three broad categories: (1) stand-alone, (2) grid-connected, and (3) grid-connected with battery backup. (These distinctions are outlined in Chapter 7 for those who aren't familiar with the terms.)

THE ANATOMY OF A MICROHYDRO SYSTEM

Microhydro systems are electrical generating systems for use on a small scale, as just noted, and usually for residential power in remote mountainous terrain. Microhydro is usually "installed" by small streams or rivers near homes — the closer the better!

To protect the stream and those creatures that depend on it, microhydro systems generally divert only a small portion of the current from the waterway. This water temporarily borrowed from the stream is diverted into a pipe or specially built channel or canal that runs alongside the waterway to a turbine some distance below the water intake. The turbine is connected to an electrical generator, described shortly.

Microhydro systems exist in two basic configurations: low-head and high-head. (Head refers to water pressure created by the vertical distance water flows, as you shall soon see.) Most homeowners install high-head systems.

AC and DC Microhydro

Microhydro systems produce both DC and AC power, depending on the design, although DC systems are by far the most commonly used in small-scale applications.

High-Head Microhydro

Figure 9-2 shows the basic components of the most widely utilized microhydro system, the high-head system. As illustrated, the system consists of a specially built water intake structure. The intake structure is constructed in a stream or river, usually along its banks, so as to minimize disturbance to the aquatic environment.

One of the key components of the water intake structure is a small settling basin that allows grit to precipitate out. Grit and silt in water can wear away the moving parts of the microhydro turbine.

Another key component of the water intake structure is a screen that removes debris such as leaves and branches that can clog the pipes and the spray nozzles on the turbine. They could also possibly damage the turbine runner (the wheel inside the turbine).

Water typically flows from the intake structure into a pipeline, called a penstock by professionals. The pipe typically runs alongside the river or stream — not in the watercourse itself — to protect the pipe from raging flood waters that can rip it apart. The pipe carries the water downhill to the turbine, usually located in a simple shelter — either a small, sturdy, waterproof vault or a small shed.

Water flowing through the turbine causes a wheel, or runner as professionals call it, inside the device to turn (Figure 9-3). A steel shaft connects the runner to the generator. When the runner and shaft spin, they cause the inner workings of the generator to spin, producing electricity. (Because the generator in a microhydro system operates like the generators in wind machines, you might want to check that section out now. See page 212.)

Water flowing through the turbine housing is then released and flows back into the stream. This return flow is referred to as the tailwater.

As noted earlier, microhydro systems produce DC and AC electricity depending on the design of the generator. As you may recall from

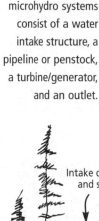

Fig. 9-2: High-head microhydro systems consist of a water intake structure, a pipeline or penstock, a turbine/generator, and an outlet.

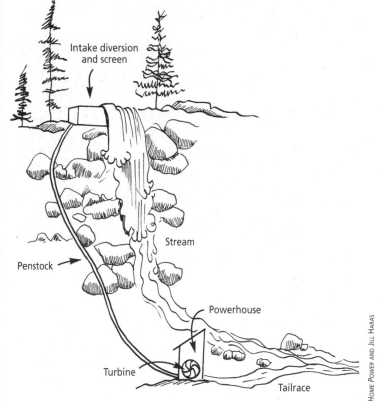

Intake diversion and screen

Penstock

Stream

Powerhouse

Turbine

Tailrace

HOME POWER AND JILL HARAS

reading previous chapters on solar electric and wind systems, low-voltage DC electricity is not used in many homes. It's AC electricity that powers our world. As a result, DC electricity produced by the generator in a microhydro system must first be sent to an inverter. It converts the DC electricity produced by the generator to the AC power required by most lights, household electronic devices, and appliances. The inverter also boosts the voltage of the current from the generator, typically either 12, 24 or 48 volts, depending on the model, to 120 volts, standard household current.

Low-Head Microhydro

Low-head microhydro systems are a bit simpler than high-head systems just described. As illustrated in Figure 9-4, they require a screened intake or a small dam across part of a stream or river with a settling basin to allow grit and silt to precipitate out. The intake structure empties into to a fairly short diversion canal that delivers water to a draft tube often only ten feet long. The water flowing through the system turns a propeller-like turbine. It is connected to a generator that produces electricity. Water is returned directly to the stream. Such systems are often built near small water falls.

ASSESSING THE FEASIBILITY OF YOUR SITE

Before you decide to purchase a microhydro system, you will need to study your site very carefully to determine whether the system

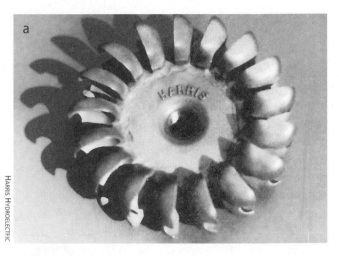

Fig. 9-3: (a) Pelton and (b) Turgo turbines.

AC Microhydro Systems

AC microhydro systems produce a form of electricity that can be used directly without conversion. In stand-alone systems, the AC electricity will, however, need to be converted back to DC to be stored in a battery bank.

would work and how much electricity it could generate.

Analyzing Your Electrical Energy Needs

Before you assess the electrical generating capacity of the stream, however, it is important, indeed essential, to analyze your electrical energy needs. This process is described in Chapter 7, so I won't repeat it here, other than to offer a few reminders.

First and foremost, when determining your electrical demand, it is important to be accurate — and generous — in your assessment. Accuracy is vital to your success, but

often difficult to achieve. Generous estimates are important because most people use a lot more electricity than they predict based on standard electrical consumption analyses.

Why?

When estimating electrical consumption for a new home, people often begin by listing all of the components of their load, that is, their household electrical demand. This includes appliances, lights, fans, pumps, coffee makers, aquariums, and an assortment of other electronic devices. They then list how much power each electronic device consumes, and how long the device is used each day.

Fig. 9-4: A typical water intake structure requires a stilling basin to allow sediment to precipitate out. It also requires a deep pool so that the pipe remains free from ice.

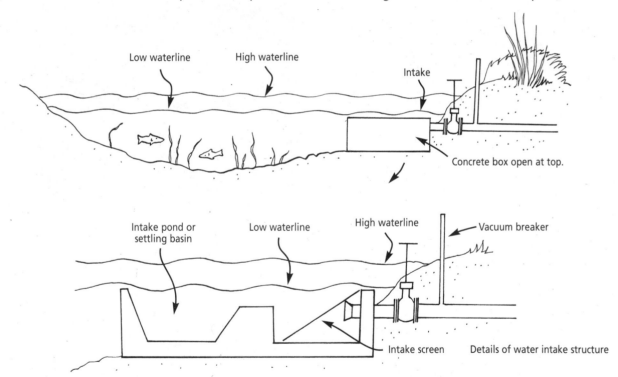

The problem with this approach is that very few people really know how long they run the TV or the toaster or the microwave each day. So estimates can be pretty inaccurate.

If you are installing a system for an existing home or work space, your task is considerably easier: you simply consult your energy bills for the past two or three years to calculate monthly electrical consumption. If you haven't saved your bills, you can contact your local utility company. They will gladly provide records. Armed with this data, you can arrive at a pretty accurate estimate of the electrical energy demands that your system will need to meet. But what can you do if you are buying a house from someone else?

Get on the phone and call the utility and ask for previous utility bills to estimate your energy consumption. Although these past bills may reflect future use, bear in mind that a previous homeowner's electrical demand may differ dramatically from yours. They may have been more miserly or much more extravagant — or somewhere in between. Their energy consumption, in short, could be quite different from yours.

Before you arrive at a final estimate of monthly and annual electrical consumption, however, remember to trim your electrical consumption. In so doing, you can dramatically reduce the cost of a renewable energy system. Changes in habits (like shutting off lights when you leave a room) and energy efficiency measures (compact fluorescent light bulbs, for instance) can dramatically reduce your monthly electrical consumption. Remember, as I've said many times before, efficiency is *the* most cost-effective means of supplying power to a home — or any building, for that matter. And, lest you forget, the more efficient you are, the smaller your system requirements. The smaller your system requirements, the less money you'll have to spend up front.

Assessing the Potential of a Microhydro Site

Once you have determined your family's electrical energy demands, it is time to assess the potential of your site. You'll need to determine how much electricity a microhydro system could produce and the percentage of your needs that it could meet. Before we do that, let's take a look an important issue you need to be aware of: continuous power vs daily power production and use.

Unlike other renewable energy systems, microhydro systems can produce power 24 hours a day, 7 days a week, 365 days a year. A system, for instance, might produce 200 watts of continuous power day in and day out. Over a 24-hour period, this system would produce 4,800 watts-hours. To determine monthly output, you can multiply the daily output by 30. That would give you 144,000 watt-hours per month or 144 kilowatt hours per month. (To determine monthly output, you can also multiply the continuous output of the system, in this case 200 watts, by 720 hours, the number of hours in a month, which gives you the same result.)

Most conventional homes — homes that don't practice much energy conservation — use 15 to 25 kWh per day or 450 to 750 kWh per month.

If the monthly electrical energy production of the system matches up to your household need, you'll be in fine shape. By the way, most conventional homes — homes that don't practice energy conservation — consume 25 kWh per day, or 750 kWh per month. The system we are looking at would fall short of those families' needs.

Comparing the output of a microhydro system to the monthly household demand is only one step in the process. You'll also need to consider periods of intense electrical demand, during which electrical consumption exceeds the continuous output of a system.

Let me explain: let's say your house uses 120 kWh of electricity per month. At first blush, it appears as if the microhydro system we've just discussed will meet your demands. Well, not necessarily.

The problem with this reasoning is that although a system that produces 200 watts of continuous power may produce enough in a given day to meet all of your household needs, what happens if you need 1,000 watts of power to run a microwave and 300 watts of power to run some lights and your computer and a television all at the same time?

And what happens when your washing machine or a power tool is turned on? As you may know, power tools and household appliances such as dishwashers and washing machines require more power to start than to run — quite a lot more. This is known as surge power.

As Scott Davis points out in *Microhydro: Clean Power from Water*, "It is entirely possible to have a system that has plenty of kilowatt hours available, but not enough capacity to start critical loads" or enough to meet demands that exceed continuous power output.

Demand in excess of continuous power output can be met by grid power or battery backup. In a grid-connected system, for instance, additional electrical power required to satisfy excess loads, including surge loads, is derived from the utility line connected to your home. In homes equipped with battery backup, electricity required to meet electrical demands that exceed the continuous output of the microhydro system comes from the battery bank. It is stored there during periods of excess.

Peak power demand can also be "managed away." That is, homeowners can avoid power consumption in excess of the continuous output of a system by managing their load better — spreading out use so as not to exceed a system's continuous power output. Peak loads can also be satisfied by using a small gas or diesel or propane electrical generator.

Assessments of the site's electrical energy production compared with household energy consumption help homeowners determine whether a site will produce enough electricity on a daily basis to meet their household needs. Understanding demand patterns, however, are also necessary. This will help homeowners decide what type of system should be installed, notably, if one needs to install battery backup or needs to connect to the grid. We'll talk more about this shortly, but for now, let's see how one assesses the potential of a site.

Assessing Head and Flow

Rather than go into minute detail on ways you determine the potential of a microhydro site, let me give you a general overview of the process. Those interested in installing a system are going to need more information than I could possibly supply here and I strongly recommend that they consult one or all of the following resources after reading this material: (1) Dan New's article in *Home Power* magazine, "Intro to Hydropower. Part 2: Measuring Head and Flow," (2) Scott Davis' book, *Microhydro: Clean Power from Water,* and (3) *Residential Microhydro Power with Don Harris,* a video produced by Scott Andrews (you can purchase a copy through Gaiam Real Goods and other outlets).

When assessing the potential of a site, you need to determine two factors: head and flow. In the words of Dan New, "You simply cannot move forward without these measurements. Your site's head and flow will determine everything about your hydro system — pipeline size, turbine type, rotational speed, and generator size. Even rough cost estimates will be impossible until you've measured head and flow." New goes on to say, "When measuring head and flow, keep in mind that accuracy is important. Inaccurate measurements can result in a hydro system designed to the wrong specs, and one that produces less electricity at a greater expense."

For these reasons, you may want to consult a professional with lots of experience in microhydro to help out or to make the necessary measurements. If you're lucky enough to have a local installer, it's not a bad idea to bring him or her in on the project. It may cost you more, but you could end up with a much better system, and more energy, than if you did all of this yourself.

So what is head?

Measuring Head

Head is an engineering term for water pressure created, in the case of microhydro systems, by the difference in elevation of the water intake and the turbine. It is usually measured in feet or meters when assessing site potential.

The difference in elevation between the intake and turbine can be measured in a variety of methods. For example, you can use an altimeter on a wrist watch, although it is not uncommon for the cheaper ones to be off by 150 feet or more, according to Dan New. You can also use a topographical map of your site to determine the differences in altitude between the intake and turbine.

While both of these methods work, they're often subject to error. As Scott Davis points out, "The accuracy of the power estimate and jet sizing ... requires measurement of head within five percent or so." As a result, experts typically recommend direct measurement.

The most accurate ways to measure vertical distances rely on some rather simple tools — a transit or a level (either a carpenter's level or a hand level) and a calibrated pole, for example, an eight-foot length of pole, marked off in feet and inches. You can even get by with a level and two people. One method is shown in Figure 9-5.

Rather than try to explain each of the methods commonly used to measure head, and confuse the whole lot of you, I strongly recommend that you read Dan New's piece in *Home Power* magazine or check out Scott Davis' book, mentioned earlier. They'll walk you through the techniques. (By the way, New's method for measuring uphill is one of the simplest you will find anywhere.) Don Harris shows the technique in his video, too.

The various techniques for measuring head allow you and an assistant to work your way up or down a hill, measuring the drop (head) from one spot to another. When done, you simply add together all of the measurements

for head from the water intake to the turbine to determine the total head.

Head can also be measured using garden hose or flexible tubing and a pressure meter. Dan New explains this technique, but points out that it works best for short distances — those in which a hose can be run from the proposed intake to the proposed turbine location. If the distance is greater than hose length, you can link several hoses together, so long as the connections are water tight. Or you can move the hose from one spot to another, taking multiple settings. The individual pressure settings are then added together to get the total head. In this case, however, head will be measured in water pressure, pounds per square inch or newtons per square meter (for those who buy a meter that's on the metric system). Read Dan New's piece before you tackle this project, as there are ways that you can get false readings.

Adding all of the measurements you've carefully taken yields the true vertical distance

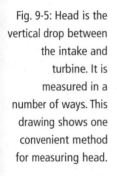

Fig. 9-5: Head is the vertical drop between the intake and turbine. It is measured in a number of ways. This drawing shows one convenient method for measuring head.

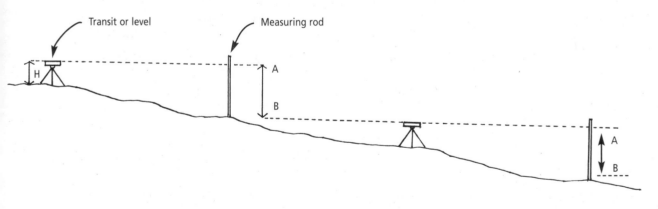

Transit or level

Measuring rod

from inlet to turbine, something that the microhydro folks call the "gross head" for a proposed site. But that's not sufficient for later calculations. You need to convert gross head to net head.

Gross head is the pressure (measured in feet or meters) in the system when the water is not flowing. It is static head. It is the pressure reading you'd get if you ran a pipe from inlet to turbine, filled the pipe with water, but capped the end of the pipe so water could not flow out. If you opened the pipe and let water flow through it, you'd see a drop in pressure. That's the net head. What accounts for this difference?

Net head, the measurement you get when water flows through the pipe, is less than gross head because of friction. Net head is less than gross head because friction slows the flow of water through the pipe. That is to say, water flowing through the pipe loses some energy due to friction losses — water molecules interacting with the interior surface of the pipe. As a result, net head is always less than gross head.

Before you can actually determine the friction loss, you will need to know the pipe length and the flow rate — how much water will flow through the pipe. I'll explain how flow is measured in a second. For now, it is important to note that the larger the pipe, the less friction loss. Conversely, the smaller the pipe, the more friction loss. Net head declines substantially in smaller diameter pipe.

But that's not all.

Friction losses also increase at higher flow rates. The faster the water flows through the pipe, the more friction.

Moreover, friction losses increase in longer pipelines.

And, as if that's not enough, bends in a pipe also increase friction losses that decrease head.

All four factors need to be considered very carefully when designing a system: diameter of the pipe, flow rate, length of the pipe, and bends in the pipe.

As a general rule, "a properly designed pipeline will yield a net head of 85 to 90 percent of the gross head you measured," says New. Greater losses will result in unacceptable reductions in electrical production. But like anything, there are exceptions and nuances to be considered. As New points out, "higher losses may be acceptable for high-head sites (100 feet plus) but pipeline friction losses should be minimized for low-head sites."

As you shall soon see, larger pipes reduce head loss resulting from friction, but they cost more; so there's often a trade-off between cost and performance. Longer

---

Four factors reduce head or pressure in a microhydro system: water flow rates, pipe diameter, pipeline length, and bends in the pipe. As a general rule, you should design your system in such a way that head loss is no more than 10 to 15 percent.

pipelines also increase head loss and cost more, too.

Before being able to calculate head loss, you will need to determine flow rate in your stream or river.

Measuring Flow Year Round

Stream flow can be measured in one of several ways. Before I briefly explain these methods, let me point out that stream flow should be measured during different times of the year. Why? To determine how much power a system can generate at high-, medium-, and low-flow regimes that are common in most perennial streams. (Perennial streams, of course, are those that flow year round.)

Fluctuations are common in perennial streams. Even in temperate rain forests like those of the Pacific Northwest there's a dry season during which stream flows are diminished. In mountainous areas, like the Sierras and the Rocky Mountains, perennial streams flow year round, but stream flows peak during the spring months in response to spring snowmelts. Flows decline dramatically as spring proceeds to summer, then fall, and into winter.

Flows in perennial streams can be reduced to a mere trickle, forcing homeowners to turn to other sources of electrical energy. Take the case of John Schaeffer, who founded Real Goods and the Solar Living Institute. John and his family live off-grid in northern California where they tap into the power of flowing water in a stream on their beautiful property. In this region of the country, rainfall is plentiful in the winter, but declines dramatically once June rolls around. As a result, the stream on the Schaeffer's property pretty much dries up in the summer and stays dry until late fall. (I know, I've seen it!) As a result, he and his family get much of their electricity from their microhydropower system during the late fall and winter and early spring when it is quite rainy. During the summer and early fall, their PV system makes up the difference, supplying virtually all of their electrical needs.

So, remember to measure flow rates, if you can, during the spring, summer, winter, and fall for the most accurate assessment of a site. Remember, too, that in climates where freezing occurs, water continues to flow in streams under the protection of a layer of ice and snow. You can tap into this energy source, even though the stream appears to be frozen over for the winter. It's wise, however, and environmentally responsible not to take all of the water from the stream then or any time of the year!

How Do You Measure Flow Rates?

Now that you understand the importance of year-round measurements, let's answer the question: how do you measure stream flows?

Stream flow can be measured by one of three methods. The simplest is the container fill method (Figure 9-6). This is particularly useful in really narrow streams. It requires a large bucket and a stop watch. To make a measurement, you simply find a narrow spot in the waterway where you can fill a single bucket. A bucket is then thrust into the spot and filled by one person. A second person runs a stop watch, timing the event. When the five-gallon bucket is full, the stop watch operator ends the session. If the five-gallon bucket fills in 15 seconds, you simply multiple 5 gallons by 4 to figure the amount of flow in a minute. In this instance, the flow rate would be 20 gallons per minute.

The second method is the float method, well described in Dan New's piece in *Home Power*. This technique is useful for larger streams but in order to do so, you will need a straight section that's about ten feet long, as shown in Figure 9-7.

In the float method, you first measure how long it takes for a floating object to travel ten feet. Let's say the object — a tennis ball, for instance — covers the ten feet in five seconds. This figure will then be used to calculate flow. But before you can do so, you need to know the average depth across a section of the stream, as shown in Figure 9-7. Depth measurements are taken every foot across a section of the river. The measurements are all added together, then divided by the number of measurements, yielding average depth. This figure is then multiplied by the width of the stream. If the stream is 6 feet wide and the average depth measurement is 1.5, the cross-sectional area is 9 square feet.

If the floating object takes 5 seconds to travel 10 feet, the stream is flowing at 2 feet

Fig. 9-6: The container fill method is one way to determine flow rates in small streams.

SCOTT DAVIS

per second or 120 feet per minute (2 feet per second x 60 seconds per minute = 120 feet per minute). If the cross-sectional area is 9 square feet, you simply multiply 120 feet per minute by 9 square feet and the result is 1,080 cubic feet per minute. That's the rate of flow.

This needs to be adjusted to take into account frictional losses along the bottom of the stream. Multiplying 1,080 cubic feet per minute by 0.83 yields the actual flow.

The next method, known as the weir method, is even more involved, but it's the most accurate of all techniques. It does, however, require construction of a temporary dam across the river with a rectangular opening in the middle of the structure. Because this technique is more complicated, and involves reference to a weir table, I'll let those interested in learning more about the method read Dan New's account in *Home Power*, Issue 104.

Basically, what you need to know is that to calculate the flow, you simply measure water level in the opening in the weir. You then refer to the weir table that provides data on flow in cubic feet per minute. You multiply this figure by the width of the opening and you're done.

Protecting the Environment

Once you have determined flow rate, you need to determine how much water can be removed from the stream without disrupting the aquatic ecosystem. Obviously, the less water that's removed, the less impact you'll have.

To make an assessment will require more training than most readers possess. I recommend that you consult an aquatic biologist for a site assessment and his or her recommendations. Your state division of wildlife may be able to help you out. Local permitting agencies may also have guidelines or may supply personnel. A professional stream biologist is apt to give you the best information about the potential impact of damming up part of the river, if necessary to divert water into your intake structure, as well as impacts that may result from the removal of water from the stream in the section between the intake and outlet.

Renewable energy is clean and great for the environment, but you don't want to trash your stream to produce clean power. So be careful and show respect for the natural world that gives so much to us.

What's the Next Step?

Once you have determined head and flow — or have had a professional do it for you — you are ready to start designing a system.

Well, not quite.

After determining head and water flow, you will need to measure the length of the pipeline. You can measure the length by pacing off the distance from the inlet to the turbine; however, it is best to measure it directly, using a 100-foot tape measure.

You'll also need to measure the distance from the turbine to your house and the battery bank. As in other renewable energy

Fig. 9-7: The float method, described in the text, is another way of determining flow rates of streams and rivers.

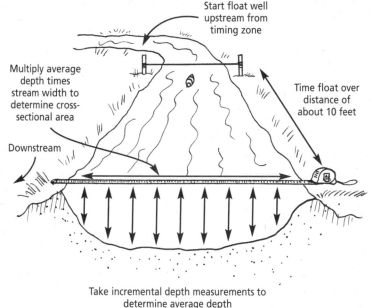

Start float well upstream from timing zone

Multiply average depth times stream width to determine cross-sectional area

Downstream

Time float over distance of about 10 feet

Take incremental depth measurements to determine average depth

CANYON HYDRO, *HOME POWER*, AND JILL HARAS

systems that produce DC power, it is best to keep the batteries as close to the source of electricity, in this case the turbine, as possible. DC electricity doesn't travel well and longer distances require larger diameter wire that is much more expensive than standard 12-gauge electrical wire.

It is also wise to keep the batteries warm year-round. Lead acid batteries, the type most commonly used in these and other renewable energy systems, perform optimally at temperatures of around 70°F (21°C). (For more on batteries, see Chapter 7.)

With this information, you can begin to design a system. You'll need to pick out a turbine that suits your purpose, and then determine pipe size. You can make these determinations yourself, or you can contact a local supplier, if you haven't already engaged his or her assistance. National suppliers of microhydro equipment, such as Gaiam Real Goods, can also lend a hand. Their staff can assist you in sizing and designing a system. They'll provide a worksheet that asks for a few pieces of relevant data. It is used to generate a design for your system via a computer-sizing program. Their computer program allows them to size plumbing and wiring with the least power loss at the lowest cost.

The best way for a home hydro builder to design a system "is to solicit proposals from equipment suppliers," recommends Dan New. "Suppliers and manufacturers have been designing systems and handling problems for years, and that experience is available and free to the home developer." New also recommends that you consider contacting microhydro expert Lee Tavenner, co-owner of Solar Plexus in Montana. "Not only can he put together a complete DC or AC system," says New, "he can design systems to use hydro, solar, and wind." Tavenner's website is <www.solarplexus1.com>.

Once the system is designed, suppliers can calculate how much electrical power the proposed system will generate.

BUYING AND INSTALLING A SYSTEM

If you are designing a system on your own, you'll need to consider each component of the system separately, starting with the intake structure. This section will help you understand a bit more about each component.

If you are relying on local or national microhydro experts to design your system, they'll specify the components and suggest the best design. Nonetheless, it is wise to read

A Good Site

The key element for a good site is the vertical distance the water drops. A small amount of water dropping a large distance will produce as much energy as a large amount of water dropping a small distance. Thus, we can get approximately the same power output by running 1,000 gallons per minute through a 2-foot drop as by running 2 gallons per minute through a 1,000-foot drop.

John Schaeffer, *Solar Living Source Book*

the material in this section so that you better understand what they're up to. The more informed you are, the more likely you are to get the system that works best for your needs and one that you will be happy with over the long haul.

Before we begin to examine the components of a microhydro system in detail, however, let me make one quick point: microhydro can be combined with any other renewable energy technology. For example, you could design a system that combines PVs and microhydro or a wind generator and microhydro, or perhaps all three. Microhydro systems can even be coupled with grid power or a diesel or propane generator. The sky's the limit.

Combining systems not only ensures better year-round service, it also means that you may be able to save some money on one or more parts of your system. For example, combining PV and microhydro will probably mean that you'll need a smaller PV system and a smaller battery bank.

With this in mind, let's look at the various components of a microhydro system, beginning with the intake structure.

Water Intake

All microhydro systems require an intake at the highest point in the system to divert water from the stream into the penstock. As noted earlier, all intakes need to be screened to prevent debris from entering the pipeline. Ideally, the screen should be self-cleansing. In other words, it should be designed so that debris washes off naturally. Otherwise, you'll have to schedule a regular inspection to remove debris that may block water flow into the pipeline. Blockages could seriously reduce your system's electrical production.

Screens are immersed in water 24 hours a day; they should be made of a durable material that won't rust. One excellent choice is the stainless steel screen. They're sold for use in irrigation systems and are available through agricultural supply outlets in rural areas where irrigation is a common practice among farmers. If your agricultural supply outlet doesn't have screens, they may be able to order one for you. You may also want to check out commercially manufactured microhydro intake screens like those made by Hydroscreen Company at <www.hydroscreen.com>.

Intake structures vary in complexity. The simplest of all intakes is a screened pipe placed into a deep pool of water in the stream. The most complex intake systems consist of small concrete diversion structures or dams that block flow across an entire stream or river. The design, of course, depends on your site.

When designing an intake, it is important to remember the function of this structure. One important function of an intake structure is to prevent air from entering the pipeline. Air flowing through a turbine reduces power output and may damage the turbine. To be sure that no air enters the system, the intake pipe needs to be fully submersed all year long.

This is done by placing the pipe in a deep pool, or building an intake structure that provides a pool that is deep enough all year round to prevent air from being sucked into the system — even during that part of the year when stream flows are at their lowest.

The intake structure also needs to provide a stilling basin — a pool that allows silt, sand, gravel, and rocks to settle out *before* stream water enters the penstock. Figure 9-4, shows a section through an intake structure. In this structure, the stilling basin empties into a second pool. Water flows from here into the pipeline. A screen over the pipe helps prevent debris from entering it.

Microhydro systems require very little maintenance. Sealed bearings in brushless generators and long-lasting runners in many systems mean that you won't be lubricating or replacing parts very often. You will, however, need to pay attention to the stilling basin and screen. Stilling basins may need to be emptied of debris and screens may need to be cleaned on a regular basis.

To reduce routine cleaning, you should consider creating an overflow in the stilling pond that naturally siphons off floating debris and returns it to the stream. The screen should be as close to vertical as possible or slanted so that it self-cleans as much as possible. The intake screen and pipe also need to be submerged below the frost line to prevent freezing. Ice buildup on the screen could slow the flow of water into your system and sharply reduce its electrical output.

Choosing a Turbine/Generator

Several different types of microhydro turbine/generators are available. Your choice of turbine depends on the characteristics of your site. For mountainous sites, characterized by fairly high pressure resulting from some favorable combination of head and water flow, you may want to consider the small Pelton wheel Harris systems (Figure 9-8). Pelton wheels are durable and require very infrequent replacement due to wear and tear. Even with dirty, gritty water, it takes at least ten years to wear out a Pelton wheel manufactured by Don Harris, according to Gaiam Real Goods. However, Harris offers a conventional automotive alternator with his system. These

Fig. 9-8: Harris turbine.

HARRIS HYDROELECTRIC

devices have bearings and brushes that need to be replaced at intervals of one to five years, depending on how hard the system works. To minimize maintenance, Harris also offers a brushless permanent magnet generator. These units cost about $700 more, but use larger, more sturdy bearings that last two to three times longer. This greatly reduces maintenance and replacement costs. It is, needless to say, well worth the extra cost.

Harris turbines are for applications with 50 feet of head and up. They produce from 1 kWh to 35 kWh per day, depending on the model and site. The unit (generator) has an instantaneous output of about 2,500 watts — enough to start many appliances and power tools. Harris microhydro turbines come in 24 and 48 volts and are manufactured in the United States.

For low-head systems that channel a lot of water through a turbine with little head (that is, flatter sites), you may want to consider a Low Head Stream Engine (Figure 9-9) or one of the newest microhydro turbine/generators, the Jack Rabbit (Figure 9-10).

The Stream Engine is a brushless permanent magnet generator with sealed bearings that minimize maintenance. These units operate in sites with heads that range from 5 to 400 feet with flow rates from 5 gallons to 300 gallons per minute, although flow rates above 150 gpm provide very little additional power. Although setup can be a bit tricky, the unit is virtually maintenance free. Output voltages are 12, 24, and 48 volts. They're manufactured in Canada.

The Jack Rabbit is an unusual microhydro turbine and generator. As shown in Figure 9-10, this submarine-like device consists of a submersible propeller and generator in a waterproof casing that's suspended in a stream in at least 13 inches of water. The generator operates

Fig. 9-9: Low Head Stream Engine.

ENERGY SYSTEMS AND DESIGN

Fig. 9-10: Jack Rabbit.

JACK RABBIT MARINE

at low speeds, ideally around 9 miles per hour, or equivalent to a slow jog. Water flowing past the device causes the propeller to spin.

In slow-moving streams, water flows can be increased by piling rocks or heavy timbers to create a funnel with the wide end facing upstream. This channels water into the narrow end of the funnel, which greatly increases its speed. (This phenomenon is known as the Venturi effect.) The Jack Rabbit is placed at the narrow part of the funnel where the water is flowing most rapidly, optimizing the performance of the generator.

Jack Rabbits are low-capacity microhydro turbines that produce 100 watts of continuous power in a 9 mile per hour stream — or about 2.4 kWh of electricity per day — and slightly less in a slower stream.

Jack Rabbits are rugged and require very little maintenance. The heavy-duty aluminum blades are not easily damaged. If struck by a log and bent, the propeller blades can be hammered back into shape. Another advantage of the Jack Rabbit is that it requires no pipeline, a feature that can save you a lot of money. Electrical lines from the generators (mounted securely in a stream) carry the current to the house. Jack Rabbits come in 12 and 24 volts models and are made in Great Britain. Proceed with caution on this one, however. Word from users is that the power output is very low and there are other problems that may make this a dubious choice.

Finally, the Low Head Stream Engine, with a turgo-type runner, is for use in sites that offer intermediate characteristics. They operate in areas with drops of 2 to 10 feet and flows ranging from 200 to 1,000 gallons per minute. Peak output is 1,000 watts, meaning that a machine operating in a good site will provide 24 kWh of electricity per day.

To learn more about these systems, I strongly recommend that you consult John Schaeffer's book, *Solar Living Source Book*. It provides a good overview of the subject and a lot of valuable information on the various microhydro turbines, including pricing. Remember, as Dan New points out, that "the turbine should be designed to match your specific head and flow. Proper selection requires considerable expertise."

AC Generators

Although most microhydro systems produce DC electricity, there are some times when AC generators are advisable, notably for larger commercial applications or for grid-connected systems. These systems can produce more than 3,000 watts of continuous power or 72 kWh per day — far more than most homes ever consume. As Dan New pointed out in an e-mail to me, these systems "can often supply *all* of the energy needs of a home." DC systems typically only provide electricity for lighting, appliances, and electronic heaters, but not space heat, hot water, or dryers. Those demands are typically satisfied by propane or natural gas. An AC microhydro system could even supply heavy duty machines, compressors, and welding and wood working equipment. "Most DC systems cannot cover most of this list," concludes New, so homeowners must rely "on nonrenewable sources of energy to accomplish these tasks."

According to Schaeffer, AC systems often involve considerable engineering, custom metalwork, formed concrete, permits, and a fairly high initial investment. AC systems also require governors to ensure that the AC generator spins at the correct speed to produce electricity of the proper frequency to match household needs. In grid-connected systems, additional controls are also required to ensure that power going onto the electric grid matches line current with respect to voltage, frequency, and phase. These controls will automatically disconnect the system from the grid if major fluctuations occur on either end.

Although AC systems cost more upfront, "AC power is almost always cheaper per kilowatt hour," says New. AC hydro systems also require no batteries and do not require inverters. AC power is used directly as it is produced. Surplus can be diverted to dump loads, usually resistance heaters, or can be diverted to the electrical grid. "So," says New, "if a homeowner can find a use for most of the power most of the time, a moderately sized AC system, say 4 kW to 15 kW, will provide the energy needed to power a home renewably for less money." (For details on grid-connected renewable energy systems, see Chapter 7.)

For those who want battery backup, in case the system must be shut down, remember that AC power can be converted to DC power by a bank of diodes and then stored in a battery bank for later use. However, also remember that to be useful, DC electricity from the battery bank must be converted back to AC power. That's a function of the inverter. As Dan New pointed out to me in his communication, systems that convert AC to DC power are rare.

AC systems can be quite costly, warns Schaeffer, so this "isn't an undertaking for the faint-of-heart or thin-of-wallet." This is not to say these systems are uneconomical. Quite the opposite: they often provide a very good return on investment. "Far more streams can support a small DC-output system," says New, "than a higher output AC system." Those who think they have a site that is suitable for low-head AC power production, can download information on these systems from the

AC vs DC Costs

Although an AC microhydro system typically costs more than a DC system, this comparison isn't fair. You're not generally comparing apples to apples. Most DC systems don't produce anywhere near as much electricity as AC systems. The result is that you will very likely need to acquire additional energy to run your home, for example, natural gas. You may also need to install additional equipment, for example, a wood-stove to provide additional heat or a gas or diesel generator to provide additional electricity to run a washing machine.

following website: <www.eere.energy.gov/RE/hydropower.html>. For more on the cost issue, see the accompanying sidebar.

Powerhouse

As noted earlier, turbines and generators must be protected against the elements to ensure longer service. Protection is provided by a powerhouse. Powerhouses range in complexity from the simple wooden or cement block boxes, designed so you can work on the system, to small sheds with room for battery banks. It's your call.

Be sure when connecting pipes to the turbine in a powerhouse to use as few elbows as possible. Bends in the pipe dramatically reduce head by creating turbulence. Reduced head, in turn, reduces system output. "Likewise," notes Dan New, "any restrictions on water exiting the turbine may increase resistance against the turbine's moving parts." This, too, reduces power output.

Drive Systems

In most systems, a steel shaft connects the turbine to the generator. This shaft couples the turbine with the generator so that rotation of the turbine's runner translates into rotation within the generator. "The most efficient and reliable drive system involves a direct 1:1 coupling between the turbine and generator," notes New. But this is not possible for all sites. In some cases, especially when AC generators are used, it may be necessary to "adjust the transfer ratio so that both the turbine and generator run at their optimum (but different) speeds," he adds. This is achieved through gears, chains, or belts with belt systems being the most popular due to their lowest cost. Unfortunately, more complex drive systems increase the cost of a system and will invariably increase maintenance requirements.

Batteries

For those who need lots of power intermittently, which is most of us, a battery system or a grid-connect may be the best route. Most microhydro systems use deep-cycle lead acid batteries. Never never never use automobile batteries. They just can't handle the deep discharging.

Because I've covered batteries for renewable energy systems at length in Chapter 7, I'll refer readers to that section rather than repeat myself. Let me point out one important fact at this point. As a general rule, microhydro systems require much smaller, and thus much less expensive, battery banks than solar electric or wind electric systems.

Why?

Because such systems only need to provide electricity for occasional heavy power usages and power surges. You're not trying to store power for three to four days of cloudy weather as in the case of a PV system or windless days in the case of a wind energy system.

The battery bank is also smaller because of rapid recharge. That is, if the batteries are drawn down during the day, they're usually recharged in the evening by the continuous power output of the system.

Occasional high output and rapid recharge not only mean fewer batteries, it also means a longer battery life, for reasons explained in Chapter 7.

Piping

After designing an intake structure and selecting a turbine, you'll need to design a pipeline. Pipelines are typically made from either four-inch PVC or smaller polyethylene pipe. PVC is used almost exclusively when the pipe in a system needs to be over 2 inches in diameter, although 1.5- to 2-inch PVC can be and is used.

Four-inch PVC pipe comes in 10- and 20-foot sections that are glued together. Assembly is quick and painless and can be mastered by anyone. PVC pipe not only goes together easily, it is relatively inexpensive. In addition, PVC pipe is very light, which makes it easy to install, which is especially helpful in steep terrain.

Two-inch polyethylene pipe is used for smaller flows. It comes in very long rolls that are laid out from intake to turbine. Because there's no gluing, unless two rolls must be connected, polyethylene pipe goes in much faster than PVC.

Although plastic pipe is fairly inexpensive, the pipeline can be a costly and time-consuming aspect of a microhydro system. "It's not unusual to use several thousand feet of pipe to collect a hundred feet of head," notes Schaeffer. Additionally, in cold climates, pipe may need to be buried below the frost line to prevent it from freezing. This can add significantly to the cost and labor required to install a system, especially if the soils are rocky and difficult to work in, which is often the case in mountainous terrain. However, Scott Davis points out that "even if the pipe is not quite below the frost line, water running through the pipe may keep it from freezing."

Burying the pipeline not only protects the pipe from freezing, it helps protect it from damage, for instance, from falling trees or tree limbs. And it helps keep the pipe from shifting around as high-pressure water flows through it. PVC pipe deteriorates in sunlight, too, necessitating burial.

Controllers

Microhydro systems also require special controllers to prevent batteries from overcharging, and hence from being permanently damaged. Unlike the charge controllers on PV and many wind systems that merely terminate the flow of electricity to the batteries, microhydro system controllers shunt excess electricity to a secondary load, typically an electric resistor or two (Figure 9-11). These resistors are typically water- or space-heating elements that put excess electricity to good use heating domestic hot water or the house. (Note: PV charge controllers should not be used in a microhydro system, as they could damage the electrical generator.)

Excess power is shunted to secondary loads when the system's batteries, if any, are full and when the household demands are being met by the system. Excess power can also be diverted onto the grid or sent to a nearby neighbor's home, if you like.

Load controllers and water heater and air heater diversion devices can be purchased from Gaiam Real Goods and other suppliers that cater to folks interested in microhydro.

Power Lines

Most microhydro systems produce low-voltage DC current that travels in a wire to the battery bank. Because this type of current doesn't travel well — it loses energy quickly over distance — it is best to keep power lines from the turbine/generator short, under 100 feet. If not, you will need to use large-gauge wire, which costs much more than standard wiring.

Permitting

Jeffe Aronson installed a low-head microhydro system on a stream running through his property in Australia. He did so by building a small concrete dam across part of the river. While friends recommended that he complete the project without permits and "let the bureaucrats find it if they could," Jeffe decided to secure the necessary permits and work with local authorities. In fact, he made a point of working with them in a cooperative fashion, and not showing anger or frustration at some of their quirks. In short, he established

AEE SOLAR

Fig. 9-11: Load diverters take excess energy and run it through resistors (shown on the right) to generate heat. They're useful in the winter to provide heat to living spaces as well as garages, sheds, and workshops.

a good working relationship, and showed them respect.

"A couple years later," Aronson writes in *Home Power*, Issue 101, a visiting angler, "who had fished this section of river for decades and considered it his own, came upon our works." The angler was outraged and, rather than consult the landowner (Jeffe), sent in a complaint to the water catchment authority. "They sent a representative with whom we'd dealt originally," said Aronson. "He thankfully found that we'd done what we'd said we'd do, and even felt the works to be 'very discreet.'"

Needless to say, that was the end of the story.

The lesson in this tale is that permitting may be a bother, but it can save you a lot of hassle and expense. In fact, government agencies can force a landowner to remove a system that cost a couple of thousand dollars to install, if they catch him or her generating microhydro without a permit.

What permits are necessary?

To answer this, you should contact a local supplier or installer. He or she can help you out. If there are no local experts, you will need to call the state's office of environmental protection or state energy office. They can steer you in the right direction.

FINDING AN INSTALLER OR INSTALLING A SYSTEM YOURSELF

Microhydro systems are pretty easy to install. In fact, those who have modest plumbing and electrical skills can install most of a system without much trouble. However, battery banks, inverters, and other controls typically installed on stand-alone systems require a higher degree of expertise than many do-it-yourselfers possess. Grid-connected systems require an even higher level of electrical expertise.

My advice is that it's always a good idea to hire a professional to help you out or to do the job for you. Experienced professionals know the tricks of the trade and can save you a lot of time, trouble, expense, and gray hairs. A professional installation will cost more, to be sure, but the added expense could very likely be well worth it. Not only will you very likely get a better system, you'll have someone to call in case something goes wrong and you can't seem to fix it.

How do you locate a professional?

I recommend contacting a local renewable energy society or, if there is none, call a manufacturer or Real Goods, and ask for references in your area.

THE PROS AND CONS OF MICROHYDRO SYSTEMS

Microhydro is a great source of reliable electrical energy, but before you go out to buy a system, you should have a full understanding of its pros and cons. On the plus side, microhydro is probably *the* most cost-effective renewable energy system on the market. According to Scott Davis, it delivers "the best bang per buck." Davis goes on to say, "Significant power can be generated with flows of two gallons per minute or from drops as small as two feet." And, says Davis, "power can be delivered in cost-effective fashion a mile or more from where it is generated to where it is being used."

What other benefits does microhydro offer?

Microhydro, unlike almost all other renewable forms of energy, certainly wind and solar, provides continuous power. That is to say, it provides electricity day and night, night and day, 7 days a week, 365 days a year. Excess power can be stored in batteries or can be shunted onto the utility grid, if it's nearby. As Figure 9-12 shows, microhydro can do a much better job of meeting your needs whereas solar and wind systems require considerable storage capacity, or a hook up to the electrical grid, to supply power when the systems are not working.

Microhydro sites owe their year-round performance in part to the fact that they can be easily winterized. Even though stream flows may slow down during the winter in snowy climates, small streams continue to offer reliable water flows (moving water doesn't freeze very readily). Burying pipes underground (below the frost line) also helps to ensure a steady flow.

Furthermore, notes Davis, microhydro can be integrated with pipelines delivering water to a house — specifically, water delivered to a house from a spring or stream located uphill from a house. Microhydro systems are inexpensive, too, costing from US

Fig. 9-12: Comparison of microhydro and hybrid solar/wind systems.

Typical Power Consumption

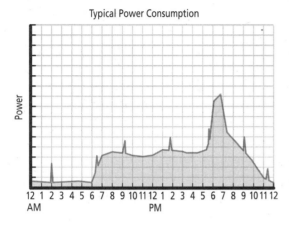

Your electrical needs vary over time.

Photovoltaic

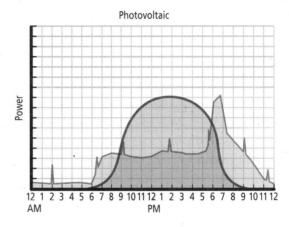

PV outputs drop to zero every night and are much reduced in winter and cloudy weather.

Wind Generator

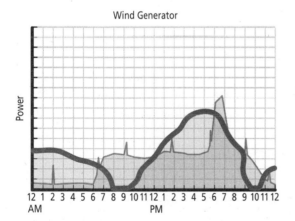

Wind system outputs go up and down irregularly.

Hydro

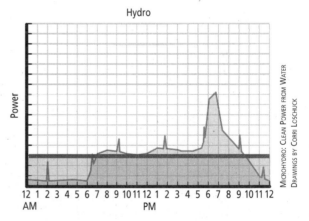

Microhydro systems have the same output all the time.

MICROHYDRO: CLEAN POWER FROM WATER
DRAWINGS BY CORRI LOSCHUCK

$2,000 to $10,000, in the case of really large systems.

Yet another advantage of microhydro is that it is applicable to a variety of different conditions from high head/low flow to low head/high flow and everything in between. The rule of thumb is, the more head, the less volume will be necessary to produce a given amount of power. The less head, the more volume you'll need.

Like all systems, there are some disadvantages to microhydro systems. First off, very few suitable sites are available, say, in comparison to solar electric or even wind energy sites. Second, microhydro systems require considerable knowledge. Third, not all sites that could be used for microhydro can be developed economically. Pipelines for the system, for instance, may be long and costly. Or they may difficult to install. Fourth, diverting water from streams can alter flows and adversely affect living things that rely on the water. You need to exert extreme caution when installing a microhydro system. Be sure to consult with a qualified stream biologist. Fifth, microhydro systems may require permits from local government agencies, which can take time and may require a financial outlay on your part — notably, for engineering costs or the costs of a biologist to examine the site for potential impact.

Like any system, you need to proceed carefully and cautiously with as complete an understanding of the system you're interested in as possible. Who knows, if you are lucky enough to live by a stream or river and can legally tap into the power of the water running by your home, you could be graced with years of very inexpensive, clean, and renewable energy.

CHAPTER 10

WHAT'S ON THE HORIZON?

NEW FUELS AND NEW TECHNOLOGIES FOR HOMES AND AUTOS

Oil and natural gas shortages — and rising fuel prices resulting from the growing rift between supply and demand — are going to figure more prominently in our lives in the coming decades. Shortfalls could affect us in many ways, as noted in the Introduction. They could, for instance, cause dramatic increases in household energy costs. And because natural gas and oil are so essential to the economy, shortfalls could dramatically increase the cost of just about every good and service we've grown accustomed to over the past 50 years of relative affluence. On a larger scale, rising fuel prices could trigger major economic woes: inflation, followed by a deep recession that could persist for years. Even more ominously, shortages could spawn global conflict as energy-hungry nations, like the United States

and China, seek to ensure, through whatever means possible, a continuing supply of fuels.

As you have seen in this book, there are many clean, reliable and affordable renewable energy resources that can meet our needs. Although we have squandered opportunities to shift to alternatives, we mustn't wring our hands in anguish. We must move forward, quickly and decisively.

First and foremost among alternatives is energy conservation: using what we need (the frugality principle) and using it efficiently. Energy conservation is to our energy future what the emergency room is to medicine. It can save us from crashing. As I've pointed out over and over in this book, energy efficiency can help homeowners dramatically reduce their use of energy and greatly ease the economic

Although we have squandered opportunities to shift to alternatives, we mustn't wring our hands in anguish. We must move on, quickly and decisively, to shift to renewable energy.

Energy conservation is to our energy future what the emergency room is to medicine.

burden of living in a world whose appetite for energy outstrips its supply.

To heat our homes, we can retrofit with passive and active solar. We can install ground- and air-source heat pumps, and an assortment of wood-burning technologies, including fireplace inserts, wood stoves, wood furnaces, masonry heaters, and pellet stoves. For domestic hot water, we can turn to active solar systems and heat pumps.

We can even increase our reliance on residential solar electricity (PVs) and wind or even microhydro to replace electricity generated from the combustion of natural gas in power plants owned and operated by public and private utilities throughout North America. But what about home cooking? And what about those dinosaurs in our garages — our beloved cars, vans, and trucks? How do we power them

in a world in which oil and natural gas supplies are slipping toward oblivion?

As we become more efficient in our use of conventional energy resources and steadily increase our reliance on renewable energy technologies, the fossil fuel resources like oil and natural gas freed up by such efforts can be utilized to power activities for which replacements are most problematic, for example, air transportation and cooking. Passive solar or solar hot water system retrofits that heat homes, for instance, could free up huge quantities of natural gas throughout North America which could then be used to cook our food, easing the crunch.

There are other options for replacing declining supplies of natural gas and oil, too, ones not previously discussed. Let's consider the most likely alternatives.

MORE FOSSIL FUELS

Dissenting voices, mostly advocates of business as usual, encourage us not to worry over declining oil and natural gas supplies. We can, they say, extract oil from abundant tar sands and oil sands. We can, they assure us, even make oil and natural gas from abundant coal supplies.

One company (Silverado Green Fuel, Inc.) has even come up with a way to use abundant low-BTU coal to replace the oil and natural gas burned in power plants. This coal, which is found in abundance in Alaska, is crushed into a fine powder and dehydrated (it contains a lot of water) in an industrial

Fig. 10-1: While there are many options for providing clean, renewable energy for our homes, what choices do we have for automobiles?

DAN CHIRAS

pressure cooker. The particles are then coated with a wax-like substance that prevents them from soaking up moisture. The coated particles are then mixed with water to create a slurry that can, says the company's literature, be transported through pipelines or by ships. At the power plant, the slurry feeds directly into the burner.

This low-sulfur coal slurry, according to the company, burns fairly cleanly, and is projected to be quite cost-effective. It does, however, continue to pour the greenhouse gas carbon dioxide into the atmosphere in an era in which many of the world's nations are striving to reduce emissions of this troublesome pollutant.

Some energy analysts believe that oil shale and tar sands could help us meet our needs. As you may recall from Chapter 1, extracting oil from oil shale and tar sands is an energy-intensive processes and, as such, is very costly. In a world where oil and natural gas supplies are declining and prices are rising, it's my belief that counting on these low net energy fuels won't save the day. They could even drive prices higher, contributing to more widespread economic worries. A world dependent on cheap oil can't afford even more expensive replacements. Moreover, continuing our use of fossil fuels will worsen other serious problems, the most important of which is the global meltdown we politely refer to as global warming. So what do we do that doesn't involve massive increases in fossil fuel use and greenhouse gas emissions?

HYDROGEN: SOLUTION OR DISTRACTION?

Many people believe that hydrogen will be the fuel of the future. Are they right or is this a blind alley?

Clean Burning and Abundant

Hydrogen is a combustible gas that can be used to heat our homes, cook food, and heat water for showers. It burns just like natural gas, without producing any carbon dioxide whatsoever. In fact, when hydrogen burns it produces heat, light, and water. You couldn't ask for a cleaner-burning fuel.

An Automotive Fuel

Hydrogen could also be used to power automobiles. It can be stored under pressure in specially built tanks (already available) and burned directly in specially designed engines (already available). Or it can be fed into a device called a fuel cell. Fuel cells are small battery-like contraptions that combine hydrogen with oxygen from the air to create electricity. Electricity generated in a fuel cell can then be used to power electric motors that power our cars, buses, and trucks. The water produced in the process can be captured and recycled.

But Where Will Hydrogen Come From?

Hydrogen can be extracted from a variety of sources. For example, it can be stripped from the organic molecules in various conventional fossil fuels — natural gas, propane, gasoline — or any hydrocarbon molecule (ethanol or methanol, for example) that contain hydrogen. Unfortunately, stripping hydrogen from fossil fuels still produces carbon dioxide — and lots of it. And why would we want to utilize finite supplies of fossil fuels to make hydrogen? Wouldn't this put us right back where we started? Why not obtain the hydrogen we need to power our cars from renewable resources, from water, for instance?

Not only is water abundant, but as just noted, it is renewable. Moreover, it is not under the control of wealthy sheiks or tyrannical leaders in the politically volatile Middle East.

Running electricity through water produces hydrogen. The electrical current splits the water molecules into their components: hydrogen and oxygen. Both hydrogen and oxygen are gases.

Besides powering our cars, hydrogen gas can be burned directly in water heaters, stoves, and even furnaces, replacing declining supplies of natural gas. If it could be pumped through the pipelines and underground pipes that currently carry natural gas to our cities and homes, we'd be able to make use of an elaborate and costly supply system that's already in place.

Unfortunately, there's a problem with this scheme.

Transporting Hydrogen

The problem is this: hydrogen is a small molecular-weight gas, much smaller than natural gas. Because of its small molecular weight, hydrogen can't be contained in existing pipelines. Put more bluntly: it would leak out.

Some proponents of a hydrogen economy suggest that we would have to rebuild all of the pipelines that carry natural gas across North America from the well heads to our cities. Would we also have to install new pipes in our cities to deliver hydrogen to every home?

If so, we're up the creek on this one. It could take decades to complete a project of this magnitude.

But maybe there's a way we can seal up the pipelines so they'd contain the stuff.

Or perhaps we could generate hydrogen on the outskirts of major cities or in the cities themselves, and then simply pipe it through the existing or even newly-laid underground pipes that deliver this vital fuel to our homes.

Where Does the Electricity Come From?

As we research the prospects of hydrogen gas as a fuel of the future, we will also need to ask how we're going to generate all of the electricity that's required to split water to make this fuel. And where are we going to get the water, especially in water-short areas of North America?

The Bush Administration embraces the idea of the hydrogen economy, but believes that we should obtain hydrogen from fossil fuels, as described above. They also support the use of nuclear energy and coal to generate the electricity needed to split water to produce hydrogen.

Renewable energy advocates disagree with this approach. Richard Engle, a hydrogen proponent at the Schatz Energy Research Center, argues that "the nuclear and coal industries are ... latching onto hydrogen as a means to assure their continued dominance of energy markets." Dominic Crea, a physics teacher who supports renewable energy argues that "a fossil-fueled hydrogen economy is a gamble at best and a nightmare at worse."

Renewable energy advocates like Engle argue that we should be using the nation's clean and abundant wind and solar energy resources to make electricity from water. It should then be used to generate hydrogen. But is this the best use of electricity generated from renewable resources?

Hydrogen: A Secondary Fuel Source

As we pursue a path to make hydrogen, it is important to remember one thing —hydrogen is *not* a primary fuel like natural gas or oil.

Companies won't be drilling into pockets of hydrogen gas in the Earth's crust.

They don't exist.

Rather, hydrogen is a fuel we manufacture. Hydrogen is a secondary fuel made by splitting water with electricity. In other words, it takes energy to make hydrogen.

Net Energy Efficiency of Hydrogen Use in Vehicles

As we pursue this fuel, we must ask: how much energy does it take to make hydrogen from electricity generated by another source?

And, more to the point, are we getting a lot more energy out of the system than we are putting into it? Ultimately, high net energy efficiency should be our goal in our quest to create an affordable fuel to replace natural gas and gasoline from oil.

Dominic Crea, mentioned earlier, is a critic of hydrogen use. His calculations suggest that it makes much more sense to use the electricity we generate from renewable energy technologies (like wind) to run cars directly than to use it to split hydrogen to power fuel cells. According to Crea, the net energy efficiency of a system that generates electricity to power electric cars is three times greater than a system that generates electricity from renewable resources to produce hydrogen to power fuel-cell cars. His work can be found in "Hydrogen: Solution or Distraction?" in *Home Power* magazine, Issue 101.

Unfortunately, electric cars require huge battery banks and can't run very far without needing recharging. They have a short range of 80 to 120 miles on a single charge. Charging takes a long time, too. You can't just buzz into a gas station and recharge your car's batteries in five minutes while you wolf down a Danish and a cup of coffee. As a result, it is very likely you won't be driving cross-country, even cross-state, in a conventional electric car unless you live in one of the spatially challenged states of the nation — those compact mini-states back east — at least until we get some lighter, higher capacity batteries. Barring major breakthroughs, then, electric cars may have

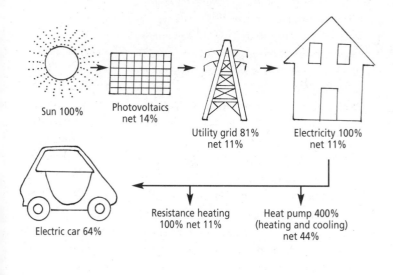

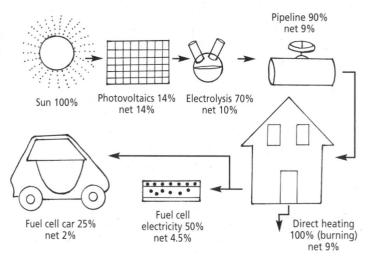

Fig. 10-2: Studying the net energy efficiency of a fuel is vital to making sound choices. This diagram from Dominic Crea's article in *Home Power* magazine, Issue 101, compares hydrogen to electricity generated from solar electricity and presents some startling findings.

only one role to play in the future: as commuter vehicles for urban residents. Don't scoff at that, though, that's the predominant use of the automobile in modern society. Most cars in North America actually travel fewer than 60 miles per day as suburbanites travel to and from work. But what about a miraculous development in battery technology?

On the bright side, researchers are working on new materials, among them carbon nanotubes, that could someday be used to make tiny, high-capacity batteries. These batteries could store a lot of electricity in a very tiny mass. On the downside, even if they prove successful, they're very likely many years from production.

And what about using hydrogen gas in our homes to cook our food? Because there are so few choices for cooking, it may make sense to replace natural gas with hydrogen generated from electricity used to split water.

And what about using hydrogen to heat our homes?

Net Energy Efficiency of Heating Homes with Hydrogen

According to Crea's calculations, heating a home with electricity, which can be quite costly, would be more efficient than heating directly with hydrogen gas (burning hydrogen gas in a furnace) (Figure 10-2). Let's look at the numbers.

Resistance heating nets 11 percent of the original energy while direct heating, burning hydrogen directly in a furnace, yields only 9 percent. (These figures take into account all of the losses that occur from production of the fuel to transport to its final point of use.)

A far better option for home heating would be to deliver hydrogen to a fuel cell at each home. It can be used to make electricity to run a heat pump. The net energy efficiency of this process is about 18 percent.

Crea's advice on this is to forget hydrogen in this instance. Power a heat pump with electricity from solar or wind power. This system has an even higher net energy efficiency of 44 percent.

Even better would be an active solar system. It has a net energy efficiency, according to Crea, of 50 percent.

Should We Pursue Hydrogen?

Clearly, at this stage, hydrogen's future is not as rosy as some would have you believe. It pains me to say this, but it is questionable whether we should be even pursuing hydrogen.

Crea believes that a renewably based hydrogen economy will require the installation of US$40 trillion worth of photovoltaic panels. His advice: go with a renewably fueled grid system. "The decision to go with a renewably fueled utility grid system, as opposed to the hydrogen system, would save enough money in photovoltaic panels alone to provide every American family with an electric car and the photovoltaic panels to run it," says Crea. "Furthermore, enough would be left over to handle all of the electricity, heating, and cooling needs for an entire house — for free!"

Will hydrogen have a bright future or any at all?

At this time, it is difficult to say whether hydrogen will become a dominant fuel source or whether it will play much of a role at all in our energy future. We don't know enough to make wise choices. The case isn't good, though, and I wouldn't count on hydrogen being our savior.

Over time, prices will help sort out the sane from the preposterous new energy ideas. But we need to get moving quickly to start gathering data and determining what are the most economical and most environmentally and socially appropriate solutions to declining natural gas and oil supplies.

THE HYBRID TRANSITION

For those interested in taking action now, I'd strongly suggest that you consider a hybrid or a diesel car (the latter powered by either biodiesel or vegetable oil).

Let's begin with the hybrid.

The hybrid is a car, truck, or minivan that has an electric motor and a small gasoline engine. The gas engine and electric motor combine forces to provide the power needed to move the vehicle forward, swiftly and economically.

But that's not all.

I've been told by reliable sources that all major US auto manufacturers also have diesel hybrid vehicles, cars that reportedly get about 80 miles per gallon using a diesel engine/electric motor combination. (They were developed during the Clinton Administration as part of

Over time, prices will help sort out the sane from the preposterous new energy ideas. But we need to get moving quickly to start gathering data and determining what are the most economical and most environmentally and socially appropriate solutions to declining natural gas and oil supplies.

Fuel Cells and Fuel Cell Cars

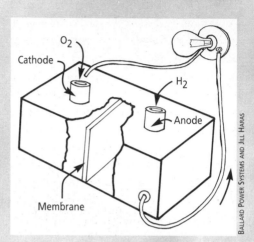

Fig. 10-3: The anatomy of a fuel cell.

Fig. 10-3a: Ballard Power Systems' fuel cell.

There's a lot of talk these days about fuel cells and fuel cell cars. Some visionaries like Jeremy Rifkin, author of *The Hydrogen Economy,* believe that someday homeowners will install fuel cells to generate electricity in their own neighborhoods.

Fuel cells are a fairly modern invention that produces electricity. Although there are many kinds of fuel cells available, one of the more popular models generates electricity by chemically combining hydrogen and oxygen.

Figure 10-3a shows a simplified view of how a fuel cell works. As illustrated, this fuel cell looks a lot like a battery. It consists of an anode and a cathode separated by a membrane.

Hydrogen gas (H_2) is fed into the anode, where it reacts to form hydrogen ions and electrons. The electrons are drawn off by a wire, creating an electrical current. It can be used to power lights, electronic equipment, and even electric motors in cars and buses.

Oxygen is introduced into the cathode. It reacts with hydrogen ions generated at the anode. They pass through a membrane that separates the fuel cell into two compartments. The hydrogen ions, oxygen, and electrons (returning from the electrical circuit) combine to form water, meaning the *only* waste product from this process is pure water.

Fuel cells can be installed in cars, trucks, and buses where they are used to generate electricity from hydrogen. Because the fuel cells powered by hydrogen are so clean and because one potential source of hydrogen, water, is so abundant, fuel cells are frequently touted as the wave of the future. Numerous pilot projects are currently underway to test them in cars and buses. In 1999, for instance, a Washington-based company introduced a hydrogen fuel-cell bus.

One of the leading manufacturers of fuel cells is a company in Canada, Ballard Power Systems. Ballard has built hydrogen fuel-cell-powered buses, which are now being tested in Chicago and British Columbia. During the public ceremony in Chicago, then-Mayor Richard Daley celebrated by drinking ☞

a glass of exhaust — water collected from the tailpipe of an idling bus — to underscore how safe the emissions are. If tests prove successful, Ballard hopes to enter full-scale production of fuel cell bus engines in the near future.

Although fuel cells can use hydrogen and oxygen, both gases are potentially dangerous. They can ignite, even explode. In addition, hydrogen gas is bulky and needs to be stored in a condensed state. How will this be achieved?

Hydrogen can be stored in special gas tanks filled with a solid yet porous material known as metal hydride. This material absorbs the hydrogen gas as the tank is being filled, then releases it when the car is operating. Unfortunately, the tanks are fairly large and heavy, and therefore seem to have fallen out of favor.

Hydrogen can also be stored under compression in a tank in the vehicle, for example, a high-strength tank built from carbon fibers. Crash tests show that these tanks are amazingly strong. But what about fires?

Although some people worry about this, crash tests show that hydrogen leaking from a tank in an accident quickly escapes into the atmosphere, dramatically reducing fire hazard, unlike gasoline tanks in conventional automobiles, which spill liquid fuel that can burn for a long time after a crash.

Fig. 10-4: This bus is powered by an electric motor. Electricity is generated by a Ballard Power Systems' fuel cell that is powered by hydrogen.

Fuel cell research and development for the auto industry is primarily focused on stripping hydrogen from fossil fuels such as natural gas, gasoline, and methanol. These fuels are fed into an onboard fuel processor (reformulator). It chemically strips the hydrogen from the organic fuel molecules. The hydrogen is then fed into the fuel cell.

This process is reportedly very clean and represents a major improvement over standard gasoline- and diesel-powered motor vehicles in all forms of emissions except the greenhouse gas carbon dioxide.

At this writing, Daimler-Chrysler, Toyota, Honda, Ford, and General Motors hope to have fuel cell vehicles on the market soon. What's my prognosis or recommendation?

As noted in the chapter, I think that it may make more sense from a net-energy yield standpoint to pursue electric vehicles for commuting to and from work or for running errands around town. Hydrogen cars may be more appropriate for long-distance trips, although biodiesel may be better from a net energy standpoint. ■

Adapted with permission from Daniel D. Chiras, *Environmental Science*, 7th edition, Jones and Bartlett Publishers, 2006.

a nationwide effort to produce super energy-efficient vehicles.) Moreover, one inventor has created a diesel hybrid train engine that, he claims, could replace the 60,000 diesel engines used on America's rail yards for moving cars here and there, dramatically reducing fuel use and pollution. In addition, General Motors has recently unveiled a diesel/hybrid locomotive for long-range trips. This 270,000-pound locomotive is designed to tow passenger-train cars at speeds of up to 110 miles per hour.

Hybrids work, and they're here to stay, even though the Bush Administration pulled support for their development in favor of hydrogen cars, a shift that, as you've just seen, may make much less sense in the long run.

I know hybrids work because I drive one. I have a Toyota Prius Gen II, which I purchased in the summer of 2004 (Figure 10-5).

Fig. 10-5: The author's Toyota Prius Hybrid, Gen II.

DAN CHIRAS

This unbelievable car is rated at 51 miles per gallon on the highway and 60 miles per gallon in the city. I've found that it consistently gets 50 to 60 miles per gallon in the summer and 40 to 50 miles per gallon in the winter driving around town, on highway, and in the city — in other words, these figures are the car's combined city and highway mileage.

Toyota's hybrid, Prius, was the first commercially available hybrid for sale in Japan. It was introduced into the United States in mid-2000, slightly after the introduction of Honda's two-seater hybrid, the Insight.

The world's leader in hybrid technology today is Honda; it currently manufactures three hybrid vehicles: a 2-seater, the Insight, that is rated at 60 miles per gallon in the city and 65 miles per gallon on the highway; the Civic, which seats 4 to 5 but gets slightly lower mileage than the Prius; and a 6-cylinder 230 horsepower Accord that gets lower mileage than the Hybrid Civic, but still greater mileage than the ordinary 6-cylinder Accord.

If you want a hybrid SUV, try Ford's Escape. It came out in late 2004, nearly four years after the Japanese manufacturers introduced their first models in North America.

If you want a hybrid pickup truck, you may want to check out GMC's Sierra or Chevy's Silverado. They get 18 miles per gallon in the city and 20 on the road.

If you want a minivan, check out Toyota's Sienna. Although it hasn't come out as of this writing, it's projected to get in the 40 miles per gallon range.

Hybrids are sleek, efficient, and affordable. You'll see a lot more of them in the coming years as oil prices continue to work their way up the ladder. Auto manufacturers seem to be rallying behind the technology. In my research for this book, I discovered that virtually all auto manufacturers have vehicles on the drawing boards or in production, including Acura, Daimler Chrylser, Jeep, Lexus, Mazda, Mercedes, Mitsubishi, Nissan, Porsche, Subaru, and Volkswagen.

How Does a Hybrid Work?

Hybrids combine an electric motor and a small gas engine to provide the propulsive force required to move a car or truck or minivan or SUV along the highway or through busy city streets. Toyota's Prius initially operates on electric power; when the car is turned on and begins to move, its electric motor provides the main propulsion. The gas engine kicks in at around 10 or 12 miles per hour. (That's why this car gets better gas mileage in the city than on the highway, as indicated in Table 10-1.)

When on the highway, however, the gas engine provides much of the thrust. The electric motor supplies boost power. In my Prius, for example, as I cruise along a fairly flat section of highway, the gas engine provides the thrust. When I need extra power, for example, to climb a hill or pass a slow-moving vehicle, like a horse and buggy as my kids like to tease me (I'm a conservative driver), the electric motor kicks in. Electricity flows from the light-weight battery (nickel metal hydride) behind the back

Table 10-1 Hybrids, Hybrids, and More Hybrids			
Manufacturer	**Model**	**City mileage**	**Highway mileage**
Honda	Insight	60	65
Honda	Civic	47	48
Honda	Accord	30	37
Toyota	Prius	60	51
Ford	Escape (SUV)	35	40
Chevy	Silverado (Pickup)	18	20
GMC	Sierra (Pickup)	18	20

<WWW.HYBRID.COM>

seat to the electric motor to provide additional power.

When slowing down or going down a hill, however, the vehicle uses very little power at all. In fact, the gas engine may shut off entirely. The instantaneous gas mileage readout in the Prius, which is located on a computer screen in the center of the dashboard, records gas mileages of 100 miles per gallon, indicating that the car is coasting.

When the vehicle comes to a stop at a stop light, the engine shuts off. When I press on the gas pedal, however, the electric motor kicks in, followed by the gas motor. I'm off and running without hesitation.

Honda's hybrids are similar in many respects. They contain a gas engine and an electric motor, but the electric motor is much smaller than the Prius'. As a result, it can't be used to start the car from a standstill.

When a Honda Civic Hybrid is turned on, then, the gas engine kicks in immediately. It provides the power to move the car and most of the propulsion from that point on. The electric motor kicks in when additional power is needed, for example, when climbing a hill or passing another vehicle. Because the gas engine starts up immediately, city mileage in all Hondas is lower than highway mileage.

In the modern language of computers, this car "defaults" to the gas engine, says Shari Prange of Electro Automotive in Felton, California, who's written many fantastic articles in *Home Power* magazine on hybrids and electric cars. Moreover, the electric motors

and the batteries in the car are not sufficient to drive the car on their own. This car will never move solely under electrical power.

In the Prius, the electric drive system is "more nearly an equal partner," notes Prange in an article in *Home Power* magazine, issue 83. As Prange notes, this car "defaults to the electric motor, and brings the gas engine online as needed." The electric motor of the Prius can drive the car, and often does at low speeds, without the assistance of the gas engine (which isn't even running at these times). The electric motor provides all of the power when the car is backing up.

But what about the batteries of a hybrid car? Do they need to be charged each night?

No. They're charged continuously by the car during normal operation.

In Honda's hybrids, for instance, the electric motor doubles as an alternator, providing propulsion and also producing electricity to charge the batteries. Battery recharging occurs when the car slows down, in a process called regenerative braking.

The Prius also recharges its batteries but in a slightly different fashion. In this car, the gas engine powers an alternator that produces electricity to recharge the batteries. It also provides electricity to the electric motor. However, Toyota's Prius also uses regenerative braking to charge the batteries.

All in all, electricity flows smoothly in and out of the light-weight batteries during various modes of operation, giving you a clean, energy-efficient ride. Like other functions in the car, it is all computer-controlled. You drive; the car figures all of this out automatically.

Hybrid car batteries are not your typical lead acid batteries. They're light-weight nickel metal hybrid batteries. As such, they're pretty expensive. Toyota warrantees its battery bank for ten years to allay fears of car buyers.

What About Cost?

Hybrids cost two to three thousand dollars more than their less frugal cousins. But federal and state incentives currently help reduce the costs dramatically. My Prius cost a little over $21,000 (I purchased it through Autobytel.com), several thousand more than a comparable Toyota Corolla. But I received nearly $3,000 back on my state and federal taxes for this purchase! (Note: at this writing [January 2006] federal tax incentives have just been introduced but won't last long.)

As much as I like gas hybrids, this technology is probably only an intermediate solution to long-term declines in oil production, because this automotive technology still relies on gasoline derived from declining supplies of oil. That said, individuals should pursue this option because it will help ease the crunch. Even so, there may be even better solutions to address the coming end of the golden age of oil.

PLUG-IN HYBRIDS

One solution that holds promise is the plug-in hybrid. A plug-in hybrid electric vehicle is a hybrid, much like those just discussed, with a couple of differences. First, plug-in hybrids contain extra lead acid batteries. Unlike the hybrids just discussed, at night these cars are plugged into a 120- or 220-volt outlet (like a dryer outlet). This charges the extra batteries. The electrical charge, in turn, powers the vehicle in most situations. According to the Institute for Analysis of Global Security, which researches transportation options that could help us free our dependence on foreign oil, "Plug-ins run on the stored (electrical) energy for much of a typical day's driving — depending on the size of the battery up to 60 miles per charge, far beyond the commute of an average American." They go on to say that when the electrical charge is used up, the car "automatically keeps running on the fuel in the fuel tank. A person who drives every day a distance shorter than the car's electric range would never have to dip into the fuel tank."

That of course leads to the second difference. Such cars need larger electric engines than hybrids currently on the market.

Because most of the energy used by plug-ins comes from electricity and not from gasoline, and because electricity can be generated efficiently and cleanly from America's abundant renewable energy resources, especially solar and wind power, hybrid electrics may help us combat the coming shortages of oil without increasing global warming and a host of other environmental problems associated with fossil fuel use.

But what about performance?

Because diesel hybrids are so efficient, and because they could burn biodiesel, they represent one of the best choices for personal transportation in an oil-short world.

According to the Institute for the Analysis of Global Security, "The plug-in hybrid drive system is compatible with all vehicle models and does not entail any sacrifice of vehicle performance or driver amenities. A mid-size plug-in can accelerate from 0 to 60 miles per hour in less than 9 seconds, sustain a top speed of 97 mph and maintain 120 mph for about two minutes even with a low battery."

BIODIESEL-POWERED VEHICLES AND HOMES

Another solution that holds great promise is the diesel hybrid, although it is not yet available. Although diesel is derived from crude oil (petroleum), a diesel-like fuel can also be manufactured from an assortment of vegetable oils, for example, corn oil, canola oil, and soy oil. The diesel-like product, known as biodiesel, is a combustible, clean-burning, and renewable fuel. It could eventually power many of the nation's trucks, cars, busses, vans, ships, and trains, perhaps even jets.

Biodiesel could also be used in diesel hybrid vehicles, assuming they make it to the market. (I'm guessing they will.)

Because diesel hybrids are so efficient, and because they could burn biodiesel, they represent one of the best choices for personal transportation in an oil-short world.

How is Biodiesel Made?

Biodiesel is made by mixing vegetable oil with a solution of methanol containing sodium hydroxide (lye). The oil is usually heated. The methanol-lye mixture is then added to the vegetable oil. This solution is heated some more, then stirred for a period of time, usually about an hour. When the chemical reaction is complete, out comes biodiesel — long-chain fatty acids that burn very nicely in diesel engines. The only waste product is glycerol, a dark, thin, oily substance that can be purified and turned into soap. (For those who want to know more about biodiesel production, see the accompanying sidebar)

Biodiesel can be burned directly in virtually all diesel engines without any modification of the engine. The only exception is older diesel engines. (For advice on older diesel engines see the sidebar on the next page.)

The Chemistry of Biodiesel Production

Biodiesel is made by first mixing methanol (methyl alcohol), derived from natural gas, with sodium hydroxide or lye. The result is a chemical called sodium methoxide. It is then reacted with vegetable oil consisting of triglycerides. Triglycerides consist of a single molecule of glycerol chemically bonded to three fairly long-chain fatty acids. The chemical reaction between sodium hydroxide and triglycerides in vegetable oil slices off the long-chain fatty acids. The fatty acids are bonded with the methanol, creating biodiesel (with glycerol as a by-product). Both methanol and lye must be handled very carefully. Skin and eyes should be covered and workers should be careful not to breathe the fumes from any open reactions.

Biodiesel can be burned full strength or can be mixed with ordinary petroleum-derived diesel, a biodiesel blend.

Pros and Cons of Biodiesel

Biodiesel is a renewable fuel that could help us meet our needs for transportation fuels as the age of oil winds down.

But that's not its only plus.

Biodiesel can help stimulate our nation's economy, in part, by reducing its reliance on foreign oil. It could also help stimulate rural economies. In the coming years, many farmers will be enlisted to produce "fuel grains" for the biodiesel market. Their seed crops will be converted to vegetable oil by local biodiesel manufacturers. Crop production and local manufacturing not only create stronger local and regional economies, they help forge the path to a more decentralized and sustainable

Supporting Local Economies

Adding to biodiesel's many benefits, oils used to make it can be grown locally by farmers, providing a much needed shot in the arm to rural economies and the people who live in rural areas of North America. Furthermore, the oil-rich seeds can then be shipped to local production facilities, greatly reducing transportation costs and our dependence on foreign oil. Farmers could even create cooperatives to make their own oils or even their own biodiesel.

Got an Older Diesel Car?

Biodiesel works fine in older cars, but can create problems when first used in them. That's because biodiesel is a solvent that cleans diesel engines, fuel lines, and fuel tanks, loosening the gook that may have accumulated in them from petroleum diesel, especially in the fuel tank. This material then flows into the fuel lines and through the fuel filter, where it can obstruct the flow of fuel.

But as I just said, that doesn't mean you can't use biodiesel in an older car.

Not at all; you just have to start slowly.

In order to use biodiesel in an older vehicle, you should start with a blend of biodiesel and regular diesel — around 10 to 20 percent biodiesel, for instance. Run the car on this for a while, being sure to change fuel filters frequently until the tank and fuel lines are cleaned.

Next, increase the concentration of biodiesel blend a bit more. Continue to change the fuel filter until you are sure that the gunk has been purged. When the fuel tank and fuel lines are clean, you can then switch to 100 percent biodiesel. If your vehicle is older than 1995, you may have to replace the rubber seals and fuel lines with a synthetic material, Viton, that is resistant to biodiesel.

system of fuel production. In Colorado, for example, a leader in biodiesel production, known as Blue Sun, makes biodiesel from seed crops, such as rapeseed (canola), grown by local farmers. They currently sell their product at 16 gas stations in the state.

There's also good news about biodiesel on the net-energy efficiency front. Unlike other options, such as hydrogen, oil shale, and tar sands, biodiesel production is amazingly energy efficient. According to Marc Franke, an Iowa-based proponent of biodiesel, the net energy efficiency of biodiesel production from soy oil is 3.2; from canola or rapeseed oil it is 4.3. What these figures mean is that for every unit of energy invested in biodiesel production, you get 3.2 units of energy output from soy oil and 4.3 units of energy from canola oil. According to Franke, it would take 7 acres of soybeans to supply soybeans to extract the oil needed to make biodiesel for a diesel car that travels 15,000 miles per year and gets 44 miles per gallon. It would take 2.7 acres of canola oil to do the same thing.

Seed crops are not the only potential source of biodiesel, however. Biodiesel can also be produced from vegetable oils discarded by local restaurants, reducing their disposal costs while providing a valuable renewable liquid transportation fuel. According to Franke, US restaurants, including all the fast-food chains, produce an estimated three billion gallons of waste vegetable oil per year!

There are a lot of other sources, too. For example, biodiesel can be manufactured from algae, another potentially renewable source. Algae could be grown in ponds associated with sewage treatment plants, helping reduce pollution while generating liquid fuel for North America's transportation system.

Diesel fuel can also be produced from organic waste, such as that generated at turkey farms, using a process known as Thermal De-Polymerization (TDP). Agricultural organic wastes, says Franke, produce enough material to make four billion barrels of biodiesel each year!

But how does biodiesel perform? Will car owners be sacrificing performance?

According to Franke, biodiesel offers the same performance as regular diesel, but dramatically reduces tailpipe emissions. For example, biodiesel contains no sulfur, so combustion of this fuel source eliminates sulfur oxide emissions that contribute to acid rain and snow, a big problem with conventional diesel vehicles.

Moreover, says Franke, there's no black smoke spewing from tailpipes of cars or trucks powered by biodiesel as they pass other vehicles or power up a hill. Complete-cycle carbon dioxide production from the manufacture of the fuel and use of biodiesel cars and trucks is 78 percent lower than from vehicles powered by standard diesel fuel. (For reasons beyond the scope of this book,) "Biodiesel is a viable fuel, not just a new technology," says Jeff Probst, CEO of Blue Sun. According to the US Department of Energy, biodiesel is the fastest growing renewable energy fuel on the market today. Moreover, notes Lizzy Scully in "Wanted: Cleaner and Greener Wheels" in *Home Power*, Issue 103, "More than 400 U.S. fleets — public and private companies with large number of vehicles — now use biodiesel."

Yet another advantage of biodiesel is that the transition to this fuel won't require major changes in the distribution system. Biodiesel could be produced locally and sold at area filling stations using the same facilities that are used to dispense regular diesel fuel.

And here's another plus: biodiesel can also be run in space heaters and oil furnaces, even forklifts, tractors, and electric generators that currently use diesel. Your home someday could be heated with biodiesel.

"Undeniably, biodiesel fuel could change the face of the North American transportation industry," remarks Scully. "Biodiesel is a smart fuel for anyone to use," she adds. "For me, it's plain and simple: using biodiesel means reducing the emissions of harmful pollutants, while supporting the U.S. economy and U.S. farmers – instead of propping up an out-of-control, oil import infrastructure. And driving a biodiesel-fueled vehicle instead of my petroleum-guzzling Chevy also could ease my eco-conscience during my frequent commutes and road trips."

Despite these benefits, biodiesel does have a few problems. For one, it is not yet widely available, although I suspect this will change. Second, in the United States, commercially manufactured biodiesel costs a bit more than standard petroleum-derived diesel. This, of course, is largely the result of the fact that biodiesel is only produced by small-scale production facilities. Increasing the scale of production could bring the cost down substantially. As oil prices rise and biodiesel production ramps up, costs could come down even more, making biodiesel an important fuel of the future. Improving matters, starting in January 2004, producers will receive a federal tax incentive of up to one dollar per gallon of biodiesel. With this incentive, biodiesel may now cost the same or even less than petroleum diesel.

You can also make your own biodiesel at bargain basement prices in your basement. Biodiesel Solutions, a company in Fremont, California, sells equipment you can set up in your basement or garage to manufacture biodiesel. They claim that it currently costs only about $0.75 per gallon to make, far lower than standard diesel, which is currently running about $2.50 per gallon (Figure 10-6). The unit costs about $3,500.

Another, much less expensive, option is the residential biodiesel reactor produced by BioFuels Technology in Denver, Colorado. This company sells a kit containing the pipe, pumps, and valves needed to assemble a biodiesel reactor using a used electric water heater (that will require 220-volt AC electricity). You can obtain the water heater locally to save on shipping costs. Their reactor produces 25 to 75 gallons of biodiesel at a time, depending on the size of the water heater you buy. You can contact the company at samissile@idcomm.com.

Another problem with biodiesel is that soy biodiesel gels around 32°F (0°C), and therefore can't be used at full strength when

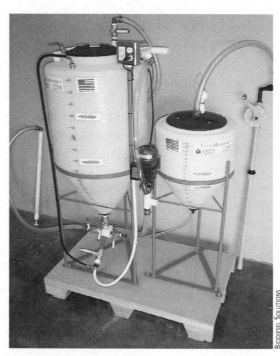

Fig. 10-6: The FuelMeister and similar systems create biodiesel at a fraction of the cost of gasoline, diesel, and commercially available biodiesel.

the weather gets cold (rapeseed biodiesel gels at a lower temperature). To get around this, biodiesel is ordinarily mixed with conventional diesel. Why?

Manufacturers add an anti-gelling agent to winter petroleum diesel. As shown in the sidebar, the lower the temperature the less biodiesel you can blend with normal petroleum-based diesel. (Note that anti-gelling agents can be added directly to biodiesel.)

Last, but not least, large-scale biodiesel production will put increasing demand on farmland. Production could, if large enough, even reduce the exports of food crops. Although farmers won't suffer, those who rely on food from North America could find themselves in a bind. One way to lessen the impact of widespread biodiesel production would be to make it from algae and waste from turkey and hog farms.

VEGETABLE OIL AS A FUEL?

Biodiesel isn't the only renewable liquid fuel available to us. Some car owners are currently burning vegetable oil directly in their diesel vehicles.

That's right, your eyes aren't deceiving you, they're burning vegetable oil in cars and trucks and buses equipped with diesel engines. Some individuals acquire their fuel from vegetable oil they purchase in bulk. Others salvage vegetable oil from fast-food chains and other restaurants.

How can vegetable oil be burned in a diesel car?

Cold Weather Soy Biodiesel Mixes

Temperatures above 40°F (4°C) — 100 percent biodiesel

Temperatures in the 20° to 40°F (-6° to 4°C) range — 50 percent biodiesel blend

Temperatures in the 0° to 20°F (-20° to -6°C) range — 20 percent biodiesel blend

To run a vehicle on straight vegetable oil, which is thicker (more viscous) than biodiesel or conventional diesel fuel, car and truck owners must make some modifications to their vehicles. To make these vegetable oil conversions simpler, several companies now manufacture conversion kits costing $300 to $800, depending on the quality of the kit. Individuals can install the kits themselves, if they're mechanically inclined, or can hire a professional to do the job.

Before we examine the contents of a conversion kit, it's helpful to understand the main purpose of these kits. That way the parts will make sense to you.

First, most conversion kits are designed to store vegetable oil apart from the diesel or biodiesel fuel. In the majority of cars, you can't simply fill a diesel tank with vegetable oil because veggie-oil cars and trucks can't run on 100 percent vegetable oil all of the time. The main reason for this, which will make sense soon, is that you can't start a car or truck using straight vegetable oil. (There is a new conversion kit from a German company that allows 100 percent veggie-oil operation, discussed shortly.)

Second, because vegetable oil is much thicker than diesel, it needs to be heated to around 165°F or 74°C before it can be burned in a diesel engine. Heating makes the oil thinner.

All kits provide simple yet ingenious devices that heat vegetable oil so that it flows freely into the engine. If they didn't, the oils would clog up the works!

With this in mind, let's take a look at a typical conversion kit. As just noted, all conversion kits (except for one) include a separate tank for storing vegetable oil. They're made from steel or plastic and are placed in the trunks of cars or the beds of pickup trucks.

Conversion kits also come with tubing to connect the vegetable oil tank to the combustion chambers in the diesel engine and a filter to remove impurities, if any, from the oil before it reaches the engine.

Conversion kits also include valves to control the flow of biodiesel, described momentarily. Switches that allow the operator to control the valves are typically mounted on or near the dashboard to permit ease of use (Figure 10-7). A fuel gauge is included to monitor vegetable oil in the ancillary tank.

Fig. 10-7: A switch opens a valve that starts the flow of vegetable oil to the diesel engine and shuts off the flow of diesel. The gauge monitors the fuel level in the biodiesel tank.

WILLIAM WRENTMORE

One of the most important components of the conversion kit, however, is a device to heat the vegetable oil. Some systems rely on electric (resistance) heaters. Others use heat exchangers that transfer engine heat to the vegetable oil. Both systems warm the vegetable oil to make it thin enough to flow freely to the engine.

To understand how a heating system works, let's take a look at the Greasecar Vegetable Fuel Systems conversion kits (<www.greasecar.com>). These kits rely on a heat exchanger that, like others of similar design, transfers heat from the engine's cooling system to warm the veggie fuel.

The fuel-heating component of this kit consists of three parts: (1) a copper coil that wraps around the vegetable oil filter in the fuel line, (2) a heat exchanger that's installed in the vegetable oil tank, and (3) a heat exchanger that surrounds the tubing delivering vegetable oil from the veggie oil tank to the engine. The heat comes from the engine coolant that is circulated through the coil around the vegetable oil filter, then through the heat exchanger in the vegetable oil tank, and then around the hose leading from the tank to the engine. This feat is accomplished by installing a T fitting into the coolant hose that runs from the engine to the car's heater.

To start a veggie car, the owner first turns on the engine using diesel fuel from the vehicle's diesel tank. As the vehicle warms, antifreeze from the engine's cooling system begins to circulate through the heat exchangers, warming the vegetable oil in the fuel filter, the tank, and the fuel line (the line connecting the vegetable oil tank to the engine). After five minutes or so of heating, the operator flips a switch that opens a valve. It allows vegetable oil to flow into the engine. This switch also shuts off the flow of diesel from the main fuel tank. When the valve is opened, the heated vegetable oil begins to flow into the engine; from that point on, the vehicle is operating on 100 percent clean-burning, renewable vegetable oil.

Before the engine can be shut down, however, the fuel lines must be purged of vegetable oil. Drivers must switch back to diesel fuel for five minutes — usually the last five minutes of a trip. Running conventional diesel through the lines for five minutes cleans them out, replacing vegetable oil with diesel so it will be ready for the next cold start. (Some systems contain a back-flush pump that purges the fuel lines of vegetable oil automatically when the car is shut off. That way, the driver doesn't have to remember to switch back to diesel five minutes before he or she arrives at his or her destination.)

The lines are purged after each use because, since vegetable oil is thicker than diesel, it can clog the fuel lines, making a car difficult, if not impossible to start cold.

Pros and Cons of Vegetable Oil as a Fuel

Vegetable oil is an ideal fuel but one needs to understand the pros and cons of this approach to compare it to other options, especially biodiesel.

Let's start on the upside.

One of the biggest advantages of vegetable oil is that the fuel is widely available. You can stop and fill up anywhere in North America so long as there's a restaurant that deep-fries its food in vegetable oil. (You'll have to filter the gunk out of the deep-fryer oil first, however.)

Not only is the fuel abundant and widely available, so are diesel engine conversion kits. You can purchase them on the Internet.

Like other options discussed in this book, this fuel is renewable and can be picked up for free, for example, from fast-food restaurants whose owners are typically pleased to give it away, rather than pay for disposal!

Vegetable oil burns cleanly and thus helps solve another thorny issue — air pollution from conventional fossil fuels. Like biodiesel, vegetable oil use reduces carbon dioxide emissions. The fuel itself is often called carbon neutral but that's not entirely true. Sure, the amount produced during combustion equals the amount the plants take up during photosynthesis, but remember, it takes energy to make this fuel (gasoline to power a tractor, for instance). The consumption of energy, in turn, produces carbon dioxide. Even so, the fuel is light years ahead of conventional fossil fuels in the greenhouse gas production department.

Another advantage of vegetable oil is that it dramatically improves the range of a car. Gary Liess of Santa Rosa, California, for instance, can drive his Mercedes more than — get this — 800 miles on a tank of diesel (or biodiesel) and a tank of vegetable oil. His partner, with a slightly more fuel-efficient vehicle, can travel 1,000 miles between fill ups, if she wanted, using diesel or biodiesel and vegetable oil. (Their story is told in *Home Power*, Issue 95.)

Like virtually anything we do in life, vegetable oil fuels have some disadvantages. The conversion kits and installation of the kits cost money. Expect to pay $800 to $1,600 for a good kit and installation. In addition, the additional fuel tank takes up a considerable amount of trunk space (Figure 10-8). And you'll need to still use diesel or find biodiesel to fill the car's main fuel tank.

Fig. 10-8: This tank, mounted in the trunk of the car, holds the vegetable oil. It is part of a kit designed to retrofit standard diesel vehicles for vegetable oil.

You'll also need to find a source of vegetable oil and be willing to collect and store it. Another problem is that the vegetable oil may clog the fuel injectors of a diesel engine over time, according to Sam Anderson of BioFuels Technology, a Denver-based company. For more on this topic see the accompanying sidebar.

Another disadvantage is that you need to switch the fuel on and off, although back-flush pumps that come with the more expensive kits avoid this task. (You'll recall that they automatically purge the fuel lines after the ignition switch is shut off.) As noted earlier, however, Elsbett, a German manufacturer, now provides a bare-bones conversion kit that allows vehicles to be cold-started on veggie oil (to learn about it go to <www.elsbett.com>). This system uses only the fuel tank that comes with the car. This kit doesn't require extra switches and hoses like others. It comes with glow plugs (to warm the fuel in the tank), special fuel injectors, and an in-line heater that permit the car to operate on 100 percent vegetable oil.

If you own a diesel car, biodiesel or vegetable oil may be just the thing. If you are thinking about a new car and wondering what vehicle makes the most sense, given the decline in global oil production, you may want to give

Some Problems with Straight Vegetable Oil

According to Marc Franke and other experts on alternative fuels, more recent diesel cars with high-pressure injection systems have a more difficult time burning straight vegetable oil (SVO) than older models. The fuel pumps struggle a bit more to propel SVO through the injectors than they do with biodiesel or conventional petroleum-based diesel. The diesel vehicles that work best are the older VWs and Mercedes that don't use direct injection. Instead, these older diesel vehicles have a pre-chamber to get the burn started in each cylinder and therefore don't need such high pressures.

Another problem, says Franke, is that the thicker SVO apparently doesn't burn completely and "cokes" (leaves deposits) on the valves and possibly the injectors. The unburned vegetable oil polymerizes into a hard goo that sticks to the engine.

I contacted a couple of individuals who use SVO in their diesel cars to determine whether these concerns were valid. One colleague who has burned SVO in a relatively new pickup truck reported no problems whatsoever in over 40,000 miles of driving. The other who has logged over 400,000 miles on a diesel truck also reported no problems. In fact, when the engine of his truck finally died, he hired a mechanic to disassemble it to see if he could detect problems. They could find none. Readers are advised to research this issue before switching to SVO.

strong consideration to a diesel vehicle. Neither biodiesel nor vegetable oil will be immune to the rising prices of gasoline and conventional diesel, because it takes energy to make them, but they may be less severely affected. I envision a time when biodiesel and vegetable oil are used to power the tractors and trucks on farms that produce these renewable fuels, perhaps even the facilities that produce these fuels.

WHAT ABOUT ETHANOL?

Another liquid fuel that's already being used in the transportation sector is ethanol or ethyl alcohol. Derived from corn and other sugar-rich crops such as sugar cane, ethanol is the same chemical substance that's found in alcoholic beverages. Today, many states in the United States add small amounts of ethanol (ten percent) to gasoline in the winter to help reduce air pollution during winter months.

Unfortunately, ethanol has a low net energy efficiency. In fact, for many years, it actually took more energy to make a gallon of ethanol than you got out of burning it. It had, in other words, a negative net energy efficiency. That, of course, rendered ethanol a highly questionable fuel source.

Ethanol's early performance has given it a black eye and many folks still continue to dismiss it for this reason. Fortunately, ethanol's prospects are changing. Research over the past 20 years has helped ethanol claw its way into the positive net-energy yield category. According to Marc Franke, ethanol currently yields 1.67 units of energy for every unit invested. That's still not great, but don't count ethanol out.

New processes are under development that could dramatically boost the net energy efficiency of ethanol production. One Canadian company, for instance, has developed a way to generate ethanol from cellulose in corn stalks and wheat straw, both of which are considered waste materials. By using waste products from the production of corn and wheat, manufacturers could dramatically improve the net energy efficiency. Although it is too early to tell, some think that the net energy efficiency could be as high as seven. Translated, that means that for every unit of energy invested in the production of ethanol, you'd get back seven.

Making ethanol production more energy efficient is one of the goals of the US Department of Energy's National Renewable Energy Laboratory (NREL) in Golden, Colorado. It is part of their program to study and develop ways of obtaining energy from biomass. Biomass refers to biological materials, principally plant matter, that can be used to produce energy, either by direct combustion or by processing (fermentation, for instance) to create liquid or gaseous fuels such as ethanol or methane.

Much of NREL's biomass program focuses on ethanol. And much of NREL's research on ethanol concentrates on using "corn stover"— stalks, leaves, and corn cobs, the leftover by-products of corn harvest. NREL scientists have concluded that manufacturers could use about one-third of the nation's corn stover to produce ethanol for fuel without harming North America's agricultural soils.

Although ethanol production currently costs approximately twice as much as gasoline, primarily because of its low net energy yield, NREL scientists are confident that they can lower costs. To do so, they're working with specially developed enzymes plucked from bacteria that grow in hot springs. It's their hope that by manipulating these enzymes they'll be able to dramatically increase ethanol production and lower energy input — lowering the cost to the general public.

If these and other efforts are successful, ethanol could someday join vegetable oil and biodiesel as a major component of North America's liquid transportation fuel supply. It can be mixed with gasoline, as noted above, and can be burned at nearly full strength, for example, in mixtures containing 85 percent ethanol and 15 percent gasoline.

This blend, called E-85, is currently being sold in select gas stations in North America. At this writing, E-85 was selling for 40 cents per gallon less than unleaded regular gasoline in Denver.

It is important to note, however, that not all cars or trucks can use E-85. To operate on E-85, the vehicle needs to be modified. Fortunately, a growing number of auto manufacturers now produce flexible-fuel vehicles that run on either 100 percent gasoline or E-85, including a number of sedans, pickup trucks, and minivans.

Before you fill your tank with E-85, be sure your car is rated for its use. You'll find a small sticker on the inside of the gas tank door that will tell you if your car can use this fuel.

Leon Corzine is a corn farmer in Assumption, Ill., and president of the Illinois Corn Growers Association. He drives a Ford Ranger pickup truck that burns E-85. Like other progressive-minded farmers, Corzine hasn't had to contend with the soaring gas prices that have plagued the rest of us in recent years.

Skyrocketing oil prices should serve as a wake-up call to the public about the dangers of the nation's reliance on imported oil. But it also makes the case for ethanol, according to Corzine. "OPEC (Organization of Petroleum Exporting Countries) has us by the throat," he says.

How valuable is E-85? Corzine notes that 2.5 gallons of ethanol can be produced from a single bushel of corn. Moreover, it takes about 24 gallons of ethanol to displace the gasoline generated from one barrel of oil. (In this equation 10 bushels of corn produce the equivalent of one barrel of oil.)

"Right now," notes Corzine, "ethanol replaces 125,000 barrels of oil per day. We could double that in four years."

Corzine is not alone. The US Department of Energy foresees a sharp rise in the use of E-85 gasoline, starting early in the twenty-first century, eventually reaching more than

1.5 billion gallons a year. In its survey, "Annual Energy Outlook 1998" with projections to the year 2020, the department's Energy Information Administration predicts average annual growth rates of more than 20 percent for E-85 ethanol starting in 2004.

Ethanol is renewable and home-grown. It can help us slash our dependence on foreign oil. Ethanol fuel reduces tailpipe emissions, yet provides performance similar to gasoline. It also results in cleaner engines. Burning this fuel creates jobs in North America, pumps millions of dollars into rural economies, and creates thousands of jobs. Will E-85 become a fuel of the future?

Only time will tell.

METHANE DIGESTERS

By now, you can see that we have lots of clean-burning alternatives to declining fossil fuels, and many of them could be cost-effective, too. One additional fuel that receives very little attention is methane produced by the decay of organic matter — human or livestock wastes and even municipal garbage — under anaerobic conditions (the absence of oxygen).

Methane, of course, is the main component of natural gas, derived from ancient plants and algae. This highly combustible gas can also be produced naturally in landfills. It can also be produced at sewage treatment plants by the natural decomposition of human solid waste. Interestingly, many sewage treatment facilities capture this valuable fuel and put it to good use.

Sewage treatment plants capture the methane produced from the waste they receive each day, and then burn it on-site to generate electricity and heat to power their operations. Landfills sometimes pipe the methane to nearby buildings like schools that use it for heating.

Methane can also be produced in devices called methane digesters. A methane digester is a tank made from metal or concrete that accepts organic waste, for example, from cattle or other livestock. The waste is mixed with water and enters the tank as a slurry. Here it decomposes anaerobically (in the absence of oxygen) to produce methane gas. The methane is then piped out of the system and used for heating or cooking or generating electricity. (To learn more about methane digesters, see the accompanying box.)

Although methane digesters are a great idea, and are widely used in less developed countries, they're terribly underutilized in the more developed countries. In time, as natural gas supplies fall, though, methane digesters could be used to take up the slack. I even envision the day when septic tanks in rural settings could be used to produce small amounts of methane for homes. Methane produced in the tank could be captured and piped to the house where it would be burned in gas ranges, gas water heaters, and even gas furnaces and boilers.

THE BOTANICAL REVOLUTION

Oil and natural gas are not just used to heat homes and provide for other energy needs. They're vital components of many other human

Today hundreds of high-value chemicals are derived from petroleum refineries. Gasoline is one of the least valuable of all the chemicals in crude oil!

activities as well. Oil, for instance, contains a wide assortment of organic chemicals that are used to make a variety of products from moth balls to paint thinner to beach balls to computers and cameras. You may be surprised to learn that many medicines in your medicine cabinet are derived from chemicals extracted from crude oil. So are synthetic fabrics and virtually all plastics.

Natural gas, while less useful as a feedstock to industry, is a source of artificial fertilizer.

So how will we meet our needs for this enormous number of chemicals as oil and natural gas enter their retirement years?

Many people think that plants could supply human society with all of the chemicals needed to meet these nonfuel resource needs. It may surprise many readers to learn that for many years the world economy depended almost entirely on plant matter. As a young boy in the 1950s and 1960s, the rope we used was made from hemp rather than plastic or

Methane Digester Designs

Anaerobic digesters are made out of concrete, steel, brick, or plastic. They are shaped like silos, troughs, basins, or ponds, and may be placed underground or on the surface. All designs incorporate the same basic components: a pre-mixing area or tank, a digester vessel(s), a system for using the biogas, and a system for distributing or spreading the effluent (the remaining digested material).

There are two basic types of digesters: batch and continuous. Batch-type digesters are the simplest to build. Their operation consists of loading the digester with organic materials and allowing it to digest. The retention time depends on temperature and other factors. Once the digestion is complete, the effluent is removed and the process is repeated.

In a continuous digester, organic material is constantly or regularly fed into the digester. The material moves through the digester either mechanically or by the force of the new feed pushing out digested material. Unlike batch-type digesters, continuous digesters produce biogas without the interruption of loading material and unloading effluent. They may be better suited for large-scale operations. There are three types of continuous digesters: vertical tank systems, horizontal tank or plug-flow systems, and multiple tank systems. Proper design, operation, and maintenance of continuous digesters produce a steady and predictable supply of usable biogas.

Many livestock operations store the manure they produce in waste lagoons or ponds. A growing number of these operations are placing floating covers on their lagoons to capture the biogas. They use it to run an engine/generator to produce electricity.

Source: US Department of Energy

other synthetic materials like nylon, which are common today.

Most chemicals in use at the time also came from plants. Even soaps, resins, textiles, and inks were derived from plants. And of course, building supplies have long been made from trees and other members of the plant kingdom.

But then came oil.

Over the years, researchers found many uses for the chemicals contained in oil. It wasn't too long before the plant-based economy was replaced by the oil-based economy. But with oil in its sunset years, plants may once again rise to a pre-eminent position, providing renewable fuels such as biodiesel, vegetable oil, and ethanol, and a wide variety of chemicals needed to produce the medicines, plastics, and synthetic fabrics we've grown so accustomed to.

More Hemp in Our Future?

Believe it or not, hemp may be one of the main contributors to the next industrial revolution. This isn't marijuana-type hemp, though. It's a related species without the THC.

Hemp has been used to make ropes for many years and was also once utilized by the Sherman Williams Paint Company in many of its products. In fact, until the 1930s linseed and hemp oils were used to produce the majority of the resins, paints, shellacs, and varnishes sold in the United States.

Hemp has long been used as a food source for animals. Most birdseed mixes, in fact, contain hemp seeds. Hemp is also used to make a high-protein food for cattle, chickens, and household pets. And, believe it or not, hemp is being used to produce human food, for example, hemp cheese, milk, and ice cream. Hemp seed flour is even added to bread, pastas, cakes, and cookies.

Hemp is also currently being used to make kitty litter and bedding for horses and smaller pets, such as guinea pigs, rabbits, and hamsters. Hemp seeds can be crushed to liberate oil, as well. Hemp oils are being incorporated in a variety of personal care products including soaps, shampoos, lip balm, massage oil, and perfumes. Some manufacturers are using it to make paper as well.

Still more surprisingly, the auto manufacturer BMW is currently using hemp fiber in its airbag system. Industrial hemp may also one day be used to manufacture floor mats, seat covers, and gaskets. As if that's not enough, hemp is even being used to produce materials such as fiberboard, paints, and sealants.

Besides having many practical uses, hemp grows quickly, even in fairly poor soil. It also thrives in most climates and is naturally resistant to diseases and insects. Hemp discourages weed growth, even after it has been harvested. In addition, hemp adds nutrients to the soil.

Although grown in Europe, industrial hemp is not legal in the United States. The federal government still views it as a possible source of drugs. Unfortunately, they're dead wrong on this issue. "If one were to roll leaves from an industrial hemp plant into cigarettes and smoke them, no euphoric effect would be

Who knows ... in the future you may fill up your car's gas tank with ethanol made from corn stalks, bathe with soap made from hemp, write on paper made from kenaf, and take medicines manufactured from chemical feedstocks produced from corn stalks in a biorefinery.

experienced, even if a thousand hemp cigarettes were smoked," says John Roulac, author of *Hemp Horizons*.

On the subject of the US government's long-standing opposition to industrial hemp, Roulac asks, "Should garden poppies be plowed under because another closely related member of the genus is grown for heroin?"

Hemp is just one of a number of plants that could support the re-emergence of the carbohydrate economy. Over the years, jute, flax, kenaf, ramie, and urena will also very like become part of this botanical revolution. Like hemp, many of these plants grow rapidly in poor soils, helping farmers put agricultural land that has been ravaged by poor farming practices back into production. Kenaf, a plant native to Africa, for instance, reaches harvestable size in 120 to 150 days. Grown commercially in Switzerland, China, India, and the United States, at least on a small scale, kenaf can be used to make paper and several building products.

With oil and natural gas on the decline, corn, soybeans, rapeseed, and a host of others will very likely become the foundation of the world economy. Ethanol from corn and other crops, for instance, could also be used to replace chemical feedstocks. Researchers at the National Renewable Energy Lab hope that ethanol will someday be used to produce a host of useful chemicals that can be used to manufacture medicines, plastics, dyes, and other products that are now derived principally from a nonrenewable source: petroleum.

"What is a cornstalk but oil without the benefit of years of heat and pressure?" quips NREL's George Douglas. "Everything that can be produced from oil could come from corn and other vegetation in special biorefineries. All you need to do is rearrange the molecules in a beneficial way to produce a wide array of useful chemicals — all from a renewable source — without increasing the amount of carbon dioxide released into the atmosphere."

So who knows ... in the future you may fill up your car's gas tank with ethanol made from corn stalks, bathe with soap made from hemp, write on paper made from kenaf, and take medicines manufactured from chemical feedstocks produced from corn stalks in a biorefinery.

CONCLUSION

In this book, we've explored many ways to use energy more efficiently to get the most for your energy dollar. We've also explored a wide range of options for tapping into renewable energy. But energy efficiency and renewable energy aren't the only ways to achieve greater self-reliance. There's much more you can do to achieve a greater level of independence, like growing some of your own food, but that's the topic of another book. For ideas on that I recommend that you take a look at a book I co-authored with Dave Wann, called *Superbia! 31 Ways to Create Sustainable Neighborhoods*. It offers a wealth of advice on many other aspects of your life.

Well, that's it. There's not much more I can say. At this point, it is up to you. Study your options carefully. Keep your eye on the prize always, and proceed forward with confidence that you're not only helping to create a better future for yourself and your family, you're helping to build a sustainable future for all human beings and the millions of species that share this planet with us.

I wish you the best of luck!

Appendix

Metric Conversions		
If you know:	**Multiply by:**	**To find:**
Inches	2.5	centimeters
Feet	0.3	meters
Miles	1.6	kilometers
Gallons	4.5	liters
Pounds	0.45	kilograms
Acres	0.4	hectares
Square feet	0.09	square meters
Miles per hour	1.6	kilometers per hour

To convert miles per gallon to liters per 100 kilometers, divide 282 by the number of miles per gallon. For example, 30 miles per gallon is 282/30 = 9.4 liters per 100 kilometers.

Resource Guide

This resource guide contains a wealth of information on renewable energy listed by chapter. Information is periodically updated on my website: <www.danchiras.com>.

Introduction

Publications

Campbell, C. J. *The Coming Oil Crisis*, Petroconsultants Sa, 1997. Detailed and authoritative analysis of world oil supplies. Paints a rather dismal future.

Campbell, C. J. "The Oil Peak: A Turning Point," *Solar Today* 15(4), 2001. A brief analysis of the future of global oil.

Darley, Julian. *High Noon for Natural Gas: The New Energy Crisis*. Chelsea Green, 2004. A look at natural gas supplies and the impacts of the imminent peak in global natural gas production.

Hartmann, Thom. *The Last Hours of Ancient Sunlight: Warming Up to Personal and Global Transformation*. Three Rivers Press, 1999. A philosophic look at the decline in oil.

Heinberg, Richard. *The Party's Over: Oil, War and the Fate of Industrial Societies*. (Revised and Updated Version) New Society Publishers, 2005. A grim look at the prospects for human society as global oil production peaks.

Heinberg, Richard. *Power Down: Options and Actions for a Post-Carbon World*. New Society Publishers, 2004. A frank discussion of our options as global oil production peaks.

Howe, John. *The End of Fossil Energy: A Plan for Sustainability*. McIntire Publishing, 2003. A short overview of energy problems and what we can do about them.

Rifkin, Jeremy. *The Hydrogen Economy: The Creation of the World-Wide Energy Web and the Redistribution of Power on Earth*. Tarcher/Putnam, 2002. Excellent analysis of world energy troubles and an optimistic look at the role hydrogen could play in our future.

Udall, Randy and Steve Andrews. "Methane Madness: A Natural Gas Primer," *Solar Today* 15(4), 2001. A frightening look at natural gas production.

Udall, Randy and Steve Andrews. "When Will the Joyride End?" *Home Power* 81, 2001. An insightful look at oil production and consumption with emphasis on peak oil production.

Udall, Randy. "From Cleopatra to Columbia," *Home Power* 100, 2004. An insightful look at energy in an historical perspective.

Videos

The End of Suburbia: Oil Depletion and the Collapse of The American Dream. A gripping video on the impacts of peak oil and natural gas production. Paints a dim future for human culture. To order a copy contact: www.endofsurburbia.com.

Organizations

Global Public Media. This organization helps to spread the word about peak oil and natural gas and tracks important developments.
Website: www.globalpublicmedia.com.

PeakOilAction.org is another group dedicated to helping spread the word about the proximate peaks in global oil and natural gas production.
Website: www.peakoilaction.org.

The Post Carbon Institute is working to spread the word about the proximate peaks in global oil and natural gas production.
Website: www.postcarbon.org.

Chapter 1
Renewable Energy: Clean, Reliable, and Affordable

Publications

Aitken, Donald W. "Germany Launches Its Transition," *Solar Today* 19(2), 2005. A fascinating look at Germany's plans to achieve 100 percent of its energy from renewable sources.

Aitken, Donald W. "The Renewable Energy Transition: Can it Really Happen?" *Solar Today* 19(1), 2005. A valuable look at a very important question.

Asmus, Peter. "Power Solutions in Our Own Backyards," *Solar Today* 15 (1), 2001. An interesting look at dispersed energy production.

Bihn, Dan. "Japan Takes the Lead," *Solar Today* 19(1), 2005. A look at Japan's aggressive pursuit of renewable energy.

Brown, Lester R. "Harnessing the Wind for Energy Independence," *Solar Today* 16(2), 2002. A good overview of wind energy.

Brown, Lester R. "The Short Path to Oil Independence," *Mother Earth News* 208, 2005. How hybrid cars and wind energy can slash our oil imports.

Chiras, Daniel D. *Lessons From Nature: Learning to Live Sustainably on the Earth.* Island Press, 1992. Describes transitional steps to a renewable energy economy.

Chiras, Dan. "All About Insulation," *Mother Earth News* 195, 2003. A detailed look at insulation options.

Chiras, Daniel D. *Environmental Science, 7th ed.* Jones and Bartlett, forthcoming, 2006. Offers a detailed overview of renewable and nonrenewable energy issues and solutions.

Dunn, S. "Decarbonizing the Energy Economy," *State of the World 2001.* Linda Starke, ed. Norton, 2001. Important reading on renewable energy.

Flavin, C. "Rethinking the Energy System," *State of the World 1999.* Linda Starke, ed. Norton, 1999. Part of an ongoing series on ways to restructure the global energy system that are good for people and the environment.

Flavin, C. "Harnessing the Sun and the Wind," *State of the World 1995.* Linda Starke, ed. Norton, 1995. Important reading.

Flavin, C. and N. Lenssen. "Reshaping the Power Industry," *State of the World 1994.* Linda Starke, ed. Norton, 1994. Important insights into changes under way in the power industry, especially those related to energy conservation.

Home Power Staff. "Clearing the Air: Home Power Dispels the Top RE Myths," *Home Power* 100, 2004. Superb piece for those who want to learn more about the many false assumptions and beliefs about renewable energy.

Kohn, Lin. "Solar in San Francisco," *Solar Today* 1 (4), 2003. An exciting look at what one progressive city is doing to increase its reliance on renewable energy.

Perlin, J. *From Space to Earth: The Story of Solar Electricity.* Aatec Publications, 1999. A wonderfully readable history of solar electricity.

Perlin, John, Lawrence Kazmerski, and Susan Moon. "Good as Gold: The Silicon Solar Cell Turns 50," *Solar Today* 28(1), 2004. A brief history of PV research and development.

Prugh, Tom, Christoper Flavin, and Janet L. Sawin. "Changing the Oil Economy," *State of the World 2005.* Linda Starke, ed. W. W.

Norton, 2005. Examines oil production declines from the standpoint of national security.

Renner, M. "Creating Jobs, Preserving the Environment," *State of the World 2000*. Linda Starke, ed. W. W. Norton, 2000. Shows the economic and employment benefits of renewable energy.

Renner, M. "Employment in Wind Power." World Watch 14(1), 2001. Fascinating look at the employment boom in the wind energy sector.

Roodman, D. M. "Reforming Subsidies." In *State of the World 2000*. Linda Starke, ed. Norton, 2000. Extremely important reading.

Sawin, Janet L. "Charting a New Energy Future," *State of the World 2003*. Linda Starke, ed. Norton, 2003. An overview of renewable energy potential and what other nations are doing to create a sustainable energy future.

Sawin, Janet L. *Mainstreaming Renewable Energy in the 21st Century*, Worldwatch Paper 169, Washington, D.C.: Worldwatch Institute, 2004. Overview of the prospects of renewable energy.

Sawin, Janet L. "Making Better Energy Choices," *State of the World 2004*. Norton, 2004. An overview of what people are doing worldwide to switch to a renewable energy strategy.

Sindelar, Allan and Phil Campbell-Graves. "How to Finance Your Renewable Energy Home," *Home Power* 103, 2004. Very useful article.

Starrs, Tom. "Green Tags: A New Way to Support Renewable Energy," *Solar Today* 15 (4), 2001. Describes ways that individuals can support renewable energy production without having to install a system on their homes.

Stronberg, Joel B. "A Common-Sense Solution," *Solar Today* 19(2), 2005. A look at the renewable energy strategy in light of current affairs.

Strong, Steven J. "Beyond Petroleum," *Solar Today* 15(2), 2001. One of my all-time favorite stories: British Petroleum's shift to renewable energy.

Swain, J. "Charting a New Energy Future," *State of the World 2003*. Linda Starke, ed. Norton, 2003. Examines the potential of renewable energy resources and many other important subjects.

Sweezy, Blair and Lori Bird. "Businesses Lead the 'Green Power' Challenge," *Solar Today* 15(1), 2001. What some major corporations like Toyota are doing to increase their reliance on renewable energy.

Sweezey, Blair and Lori Bird. "Buying Green Power — You Really Can Make a Difference," *Solar Today* 17(1), 2003. An in-depth look at ways, such as green tags, that homeowners can tap into renewable energy without installing a system on their home.

Wilkerson, Mark W. "Solar in the Heartland," *Solar Today* 14(5), 2000. An inspiring tale of a small unincorporated village in north-central Illinois that has gone solar.

Yerkes, Bill. "40 Years of Solar Power," *Solar Today* 18(1), 2004. A historical look at PV development from an insider.

Yewdall, Zeke. "Alternatives that Don't Cost an Arm and a Leg," *Home Power* 101, 2004. A useful article on energy efficiency and other ways to acquire electricity from renewable sources if your site is not ideally suited for them or your pocketbook prohibits the investment.

Chapter 2
Conservation Rules: The Keystone to Your Energy Future

Energy-Efficient Building Envelopes

Publications

Bailes, Allison A. "How Efficient is Your House?" *Home Power* 106, 2005. Great article on home energy ratings and blower door tests.

Barker, Jennifer. "Buying an Energy-Efficient Refrigerator," *Home Power* 104, 2005. For those interested in upgrading their refrigerators, this article is a must.

Chiras, Dan. "Hunting Phantom Loads," *Home Power* 82, 2001. My own experience with phantom loads in my solar electric home and advice on eliminating them.

Chiras, Dan. "Minimize the Digging: Frost-Protected Shallow Foundations," *The Last Straw* 38, 2002. A brief overview of frost-protected shallow foundations.

Chiras, Dan. "Retrofitting a Foundation for Energy Efficiency, *The Last Straw* 38, 2002. Describes ways to retrofit foundations to reduce heat loss.

Chiras, Daniel D. "The Energy-Efficient Home," *Solar Today* 18(5), 2004. A primer on energy-efficient home design.

Carmody, John, Stephen Selkowitz, and Lisa Heschong. *Residential Windows: A Guide to New Technologies and Energy Performance.* Norton, 1996. Important resource for energy-efficient home designers.

Fine Homebuilding. *The Best of Fine Homebuilding: Energy-Efficient Building.* Taunton Press, 1999. A collection of detailed articles on a wide assortment of topics related to energy efficiency including insulation, energy-saving details, windows, and heating systems.

Hurst-Wajszczuk, Joe. "Save Energy and Money – Now!" *Mother Earth News* 189, 2001. More ideas on ways to save energy in your home.

Kerr, Andy. "Doing Well While Doing Good: Conservation of Energy as a Rational Financial Investment," *Home Power* 86, 2002. A look at the economics of household energy savings.

Johnston, David and Kim Master. *Green Remodeling: Changing the World One Room at a Time.* New Society Publishers, 2004. Superb coverage of many ideas on ways to boost energy efficiency in existing homes.

Loken, Steve. *ReCraft 90: The Construction of a Resource-Efficient House.* National Center for Appropriate Technology, Center for Resourceful Building Technology, 1997. Field notes, lessons learned, and other information obtained from experience building a demonstration home in Missoula, Montana.

Lstiburek, Joe, and Besty Pettit. *EEBA Builder's Guide–Cold Climate.* Energy Efficient Building Association, 1999. Superb resource for advice on building in cold climates.

Lstiburek, Joe, and Besty Pettit. *EEBA Builder's Guide–Mixed Humid Climate.* Energy Efficient Building Association, 1999. Superb resource for advice on this climate.

Lstiburek, Joe, and Betsy Pettit. *EEBA Builder's Guide–Hot-Arid Climate.* EEBA, 1999. Superb resource for advice on building in hot, arid climates.

Magwood, Chris, ed. "Roofs and Foundations," *The Last Straw* 38, 2002. An excellent resource for those who want to learn about efficient foundations.

Mumma, Tracy. *Guide to Resource Efficient Building Elements.* National Center for Appropriate Technology, Center for Resourceful Building Technology, 1997. A handy guide to materials that help improve the efficiency of homes and other buildings. Available in updated versions online and free at www.crbt.org.

National Association of Home Builders Research Center. *Design Guide for Frost-Protected Shallow Foundations.* NAHB Research Center, 1996. Also available online at www.nahb.org.

Pahl, Greg. *Home Heating Basics.* Chelsea Green, 2003. A detailed overview of natural home heating options.

Pinkham, Linda and Joe Schwartz. "Washing Machine Spin-Off: Maytag Neptune vs.

Frigidaire Gallery vs. Thrift Store Model," *Home Power* 103, 2004. A good comparison of several of your options for energy- and water-efficient washing machines.

Salomon, Thierry and Stephane Bedel. *The Energy Saving House*. Centre for Alternative Technology Publications, 1999. Good guide to home energy savings.

Scheckel, Paul. *The Home Energy Diet*.New Society Publishers, 2005. A great guide for energy conservation in homes.

Sikora, Jeannie L. *Profit from Building Green: Award Winning Tips to Build Energy Efficient Homes*. BuilderBooks, 2002. A brief, but informative overview of energy conservation strategies.

Williams, Jeff. "Warm Light, Cool Savings," *Solar Today* 19(2), 2005. An introduction to energy-efficient windows and doors.

Wilson, Alex. "Windows: Looking through the Options," *Solar Today* 15(2), 2001. A great overview of windows with a useful checklist for those in the market to buy new windows.

Yost, Harry. *Home Insulation: Do It Yourself and Save as Much as 40%*. Storey Communications, 1991. Extremely useful book for anyone building his or her own home.

Organizations

American Council for an Energy-Efficient Economy. 1001 Connecticut Avenue NW, Suite 801, Washington, D.C. 20036. Tel: (202) 429-0063, Website: www.aceee.org. Numerous excellent publications on energy efficiency, including *Consumer Guide to Home Energy Savings*.

Building America Program. US Department of Energy. Office of Building Systems, EE-41, 1000 Independence Avenue SW, Washington, D.C. 20585. Tel: (202) 586-9472. Leaders in promoting energy efficiency and renewable energy to achieve zero-energy buildings.

Cellulose Insulation Manufacturers Association. Your place to shop for information on cellulose insulation. 133 S. Keowee St., Dayton, OH 45402. Tel: (937) 222-2462. Website: www.cellulose.org.

Consumers Union. Tel: (800) 500-9760. Publishes *Consumer Reports* and *Consumer Reports Annual Buying Guide*, which rates appliances for reliability, convenience, and efficiency.
Website: www.consumerreports.org.

Energy Efficiency and Renewable Energy Clearinghouse. P.O. Box 3048, Merrifield, VA 22116. Tel: (800) 363-3732. Great source for a variety of useful information on energy efficiency.

Energy Efficient Building Association. 490 Concordia Ave., P.O. Box 22307, Eagen, MN 55122. Tel: (651) 268-7585. Offers conferences, workshops, publications and an on-line bookstore. Website: www.eeba.org.

National Fenestration Ratings Council. 1300 Spring St., Suite 120, Silver Springs, Md. Tel: (301) 589-6372. For information on the energy efficiency of windows. Website: www.nfrc.org.

National Insulation Association. 99 Canal Center Plaza, Suite 222, Alexandria, VA 22314. Tel: (703) 683-6422. Offers a wide range of information on different types of insulation. Website: www.insulation.org.

US Department of Energy and Environmental Protection Agency's ENERGY STAR program. Tel: (888) 782-7937. Website: www.energystar.gov.

Energy-Efficient Appliances and Heating Systems

Publications

Fine Homebuilding. *Energy-Efficient Building.* Taunton Press, 1999. Contains a collection of extremely useful articles on mechanical heating systems.

Fust, Art. "A Simple Warm Floor Heating System," *The Last Straw* 32, 2000. Contains much useful information on radiant floor heat.

Grahl, Christine L. "The Radiant Flooring Revolution," *Environmental Design and Construction* January/February, 2000. Superb introduction to radiant-floor heating.

Hyatt, Rod. "Hydronic Heating on Renewable Energy," *Home Power* 79, 2000. Practical advice on installing a radiant-floor heating system using renewable energy.

O'Connell, John, and Bruce Harley. "Choosing Ductwork," *Fine Homebuilding* June/July, 1997. Essential reading for anyone interested in installing a forced-air heating system.

"Hydronic Radiant-Floor Heating," *Fine Homebuilding,* October/November, 1996. Extremely useful reference. Well-written, thorough, and well-illustrated.

Siegenthaler, John. *Modern Hydronic Heating.* Delmar Publishers, 1995. Everything you would ever want to know about hydronic heating.

Thorne, Jennifer, John Morrill, and Alex Wilson. *Consumer Guide to Home Energy Savings,* 8th ed. American Council for an Energy-Efficient Economy, 2003. Excellent resource, full of vital information on energy-saving appliances.

Weaver, Jennifer. "Tankless Is In," *Home Power* 105, 2005. Excellent overview of tankless water heaters.

Wilson, Alex. "A Primer on Heating Systems," *Fine Homebuilding*, February/ March, 1997. Superb overview of furnaces, boilers, and heating systems.

Wilson, Alex. "Radiant-Floor Heating: When It Does — and Doesn't — Make Sense," *Environmental Building News* 1, 2002. Valuable reading.

Organizations

Consumer Product Safety Commission. Office of Information and Public Affairs, CPSC, Washington, D.C. 20207 or call their hotline at (800) 638-2772. Offers a wealth of information on space heaters, including safety precautions. Website: www.cpsc.gov.

Radiant Panel Association. 1433 West 29th Street, Loveland, CO 80539. Tel: (970) 613-0100. Professional organization consisting of radiant heating and cooling contractors, wholesalers, manufacturers, and professionals.
Website: www.radiantpanelassociation.org.

Energy-Efficient Landscaping

Publications

Dramstad, Wenche E., James D. Olson, and Richard T. Forman. *Landscape Ecology: Principles in Landscape Architecture and Land-Use Planning*. Island Press, 1996. A useful textbook on the subject.

Moffat, Anne Simon, Marc Schiler and the staff of Green Living. *Energy-Efficient and Environmental Landscaping*. Appropriate Solutions Press, 1994. Contains an abundance of information on energy-efficient landscaping strategies and plant varieties suitable for various climate zones.

NREL. *Landscaping for Energy Efficiency*. DOE Office of Energy Efficiency and Renewable Energy, 1995. DOE/GO-10095-046. Provides a decent, though somewhat disorganized, overview on the topic.

Striefel, Jan and Wesley A. Groesbeck. *The Resource Guide to Sustainable Landscapes*. Environmental Resources, Inc., 1995. Excellent resource.

Magazines

Earthwood Journal. Eos Institute, 580 Broadway, Suite 200, Laguna Beach, Ca. 92651. Phone: 1-714-497-1896. A glossy permaculture magazine published by Eos Institute and the Permaculture Institute of Southern California. Geared to the professional designer, architect, and land-use planner.

The Permaculture Activist. P.O. Box 1209W, Black Mountain, N.C. 28711. Tel: (828) 298-2812. Publishes articles on a variety of

subjects related to permaculture; includes an updated list of permaculture design courses.
Website: www.permacultureactivist.net.

Permaculture Drylands Journal. Permaculture Drylands Institute, P.O. Box 156, Santa Fe, N.M. 87504. Tel: (505) 983-0663. Quarterly journal that focuses on the practice of permaculture in arid lands, especially Arizona and New Mexico.
Website: www.permaculture.net.

Permaculture Edge. Permaculture Nambour, Inc. P.O. Box 148, Inglewood 6050, Western Australia. Reports on cutting-edge developments in permaculture.

Permaculture Magazine. Permanent Publications, Hyden House Limited, Little Hyden Land, Clandfield, Hampshire PO8 ORU, England. A quarterly journal published in cooperation with the Permaculture Association of Great Britain, containing articles, book reviews, and solutions from Britain and Europe.
Website: www.permaculture.co.uk.

Permaculture Resources. P.O. Box 65, 56 Farmersville Road, Califon, N.J. 07830. Tel: (800) 832-6285. An educational publisher and distributor of permaculture resources and publications.

The Last Straw. TLS, P.O. Box 22706, Lincoln, NE 68542. Tel: (402) 483-5135.

This journal publishes articles on natural building and features articles on passive solar heating and cooling.
Website: www.strawhomes.com.

Organizations

Appropriate Technology Transfer for Rural Areas, P.O. Box 3657, Fayetteville, AR 72702. Tel: (800) 346-9140. This organization is actively involved in the permaculture movement.

International Permaculture Institute. An international coordinating organization for permaculture activities such as accreditation. P.O. Box 1, Tyalgum, NSW 2484, Australia. Tel: (066) 793 442.

Chapter 3
Solar Hot Water

Publications

Butler, Barry. "Solar Wand: Hot Water Assist for Cold Climates," *Home Power* 104, 2005. Illustrates and describes a quick retrofit for existing water tanks.

Galloway, Terry. *Solar House: A Guide for the Solar Designer.* Architectural Press, 2004. A technical guide on a wide range of solar designs, including active solar.

Lane, Tom. "Solar Pool Heating Basics, Part 1," *Home Power* 94, 2003. Excellent overview of solar pool heating systems.

Lane, Tom. "Solar Pool Heating Basics, Part 2," *Home Power* 95, 2003. Excellent overview of solar pool heating systems.

Johnston, David and Kim Master. *Green Remodeling: Changing the World One Room at a Time.* New Society Publishers, 2004. Contains many ideas to boost energy efficiency in existing homes and increase one's reliance on renewable energy, including active solar.

Lane, Tom and Ken Olson. "Solar Hot Water for Cold Climates, Part II: Drainback Systems," *Home Power* 86, 2002. Detailed look at drainback systems. (Part I of this series is Olson's article on closed-loop antifreeze systems, listed below. Part III, written by Marken and Olson, is also listed below.)

Marken, Chuck. "Heat Exchangers for Solar Water Heating," *Home Power* 92, 2003. Great overview of heat exchangers.

Marken, Chuck and Ken Olson. "Installation Basics for Solar Domestic Water Heating Systems," *Home Power* 94, 2003. The first in a series of three articles for those who would like to install their own solar hot water systems.

Marken, Chuck and Ken Olson. "One-Tank SDHW Storage with Electric Backup," *Home Power* 96, 2003. All about retrofitting an existing electric water heater tank for solar hot water.

Marken, Chuck and Ken Olson. "SDHW Installation Basics. Part III: Drainback System," *Home Power* 97, 2003. Excellent reference for installers and do-it-yourselfers.

Marken, Chuck. "New Life for Your Old Water Heater: Water Heater and Solar Tank Anode Rods," *Home Power* 106, 2005. A must read for anyone who has a conventional water heater.

Olsen, Ken. "Solar Hot Water: A Primer," *Home Power* 84, 2001. Excellent overview of solar hot water systems and your options.

Olson, Ken. "Solar Hot Water, Homebrew Style," *Home Power* 88, 2002. For those who want to learn more about drainback systems.

Olson, Ken. "Solar Hot Water for Cold Climates, Part I: Closed Loop Antifreeze System Components," *Home Power* 85, 2001. For those interested in installing a solar hot water system in a climate where wintertime freezing is a regular occurrence.

Owens, Bob. "Florida Batch Water Heater," *Home Power* 93, 2003. For those interested in installing a solar batch heater.

Owens, Bob. "My Solar Heated Hot Tub," *Home Power* 105, 2005. For those interested in solar hot tubs, this article is a must.

Perlin, John. "Solar Hot Water History," *Home Power* 100, 2004. A great overview of the history of solar hot water.

Sindelar, Allan and Phil Campbell-Graves. "How to Finance Your Renewable Energy Home," *Home Power* 103, 2004. Very useful article.

Sklar, Scott. "Selecting a Solar Heating System," *Solar Today* 18(5), 2004. A good look at the economics of solar hot water systems.

Sklar, Scott, and Kenneth Sheinkopf. *Consumer Guide to Solar Energy: More Ways to Reduce Your Energy Bills and Save the Environment.* Bonus Books, 1995. Delightful introduction to many different solar applications, including solar hot water.

Tonnessen, Roy W. "Solar Water Heating," *Home Power* 91, 2002. A case study worth your while to read.

Weaver, Jennifer. "Tankless Is In," *Home Power* 105, 2005. Excellent overview of tankless water heaters.

Wilson, Jib. "Hawaiian Heat," *Solar Today* 14(3), 2000. Production builders are

adding domestic solar hot water systems with help of the state.

Magazines and Newsletters

Backwoods Home Magazine. P.O. Box 712, Gold Beach, OR 97444. Tel: (800) 835-2418. Publishes articles on all aspects of self-reliant living, including renewable energy strategies such as solar. Website: www.backwoodshome.com.

The CADDET Renewable Energy Newsletter. 168 Harwell, Oxfordshire OX11 ORA, United Kingdom. Tel: +44 123335 432968. Quarterly magazine published by the CADDET Centre for Renewable Energy. Covers a wide range of renewable energy topics.

Earth Quarterly (formerly *Dry Country News*). Box 23-J, Radium Springs, NM 88054. Tel: (505) 526-1853. A new magazine devoted to living close to, and in harmony with nature. Covers all aspects of natural life including homebuilding and renewable energy. Website: www.zianet.com/earth.

EREN Network News. Newsletter of the Department of Energy's Energy-Efficiency and Renewable Energy Network. See listing under organizations.

Home Energy Magazine. 2124 Kittredge Street, No. 95, Berkeley, CA 94704. Great resource for those who want to learn more about ways to save energy in conventional home construction.

Home Power P.O. Box 520, Ashland, OR 97520. Tel: (800) 707-6585. Publishes numerous extremely valuable how-to and general articles on renewable energy, including solar hot water, PVs, wind energy, microhydroelectric, and occasionally an article or two on passive solar heating and cooling. This magazine is a gold mine of information, an absolute must for anyone interested in learning more. The magazine also contains important product reviews and ads for companies and professional installers. CDs containing back issues can be purchased from *Home Power* website: www.homepower.com.

Inside and Out. Newsletter of the Passive Solar Industries Council. See listing under organizations.

Mother Earth News. 1503 SW 42nd St., Topeka, KS 66609. One of my favorite magazines. Usually publishes a very useful article in each issue on some aspect of renewable energy.
Website: www.motherearthnews.com.

Solar Today. ASES, 2400 Central Ave., Suite G-1, Boulder, CO 80301. Tel: (303) 443-3130. This magazine, published by the American Solar Energy Society, contains lots of good information on passive solar, solar thermal, photovoltaics, hydrogen, and other topics, but not much how-to information. Also lists names of engineers, builders, and installers and lists workshops and conferences.
Website: www.solartoday.org.

Organizations

American Solar Energy Society. 2400 Central Avenue, Suite G-1, Boulder, CO 80301. Publishes *Solar Today* magazine and sponsors an annual national meeting. Also publishes an online catalogue of publications and sponsors the National Tour of Solar Homes. Contact this organization to find out about an ASES chapter in your area. Website: www.ases.org.

Center for Building Science. Lawrence Berkeley National Laboratory's Center for Building Science works to develop and commercialize energy-efficient technologies and to document ways of improving the energy efficiency of homes and other buildings while protecting air quality. Website: www.eetd.lbl.gov.

Center for Renewable Energy and Sustainable Technologies (CREST). CREST, 1612 K St. NW, Suite 410, Washington, D.C. 20006. Tel: (202) 293-2898. Nonprofit organization dedicated to renewable energy, energy efficiency, and sustainable living. Website: http://solstice.crest.org.

El Paso Solar Energy Association. P.O. Box 26384, El Paso, TX 79926. Active in solar energy, especially passive solar design and construction.
Website: www.epsea.org/design.html.

Energy Efficiency and Renewable Energy Clearinghouse. P.O. Box 3048, Merrifield, VA 22116. Tel: (800) 363-3732. Great source of a variety of useful information on renewable energy.

Florida Solar Energy Center. FSEC, 679 Clearlake Road, Cocoa, FL 32922. Tel: (321) 638-1000. A research institute of the University of Central Florida Research and education on passive solar, cooling, and photovoltaics.
Website: www.fsec.ucf.edu.

Midwest Renewable Energy Association. P.O. Box 249, Amherst, WI 54406. Tel: (715) 824-5166. Actively promotes solar energy and offers valuable workshops and a superb annual energy fair.
Website: www.the-mrea.org.

National Renewable Energy Lab. NREL, 1617 Cole Blvd., Golden, CO 80401. Tel: (303) 384-7349. Center for Buildings and Thermal Systems. Key players in research and education on energy efficiency and passive solar heating and cooling.
Website: www.nrel.gov/buildings/highperformance.

North Carolina Solar Center. Box 7401, Raleigh, NC 27695. Tel: (919) 515-3480. Offers workshops, tours, publications, and much more.
Website: www.ncsc.ncsu.edu.

Renewable Energy Training and Education Center. 1679 Clearlake Road, Cocoa, FL 32922. Tel: (407) 638-1007. Offers hands-on training and certification courses in US and abroad for those interested in becoming certified in solar installation.

Solar Energy International. P.O. Box 715, Carbondale, CO 81623. Tel: (970) 963-8855. Offers a wide range of workshops on solar energy, wind energy, and natural building. Website: www.solarenergy.org.

Solar Living Institute. P.O. Box 836, Hopland, CA 95449. Tel: (707) 744-2017. A nonprofit organization that offers frequent hands-on workshops on solar energy and many other topics. Be sure to tour their facility if you are in the neighborhood. Website: www.solarliving.org.

Chapter 4
Free Heat: Passive Solar, Active Solar, and Heat Pumps
Passive Solar
Publications

Chiras, Daniel D. "Build a Solar Home and Let the Sunshine in," *Mother Earth News*

193, 2002. A survey of passive solar design principles and a case study showing the economics of passive solar heating.

Chiras, Dan. "Learning from Mistakes of the Past," *The Last Straw* 36, 2001. Describes common errors in passive solar design.

Chiras, Daniel D., ed. "Solar Solutions," *The Last Straw* 36, 2001. Over a dozen articles, many by me, on passive solar heating, integrated design, thermal mass, and more.

Chiras, Dan. "Sunshine from a Tube," *Mother Earth News* 202, 2004. Brief introduction to solar tube skylights.

Chiras, Daniel D. *The Solar House: Passive Solar Heating and Cooling.* Chelsea Green, 2002. A detailed, readable guide for designing and building homes for passive solar heating and cooling.

Chiras, Dan. "Sun-Wise Design: Avoid Passive Solar Design Blunders," *Home Power* 105, 2005. Important look at the most costly and most common mistakes in passive solar design.

Cole, Nancy, and P.J. Skerrett. *Renewables Are Ready: People Creating Renewable Energy Solutions.* Chelsea Green, 1995. Numerous case studies showing how people have applied various solar technologies, including passive solar.

Crosbie, Michael. J., ed. *The Passive Solar Design and Construction Handbook.* John Wiley and Sons, 1997. A fairly technical manual on passive solar homes. Contains detailed drawings and case studies.

Crowther, Richard I. *Affordable Passive Solar Homes: Low-Cost Compact Designs.* SciTech Publishing, 1984. Contains some valuable background information on passive solar design and numerous designs for passive solar homes.

Energy Division, North Carolina Department of Commerce. *Solar Homes for North Carolina: A Guide to Building and Planning Solar Homes.* North Carolina Solar Center, 1999. Available online at the North Carolina Solar Center's website.

Galloway, Terry. *Solar House: A Guide for the Solar Designer.* Architectural Press, 2004. Fairly technical guide on a wide range of solar designs, including passive solar.

Gillett, Drew and Nick Pine. "Soldier's Grove Soldiers On," *Solar Today* 17(6), 2003. Inspiring look at a solar town in Wisconsin that uses passive and active solar technologies to provide heat to homes and stores.

Johnston, David and Kim Master. *Green Remodeling: Changing the World One Room at a Time.* New Society Publications, 2004.

Many ideas that boost energy efficiency in existing homes and increase reliance on renewable energy, including passive solar.

Kriescher, Paul. "New England Style Passive Solar," *Solar Today* 14(3), 2000. An interesting case study in residential passive solar heating.

Kachadorian, James. *The Passive Solar House.* Chelsea Green, 1997. Presents a lot of good information on passive solar heating and an interesting design that has been fairly successful in cold climates.

Kubusch, Erwin. *Home Owner's Guide to Free Heat: Cut Your Heating Bills Over 50%.* Sunstore Farms, 1991. A self-published book with lots of good basic information.

Little, Amanda Griscom. "Super Solar Homes Everyone Can Afford," *Mother Earth News* 207, 2005. Those interested in building a new home should check out this article.

Marken, Chuck. "Solar Hot Air System Design," *Home Power* 98, 2004. Valuable resource for those who can't retrofit for passive solar or solar hot water heating systems.

Marken, Chuck. "Solar Hot Air Systems, Part II," *Home Power* 99, 2004. Valuable resource.

Miller, Burke. *Solar Energy: Today's Technologies for a Sustainable Future.* American Solar Energy Society, 1997. Extremely valuable resource; contains numerous case studies showing how passive solar heating can be used in different climates, even in some solar-deprived places.

Moore, Steve and Carol. "Winter Food Production in Pennsylvania – Without Fossil Fuels," *Home Power* 99, 2004. Learn to grow much of your own food year-round without artificially heating a greenhouse.

Niklas, Mike. "High Performance Schools – It's a No-Brainer," *Solar Today* 16I (3), 2002. A fascinating look at the greening of a high school in Oregon, including energy efficiency, passive solar heating, passive cooling, and daylighting.

Olson, Ken and Joe Schwartz. "Home Sweet Solar Home: A Passive Solar Design Primer," *Home Power* 90, 2002. Superb introduction to passive solar design principles.

Passive Solar Industries Council. *Passive Solar Design Strategies: Guidelines for Home Builders.* PSIC, undated. Extremely useful book with worksheets for calculating a house's energy demand, the amount of back-up heat required, the temperature swing one can expect given the amount of thermal mass you've installed, and the estimated cooling load. You can order a copy from the Sustainable Buildings Industry Council (SBIC, formerly the PSIC) with detailed information for your state, so you can design a home to meet the requirements of your site.

Potts, Michael. *The New Independent Home: People and Houses that Harvest the Sun, Wind, and Water.* Chelsea Green, 1999. Delightfully readable book with lots of good information.

Reynolds, Michael. *Comfort in Any Climate.* Solar Survival Press, 1990. A brief but informative treatise on passive heating and cooling.

Sklar, Scott, and Kenneth Sheinkopf. *Consumer Guide to Solar Energy: More Ways to Reduce Your Energy Bills and Save the Environment.* Bonus Books, 1995. Delightful introduction to many different solar applications, including passive solar heating.

Solar Survival Architecture. "Thermal Mass vs. Insulation." *Earthship Chronicles.* Solar Survival Architecture, 1998. Basic treatise on passive solar heating and cooling.

Sustainable Buildings Industry Council. *Designing Low-Energy Buildings: Passive Solar Strategies and Energy-10 Software.* SBIC, 1996. A superb resource! This book of design guidelines and the *Energy-10* soft-ware that comes with it enables builders to analyze the energy and cost savings in building designs. Helps permit region-specific design.

Taylor, John S. *Shelter Sketchbook: Timeless Building Solutions.* Chelsea Green, 1983. Pictorial history of building that will open your eyes to intriguing design solutions to achieve comfort, efficiency, convenience, and beauty.

Van Dresser, Peter. *Passive Solar House Basics.* Ancient City Press, 1996. A brief book that provides basics on passive solar design and construction primarily of adobe homes. Contains sample house plans, ideas for solar water heating, and much more.

Videos

Buildings for a Sustainable America. A concise overview of passive solar buildings and their benefits. Available from the Sustainable Buildings Industry Council (SBIC), 1331 H Street NW, Suite 1000, Washington, D.C. 20005. Tel: (202) 628-7400. Website: www.sbicouncil.org.

Organizations

Sustainable Buildings Industries Council. SBIC, 331 H. Street NW, Suite 1000, Washington, D.C. 20005. Tel: (202) 628-7400. This organization has a terrific website with information on workshops, books and publications on energy-efficient, passive solar design, and links to many other international, national, and state solar energy organizations. Publishes a newsletter, *Buildings Inside and Out*. Website: www.psic.org.

Active Solar Hot Water for Space Heat

Publications

Gillett, Drew and Nick Pine. "Soldier's Grove Soldiers On," *Solar Today* 17(6), 2003. An inspiring look at a solar town in Wisconsin that uses passive and active solar technologies to provide heat to homes and stores.

Hyatt, Rod. "Hydronic Heating on Renewable Energy," *Home Power* 79, 2000. Provides a lot of practical advice on building your own radiant floor heating system and powering it with photovoltaic panels.

Kriescher, Paul. "Energy Performance on a Budget," *Solar Today* 14(5), 2000. A fascinating case study in residential active and passive solar heating in New Hampshire. A must read.

Marsden, Guy. "Solar Heat for My Main Workshop," *Home Power* 89, 2002. A case study worth reading by those interested in using solar hot water to provide space heat.

Pine, Nick. "Solar Heat in Snow Country," *Solar Today* 17 (1), 2003. An inspiring

story about active solar heating in a US Customs border station in Vermont.

Simpson, Walter. "Adventure in Solar Living," *Solar Today* 17(5), 2003. An inspiring tale of a passive solar/solar hot water heated home in Buffalo, New York.

See additional listings on active solar systems for Chapter 3.

Heat Pumps

Publications

Malin, Nadav, and Alex Wilson. "Ground-Source Heat Pumps: Are They Green?" *Environmental Building News* 9(1), 2000. Detailed overview on ground-source heat pumps.

National Renewable Energy Lab. "Geothermal Heat Pumps," published online at www.eere.energy.gov/geothermal/ heatpumps. Great overview of ground-source heat pumps.

Persons, Jeff. "The Big Dig," *Mother Earth News* 185, 102. A brief introduction to ground-source heat pumps.

Organizations

Geo-Heat Center, Oregon Institute of Technology, 3201 Campus Dr., Klamath, OR. 97601. Tel: (541) 885-1750. Technical information on heat pumps. Website: http://geoheat.oit.edu.

Geothermal Heat Pump Consortium, Inc. 701 Pennsylvania Ave, NW, Washington, D.C. 20004-2696. Tel: (888) 333-4472. General and technical information on heat pumps.
Website: www.ghpc.org.

International Ground Source Heat Pump Association. 490 Cordell South, Stillwater, OK. 74078-8018. Tel: (405) 744-5175. Provides a list of equipment manufacturers, installers by state, and numerous other resources for contractors, homeowners, students, and the general public.
Website: www.igshpa.okstate.edu.

US Department of Energy, Office of Geothermal Technologies. EE-12, 1000 Independence Avenue, S.W., Washington, D.C. 20585-0121. Tel: (202) 586-5340. Carries out research on GSHPs and works closely with industry to implement new ideas.

Chapter 5
Wood Heat

Publications

Barden, Albert A. AlbiCore™ Construction Manual. Maine Wood Heat Company, 1996. Detailed construction manual for one type of masonry heater.

Barden, Albert A. *The Finnish Fireplace: Construction Manual.* Maine Wood Heat Company, Inc., 1984. The only complete English language primer on making masonry heaters. Available through the Maine Wood Heat Company.
Website: www.mainewoodheat.com.

Barden, Albert A. and Keikki Hyytiainen. *Finnish Fireplaces: Heart of the Home.* Building Book Ltd., 1988. A valuable resource for anyone wanting to learn more about Finnish masonry stoves. Available through the Maine Wood Heat Company listed above.

British Columbia Ministry of Environment, Land, and Parks. "Reducing Wood Stove Smoke: A Burning Issue," Sept.1994. Website: www.env.gov.bc.ca/epd/epdqa/ar/particulates/rwssabi.html

Gulland, John. "The Art of the Wood Cookstove," *Mother Earth News* 207, 2005. A detailed look at wood cookstoves.

Gulland, John. "Woodstove Buyer's Guide," *Mother Earth News* 189, 2002. Superb overview of woodstoves with a useful table to help you select a model that meets your needs.

Gulland, John. "Responsible Wood Heating: A Kind-to-the-Environment Guide," *Home Power* 99, 2004. For those who want to burn wood responsibly, that is, with minimal impact, this article is a must.

Johnson, Dave. *The Good Woodcutter's Guide: Chain Saws, Portable Sawmills, and Woodlots.* Chelsea Green, 1998. A practical guide to felling trees and cutting fire wood safely.

Lyle, David. *The Book of Masonry Stoves: Rediscovering an Old Way of Warming.* Chelsea Green, 1984. This book contains a wealth of information on the history, function, design, and construction of masonry stoves.

Mink, Kate. "Living with a Masonry Stove," *Home Power* 103, 2004. A personal account of what it is like to live with a masonry heater; well worth reading.

Pahl, Greg. "Wood-Fired Central Heat," *Mother Earth News* 196, 2003. For additional information on wood furnaces.

Organizations

Hearth, Patio, and Barbecue Association. (Formerly the Hearth Products Association.) International trade association that promotes the interests of the hearth products industry. 1601 North Kent Street, Suite 1001, Arlington, VA. 22209. Offers lots of valuable information.
Website: http://hpba.org.

Masonry Heater Association of North America. 1252 Stock Farm Road, Randolph, VT. 05060. Tel: (802) 728-5896. Publishes a valuable newsletter and has a website with links to dealers and masons who design and build masonry stoves. Website: www.mha-net.org.

Wood Heat Organization. 410 Bank Street, Suite 117, Ottawa, Ontario Canada K2P 1Y8. Promotes safe, responsible use of wood for heating.
Website: www.woodheat.org.

Chapter 6
Passive Cooling: Staying Cool Naturally

Chiras, Dan. "Sunshine from a Tube," *Mother Earth News* 202, 2004. A brief introduction to solar tube skylights, a device that helps reduce heat gain in the summer.

Mossberg, Cliff. "Passive Cooling. Part 1 – Basic Principles," *Home Power* 82, 2001. A fairly technical, but very valuable resource on passive cooling.

Mossberg, Cliff. "Passive Cooling. Part 2 – Applied Construction," *Home Power* 82, 2001. Part 2 of the piece described above.

Galloway, Terry. *Solar House: A Guide for the Solar Designer.* Architectural Press, 2004. Fairly technical guide on a wide range of solar designs, including passive cooling.

Givoni, Baruch. *Passive and Low Energy Cooling of Buildings.* John Wiley and Sons, 1994. A fairly technical book, but one of the few resources on the subject.

Niklas, Mike. "High Performance Schools – It's a No-Brainer," *Solar Today* 16 (3), 2002. A fascinating look at the greening of a high school in Oregon, including energy efficiency, passive cooling, and daylighting.

See resources for passive solar heating, as many concepts and techniques that make passive solar heating work, also function to passively cool a home.

Chapter 7
Solar Electricity

Publications

Berton, John. "Off-Grid in Chicago," *Home Power* 80, 2001. For those who are skeptical about solar electricity in a city, this is a must read.

Butti, Ken and John Perlin. *Golden Thread: 2500 Years of Solar Architecture and Technology.* Cheshire Books, 1980. Delightful history of solar energy.

Carnes, Richard. "To PV or Not to PV," *Mother Earth News* 184, 2001. One family's venture into solar electricity.

Dankoff, Windy. "Solar Water Pumping Makes Sense," *Home Power* 97, 2003. Great

primer by the nation's leading expert on the subject.

Davidson, Joel. *The New Solar Electric Home: The Photovoltaics How-To Handbook.* Aatec Publications, 2005. Comprehensive and highly readable guide to photovoltaics, a brand new edition.

Ewing, Rex A. *Power With Nature: Solar and Wind Energy Demystified.* PixyJack Press, 2003. Skip to the second half if you want to get to the meat of the matter.

Galocy, Baran. "Build Your Own Adjustable PV Mount," *Home Power* 97, 2003. Instructions on how to build an adjustable PV rack.

Gourley, Colleen. "Production Builders Go Solar," *Solar Today* 16(1), 2002. Inspiring story about the incorporation of solar electricity into homes in California by large-scale production builders.

Hackleman, Michael and Claire Anderson. "Harvest the Wind," *Mother Earth News*, June/July, 2002. A wonderful introduction to wind power.

Jeffrey, Kevin. *Independent Energy Guide: Electrical Power for Home, Boat, and RV.* Orwell Cove Press, 1995. Contains a wealth of information on solar electric systems and wind generators. Fairly easy to read.

Kazmerski, Lawrence L. "Photovoltaic Myths – The Seven Deadly Sins," *Solar Today* 16 (4), 2002.

Kelin, Ken and Paul Hanley. "Winter Cattle Watering with Automated Solar Pumps," *Home Power* 98, 2004. To learn more about ways to pump water with solar electricity.

Kohn, Lin. "Solar in San Francisco," *Solar Today* 1(4), 2003. A great look at what one progressive city is doing to increase its reliance on renewable energy.

Komp, Richard J. *Practical Photovoltaics: Electricity from Solar Cells*, 3rd ed. Aatec Publications, 1999. Fairly popular book on PVs.

Linkous, Clovis A. "Solar Energy Hydrogen– Partners in a Clean Energy Economy." *Solar Today* 13(4), 1999. A detailed and somewhat technical, article on hydrogen production using solar electricity.

Moates, Tom. "Grid-Free Forever," *Mother Earth News* 186, 2001. A personal tale of energy independence.

NREL. *The Colorado Consumer's Guide to Buying a Solar Electric System*. National Renewable Energy Lab, 1998. Provides basic information about purchasing, financing, and installing photovoltaic systems in Colorado that is applicable to many other states and countries as well.

Contact NREL's Document Distribution Service at (303) 2754363 for a free copy.

NREL. *The Borrower's Guide to Financing Solar Energy Systems*. National Renewable Energy Lab, 1998. Provides information about nationwide financing programs for photovoltaics and passive solar heating. Contact NREL's Document Distribution Service at (303) 275-4363 for a free copy.

Pahl, Greg. "Choosing a Backup Generator," *Mother Earth News* 202, 2004. Fairly detailed overview of what to look for when buying a backup electrical generator for an RE system.

Peavy, Michael A. *Fuel from Water: Energy Independence with Hydrogen*, 8th ed. Merit, Inc., 1998. Technical analysis for engineers and chemists.

Perez, Richard. "To Track … or Not to Track," *Home Power* 101, 2004. Great little piece on tracking devices for PVs and whether they make sense for your site.

Perez, Richard. "Flooded Lead-Acid Battery Maintenance," *Home Power* 98, 2004. Read and memorize this and put the advice into practice if you plan on installing a stand-alone system.

Perlin, J. *From Space to Earth: The Story of Solar Electricity*. Aatec Publications, 1999.

A wonderfully readable history of solar electricity.

Perlin, John, Lawrence Kazmerski, and Susan Moon. "Good as Gold: The Silicon Solar Cell Turns 50," *Solar Today* 28(1), 2004. A brief history of PV research and development.

Pinkham, Linda. "From the Ground Up: My RE System Design Choice," *Home Power* 106, 2005. A personal account that walks readers through the issues one woman faced when considering a solar electric system.

Price, Stuart V. "4 Times Square – Urban Solar Flair," *Solar Today* 16(3), 2002. An inspiring story of what can be done to green a skyscraper. One of my all-time favorite articles!

Radoff, Joshua H. "Solar in the City," *Solar Today* 18(5), 2004. An interesting look at solar electric installations in New York City.

Rastelli, Linda. "Energy Independence with all the Comforts," *Solar Today* 16(1), 2002. An inspiring story about a passive solar/solar electric home in Washington, D.C.

Roberts, Simon. *Solar Electricity: A Practical Guide to Designing and Installing Small Photovoltaic Systems*. Prentice-Hall, 1991. Good reference but a bit dated.

Russell, Scott. "Solar-Electric Systems Simplified," *Home Power* 104, 2005. Good, solid, and well-illustrated introduction to the components of a solar electric system.

Russell, Scott. "Starting Smart: Calculating Your Energy Appetite," *Home Power* 102, 2004. Great little introduction to household load analysis to determine household electrical demand.

Schaeffer, John and the Real Goods staff. *Solar Living Source Book, 10th ed.* Real Goods, 1999. Contains an enormous amount of background information on wind, solar, and microhydroelectric.

Schwartz, Joe. "What's Going On—The Grid?" *Home Power* 106, 2005. An excellent look at inverters for grid-connected systems.

Schwartz, Joe. "Go Configure: Configuring Your PV Array," *Home Power* 87, 2002. Guide to wiring PV arrays. Very useful.

Seuss, Terri and Cheryl Long. "Eliminate Your Electric Bill: Go Solar, Be Secure," *Mother Earth News* 190, 2002. Excellent discussion of solar roofing materials.

Sindelar, Allan and Phil Campbell-Graves. "How to Finance Your Renewable Energy Home," *Home Power* 103, 2004. Very useful article.

Sklar, Scott, and Kenneth Sheinkopf. *Consumer Guide to Solar Energy: More Ways to Reduce Your Energy Bills and Save the Environment.* Bonus Books, 1995. Delightful introduction to many different solar applications, including solar electricity.

Solar Energy International. *Photovoltaic Design Manual, Version 2.* Solar Energy International. A manual on designing, installing, and maintaining a PV system. Used in SEI's PV design and installation workshops.

Stockman, Douglas. "The Hard Part About Wind Turbines," *Home Power* 86, 2002. Personal tale about the difficulties of siting a wind machine in a rural area.

Strong, Steven and William G. Scheller. *The Solar Electric House: Energy for the Environmentally Responsive, Energy-Independent Home.* Sustainability Press, 1993. Comprehensive and technical guide to solar electricity.

Symanski, Paul. "Money from the Sun: An Investor's Guide to Solar-Electric Profits," *Home Power* 100, 2004. Very interesting comparison of the economic payback of grid-connected solar electric systems in Arizona with small rebates to an investment in the stock market.

Taylor, Phillip L. "The Agony and the Ecstasy—My Solar Odyssey," *Solar Today* 16(2), 2002. A personal tale of a college professor who installs solar electric panels on his Midwestern home.

Woofenden, Ian. "Battery Filling Systems of the Americas: Single-Point Watering System," *Home Power* 100, 2004. This article is a must for those who would like to reduce battery maintenance.

Yerkes, Bill. "40 Years of Solar Power," *Solar Today* 18(1), 2004. A historical survey of PVs from an insider.

Yewdall, Zeke. "PV Orientation," *Home Power* 93, 2003. A must read for those with less-than-perfect solar sites.

Videos

An Introduction to Residential Solar Electricity with Johnny Weiss. Good basic introduction to solar electricity. Produced by Scott S. Andrews, P.O. Box 3027, Sausalito, CA 94965. Tel: (415) 332-5191. Also available through Gaiam Real Goods.

An Introduction to Solar Water Pumping with Windy Dankoff. A very useful introduction to the subject. Produced by Scott S. Andrews, P.O. Box 3027, Sausalito, CA 94965. Tel: (415) 332-5191. Also available through Gaiam Real Goods.

An Introduction to Storage Batteries for Renewable Energy Systems with Richard Perez. This is one of the best videos in the series. It's full of great information. Produced by Scott S. Andrews, P.O. Box 3027, Sausalito, CA 94965. Tel: (415) 332-5191. Also available through Gaiam Real Goods.

The Solar-Powered Home with Rob Roy. An 84-minute video that examines basic principles, components, set-up, and system planning for an off-grid home featuring tips from America's leading experts in the field of home power. Can be purchased from the Earthwood Building School at 366 Murtagh Hill Road, West Chazy, N.Y. 12992. Tel: (518) 493-7744.
Website: www.cordwoodmasonry.com.

Organizations

American Solar Energy Society: see listing in Chapter 3.

Center for Alternative Technology. Address: Machynlleth, Powys SY20 9Az., UK. Tel: 01654 703409. This educational group in the United Kingdom offers workshops on alternative energy, including wind, solar, and microhydroelectric.
Website: www.cat.org.uk.

Center for Renewable Energy and Sustainable Technologies: see listing in Chapter 3.

Real Goods Solar Living Institute. P.O. Box 836, Hopland, CA 95449. Tel: (707) 744-2017. A non-profit organization that offers frequent hands-on workshops on solar energy and many other topics. Website: www.solarliving.org.

Solar Energy International: see listing in Chapter 3.

Chapter 8
Wind Power: Meeting Your Needs for Electricity

Publications

Brown, Lester R. "Harnessing the Wind for Energy Independence," *Solar Today*16(2), 2002. Good overview of wind energy.

Ewing, Rex A. *Power With Nature: Solar and Wind Energy Demystified.* PixyJack Press, 2003. Skip to the second half if you want to get to the meat of the matter.

Green, Jim. "Small Wind Installations in Colorado," *Solar Today* 14 (1), 2000. Several case studies of wind installations.

Gipe, Paul. "Small Wind Systems Boom," *Solar Today* 1 (2), 2002. Good overview of small wind energy systems by one of America's leading experts on the subject.

Gipe, Paul. *Wind Power for Home and Business: Renewable Energy for the 1990s and Beyond.* Chelsea Green, 1993. Somewhat technical introduction to small and medium-sized wind generators.

Gipe, Paul. *Wind Energy Basics: A Guide to Small and Micro Wind Systems.* Chelsea Green, 1999. A brief introduction to wind energy for newcomers.

Hackleman, M. and C. Anderson. "Harvest the Wind." *Mother Earth News* 192, 2002. An easy-to-read and fact-filled article on wind power.

Kuebeck, Sr., Peter and Peter Kuebeck, Jr. "Old Jacobs – Current Again," *Home Power* 89, 2002. Personal story about one of the best wind machines on the market.

Laughlin, Don. "You Gotta Have Height: A Tower Construction Project in Iowa," *Home Power* 92, 2003. Interesting case study. Well worth reading to learn more about tower construction and erection.

Osborn, D. "Winds of Change." *Solar Today* 17(6), 2003. Looks at a number of important issues, including bird kills by wind towers compared to other sources.

Pahl, Greg. "Choosing a Backup Generator," *Mother Earth News* 202, 2004. A fairly detailed overview of what to look for when buying a back-up electrical generator for an RE system.

Pearen, Craig. "Brushless Alternators," *Home Power* 97, 2003. Brief but interesting look at brushless (low-maintenance) alternators for wind machines.

Piggott, Hugh. "Estimating Wind Energy," *Home Power* 102, 2004. A brief piece that will help you determine how much electrical energy you can produce on your site.

Perez, Richard. "Flooded Lead-Acid Battery Maintenance," *Home Power* 98, 2004. Read and memorize this and put the advice into practice if you plan on installing a stand-alone system.

Preus, Robert. "Thoughts on VAWTs: Vertical Axis Wind Generator Perspectives," *Home Power* 104, 2005.

Rastelli, Linda. "Energy Independence – with all the Comforts," *Solar Today* 16(1), 2002. The story of a mass-marketed passive solar/solar electric home.

Russell, Scott. "Starting Smart: Calculating Your Energy Appetite," *Home Power* 102, 2004. Great little introduction to household load analysis (to determine household electrical demand).

Sagrillo, Mick. "Apples and Oranges 2002: Choosing a Home-Sized Wind Generator," *Home Power* 90, 2002. The most valuable resource you will find on selecting a wind generator. Worth its weight in gold!

Sagrillo, Mick. "Being Your Own Utility," *Solar Today* 17(5), 2003. For those who are considering going off-grid.

Sagrillo, Mick. "On Intimate Terms with a Wind Generator," *Solar Today* 17(1), 2003. An inspiring tale about one do-it-yourselfer and his wind machine.

Short, Walter and Nate Blair. "The Long-Term Potential of Wind Power in the U.S." *Solar Today* 17(6), 2003. Important study of wind power's potential.

Sindelar, Allan and Phil Campbell-Graves. "How to Finance Your Renewable Energy Home," *Home Power* 103, 2004. Very useful article.

Sweezy, Blair and Lori Bird. "Businesses Lead the 'Green Power' Challenge," *Solar Today* 15(1), 2001. An interesting look at what some major corporations like Toyota are doing to increase their reliance on renewable energy.

Sweezey, Blair and Lori Bird. "Buying Green Power – You Really Can Make a Difference," *Solar Today* 17(1), 2003. An in-depth look at ways homeowners can tap into renewable energy (such as green tags) without installing a system on their home.

Woofenden, Ian. "Wind Generator Tower Basics," *Home Power* 105, 2005. Excellent overview of an important subject.

Woofenden, Ian. "Battery Filling Systems of the Americas: Single-Point Watering System," *Home Power* 100, 2004. This article

is a must for those who would like to reduce battery maintenance.

Videos

An Introduction to Residential Wind Power with Mick Sagrillo. Produced by Scott S. Andrews, P.O. Box 3027, Sausalito, CA 94965. Tel: (415) 332-5191. A very informative video, especially for those wishing to install a medium-sized system.

Organizations

American Wind Energy Association. 122C Street, NW, Suite 380, Washington, D.C. 20001. Tel: (202) 383-2500. This organization also sponsors an annual conference on wind energy. The website contains a list of publications, an online newsletter, frequently asked questions, news releases, and links to companies and organizations. Website: www.ogc.apc.org/awea.

British Wind Energy Association. 26 Spring Street, London W2 1JA. Tel: 0171 402 7102. Actively promotes wind energy in Great Britain. Check out the website for fact sheets, answers to frequently asked questions, links, and a directory of companies. Website: www.bwea.com.

Center for Alternative Technology. Machynlleth, Powys SY20 9Az., UK. Tel: 01654 703409. This educational group in the United Kingdom offers workshops on alternative energy, including wind, solar, and micro-hydroelectric. Website: www.cat.org.uk.

Center for Renewable Energy and Sustainable Technologies. See listing in chapter 3.

European Wind Energy Association. Rue du Trone 26, B-1000, Brussels, Belgium. Tel: +32 2 546 1940. Promotes wind energy in Europe. The organization publishes the *European Wind Energy Association Magazine*. The website contains information on wind energy in Europe and offers a list of publications and links to other sites. Website: www.ewea.org.

National Wind Technology Center of the National Renewable Energy Laboratory. 1617 Cole Blvd., Golden, CO 80401-3393. Tel: (303) 275-3000. The website provides a search mode so you can check out the site, and provides a great deal of information on wind energy, including a wind resource database. Website: www.nrel.gov/wind.

Real Goods Solar Living Institute. P.O. Box 836, Hopland, Ca 95449. Tel: (707) 744-2017. Website: www.solarliving.org. A nonprofit organization that offers frequent hands-on workshops on solar and wind energy and many other topics.

Solar Energy International: see listing in Chapter 3.

Chapter 9
Microhydropower: Generating Electricity from Running Water

Publications

Aronson, Jeffe. "Choosing Microhydro … Clean Electricity in the Outback," *Home Power* 101, 2004. Valuable reading for anyone interested in low-head microhydro.

Isley, Bill. "Happy on One Kilowatt," *Mother Earth News* 180, 92, 2000. A story of one couple's quest for energy independence through microhydro.

Maxwell, Steve. "Homestead Hydropower," *Mother Earth News* 208, 2005. A good overview of the subject.

New, Dan. "Intro to Hydropower. Part 2: Measuring Head and Flow," *Home Power* 103, 2004. The first piece in a superb series.

New, Dan. "Intro to Hydropower. Part 2: Measuring Head and Flow," *Home Power* 104, 2004. The second piece in a superb series; this one covers important information on assessing a site.

New, Dan. "Intro to Hydropower. Part 3: Power, Efficiency, Transmission & Equipment Selection," *Home Power* 105, 2005. The final piece in this superb series.

Pahl, Greg. "Choosing a Backup Generator," *Mother Earth News* 202, 2004. A fairly detailed overview of what to look for when buying a back-up electrical generator for an RE system.

Perez, Richard. "Flooded Lead-Acid Battery Maintenance," *Home Power* 98, 2004. Read and memorize this, and put the advice into practice if you plan on installing a stand-alone system.

Russell, Scott. "Starting Smart: Calculating Your Energy Appetite," *Home Power* 102, 2004. Great little introduction to household load analysis (to determine household electrical demand).

Woofenden, Ian. "Battery Filling Systems of the Americas: Single-Point Watering System," *Home Power* 100, 2004. This article is a must for those who would like to reduce battery maintenance.

Videos

An Introduction to Residential Microhydro Power with Don Harris. Produced by Scott S. Andrews. P.O. Box 3027, Sausalito, CA 94965. Tel: (415) 332-5191. Outstanding video packed with lots of useful information.

Chapter 10
What's on the Horizon: New Fuels and New Technologies

Brown, Mike and Shari Prange. "PV and EV: Photovoltaics and Electric Vehicles," *Home Power* 103, 2004. Describes use of PVs on homes to power electric vehicles.

Dunn, S. 2000. "The Hydrogen Experiment." *World Watch* 13(6). Tells how the country of Iceland is planning to convert to hydrogen power by the year 2030.

Durkee, Scott. "Getting Off the Petroleum Grid with Biodiesel, *Home Power* 93, 2003. A how-to guide to making your own biodiesel, simply and efficiently.

Engle, Richard and Dominic Crea. "Hydrogen: Solution or Distraction?" *Home Power* 101, 2004. A must-read for anyone interested in hydrogen.

Hackleman, Michael. "Clean, Green Electric Machines," *Mother Earth News* 194, 2002. A detailed look at electric cars.

Kerr, Andy. "Toyota Prius: Ready for Prime Time," *Home Power* 85, 2001. Description of the first generation Toyota Prius with the author's personal experiences woven in.

Kliesch, James. "Buying a Green Vehicle," *Solar Today* 15(6), 2001. A good overview of some of your environmentally friendly vehicle options.

Kolod, Emily. "Going Pro with Biodiesel," *Home Power* 89, 2002. Interesting case study for those who want to learn more about biodiesel production.

Moné, Carol E. "My Chrysler is a Furnace and It Runs on Biodiesel," *Home Power*

97, 2003. Describes Carol's personal experience using biodiesel to run her home's furnace.

Patterson, Allen. "The 2004 Toyota Prius," *Home Power* 102, 2004. Great but somewhat technical piece on this exciting hybrid.

Prange, Shari. "Fuel Cell Cars," *Home Power* 76, 2000. A brief introduction to fuel cell car technology.

Prange, Shari. "Driving Miss DC: How to Drive an EV, Part I," *Home Power* 81, 2000. Useful advice for those who own or are thinking about buying an electric vehicle.

Prange, Shari. "Zen and the Art of EV Driving: How to Drive an EV, Part II," *Home Power* 80, 2001. More useful advice for those who own or are thinking about buying an electric vehicle.

Prange, Shari. "A Horse of a Different Color," *Home Power* 83, 2001. A detailed look at the Toyota Prius Gen I.

Prange, Shari. "Good Things in Small Packages," *Home Power* 87, 2002. Delightful look at very small, highly functional commuter cars.

Prange, Shari. "Charge Your EV, Part 1," *Home Power* 89, 2002. A primer on charging electric vehicles.

Prange, Shari. "Hitting the Juice Bar," *Home Power* 90, 2002. Part 2 of Shari's piece listed above.

Prange, Shari. "Sorting out the Alternatives: EVs, Hybrids, and Fuel Cell Vehicles," *Home Power* 94, 2003. Good overview of three top contenders for car of the future.

Prange, Shari. "Honda's Hybrid Duo," *Home Power* 101, 2004. Examines the hybrid Honda Civic and Insight.

Prange, Shari. "EV Range: How Much is Enough?" *Home Power* 106, 2005. A brief but important discussion of things you must consider when selecting an electric vehicle.

Scully, Liz. "Wanted: Cleaner and Greener Wheels," *Home Power* 103, 2004. Brief but interesting introduction to biodiesel.

Selected Titles by the Author

Here Stands Marshall (novel)

The New Ecological Home

The Solar House: Passive Solar Heating and Cooling

The Natural Plaster Book: Earthen, Lime, and Gypsum Plasters for Natural Homes

The Natural House: A Complete Guide to Healthy, Energy-Efficient, Environmental Homes

Superbia! 31 Ways to Create Sustainable Neighborhoods

EcoKids: Raising Children Who Care for the Earth·

Lessons from Nature: Learning to Live Sustainably on the Earth

Beyond the Fray: Reshaping America's Environmental Movement

Voices for the Earth: Vital Ideas from America's Best Environmental Books

Environmental Science

Natural Resource Conservation: Management for a Sustainable Future

Human Body Systems

Human Biology

Biology: The Web of Life

Study Skills for Science Students

Essential Study Skills

Index

About the Author

Dan Chiras paid his last electric bill in June of 1996 and pays about $13 per month for natural gas to power his superefficient, solar and wind-powered home in Colorado. He has not disavowed the use of electricity or natural gas, and the modern conveniences they afford, but rather has turned to other sources, the sun and wind, to power his home and office.

In 1996, Dan installed solar electric panels on the roof of his state-of-the-art environmental home in Evergreen, Colorado, built from straw bales and rammed earth tires and many recycled materials. A year later, he installed a small wind generator to boost his electrical supply. Since that time he has met nearly all of his electrical needs for his home and office from these clean, renewable sources.

SKYLER CHIRAS

Dan heats his home, which sits in the foothills of the Rocky Mountains 8000-feet above sea level, with energy from the sun through passive solar design. For backup heat on those cold winter nights, he burns a little wood, about a cord a year. His annual gas bill for showers, dishwashing, and cooking, runs about $130 a year.

Dan has spent much of the past 30 years studying renewable energy and energy efficiency and other aspects of sustainable design and has been applying what he has learned in these areas to residences. For the last ten years, he has been sharing the practical knowledge he has gained through writing, lectures, slide shows, and workshops.

Dan is a visiting professor at Colorado College where he teaches courses on renewable energy, sustainable development, green building, and ecological design.

Dan has published nearly 250 articles on environmental issues, sustainable development, green building, and renewable energy in a variety of magazines, journals, newspapers, and encyclopedias. He has also published numerous books — 22 all told — including *The Solar House: Passive Solar Heating and Cooling*; *The Natural House*; *The New Ecological Home*; *The Natural Plaster*; *Superbia! 31 Ways to Create Sustainable Neighborhoods, and EcoKids: Raising Children Who Care for the Earth*. In 2006, he published his first novel, *Here Stands Marshall*.

Dan consults on residential passive solar heating and cooling design and green building through his company, Sustainable Systems Design, Inc. For more information, you may want to visit his web pages at <www.danchiras.com>.

If you have enjoyed *The Homeowner's Guide to Renewable Energy*
you might also enjoy other

BOOKS TO BUILD A NEW SOCIETY

Our books provide positive solutions for people who want to
make a difference. We specialize in:

**Environment and Justice • Conscientious Commerce
Sustainable Living • Ecological Design and Planning
Natural Building & Appropriate Technology • New Forestry
Educational and Parenting Resources • Nonviolence
Progressive Leadership • Resistance and Community**

For a full list of NSP's titles, please call **1-800-567-6772** *or check out our website at:*

www.newsociety.com

NEW SOCIETY PUBLISHERS